The Ruin of the Eternal City

The Ruin of the Eternal City

Antiquity and Preservation in Renaissance Rome

DAVID KARMON

OXFORD
UNIVERSITY PRESS

OXFORD
UNIVERSITY PRESS

Oxford University Press, Inc., publishes works that further
Oxford University's objective of excellence
in research, scholarship, and education.

Oxford   New York
Auckland   Cape Town   Dar es Salaam   Hong Kong   Karachi
Kuala Lumpur   Madrid   Melbourne   Mexico City   Nairobi
New Delhi   Shanghai   Taipei   Toronto

With offices in
Argentina   Austria   Brazil   Chile   Czech Republic   France   Greece
Guatemala   Hungary   Italy   Japan   Poland   Portugal   Singapore
South Korea   Switzerland   Thailand   Turkey   Ukraine   Vietnam

Published by Oxford University Press, Inc.
198 Madison Avenue, New York, New York 10016

www.oup.com

Oxford is a registered trademark of Oxford University Press.

Library of Congress Cataloging-in-Publication Data
Karmon, David E.
The ruin of the Eternal City: antiquity and preservation in Renaissance Rome/David E. Karmon.
   p.   cm.
Includes bibliographical references and index.
ISBN 978-0-19-976689-5
1. Rome (Italy)—Antiquities. 2. Renaissance—Italy—Rome. 3. Historic preservation—Italy—
Rome—History—To 1500. 4. Historic preservation—Italy—Rome—History—16th century.
5. Rome (Italy)—Antiquities—Collection and preservation. 6. Historic buildings—Conservation
and restoration—Italy—Rome. 7. Rome (Italy)—Buildings, structures, etc. I. Title.
DG63.5.K37   2011
363.6'9094563209024—dc22   2010033357

9 8 7 6 5 4 3

Printed in the United States of America
on acid-free paper

To my parents
Oshri and Harriet Karmon

Acknowledgments

I would like to thank the following institutions and grant agencies for their generous support in helping me research and write this book: the National Endowment for the Humanities, the Holy Cross Research and Publications Committee, the Graham Foundation for Advanced Studies in the Fine Arts, the Society of Architectural Historians, the American Philosophical Society, the Batchelor Foundation, and the Canadian Centre for Architecture.

I would also like to thank the following archives and libraries. In Rome I consulted the collections of the Archivio Segreto Vaticano, the Archivio Storico Capitolino, the Archivio della Reverenda Fabbrica di San Pietro, and the Archivio di Stato. In my work at these repositories I was fortunate to have the expert guidance of Arnold Esch, Michele Franceschini, Massimo Miglio, Anna Modigliani, and Orietta Verdi. Of the many libraries in Rome, I worked most often at the American Academy, the École Française, the Deutsches Archäologisches Institut, the Biblioteca Hertziana, the Biblioteca Casanatense, and the Vatican Library, and the courteous assistance of their staffs made my research in Rome a pleasurable experience.

Special thanks go to James Ackerman, who stimulated my thinking on the history of Italian Renaissance architecture and questions of preservation from the very beginning and who has remained a key mentor throughout. I have also been fortunate to benefit from the counsel of Howard Burns, Henry Millon, and John Shearman. In addition I would like to thank Aloisio Antinori, Hilary Ballon, Lex Bosman, Cammy Brothers, Kathleen Christian, Georgia Clarke, Robert Coates-Stephens, Cinzia Conti, Tracy Cooper, Franceso Paolo Di Teodoro,

Cesare d'Onofrio, Paolo Fancelli, Maurizio Gargano, Robert Gaston, Anthony Grafton, Marcia Hall, Dale Kinney, Pamela Long, Giangiacomo Martines, Arnold Nesselrath, Laurie Nussdorfer, Jorge Otero-Pailos, Pier Nicola Pagliara, Susanna Pasquali, Angela Quattrocchi, Katharine Rinne, Ingrid Rowland, Carlos Sambricio, Salvatore Settis, Rabun Taylor, William Tronzo, Richard Tuttle, Christof Thoenes, Vitaliano Tiberia, and William Wallace for welcoming my questions, providing encouragement, and sharpening my thinking.

I have had wonderful colleagues who have shown me many kindnesses. I am especially grateful for the warmth of Ann Harris, Kirk Savage, and Frank Toker while I was a visiting scholar at the University of Pittsburgh, and that of Brian Curran, Charlotte Houghton, and Elizabeth Smith while I was at the Pennsylvania State University. The community of Renaissance scholars in Chicago, including Paul Gehl, Diana Robin, Carla Zecher, and Rebecca Zorach, made my residency at the Newberry Library a pleasure. At Holy Cross, Michael Beatty, Todd Lewis, Sarah Luria, Robert ParkeHarrison, Virginia Raguin, Cristi Rinklin, John Reboli, Susan Schmidt, and Jody Ziegler have been the best colleagues anyone could wish for. I would also like to thank the President and the Dean's Office for the Junior Leave which allowed me to complete this book.

Much of the final manuscript was written in residency at the Canadian Centre for Architecture, and I am grateful to Phyllis Lambert and Alexis Sornin for making the Study Center such a wonderful place in which to think and to share ideas. Thanks also to Pierre-Édouard Latouche, Indra McEwen, and Frances Richard, who each offered advice and encouragement at critical moments. Stefan Zebrowski-Rubin read the entire manuscript and helped me to clarify important passages. Elspeth Cowell helped smooth the way with preparing images for publication. Equally wonderful was the work of Milton Kooistra who improved my translations and transcriptions of archival sources. The keen interest expressed in the project by Stefan Vranka at Oxford University Press, and the valuable constructive comments of anonymous readers, spurred me to complete the manuscript. I have also benefited from the kind assistance of Deirdre Brady and Tamzen Benfield.

The value of enduring friendship acquires new significance when thinking about preservation practices. Throughout the years of working on this project I have been renewed and sustained by affection and support from family and friends, although often separated by great distances. Ever since architecture school I have been revitalized by the wonderful conversations and friendship of Christy Anderson, Kevin Gallagher, and Innis Anderson-Gallagher. I was fortunate to have Turner Brooks as a first-year critic: his design for Il Risorgimento, the winged obelisk that for a brief time floated among the massive monuments of Rome, showcased the intriguing paradox of impermanence in the Eternal City. My first professional contact with the preservation of antiquity, however, happened in the extraordinary architectural office of Steve Farneth, thanks to the goodwill of Betty Rintoul and Robin Jeffers.

I would also like to thank Jane and Raynor Clark, Heather and Jamie Clark, Holly and Scott Clark, Kathy and Charles Hosack, Ayelet and Haim Izraeli-Karmon, Orit and Yoram Karmon, Elizabeth and Paul Reynolds, Kate Bentz, Persis Berlekamp, Julia and Kevin Bernard, Ellen Cianciarulo, David Ciarlo, Anne Leonard and Alex Millet, Grete and Bjarne Nielsen, Barbara, Phil, and Nicole O'Hay, Linda Reeder and Chris Anderson, Vicky Solan and Daniel Trutt, Alison Stone and John Weiss, Lisa Tetrault, and Beany and Dick Wezelman, all of whom have made things better along the way. The unfailing kindness of Serena D'Ambrogi was proved yet again when she stepped in to guarantee the delivery of archival documents from Rome.

My parents, Harriet and Oshri Karmon, and my sister Gabrielle have believed in the project all along: I have them to thank for unfailing faith and support. And while Sarah Karmon is my greatest editor and critic, that's only just the beginning. The much-anticipated delivery of the proofs for this book was made even more marvelous by the arrival, that same week, of our son Wyn.

Contents

The Ruin of the Eternal City

Introduction

In *Civilization and Its Discontents*, Sigmund Freud addressed the layered archaeological residue of Rome as an intriguing analogy by which to explore the process of memory.[1] Freud argued that even if the mind managed to suppress certain experiences and memories, the unconscious still retained an indelible imprint of these forgotten things and events. This mental record could be conjured up again, even when the subject believed it had been completely erased. According to Freud, the evidence of preserved artifacts at Rome offered a parallel to this mental process in the external, physical world.

To explore this parallel in further detail, Freud first observed that Rome revealed an extraordinary variety of physical conditions, where some structures remained almost perfectly intact, others suffered major changes, and still others had been obliterated or supplanted by new construction. Freud sought to clarify this jumble of past remains by inviting the reader, in "a flight of the imagination," to see Rome "not as a human habitation, but as a psychical entity," in which "nothing that has once come into existence will have passed away; and all the earlier phases of development continue to exist alongside the latest one." In this imaginary Rome, everything would be "somehow preserved." We would see not just the Colosseum or the Pantheon, as they stood in the Rome of the present, but simply by changing the direction of our glance or position, we would also see the city at other moments in its history: the Domus Aurea of Nero, leveled to make room for the Amphitheatrum Flavium, and the original Pantheon of Agrippa, later supplanted by Hadrian's

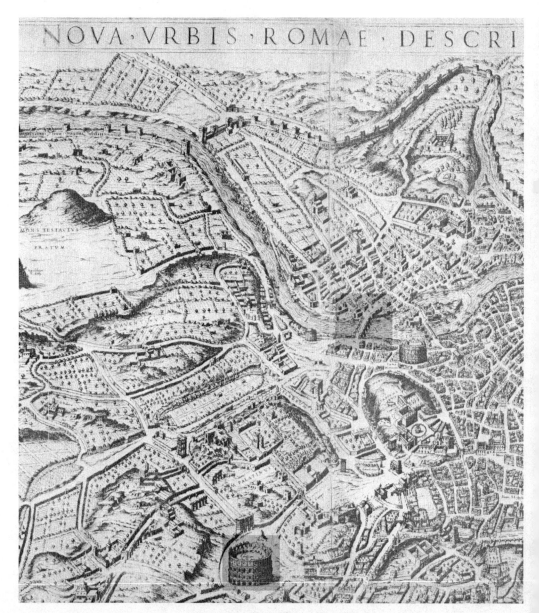

FIGURE 0.1. Etienne Dupérac, Map of Rome (upper half), 1577.

present structure. We would see not just the present truncated stub of the Ponte Santa Maria, better known today as the Ponte Rotto, but the earliest version of this bridge, and all of its subsequent permutations as these took form over time. In this imaginary Rome, all things would coexist simultaneously, allowing the viewer to see every different stage of an archaeological site at once.

Archaeologists, like Freud, are deeply interested in recuperating such losses, and many students of classical archaeology will recognize a routine practice in this Freudian exercise. It is a standard convention in archaeological training to reconstruct an ancient site to its earliest supposed condition and to envision this reconstruction alongside its later iterations and transformations. Of course, such practices have a very long pedigree at Rome itself, going back to the sixteenth century with Raphael's first systematic plan of ancient Rome. Rodolfo Lanciani's *Forma Urbis* provided new stratigraphic clarity at the turn of the twentieth century, while the famous *plastico di Roma* of Italo Gismondi, on display at Mussolini's EUR, gave this paper reconstruction new three-dimensionality in the 1930s. Now virtual reconstructions such as Google Ancient Rome are taking this venerable tradition into the digital age.[2] Confronted by the bewildering archaeological landscape of Rome, we can only make sense of it through reconstruction: this explains the perennial appeal of tourist guidebooks with trace overlays that allow us to flip back and forth between views of the Roman Forum as it appeared in antiquity and as it appears today.

But our impulse to reconstruct can also affect the way we see these sites in the present. When we juxtapose past and present in this way, our tendency is to focus upon the destruction and losses that have occurred since these ancient buildings were first built. Even in the case of the most exceptionally well-preserved monuments, such as the Pantheon, substantial changes and losses have occurred. Complete preservation begins to appear an impossible ideal. Freud himself concluded that the preservation of physical objects at Rome was at best a sketchy, incomplete process, and only the mind itself offered the possibility for a more total kind of preservation.[3]

Leaving aside Freud's ideas about how preservation works in the mind, this same analogy also invites us to reconsider how preservation works in the distinctive built environment of Rome. The densely superimposed archaeological stratigraphy of Rome invites us to think more carefully about the very real, tangible problem of how things endure over time. Indeed, this essential process has been all too quickly elided, not only by tourist guidebooks with their trace overlays, but by the general archaeological literature. Freud observed that certain conditions seemed to favor preservation, and as we will see, the history of Rome during the Renaissance allows us to explore this question—at least in terms of the built environment—with an extraordinary degree of detail.[4] This is the pivotal idea of this book: while it has long been a commonplace that the Renaissance, though it claimed to hold antiquity in the highest possible regard, was responsible for more destruction of ancient monuments in Rome than any other period in history, *The Ruin of the Eternal City* asserts that pragmatic and essential advances in preservation practices also took place at this time.

The entrenched bias of the literature on the history of archaeology in Rome is overwhelmingly skewed in the direction of Renaissance destruction. This way of thinking is one that evolved gradually and over the course of many centuries, so that it has become nearly an automatic reflex for writers to overlook or otherwise ignore the evidence for Renaissance preservation practices. Given the overwhelming impression of destruction apparent in the Eternal City, many scholars and thinkers who reflected upon the fate of ancient Rome focused upon the epic problem of material degradation and decay. Paradoxically, the anxiety of loss that has pervaded the historiography of Roman archaeology from its inception emphasizes above all the archaeological destruction caused in the context of Renaissance Rome, the period best known for its reverent admiration of antiquity.[5] But it was Renaissance artists and scholars themselves who helped to lay the foundations for this particular way of thinking. Their devotion to ancient Rome caused them to focus almost exclusively upon the evidence for relentless destruction. To them, the evidence for preservation appeared inconsequential in comparison to the ongoing excavation and demolition of ancient sites that was then underway in the papal capital. Petrarch, writing in the fourteenth century, was keenly aware of the destruction of ancient artifacts both in Rome and in Italy, and he denounced these losses with great vehemence in his letters, emphasizing the urgent need to stem the ongoing erosion of the past.

As the chorus of humanist voices condemning archaeological destruction in Rome grew steadily louder over the course of the Renaissance, this only further diverted attention away from contemporary preservation practices. Influential writers such as Ghiberti and Vasari reinforced this pattern by underscoring the iconoclastic destruction of antiquity caused by the Roman church, as the leading temporal authority and political power in the ancient city. The most famous text to address the problem of preserving antiquity in Renaissance Italy, the "Letter to Leo X" by Raphael and Baldassare Castiglione, appealed to the pope to defend the threatened ancient patrimony of Rome. But at the same time, this appeal also disguised the fact that long-standing preservation practices were already in place. Canonical texts for the history of Italian Renaissance art and architecture thus successfully perpetuated the notion that the rulers of Renaissance Rome took only nominal interest in preservation practices.

The emergence of modern conservation theory helped to cast the history of Renaissance preservation practices into further obscurity. The professional and academic discipline of conservation as we know it today, forged in the wake of the Enlightenment and the French Revolution, promoted the development of normative conservation principles.[6] But by the same token, this process also helped to inculcate a teleological approach to conservation, where protective interventions conducted on historic remains prior to the late eighteenth century now appeared naive and irrelevant.

The advent of scientific archaeology in the nineteenth century, strengthened by the invention of new technologies as well as by positivist claims to greater objectivity, further reinforced these ingrained habits of dismissing earlier protective interventions upon archaeological artifacts as imperfect and mistaken. Moreover, the complaints of Renaissance humanists directed at the destruction of the ancient past now served to reinforce the progress and achievements accomplished by modern archaeologists. This was above all evident in Rodolfo Lanciani's multivolume series published beginning in 1902, the *Storia degli scavi di Roma*, an exhaustive survey of excavations that has been the essential reference point for the history of archaeology for more than a century.[7] By privileging the scientific practices of modern archaeology over the past, Lanciani hampered the judicious assessment of Renaissance preservation measures. His handsomely crafted and persuasive prose conveyed with gusto the idea that because people in Renaissance Rome lacked the theoretical insights and technological advantages afforded by modern archaeology, they were inevitably fated to misunderstand the intrinsic significance and complexity of preservation practices. As the historian Ilaria Bignamini has observed, such an outlook had a defining impact upon the history of archaeology, where it caused archaeology to "gradually lose the memory of its own past."[8]

Later studies, including the key work of Roberto Weiss, *The Renaissance Discovery of Classical Antiquity*, accepted Lanciani's authoritative position without question. Although modern scholars generally acknowledge that the Italian Renaissance marked a turning point for the development of modern conservation theory, they have insisted upon evaluating these earlier interventions based upon the normative standards generated by the same modern conservation theory that took form in the centuries following the French Revolution. Thus, following the pattern established by Lanciani, they are reluctant to consider Renaissance interventions as valid preservation practices, and instead regard them with skepticism if not outright dismay.[9]

As a result, parallel with the rise of modern archaeology as a discipline, we have become convinced that excavations in Renaissance Rome caused only reckless and reprehensible destruction. We have been persuaded that the ruinous behavior of earlier generations only came to an end with the advent of modern archaeological practices, to which we remain indebted for the conscientious and methodical salvation of the Eternal City. But to accept this argument at face value is to overlook the abundant evidence for the preservation of antiquity throughout the history of Rome, and above all during the unsettled and exciting period of the Renaissance. The extraordinary preservation of so many ancient monuments in Rome, standing serene and undisturbed long before the invention of scientific archaeology, was not mere coincidence. Neither could it be simply attributed to the favorable climatic and geographic conditions of Rome, or to the extraordinary skill of Roman architects and engineers, although certainly both of these were important factors. On the contrary, the survival of ancient Roman structures bears witness to the enduring importance of the preservation of antiquity as an essential cultural tradition in Rome throughout its history, and above all at a time known to have posed a significant danger to these remains: during the construction of the new papal capital in the fifteenth and sixteenth centuries. It is an underlying premise of this book that at this precise moment, during the recovery and rejuvenation of Rome, the existing Roman practice and tradition of preservation became more robust, more focused, and more effective than ever before.[10]

Our narrative begins with a survey of preservation practices in antiquity and in the context of the postclassical city, to provide the essential background for the distinctive and characteristic Roman culture of preservation. The year 1420, however, marked a vital turning point: with the arrival of Martin V in the papal capital, preservation practices began to be implemented with new energy and ingenuity, in response to the complex and difficult conditions posed by inhabiting and building upon the remains of ancient Rome. Our survey of Renaissance preservation practices culminates with the reign of the preservation-minded Paul III, who introduced preservation measures of an unprecedented scope in his transformation of the city.

Arguing that preservation practices were rethought, recast, and fundamentally transformed in the new light of the Renaissance, this book points to several critical and interconnected elements as certain conditions, following Freud's idea, that favored preservation in Renaissance Rome. The survival of the ancient monuments themselves depended upon specific design features, including engineering details and the strength of component materials. From shifts in population density to the movement of tectonic plates, a variety of demographic and geographic factors played a key role in determining the fate of a given ancient structure. But during the Renaissance, the close study of antiquity by humanists and scholars who drew renewed attention to the physical conditions of these ancient artifacts also helped to lay the essential foundations for a more precise and exacting approach to preservation.

In Renaissance Rome the preservation of antiquity had acute political relevance, just as it does today, confirmed by the fact that antiquarian writings repeatedly presented the preservation of ancient remains as a key priority for the rulers of the city. The specific political conditions of Renaissance Rome exercised a profound impact upon the direction and forms of emerging preservation practices. Above all, the institution of the papacy, absorbed in the process of establishing and consolidating absolute temporal power over the Eternal City at exactly this time, played an indispensable role in shaping preservation practices in the papal capital. Although it has tended to go unnoticed, the rule of the Renaissance popes also coincided with the vigorous implementation and enforcement of an unprecedented, systematic, and comprehensive form of preservation legislation.

It is important to note, however, that despite their often ruthless pursuit of power, the Renaissance popes never managed to consolidate exclusive jurisdiction over the preservation of antiquity in Renaissance Rome. Rome was unique among Italian cities in that it had two rival ruling administrations, where supreme papal power concentrated at the Vatican overlapped the authority of the municipal government, the self-appointed successors of the ancient Roman Senate, founded in the twelfth century on the Capitoline Hill. The fact that not just the popes but also the magistrates of the civic administration counted preservation among their responsibilities rendered this an intense and conflicted political issue in the postclassical city.

Despite the definitive subordination of the civic magistrates to papal power at the outset of the Renaissance, these officials—known as the Conservators—managed to retain official custody of the city's ancient remains. Over the course of the fifteenth and sixteenth centuries, with papal consent, the preservation of the ancient past became a defining part of the Conservators' identity. Thus preservation practices evolved into a shared management of ancient remains, uneasily administered by two entities with sometimes parallel and sometimes opposing agendas. In this context, against the backdrop of the rapid reconstruction of the new papal capital, preservation became a vital instrument with which to negotiate power.

By exploring such problems, this book traces the ceaselessly shifting dialogue of the present with the past. During the Renaissance, as today, this relationship was fraught with rival and conflicting interests. Efforts to ensure the survival and protection of historic artifacts inevitably reflected different social and political demands of the competing constituencies, and *The Ruin of the Eternal City* invites us to explore a critical moment in this ongoing and unresolved debate. By extension, it also invites us to expand our conventional understanding of preservation and conservation practices in the present. Since the nineteenth century, preservation and conservation have become fully formed disciplines supported by specialized theories and established academic discourses. However, it is essential to acknowledge that despite the definitive impression imparted by disciplinary formation, preservation practices are always radically open to transformation. They must be constantly modified to respond not only to the specific requirements of individual cases and changing technical capacities, but also to a dizzying constellation of different cultural, political, and economic forces.[11] The boundaries of preservation are nothing if not fluid.[12]

The critique of preservation practices in Renaissance in Rome leveled by scientific archaeology was predicated upon the assumption that modern approaches were of necessity superior to those of the past. According to this view, new insights regarding archaeological remains reached since the Renaissance automatically rendered earlier interventions on ancient sites irrelevant and obsolete. But to condemn the knowledge of the past is a counter-productive move, one that ignores a useful source of information and ideas.[13] By recognizing that Renaissance interventions on ancient sites also had value in terms of preservation, we recognize that preservation itself is a process undergoing constant redefinition and reinterpretation. Perhaps a more modest approach, one that is less quick to judge, will allow us to gain new perspective both on the past and on ourselves.[14]

New Approaches to Preservation Problems

Historic preservation in the United States may have first come to the attention of the general public with the demolition of Pennsylvania Station in the late 1960s, but the intervening decades have revealed that this problem is infinitely more complex than just a reactionary attempt to stop the wrecking ball. There has been a new groundswell of interest in preservation especially in the last decade, where the notion of preservation has become increasingly perceived as a vital aspect of cultural identity and a driving force in cultural politics. Globalization has made the notion of cultural identity and heritage preservation all the more urgent, with a boom in specialized programs and publications responding to this rising demand. According to Frank Matero, chair of the graduate program in historic preservation at the University of Pennsylvania, "over the past decade, historic preservation has come center stage in the discourse on place, cultural identity, and ownership of the past."[15]

More than ever, the preservation of the past is now recognized as an issue of global importance that transcends national and cultural boundaries. The provocative question of who owns antiquity, posed by James Cuno, responds to the competition for custody of ancient artifacts as this becomes ever more litigious and contested on the international level.[16] But at the heart of this debate rests the enduring question: how do we confront the complex problem of preserving the past?

At Rome itself the preservation of antiquity has also come under the media spotlight, especially in preparation for the Jubilee of 2000 and in the continued expansion of the city in the following years. The demolition of the pavilion constructed by Mussolini to shelter the Ara Pacis, and its subsequent replacement by Richard Meier, provoked vigorous public debate over the legitimacy of promoting large-scale construction in Rome's venerable core. Other ambitious projects in the *centro storico*, such as the projected expansion of the metropolitan subway system, have focused renewed public scrutiny upon the authorities responsible for the preservation of antiquity.[17] In a series of recent publications, Salvatore Settis, director of the Scuola Normale at Pisa, has addressed the distinctive problems Italy faces as a modern nation in administering its legendary ancient patrimony, as an incomparable legacy as well as a tremendous burden, while also investigating the ongoing vitality and importance of the classical tradition within an increasingly globalized society. To borrow from Settis, recent trends indicate that we have reason for anxiety, but also reason for tremendous excitement, regarding the "future of the past."[18]

Nonetheless, despite this skyrocketing profile of historic preservation, the question of how the preservation of antiquity was conceived and practiced in Renaissance Rome has remained remarkably little explored. This book seeks to take advantage of the unparalleled abundance of resources available in Rome to help us recuperate this process and thus to add to this growing dialogue. A fuller understanding of Renaissance preservation practices may afford us not only new insight into preservation as we practice it in the present, but also how we might practice it in the future.

Three primary deposits of evidence will be used to explore how the preservation of antiquity occurred in Renaissance Rome. The first of these is the surviving record of the physical artifacts themselves, based upon the evidence of archaeological excavations as well as on-site analysis. Second are the numerous antiquarian drawings after ancient remains that were first produced in quantity in Renaissance Rome, an exemplary body of visual materials that offers a unique resource to investigate the conditions of ancient remains in the Renaissance and how contemporary preservation efforts were implemented.[19] Finally, key documentary collections, in particular those of the Vatican and Capitoline archives, provide an essential record of mandates and regulations regarding ancient remains in Renaissance Rome. By weaving together the evidence of these different sources, we can begin to see how the preservation of antiquity remained a primary concern in the Renaissance capital and better define and interpret the distinctive Renaissance approaches developed in response to these long-standing problems.

The book is conceived in two parts. Part I consists of three chapters that reconstruct important moments in the preservation of antiquity in Rome, culminating with the critical advances made during the fifteenth and sixteenth centuries. This provides a broader, diachronic discussion of emerging strategies for the management and preservation of ancient remains in the rapidly changing context of Renaissance Rome. Part II shifts focus to consider the Renaissance history of three individual ancient monuments: the Colosseum, the Pantheon, and the Ponte Santa Maria. These chapters, conceived as object biographies, represent a form of extended archaeological site investigation. Each chapter investigates how preservation projects took shape at each of these very different monuments during the fifteenth and sixteenth centuries and prompts us to consider how Renaissance preservation strategies responded to unique, site-specific concerns.

Chapter 1 serves as a rapid survey of preservation traditions as these can be reconstructed for ancient and medieval Rome. The Roman interest in preservation was critically reinforced in both cultural and institutional terms under

Augustus, and successive rulers continued to have recourse to this established tradition. Even as imperial authority diminished and as the deterioration of Rome increased, preservation afforded a strategic means to claim political power in the ancient capital. The twelfth-century establishment of the civic government on the Capitoline Hill marked a critical turning point for the history of preservation, where this new institutional entity deployed the preservation of antiquity as a potent political strategy in its feuds with the popes and the Roman aristocracy.

Chapter 2 explores the changing cultural and political significance of the preservation of antiquity in the context of fifteenth-century Rome. Following the return of Martin V to Rome in 1420, the preservation of ancient remains afforded a vital means to achieve the key papal objective of acquiring and extending temporal power over the ancient city. By issuing licenses in the fifteenth century, the popes appropriated and reformed the existing system operated by the civic government but also made it more efficient through the introduction of modern bureaucratic practices. This in turn enabled the popes to regulate the ancient remains of the city with increased precision. At the same time that the civic magistrates were steadily drawn into the orbit of supreme papal power, these officials also became ever more deeply invested in the preservation of antiquity. The Renaissance popes chose to reinstate their historic authorities as the custodians of Rome's ancient past and, by the end of the century, preservation was administered jointly and collaboratively by the Vatican and the Campidoglio, thereby providing a strategic currency that allowed the Conservators to negotiate power in the papal capital.

Chapter 3 addresses the accelerating destruction of antiquity during the sixteenth century, spurred by the voracious demand for construction materials at the New St. Peter's. Following its inauguration in 1506, ancient sites in Rome were excavated with renewed zeal to produce sufficient building stone for what would soon become the largest building site in Europe. Rodolfo Lanciani condemned sixteenth-century papal excavations for unleashing "a meteor through the Roman Forum." Yet such inflammatory rhetoric has caused us to overlook the ways that preservation practices were understood and implemented in the sixteenth century. Despite the notorious disregard Julius II and Bramante are supposed to have had for the protection of ancient Rome, both the pope and his architect were profoundly concerned with preservation problems. As architect of the New St. Peter's for Leo X, Raphael also advanced greater awareness of the urgent need to safeguard ancient remains. Excavation licenses issued by both the papal administration and the civic government prove that new preservation strategies were in place by 1520, the year of Raphael's death, and these continued to be refined over the following decade, culminating in 1534 when Paul III appointed Latino Giovenale Manetti as the papal commissioner of antiquity. Despite ongoing destruction, the preservation of antiquity always remained a vital papal priority. Even the excavations conducted for Paul III in the heart of the ancient Roman Forum, although excoriated by Lanciani, conformed to the ideals of sixteenth-century preservation legislation.

Part II consists of the three object biographies. It begins with chapter 4 on the Colosseum, examining the afterlife of a landmark that is not only the most famous symbol of Rome but also the most infamous symbol of the Renaissance plundering of antiquity (figure 0.2). Historians and archaeologists have long pointed to Renaissance builders and their insatiable quest for building stone as the chief culprits responsible for the ongoing evisceration of this iconic landmark. And yet this chapter reverses this long-standing perception by exploring how interventions at the site actually adhered to strict Renaissance preservation practices. Despite our expectations to the contrary, early modern excavators did not have free rein when they wished to collect stone at this site. On the contrary, they were obliged to obey precise legislative measures implemented specifically to ensure its preservation. By the same token, this chapter also explores the evidence of the Passion Plays staged at the Colosseum as a noteworthy instance of the popular adaptive reuse of an ancient monument in Renaissance Rome. The inexplicable decision by Paul III to terminate the

· THEATRVM· SIVE · COLISEVM · ROMANVM

FIGURE 0.2. Colosseum, printed by Antonio Lafréry, before 1558. This view, taken from the south, emphasizes the ruinous condition of the ancient amphitheater. Note the holes gouged into the masonry joints where metal was extracted by scavengers. The collapsed stone along the southern perimeter stands considerably higher than the figures walking along the path in the right foreground.

wildly popular performances in 1539 becomes more understandable when we consider that growing papal anxiety about the appropriate conduct and behavior of the audience reflected directly upon the pope's mission to ensure the safety and preservation of the venerable Colosseum itself.

Chapter 5 turns to the Pantheon, at the opposite end of the spectrum as the best-preserved monument surviving from ancient Rome (figure 0.3). Yet the superb architectural integrity of the Pantheon was not inevitable: on the contrary, this was the result of constant, solicitous repairs and maintenance undertaken by the popes. In the fifteenth century, during the reign of Eugenius IV, the Pantheon was the subject of a remarkable and prescient papal-sponsored restoration designed to recover and reinstate the earlier historic condition of this famous landmark. The controversy this generated, however, suggests that papal intervention on this site was also liable to be interpreted by the community as

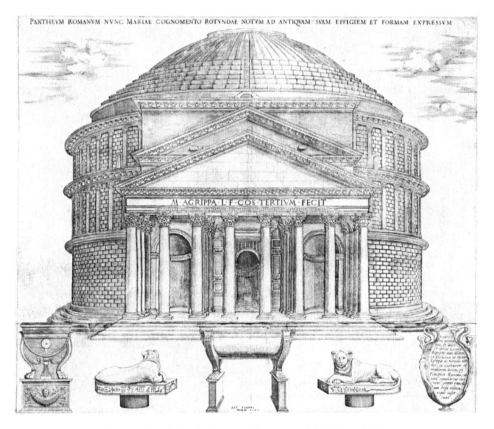

FIGURE 0.3.   Pantheon, printed by Nicolas Beatrizet, 1549. This frontal view, presenting the Pantheon as it might have appeared in antiquity, underscores the remarkable preserved state of this monument. During the Renaissance the ancient porphyry sarcophagus and the pair of basalt Egyptian lion sculptures depicted in the foreground stood in the square in front of the Pantheon portico.

an invasive form of political aggression. While the unique design of the Pantheon embodied Renaissance architectural ideals, Renaissance audiences paid
very close attention to the Pantheon's remarkable state of preservation. Above
all, the artist Raphael played a leading role in determining its future preservation history when he decided to erect his own tomb in the rotunda.

   In contrast to the proverbial examples of the half-ruined Colosseum and
the perfectly preserved Pantheon, the subject of chapter 6, the third object
biography, is virtually unknown: the bridge now called the Ponte Rotto, standing
in the rapids below the island in the Tiber (figure 0.4). While only a fragment
still survives today, during the Renaissance this bridge, known as the Ponte
Santa Maria, served as a linchpin in the urban network. The ongoing maintenance of this vital transportation corridor was a primary preoccupation for the
popes, the civic magistrates, and the Roman populace: Renaissance expenditures to preserve this bridge far surpassed those at either the Colosseum or the

FIGURE 0.4.   The remains of the Ponte Santa Maria, photographed by Eugène
Constant, ca. 1853–55. Following the loss of two piers in the flood of 1598, the bridge
was accessible only from Trastevere, until the construction of a metal suspension
bridge under Pius IX. This in turn was removed in 1885 with the construction of the
Tiber embankments and the Ponte Palatino.

Pantheon. During the sixteenth century, as its condition deteriorated, an enormous preservation campaign was organized to reinforce the structure. Even Michelangelo was involved in this work. Although the Ponte Santa Maria finally collapsed in 1557, there is evidence to suggest that this failure was caused not so much by the fault of its designers as by the project sponsors, who imposed limitations upon how this work could take place. In a surprise inversion of the conventional narrative, it was not the reckless Renaissance disregard for antiquity but rather too rigid and exacting Renaissance preservation requirements that led to this disaster.

In conclusion, it seems only appropriate that Freud's disquisition on the operation of the human mind should have been inspired by the fabulous panorama presented by ancient Rome. The strange and remarkable juxtapositions of past and present that are commonplace in this unique setting, realized through the simultaneous and ongoing processes of destruction, preservation, and rebirth, have provided endless sources of fascination and pleasure for the collective imagination. Freud's investigation reminds us that throughout history, ancient remains continued to go through progressive renewal. But by the same token, his argument also makes it clear that the physical vulnerability that they embody, registering the slow and inexorable process of change, also has its own distinctive value. Indeed, this is the unforgettable lesson of Rome, where scooters jostle casually next to monumental marble remains: it is in the context of the living, breathing present that our experience of the Roman past is at its most intense and magically alive.

Note on Terminology

The study of early modern Italian architectural and antiquarian treatises reveals not only that the use of terms such as *preservation* and *restoration* was common practice among Renaissance authors, but that such writers also used these words to make sophisticated and precise distinctions between different types of interventions upon an existing structure or urban organism. The writings of the leading mid-fifteenth-century antiquarian scholar Biondo Flavio provide a vital source in the effort to better understand these critical Renaissance distinctions. Biondo's *Roma instaurata*—translated as "Rome Revived" or "Rome Restored"—remained unsurpassed as the most important antiquarian guide to Rome for well over a century, and we can conclude that the definitions proposed by Biondo in this text represented the canonical Renaissance understanding of these words as they were employed and understood by literate audiences. The popular success of this text indicates that Biondo's use of these terms soon percolated into common parlance.[20]

In the dedicatory introduction of *Roma instaurata*, addressed to the reigning pontiff, Eugenius IV, Biondo distinguished between the different values that he assigned to these particular words, just as Rome began to experience the first stages of its progressive transformation into the papal capital. A clear definition for the word *preservation* appeared in a passage where Biondo explained the motives for his work. Above all, his composition of *Roma instaurata* had been prompted by the desire to dispel the fabulous stories in circulation about the ancient ruins, which had obscured the true meaning and virtue of ancient Rome. But in addition to serving as a necessary corrective, Biondo's work also served to celebrate the recent transformation of the city under papal rule. As he affirmed, the presence of the Holy See had finally brought stability and order to Rome, and this had been both "useful and necessary for the *preservation* of the city."[21] Biondo's use of the Latin term *conservare* at this juncture may be translated as "to preserve," as papal rule had ensured the survival and preservation of Rome itself. Thanks to the pope's decision to return to Rome, the city had narrowly escaped continued deterioration and even possible extinction. Biondo provided further corroboration for this in the next sentence, where he affirmed that with the continued absence of the papacy, Rome would have faced total collapse within ten years.

At this point, Biondo provided a clear definition for the term *restoration*. He praised Eugenius IV for his active efforts to improve existing conditions in the city, noting that the pope had renewed the city and revitalized it through new construction: "in many places and at great expense you have rebuilt and *restored* many ancient buildings."[22] Biondo's use of *instaurare*, the same word he chose for the title of his volume, can again be translated as "to revive" or "to restore." This verb described a more active transformation of the original artifact than that implied by the verb *conservare*, where restoration signaled a more energetic process of renewal rather than simply maintaining the status quo. Strategic interventions in the urban fabric by the pope had infused new vitality into defunct structures and ruinous districts, thereby lending new value and relevance to these in the present city as well as for the future.[23]

Broadly speaking, Biondo's distinction between preservation and restoration still corresponds to the way that these two terms are used in conservation theory today.[24] Preservation has the goal of stabilizing, extending the life expectancy, or otherwise maintaining the integrity of a historic structure by minimizing its ongoing deterioration. This outlook privileges the value of the structure as a historical artifact and seeks to ensure the structure remains in that state going forward into the future. Restoration, on the other hand, is more present focused: its chief objective is to reanimate the structure to fulfill contemporary goals, even if this may sometimes involve obscuring or destroying historic features. Restoration generally implies a more invasive operation, and although we may or may not agree with the views of the influential nineteenth-century critic John Ruskin, who denounced the restoration of a structure "as a lie from beginning to end," it clearly does involve the significant transformation of an existing artifact.[25]

The distinctions made by Biondo between preservation and restoration provide useful categories for a more historically informed discussion of what in this book we will call Renaissance or early modern *preservation practices*. The use of this kind of umbrella term has the advantage of situating these practices firmly in their own time, even as we must remain sensitive to the reality of differing local considerations and conditions. It also has the advantage of avoiding the negative implications of the word *conservation*. Although conservation is currently applied as a blanket reference to a wide range of interventions on historic fabric, it is too closely connected to modern interpretations to be useful for our discussion of Renaissance preservation practices. While conservation automatically directs us toward current conservation theory and the contemporary discourse regarding appropriate interventions upon historic objects, this cannot be the route by which to investigate preservation practices as they were implemented and understood in Renaissance Rome. The notion of "Renaissance preservation practices," by contrast, provides a more flexible and open way to evaluate such historic interventions, one that seeks to refrain from judging them based upon contemporary conservation principles.

In conclusion, it is worth reflecting upon the extensive use of the word *instaurare* in Biondo's text. Biondo made repeated use of this term, along with related words such as *renovare* and *restaurare*. He further privileged *instaurare* by choosing it as the title of his work, the *Roma instaurata*. The notion of the restoration of Rome can be seen as the summation of his entire writing venture, where at the end of his dedicatory preface he made a direct comparison between the papal rebuilding of Rome and his own work as a writer and antiquarian: "Let me insist, just as you strive to restore [*instaurare*] Rome, by means of the work of many masons, architects, and carpenters, so too you should make use of the monuments set forth through the modest skill of my writing."[26] Biondo thus invoked an ancient literary conceit that claimed texts were likely to be longer-lived than even the most durable building materials. Biondo concluded that posterity will judge "whether the restoration [*instauratio*] wrought in marble, brick, cement, stone, and bronze, or the restoration in literature will last better and longer."[27]

Biondo's enthusiastic use of the term *instaurare* stands in contrast to his relatively sparing use of *conservare*, which carried more restrictive and less dynamic associations. This was obviously a deliberate choice on Biondo's part, and it serves as a useful index to his thinking about the relative significance and meaning of preservation and restoration in Renaissance Rome. While Biondo clearly considered both of these processes to be essential for the survival of the city over time, it is clear he felt that more needed to be done than simply stabilizing Rome by minimizing ongoing archaeological deterioration and extending the life expectancy of its monuments. Preservation, although indispensable, was still not enough. On the contrary, Biondo rejoiced that the popes had taken a much more active role in transforming Rome, rebuilding its ancient sites, thereby giving these and the ancient city he loved so much a new life. While conservation theory tends to regard "restoration" with suspicion, if not consternation, for Biondo, as an informed and enthusiastic Renaissance scholar of the classical past, the active, animated meaning of *instaurare* was imperative. More than simply passive preservation, Biondo affirmed that it was the active and ingenious restoration of antiquity in the present that would provide for its survival today and ensure its continued vitality tomorrow.

PART I

A History of Preservation Practices in Renaissance Rome

I

Preservation Practices
in Ancient and
Medieval Rome

The innovations made for the preservation of antiquity in Renaissance Rome did not originate in a vacuum, but rather developed within a very long tradition of preservation that was fundamentally shaped by the distinctive historic, material, and cultural circumstances of Rome itself. To better understand the process by which the preservation of antiquity took place in the fifteenth- and sixteenth-century papal capital, we must have at least a general sense of how preservation practices occurred in Rome during previous centuries, as the essential backdrop against which these new Renaissance practices would emerge. Such a sweeping overview cannot claim to be comprehensive and must also depend on the work of many others, but the study of the history of institutions and the gradual emergence of institutional practices requires that we consider the *longue durée*. Moreover, this kind of study also offers an opportunity to explore changing attitudes toward the preservation of the past over time. One of the key themes to emerge from this survey is that the reverence for antiquity which is such a defining characteristic of Rome and Roman culture was in fact a cultivated outlook, one that was carefully crafted over the centuries to fulfill strategic and precise political ends.

At its most basic level, the preservation of artifacts can be considered an instinctive form of human behavior. Humans throughout history have taken keen interest in the collection and preservation of inanimate objects, precisely because they serve to convey messages from an earlier time. The quest to establish permanent and enduring monuments, and the preservation of these monuments into the future, attests to an innate human desire to memorialize the past that transcends time and space.[1] In this sense, preservation appears a natural response to the insecurities and uncertainties of life, a way of coping with the psychological anxiety associated with the transience of human life itself. The act of safeguarding a physical artifact can thus be linked to the desire to overcome death and oblivion. By inscribing our own identities onto an object, which is preserved into the future, we seek to promote a legacy that will endure beyond our own lifetimes. Although we may perish, the preservation of such physical objects may enable them to escape what Francis Bacon characterized as the "shipwreck of time," and carry our memory forward with them into the future.[2]

But in addition to these commemorative functions, it is also imperative to note that the preservation of the past also provides a vital and often underappreciated source of power. The preservation of the past can be used to inculcate respect for one's forebears and for historic precedent. Thus a passage from the Old Testament enjoined the early Israelites to "remove not the ancient landmark, which thy fathers have set."[3] The preservation of landmarks, as a direct tie to the past that illuminates the course of history, also affords an opportunity to gain political consensus in the context of a changing world. Preservation can thus be used to introduce, sanction, and legitimize the creation of tradition in a context of rapid social and cultural change.

Perhaps nowhere is this phenomenon more apparent than at Rome. This extraordinary urban environment, with its unparalleled abundance of ancient remains and continuous occupation over the centuries, offers a remarkable opportunity to investigate changing approaches to preservation over time. Preservation has long offered a strategic means to obtain and consolidate political authority in this distinctive setting, massed with monumental architectural remains, where preserving and restoring existing structures provided a key opportunity to establish a direct connection to the venerable lineage of antiquity. By intervening upon these remains, successive rulers and regimes appropriated the distinctive authority of the ancient past and transformed it to serve their own current objectives.

This chapter will consider important precedents for fifteenth- and sixteenth-century preservation practices in Rome. Centuries before the Renaissance, the imperial rulers of Rome already placed a premium upon the preservation of the past. In the ancient city, the tradition of preserving and restoring existing structures represented an essential strategy not only to demonstrate one's piety and virtue, but also to acquire political favor and power. Above all it was Augustus, as the first emperor of Rome, who exploited the power of preservation to its fullest potential. Augustus used the preservation of existing structures to reinforce his own unquestioned dominance as the ruler of Rome, and thereby brought a long period of political uncertainty to a close. By promoting the restoration and repair of historic temples associated with his own cult, the emperor also promoted his own authority and dominance in the city. Moreover, he also critically helped to institutionalize Roman preservation practices by establishing official agencies to regulate interventions on the existing urban fabric that perpetuated these policies as an enduring legacy into the future. By canonizing the preservation of antiquity as an imperial practice, Augustus ensured that preservation practices already assumed their essential contours in the capital even by the end of his reign.

This survey of Augustan preservation measures is followed in turn by a study of the ways in which the first emperor's successors built upon these critical foundations. In later centuries, preservation problems took on new complexity as subsequent rulers sought to establish their authority among the deteriorating remains of the ancient capital. The emergence of the two leading political entities in Rome, the popes and the civic government, had vital consequences for the development of new approaches to preservation problems. On the one hand, the popes claimed not only the spiritual allegiance of the Christian world but also temporal authority over the city of Rome itself, bolstered by the famous legend of the Donation of Constantine.[4] Thus the popes were inevitably and inextricably bound to the daily affairs of the city, and they played an essential role in developing particular solutions to growing preservation problems. But on the other hand, the foundation of the Roman civic government in the twelfth century was predicated upon asserting civic independence from papal sovereignty by gaining control over the physical environment of Rome. Thus the new civic magistrates also began to take special interest in questions involving preservation, as one of the chief duties in the urban management of Rome.

The resulting tension between these rival authorities, each claiming responsibility for preservation duties, set the stage for the history of preservation in Renaissance Rome. In the papal capital, the administration of preservation practices fell into overlapping spheres of responsibility. Both the popes and the civic magistrates were well aware of the fact that the preservation of ancient fragments in Rome—as symbols of imperial power that were at the same time radically disconnected from the source of this original power itself—provided an extraordinary opportunity to reshape the past to suit their own needs. Preservation provided a means to harness these potent symbols to serve different agendas, and to legitimate and project a wide-ranging spectrum of objectives and ideals for the future. But in this new political arrangement, such agendas increasingly had to be negotiated. With both popes and civic magistrates claiming the right to preserve ancient artifacts, preservation interventions on ancient sites were increasingly subject to review, where each side could argue different positions or present alternative views. This emerging arrangement helped not only to give preservation issues greater publicity and visibility in Renaissance Rome, but at the same time, it also created an environment that was uniquely conducive to the development of new preservation ideas.

Preservation as State Policy in Augustan Rome

While the veneration of history was already long-sanctioned tradition at Rome in the first century B.C., the notion of the restoration and preservation of the past as a distinctly Roman ideology acquired extraordinary new importance during the reign of Augustus.[5] An anecdote recounted by the Greek author Dionysius of Halicarnassus provided an example of this ideology as it was put into practice at the Casa Romuli, or the hut of Romulus, one of the most sacred sites in ancient Rome:

> The hut of Romulus . . . is preserved holy by those who have charge
> of these matters; they add nothing to it to render it more stately, but
> if any part of it is injured, either by storms or by the lapse of time,
> they repair the damage and restore the hut as nearly as possible to its
> former condition.[6]

According to Dionysius, the original dwelling of the legendary founder of Rome itself stood on the southwestern slope of the Palatine Hill, not far from the banks of the Tiber.[7]

Modern archaeology has confirmed that pole foundations of Iron Age thatched structures actually exist on the site.[8] However, it is unlikely that the archaic and fragile hut of Romulus itself was still standing in Augustan Rome, as it would have been over seven hundred years old at the time. It is also unlikely that the Casa Romuli of the first century A.D. was reconstructed with any kind of scientific or archaeological precision. But even if Dionysius's account suggested that the Casa Romuli was in fact reinvented as a fiction in Augustan Rome, it was interesting for precisely this reason. Dionysius described the desire to commemorate and honor this historic structure, and the associated preservation practices necessary to keep this structure standing, as a powerful driving force in the Rome of the first century A.D., where "those who have charge of these matters" took special pains to ensure its survival.

In the context of Augustan Rome, where the construction of imperial temples and palaces had transformed the capital city, such an archaic and inconsequential hut was likely to be overshadowed by new neighbors that were both more stylish and state-of-the-art. And yet the assiduous preservation of the Casa Romuli by a vigilant staff of religious officials showcased its unique importance: the preserved physical integrity of this unchanged artifact spoke directly to profound concerns associated with the ongoing transformation of imperial Rome. Despite the sweeping changes affecting the Augustan capital, where the historic wood and terra-cotta sanctuaries of the city made way for new marble monuments, Dionysius's anecdote of the Casa Romuli affirmed that the Roman citizens continued without fail to preserve and honor the material remains of the Roman past.

The distinctive nature of Roman religion itself may have helped to encourage this curious Roman interest in the meticulous preservation of artifacts and sites. According to Simon Price, "Roman myths were in essence myths of place."[9] Roman mythology was inseparable from the physical landscape of Rome itself: it recounted the history of the area of Rome, and living tokens of this history survived in the cults of Rome. This local dimension of Roman religious practices in turn encouraged a deep-seated pious interest in preserving such sites unchanged over time.

Thus the attention to preservation manifest in the scrupulous procedures outlined by Dionysius: as he reported, the officials responsible for preserving the Casa Romuli never made any attempts to improve upon its existing physical form or to "render it more stately." On the contrary, whenever an original element failed and its replacement became necessary, every effort was made to "restore the hut as nearly as possible." It was the exact preservation of the Casa Romuli in its presumed archaic condition, as a humble thatched structure, that mattered.

At the same time, the preservation and restoration of historic sites such as the Casa Romuli also had compelling political significance for the new ruler of Rome, Augustus. The new emperor realized that the pious act of preservation afforded a unique opportunity to relate the present directly to the past.[10] Thus through his zealous preservation of historic Roman religious sites, Augustus promoted the reassuring impression of pious continuity with the past, even as the advent of his regime signaled a dramatic shift in Roman political history and equally dramatic physical changes in the city of Rome itself. Paradoxically, it was the elaboration of the traditional Roman religious focus upon preserving historic sites that enabled Augustus to implement some of his most radical transformations of Rome and Roman culture. The preservation of the Casa Romuli provided a case in point: through ongoing interventions on this legendary site Augustus reinforced his own personal connection to the founder of Rome, and thereby his own status as the ruler of the new Roman Empire.[11]

Dionysius, as a Greek who relocated to Rome at the time of Augustus's ascendancy, may have had reason to exaggerate the attentive preservation of the hut of Romulus to flatter the self-perceptions of his audience in Rome.[12] But even as an anecdote, the story of the Casa Romuli was nonetheless revealing. It demonstrated the powerful cultural and political imperative in Augustan Rome to provide for the exacting preservation and restoration of historic structures, where their enduring survival offered persuasive material proof to corroborate and verify the course of history itself.[13]

The attentive respect for the past under Augustus needs to be understood as a strategic response to complex political conditions in Rome at the end of the first century B.C. and the beginning of the first century A.D. At this time, the representative government of the Roman Republic, directed by the collective decisions taken by the Roman Senate, gave way to the imperial structure of the

Roman Empire, with Augustus as its single ruler. Competing power struggles, social upheaval, and vicious civil war marked a brutal disruption of normal life for much of Roman society during this period, before Augustus finally emerged as victor. In the aftermath, the new emperor embarked upon a cultural program calculated to disseminate the notion that this radical new constellation of power had not disrupted the ancient Republican traditions of the city, and to emphasize his support for long-standing Roman traditions and virtues. To suppress possible doubts, Augustus deployed both political and social legislation as well as inscriptions and other material artifacts to underscore the commitment of the new regime to reinstating Roman traditions that had been neglected or cast aside during the civil wars.

The notion of restoring and preserving the surviving traditions and artifacts of the past was thus central to the imperial propaganda of the Augustan state from the outset. The imperial message of triumph and peace was reinforced by the emphatic reinstatement of Roman customs and practices: this move served to surmount discord as well as to marginalize the frustration and alienation felt by the losing side. Augustus insisted that the renewal and revival of forgotten traditions was directly connected to the imperial achievement of victory and peace. This rhetoric, carried to the farthest corners of the empire, reinforced the notion of an imperial Roman culture that was deeply respectful toward venerable Roman traditions.

This emphasis upon preserving connections to history underscored the way that Augustus desired to relate the present to the past: the preservation of venerable Roman traditions provided critical support for his program of advancing the Roman state. While the cultivation of a reverent attitude toward what came before was already widespread in Roman Italy, this now became systematically integrated into all aspects of Roman life during Augustus's reign.[14] But in particular, the preservation and restoration of historic buildings, as the abiding physical fabric of Rome that was constantly present to and experienced by its inhabitants, provided a vital means to implement this program.

Thus the Augustan exaltation of history and tradition also directly influenced the way the emperor intervened upon the city of Rome itself. Conspicuous imperial interventions in the fabric of the city, subsidized by Augustus himself, served to underscore the importance the emperor assigned to the solicitous protection of historic Roman remains. These included one of the most famous restoration campaigns to take place during his reign, which was the repair of historic temples in the capital that had fallen into disrepair during the upheaval of the civil wars. Augustus publicized this pious program himself in the *Res Gestae*, where he proclaimed: "During my sixth consulate, by order of the Senate I rebuilt 82 temples of the gods in Rome and did not omit a single one which was at that time in need of renewal."[15]

Despite this token gesture of deference to the Senate, this restoration campaign was clearly intended to reinforce Augustus's own hegemony. While the rhetoric of the imperial proclamation suggested a global restoration of every temple in Rome, the interventions were in fact far from uniform. Instead, the most lavish restorations were reserved specifically for those cult buildings most closely associated with the emperor.[16] By the same token, minimal restorations at those temples that did not fit into the Augustan cultural campaign helped render them less prominent and visible.[17] Thus these restorations served to direct public attention where Augustus wanted it to go, enabling him to present his own cult temples as symbols of renewal and hope after the chaos and destruction of the civil wars. Such interventions demonstrated with enormous force how the selective preservation and restoration of existing structures had the power to shape public opinion in the present as well as in the future.

Selective preservation thus represented a key element in the strategic Augustan program by which a conservative agenda served both to disguise and to implement radical change. Augustus's rapid urban transformation of the imperial capital was commemorated by Dio Cassius, who reported Augustus recalling on his deathbed how he had turned a dusty backwater into a gleaming modern capital with the famous lines, "I found Rome a city of clay; I left it a city of marble."[18] The emperor, despite his reverent interest in guarding Roman tradition and in the preservation of the past, was also a proponent of sweeping urban renewal. He showed no hesitation in sheathing the more humble and quotidian brick of Republican Rome with an expensive and exotic veneer of imported marble. The Augustan decision to favor marble as a building material in fact marked one of the most radical physical transformations of Rome in its history. The extravagant imperial use of this prestigious stone, sanctioned by Augustus, became a defining feature of Rome as the capital of the Roman Empire. Marble became the most tangible evidence of the expansive imperial economy, which was uniquely capable of acquiring, transporting, and constructing with vast quantities of marble collected from all around the Mediterranean.[19]

Even as Augustus inaugurated this unprecedented imperial marble transformation of Rome, he also continued to emphasize his modest desire to uphold existing traditions, especially where his incursions might generate the resentment of powerful enemies. Such concerns may have affected his designs for the Forum of Augustus. According to Suetonius, "he built his Forum somewhat smaller than originally planned, because he did not dare encroach on the property of neighboring houses."[20] Thus the reconfiguration of the city to create a temple dedicated to the imperial cult of Mars was restrained by the emperor's concern to abide by historic precedents, but also by shrewd political motives. The zigzag plan of the Forum of Augustus, realized in the immense three-dimensional form of the monumental masonry wall that still defines the north edge of the Forum today, attests to this act of imperial diplomacy.[21] Augustus chose not to expropriate those properties which might have made the construction of the temple complex more convenient, but which would probably have brought him into conflict with their owners. Thus the towering ninety-foot-high stone wall twisted and turned, tracing an irregular line that inscribed the respect of the imperial house for the rights of private ownership into the heart of the imperial capital (figures 1.1 and 1.2).[22]

Such examples attest to Augustus's success at balancing the conflicting pressures of preservation and progress. While there was plenty of evidence that Augustus was in fact engaged in a radical project of rebuilding Rome from the ground up, there was also a compelling argument to be made for his conservative, abiding veneration for Roman history and traditions. The conservative program was deemed a success by Augustus's imperial successors, who continued to adhere rigorously to the norms Augustus established.[23] Thus did Augustus's creative forging of innovation and tradition enable him to achieve the seemingly impossible: as he promoted the reverent cult of the venerable Roman past, so did he also manage to implement the far-reaching transformation of Roman culture and the city of Rome itself.

FIGURE 1.1.   Part of perimeter wall of the Forum of Augustus, by Giovanni Antonio Dosio, ca. 1569. Note the three colossal columns and entablatures surviving from the Temple of Mars Ultor, crowned by the now-demolished bell tower of Santa Maria Annunziata.

FIGURE I.2. The same perimeter wall, viewed from the opposite side. Photograph by Robert Macpherson, ca. 1850–58.

Creating a Culture of Preservation:
Augustan Municipal Reforms

A system for urban maintenance or *cura urbis* had emerged by the time of the Republic, with *censors, curators,* and *aediles* assuming maintenance responsibilities.[24] By the late Republic, however, this system was showing considerable flaws, as it was unable to keep pace with the demands of a sprawling metropolis of more than a million inhabitants. The appointments to these key posts were not permanent under the Republic, but rather made on a temporary and extraordinary basis, discouraging the development of systematic approaches or uniform policies. Moreover, the posts often languished unfilled, as career-minded Roman patricians passed them over in favor of more glamorous and politically advantageous positions. The disruption of the civil wars had caused further neglect. Clearly preservation procedures at Rome prior to the advent of Augustus were at most sporadic and irregular.

All this would change under Augustus, as the emperor gradually forged a permanent municipal bureaucracy out of the constituent parts of the existing Republican framework. Under Augustus the municipal offices were reorganized, their responsibilities and geographic jurisdictions clarified, and their effective power strengthened with the addition of new staff. Extraordinary, unsalaried appointments made in response to needs as they arose were now substituted with regular, long-term, salaried appointments, funded by the state. The comprehensiveness of the Augustan reforms was epitomized by the decision to double the number of administrative regions to fourteen in 8 B.C. to cover all parts of the metropolis. This led to the creation of a permanent bureaucracy, favoring prescriptive solutions rather than reactive legislation, and the development of a professional staff of experts to address ongoing repair and maintenance problems. With these reforms, Augustus institutionalized the *cura urbis*.

Augustus's personal stake in the success of the *cura urbis* also increased its prestige. By sponsoring prominent restorations in Rome, such as the rebuilding of the city's temples, Augustus demonstrated that the care of the city was a task of the utmost importance to the city's supreme ruler. He was also assisted in this by his close associate and friend Agrippa, who assumed responsibility of important civic projects, such as the expansion and maintenance of Rome's aqueduct system. The enthusiastic participation of Rome's leading figures in major civic works encouraged others to emulate them.[25]

By stabilizing the municipal system, and by encouraging others to follow his example, Augustus played a critical role in shifting Roman cultural perceptions. His attention to and celebration of the virtues of preservation, restoration, and regular repair had a lasting legacy for Roman culture that cannot be underestimated, and the sense of civic responsibility for the maintenance of the city fabric was never entirely effaced from Roman collective memory, despite the subsequent vicissitudes of history. Indeed, the Augustan legacy of an institutional culture of preservation at Rome far outlasted even the Roman Empire itself.

Attitudes Toward Ruins in Late Antique Rome

Already in antiquity, the urban core of Rome posed special maintenance and preservation problems. Beginning with the creation of the new Forum of Caesar under Julius Caesar, the Roman Forum was progressively transformed into a monument to imperial power. With every additional conquest, another victory monument had to be shoehorned into these tight quarters. By late antiquity the Forum had thus reached a stage of intense architectural congestion, and regular maintenance of this building glut represented a formidable economic challenge. As the imperial economy slowed and faltered, the strain began to show in terms of deferred maintenance and the creation of ruins.[26] An abundance of ruins, however, offered ample scope for the development of new approaches toward the preservation of antiquity.

The late antique imperial administration, in confronting this ruinous landscape, also confronted complex preservation issues. The declining political and economic power of Rome raised a new and unexpected dilemma: how was it possible to stave off accelerating physical deterioration, while still upholding the Augustan ideals of the *cura urbis*? The effort to resolve this dilemma led to the creation of an important body of late antique preservation legislation which sought to stabilize existing conditions by slowing or interrupting the process of decay.[27] The fourth- and fifth-century edicts of the Theodosian Code and Novels explicitly condemned the cannibalization of public structures:

> It is manifest that the public buildings in which the adornment of
> the entire city of Rome consists are being destroyed everywhere. . . .
> [U]nder the pretense that the materials are needed for public works,
> the beautiful structures of ancient monuments are being scattered,
> and great things are being pulled down in order that something
> small be repaired.[28]

Such legislation affirmed that the removal of building elements or *spolia* to repair other structures, while this might seem perfectly logical to ordinary Romans, needlessly exacerbated the ruinous conditions of Rome's urban fabric. To counter the escalating destruction, punitive legislation was added to the repertoire of preservation strategies: those who dared to damage ancient buildings would be "mutilated by the loss of their hands, through which the monuments of the ancients that should be preserved are desecrated."[29] The severity of this legislation attested both to the anxiety as well as the ineffectiveness of the imperial administration in its efforts to arrest the ongoing decay of the ancient capital.[30]

In addition, the distinctive anxiety about the creation of ruins articulated by such edicts also set an important precedent for later civic legislation. As the city continued to slip into ever more grievous decay, such legislation began to demonize the ruins themselves. In this context, ruins became the antithesis of "the beautiful structures of ancient monuments" that needed to be preserved intact and whole. Ruins represented everything that the late antique rulers wanted to avoid: they were unsightly and depressing, a blight upon the capital, the physical manifestation of the collapse of Roman civil society and order. It is not surprising that late imperial preservation legislation was calculated from its inception to ward off the advance of ruins at all costs.

The influential regulations of late antiquity, however, also had another unexpected consequence: they helped to enshrine a profoundly negative outlook toward ruins in Roman civic legislation. In fact this outlook could find support among some of the most important schools of philosophy in the Western tradition. For example, Aristotle, in his investigations of different states of being and actuality, stressed the importance of attaining a state of complete development or completion, an idea that was bound to come into conflict with the fragmentary state evoked by ruins.[31] Similarly, in the *De finibus bonorum et malorum*, Cicero discussed the object of Stoic philosophy as attaining a state of perfected unity, for which ruins served as an obvious antithesis.[32] Later the medieval philosopher St. Thomas Aquinas returned to the same premises when he asserted that "a thing is called perfect to which nothing is wanting that it ought to possess."[33] According to logic, it followed that the despoiled buildings of Rome represented only flaws and imperfections. Such negative associations determined the dominant outlook toward ruins in Rome, with lasting consequences that extended into the Renaissance.

Preservation as Political Tool in Postclassical Rome

Although we are accustomed to thinking of postclassical Rome in terms of waves of barbaric invasions followed by chaos, upheaval, and destruction, important preservation efforts were still undertaken throughout this period. Later rulers who invaded and occupied Rome found it expedient to endorse preservation, thereby invoking imperial tradition and presenting themselves as the rightful heirs of imperial power.

Following his conquest of the ancient capital in the early sixth century, the Ostrogothic king Theodoric advocated with enthusiasm on behalf of the preservation of the city and its structures. Aspiring to the imperial diadem, Theodoric realized that exalting the preservation of the Roman past and thereby recalling the established imperial cultural program offered a politically useful strategy. The preservation of the past implied continuity between this "bar-barian king" and the imperial tradition, and served to reinforce his political legitimacy.[34]

At the same time, the notion of preservation could also be used by the opposite side to attack and undermine these very claims. According to the his-torian Procopius, allied with Byzantines against the Goths, whose battles he recorded in the *Gothic War*:

> more than any other people . . . the Romans are fond of their city and
> are careful to maintain and conserve everything, to ensure that none
> of the ancient beauty of Rome be lost. For even though they were for
> a long time under barbarian sway, they preserved the buildings of the
> city and most of its adornments, such as could through the excel-
> lence of their workmanship withstand so long a lapse of time and
> such neglect.[35]

Procopius presented the Romans as more invested in preservation "than any other people," taking every step to "conserve everything," and seeking to main-tain the ancient city exactly as it had been in the past. For Procopius, the pres-ervation of the past also served as an instrument of propaganda. It was precisely through the Romans' attentive preservation of the ancient city fabric that they had managed to keep their venerable history alive and preserve their distinctive cultural identity, despite the presence of alien "barbarian" populations. Exalting the conservative attitude of the Romans, Procopius pointed to the preservation of the Roman past as the fundamental proof of Roman resistance to the occu-pying Gothic forces. Further, the prestige of this protected heritage justified the struggle of the Byzantine armies to recover the ancient capital from the Gothic enemy.[36]

While the rise of Christianity at Rome may evoke images of the icono-clastic destruction of pagan cult artifacts, the new state church was also swift to recognize that the preservation of ancient remains in this historic setting of-fered an attractive and viable political strategy. Just as the acceptance of Chris-tianity can be seen as a political act of accommodation on the part of the imperial administration, so did it prove to be politically useful for the Christian rulers to accommodate and preserve the ancient history manifested with such physical abundance in Rome.[37]

For example, Gregory the Great, the influential sixth-century pope, did his best to avoid stirring up conflict with pagan traditions in Rome by advising his missionaries to preserve the existing temples of the city: "do not destroy the pagan temples but the idols that they harbor; as far as the buildings themselves are concerned, be content to sprinkle them with holy water and place your altars and relics in them." Thus a policy memorably characterized by Françoise Choay as the "appropriational practice of the hermit crab," was incorporated into official church doctrine.[38] In this way foreign bodies and traditions could

be purged of their potentially dangerous associations and adapted to fulfill current needs. Such an outlook enabled the integration of pagan structures into
the Christian world with a minimum of disruption or destruction.

Following the collapse of Byzantine rule in the eighth century, the popes
increasingly assumed the Augustan mantle of protecting and preserving antiquity in Rome. In the following centuries, often marked by violence and anarchy,
it was the popes who carried the institutional memory of preservation practices
into the future.[39]

Preservation as Rallying Cry for the *Popolo Romano*

The founding of the civic government on the Capitoline Hill in 1144 marked a
critical turning point for the preservation of antiquity in Rome. The civic government promoted an antiquarian revival, styling themselves after the ancient
Roman Senate, and reviving the classical title of the *Senatus populusque Romanus*,
or SPQR, along with the accompanying ancient dignity of senatorial title. The
new civic magistrates viewed themselves as the direct heirs to the civic ideals
and virtues of ancient Rome, and specifically those of the Roman Republic.
Thus they were vigorously opposed to the tyranny of absolute power. The hierarchy of imperial Rome, on the other hand, provided a convenient analogy to
the structure of the papacy, with the pope occupying a supreme position not
unlike that of a Roman emperor.

Charged with defending the interests of ordinary Romans against the
popes and the powerful Roman nobility, the civic magistrates also appointed
themselves the guardians of the Roman past.[40] The slogan of preserving and
restoring antiquity provided the civic leaders with a political tool of incalculable
value, which they repeatedly exploited to gain consensus, galvanizing the
Roman population to band together to resist external threats. We have already
seen that preservation in Rome had a long history as a political weapon. However, the civic government invested preservation with new meaning, reenergiz-
ing the notion of preservation in Rome as something that did not just involve
the ruling elite, but was of central interest to the general population. The
appeal of the civic magistrates to their fellow Romans to preserve and defend
the ancient remains of the city helped to transform preservation into a collective
responsibility.[41]

Papal excavations by Innocent II at the Baths of Caracalla beginning in
1140, shortly before the founding of the civic government, may have further
fueled local resentment and thus heightened the value of preservation as a
political tool (figures 1.3 and 1.4). Innocent II, as temporal ruler of Rome, decided
to make use of the imperial bath complex to supply materials for the new
basilica of Santa Maria in Trastevere. During these years workers extracted
loads of marble and other stone from the ancient site, which were then loaded

FIGURE 1.3.   The Baths of Caracalla, by Giovanni Antonio Dosio, ca. 1569. The massive
arched structure in the foreground, along with the freestanding masonry pier
in the left rear, probably supported the vault of the caldarium rotunda.

onto wagons for delivery to the basilica building site across the river. When the
new civic administration claimed right of jurisdiction over Rome's ancient
remains, the papal excavations at the Baths of Caracalla could be depicted as an
unauthorized papal incursion upon the rights of the Roman people.[42]

With the founding of the civic government, two separate political entities
in Rome—the papal administration and the civic administration—now claimed
official responsibility for the preservation of antiquity in the medieval city. This
dual administrative structure, characterized by overlapping areas of interest
and rival jurisdictional authorities, had vital implications for the future administration and management of ancient remains. Precisely because the issue of
preservation was now contested in an officially sanctioned way, it became a
topic of constant and often acrimonious controversy in Rome. The emergence
of this particular administrative system ensured that preservation remained
a subject of vigorous partisan debate, and disagreements over strategies and
approaches became a topic of general public interest.

At the same time, this division of authority also had important consequences in terms of the implementation of preservation practices. Making

FIGURE 1.4. The Baths of Caracalla, photograph by Adolphe Braun, ca. 1860–70.

preservation issues into a matter of public concern meant that different solutions could be more frequently discussed, compared, and tested against each other. Such public engagement with preservation matters favored the development of new approaches and ways of thinking about these long-standing problems.

The civic officials made strategic use of the preservation of antiquity to further their own political ends in 1162, when they issued a document specifying the preservation of the Column of Trajan "dum mundus durat," or for all eternity, and ruled that no one, upon pain of death, should deface or otherwise alter the structure in any way (figure 1.5).[43] Thus the civic administration of Rome, by threatening harsh punishment to anyone who dared infringe upon the city's ancient remains, embraced the punitive tradition of late antique preservation legislation. The classicizing culture of the twelfth century, which encouraged renewed interest in the study of Roman law, encouraged such a conscious revival of imperial legislative precedents.[44]

But clearly this preservation legislation was also calculated to answer contemporary political aims. The origins of the conflict that inspired this document are uncertain; perhaps some powerful entity, either the pope or a member of a leading noble Roman family, had designs upon the ancient landmark. In any case, this real or perceived threat to the monument spurred the civic magistrates to take action and to assume a highly aggressive and confrontational stance. Championing the preservation of the prestigious Column of Trajan, as a flagship monument in the city, became a pretext for the civic government to flex their legislative muscles. This allowed them to declare that they had the last word over its defense, as a unique and irreplaceable symbol of ancient Rome. Here preservation clearly served more than affirming continuity with the past: it was intended to galvanize patriotic sentiment, to promote a sense of solidarity and common cause (figures 1.6 and 1.7).

Immediately after the founding of the civic government, civic officials began to assume responsibility for maintaining and preserving important Roman infrastructure, as recorded in restorations both at the Aurelian Walls and on the bridges across the Tiber.[45] That the civic magistrates envisioned themselves as the direct heirs of the Roman institutional culture of preservation, however, is best attested by the eventual emergence of the officials within the civic administration known as the *maestri di strade e degli edifici*, or the masters of the streets and buildings of Rome.[46] These officials played a central role in the ongoing preservation and care of the existing urban fabric, recalling the duties of the municipal bureaucracy dedicated to such needs that had been institutionalized in Augustan Rome. Chapter 2 explores in greater detail how the *maestri* played a vital role in preserving the city's ancient remains, while also considering the key political significance of this office, which became strategically useful to the Renaissance papal administration in its efforts to promote urban reforms.

Trainni Imp. columna, cochlidis structura, in
medio eius Foro, hodie quoq erecta uisitur. Reru
à Traiano gestarum summa mirâ arte caelatam habet:
inprimis uerò Dacicum belli. intus.185. gradibus ad
summu fastigium, 40 fenestellis lucem admitten:
tibus, ascensu praebet. alta pedu.120. in summo
Traiani ossu, in pila aurea condita seruabantur.

35

FIGURE 1.5. The Column of Trajan, by Giovanni Antonio Dosio, ca. 1569. The inscription reports that the remains of Trajan were preserved at the top of the structure, "at a height of 120 feet," inside a golden sphere. Modern archaeology instead locates the imperial tombs in the pedestal chamber.

FIGURE 1.6. Panoramic view of the Column of Trajan, printed by Etienne Dupérac, published by Goert van Schayk, ca. 1621. The dome of Santa Maria di Loreto is visible to the rear. Sixteenth-century excavations liberated the pedestal of the Column of Trajan from accumulated earth and later constructions.

FIGURE 1.7. Panoramic view of the Column of Trajan, photograph by Robert Macpherson, ca. 1858–71. The eighteenth-century church of Santissimo Nome di Maria now flanks the Column of Trajan, while in the foreground archaeologists have reconstructed the colonnades of the Basilica Ulpia.

The first civic statutes of Rome, issued in the second half of the fourteenth century, further reiterated the primary importance of the preservation of antiquity for the civic government. The statutes included a specific injunction prohibiting the destruction of ancient structures, titled *De antiquis aedificiis non diruendis*:

> So that the city is not made unsightly by ruins, and so that ancient buildings might offer public decorousness, we decree that no one should dare to demolish any ancient building of the city, or have any ancient building torn down, under penalty of 100 *librarum*, of which half should go to the *Camera urbis*, and half to the accuser.[47]

This was consistent with the venerable tradition of preservation legislation in Rome that sought to restrain the demolition of existing buildings with the threat of punishment. Thus the civic magistrates threatened those who dared to demolish ancient buildings with monetary fines and offered a reward as incentive to those who reported such destruction to the authorities.

But it was not only in penalizing destruction that the civic statutes recalled earlier legislative models. The civic government continued to uphold the traditional notion that the city should not be "made unsightly by ruins," despite the fact that by the fourteenth century, much of Rome consisted of ruins. Thus the statutes continued to perpetuate the notion of preservation as it had been defined in the late antique imperial edicts, which had served as their primary model and inspiration: according to this tradition, ruins were viewed in purely negative terms. It was not ruins but ancient buildings that were the primary intended object of this legislation.

And yet ambiguity surrounded these definitions, for what really distinguished an ancient building from a ruin? Many of the ancient buildings of the city had suffered some degree of damage; which of these damaged structures were eligible for such preferential treatment, and which could be dismissed as mere rubble? Where should one draw the line that separated a decorous ancient building from an unsightly ruin? Such uncertainties, coupled with the magnitude of urban decay in early modern Rome, made it very unlikely that such legislation was very effective in safeguarding antiquity.

But if the civic government perpetuated existing notions about preservation from the past, at the same time it also took an active role in developing new methods and practices to handle the complex problem of controlling private interventions in the public realm. Excavation licenses were already in use in ancient Rome, where they served to authorize the recovery of buried valuables, and the popes had issued export licenses at least as early as the twelfth century.[48] The magistrates of the civic government, drawing upon their authority as the self-appointed guardians of Rome, claimed both of the mechanisms of excavation and export licenses as subject to their legal jurisdiction. Thus when teams of excavators seeking high-quality stone and marble to decorate the new cathedral at Orvieto descended upon Rome in the fourteenth century, they applied for excavation licenses to the civic government.[49]

The civic government collected fees when it awarded excavation licenses, and this has given rise to the assumption that excavation and export licenses were intended primarily as tools to generate income.[50] But it is also true that this legislation provided a vital means to regulate the growing lucrative trade in precious stone and marble throughout the Italian peninsula, which zeroed in upon Rome as perhaps its most important source. Thus these licenses afforded the civic government a means to control excavations and to restrict the kind of excavations and exports that could take place. While this protective dimension has generally been disregarded by much of the archaeological literature, excavation and export licenses clearly played an essential role in safeguarding ancient Roman remains from reckless or uncontrolled damage.

On the contrary, preservation at Rome was never an issue that could be easily dismissed. As we have seen with the active involvement of the civic magistrates, invoking preservation objectives offered a vital means to promote a sense of community. By celebrating the ideals of the ancient Republic and making overt efforts to recall and reinstate the grandeur of ancient Rome in the present, the civic government popularized the notion of preservation. Local pride was at stake in the defense of antiquity: the project of safeguarding what remained of ancient Rome was increasingly perceived as a common objective and shared responsibility. Ordinary Romans participated by decorating their houses with elaborate inscriptions recalling ancient Roman achievements, which declared their sense of civic pride.[51] Thus the active interest in preservation by the medieval civic government helped to disseminate an interest in preservation across Roman society from top to bottom.

Such was the case in the popular movement headed by Cola di Rienzo in fourteenth-century Rome, where Cola capitalized upon the ubiquitous ancient remains to promote common cause against the threat of papal power. In a famous incident, Cola used his renowned epigraphic skills to decipher the mysterious bronze tablet of the *lex de imperio Vespasiani*. His reading of this tablet served as the basis for a powerful political assertion: as Vespasian had acknowledged the ancient jurisdictional authorities of the *popolo romano* in antiquity, so by extension the pope should accord these same rights to the people of medieval Rome.[52] This famous act of interpretation emphasized the extraordinary value of such fragmentary ancient artifacts: they were coded with rights and honors that could be maintained only as long as these artifacts were preserved. Cola's discovery could only have reinforced to the Roman populace the immense significance of preservation. The implications of preservation extended all the way down through society even to the ordinary individual.

And yet nonetheless, it is clear that the civic government was ultimately ill equipped to cope with the immense challenge of preserving antiquity in Rome. Despite the important advances for preservation made under the rule of the

Via sacra, quae à Oris ueteri prope arcem Constantini Imp incipiens, ad Capitolij radices peringebat.

FIGURE 1.8. Panoramic view of the Roman Forum, by Giovanni Antonio Dosio, ca. 1569. Titled "Via Sacra," this view shows the ancient processional route across the Forum to the Capitoline Hill, with the sun rising over the Colosseum.

civic government—both in terms of legislation and above all in terms of encouraging broader popular interest in the preservation of the past—the implementation of these actual practices remained vague and unclear. This was especially true in the context of a city that was now dominated by ruins (figure 1.8).

Moreover, the preservation of the remains of ancient Rome was a burden that far outstripped the capacities of the civic government. Although the Augustan legacy of caring for the urban environment of Rome continued to persist across the centuries, in part because the notion of preservation itself offered such potent political opportunities, the civic magistrates lacked not only the financial clout but also the sophisticated bureaucracy necessary to ensure the close monitoring of this immense ancient landscape, subject to constant change. The situation was of course only magnified by the advanced state of ruin and deterioration that afflicted much of the city. Finally, the removal of the papacy to Avignon during the fourteenth century proved beyond a doubt that Rome was dependent upon the papacy for its livelihood and income, when the city is estimated to have reached the lowest population in its entire millennial history. Such an environment of diminishing resources and a faltering economy was not a propitious one for the active preservation and regulation of antiquity.[53]

The return of the papacy to Rome in the early fifteenth century would restore papal power and wealth to the ancient capital. By the same token, the return of the Holy See also brought the highly organized apparatus of a hierarchical, bureaucratic state to bear upon the governance of this complicated built environment. Chapter 2 explores how the permanent reestablishment of the papal bureaucracy in fifteenth-century Rome signaled a watershed moment for the preservation of antiquity in the Eternal City. At the same time, the implementation of new fifteenth-century preservation strategies also signaled a new way of thinking about this ruinous landscape. Slowly but surely, papal legislation began to treat Rome not just as an inhabited city but as an inhabited archaeological site.

2

Inventing a
Preservation Program
in Fifteenth-Century Rome

The artist rendering the view of Rome for the *Nuremberg Chronicle* of Hartmann Schedel, printed circa 1493, compressed a panoramic view of the sprawling city into a remarkably shallow plane (figure 2.1). The Aurelian Walls extended across the low foreground, while just beyond, the rounded ridges of the Esquiline, Viminal, and Quirinal hills descended toward the flat terrain of the Campus Martius along the Tiber. At the center of the image, on the opposite side of the river, the Mons Vaticanus framed the ancient Basilica of St. Peter, its high roofs and towers enclosed within the protective embrace of the Leonine Walls. Despite its compactness, the image conveyed the impression of a strange, complex, and highly varied townscape, where immense ancient monuments in every state of repair loomed unexpectedly above clusters of little houses.

Closer examination suggests the different urban conditions that surrounded each of the individual ancient structures. The north arcades of the Colosseum, for example, depicted at the left edge, stood in isolation above the emptiness of the *disabitato*, linked to the rest of the city only by beaten footpaths. Beyond the Capitoline Hill, the Ponte Santa Maria connected the shattered Theater of Marcellus to Trastevere, shown as a walled precinct with houses and towers huddled along the edge of the Tiber. Upriver stood the Ponte Sant'Angelo, the only other bridge included in this view, the primary crossing for pilgrims to St. Peter's entering the city from the northern gate of the Porta del Popolo. This was the *abitato*, the most densely populated part of the postclassical city, extending from the Castel Sant'Angelo, the papal fortress dominating the river and built upon the remains of

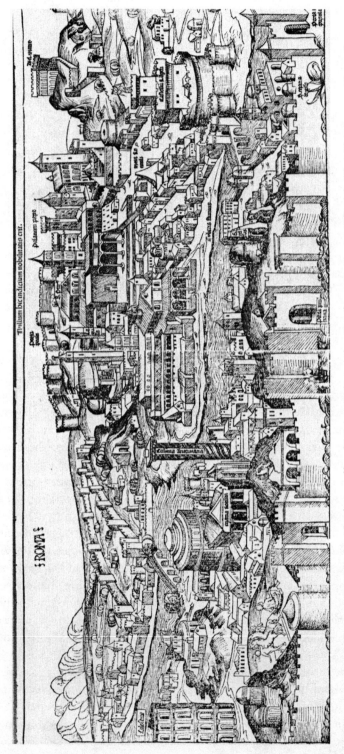

FIGURE 2.1. View of Rome, by Wilhelm Pleydenwurff and Michel Wolgemuth, print from Hartmann Schedel, *Liber Chronicarum*, Nuremberg 1493.

Hadrian's Mausoleum, to the spiraling column shaft labeled the Colonna Antoniana, otherwise known as the Column of Marcus Aurelius, its high pedestal
obscured by surrounding roofs. At the heart of the *abitato*, looming above a
thick knot of houses and churches, stood the Pantheon, depicted as a vertical
cylinder crowned by a tapering, diminutive dome, its portico labeled simply
Maria Rotunda.

The Florentine humanist Paolo Vergerio reported a similar impression of
Rome when he visited the city for the first time in 1398.[1] Like the artist of the
Nuremberg Chronicle, Vergerio noted the sharp contrast between the crowded
abitato along the river and the empty *disabitato* on the higher ground, and
marveled at the difference between the gigantic ancient monuments and the
diminutive newer structures, some of them perched on massive ancient foundations. The highest spires of the fifteenth-century city appeared miniscule in
comparison to the disintegrating grandeur of ancient Rome.

Even with the benefit of modern studies that seek to reconstruct the urban
shape and topography of fifteenth-century Rome, it requires a vigorous imagination to approximate the extraordinary appearance of the city at this particular moment in its history.[2] This was the magical landscape of the *Mirabilia
Urbis*, a fantastic world dominated by ruins of every kind, some fractured and
splintered beyond recognition but others remarkably intact, made even more
exotic by legends woven over time for the benefit of the curious, which then
only veiled them with further mystery. This was the setting that greeted Martin
V on 28 September 1420, when after extended negotiations at the Council of
Basel in Switzerland, followed by a long voyage from the Alps and down the
peninsula, the pope and his retinue arrived in the city. After an absence of
nearly a century, the pope had returned to Rome. Martin V's decision to take
up permanent residence in this ancient landscape had immediate and significant consequences for the preservation of antiquity in the Eternal City.

As recorded by the Roman chronicler Stefano Infessura, the citizens of the
city received the pope with great joy. Infessura described the people gathering
to welcome the pope on his arrival, and noted that the civic magistrates led the
festivities: "the Conservators and the *caporioni*, with many citizens of Rome,
paraded for many nights carrying aloft burning torches, calling out *Viva Papa
Martino, Viva Papa Martino*."[3] The prominent participation of the Conservators, the leading magistrates of the civic government of Rome, along with district representatives from each part of the city, revealed the palpable sense of
relief felt by the local government administration following the pope's decision
to return to the Eternal City.

The arrival of Martin V and the papal court was acclaimed in providential
terms as the longed-for conclusion to the period of decline and stagnation that
had settled upon Rome following the relocation of the papal court to France in
the previous century. Invoking the celebrated Augustan paradigm, Martin V
was heralded as the leader of a long-awaited *instauratio* or restoration of Rome.

Not unlike Augustus, Martin V and his successors would make good on this claim: the revival of Rome's ancient glory and supremacy became one of the primary objectives of the Renaissance popes. The entry of Martin V thus marked the formal inauguration of a far-reaching urban transformation project that ultimately remade this deteriorating ancient landscape into one of the leading capitals of the world.[4]

Not surprisingly, most archaeologists and historians have long taken a dim view of the momentous transformation of ancient Rome that occurred during the Renaissance. The impact of this urban renewal campaign had predictable consequences in terms of the fate of ancient remains: by launching new building projects it not only encroached upon archaeological sites but consumed and destroyed ancient building materials in the process. One of the foremost archaeological guides to Rome thus rehearses a received truth by stating that "the worst devastation occurred during the fifteenth and sixteenth centuries, when the ruins were systematically plundered for materials with which to build and decorate the churches and palaces of papal Rome."[5] The condemnation of the egregious Renaissance destruction of antiquity in fact draws upon a venerable tradition, given that many writers already expressed a similar bleak outlook even during the Renaissance itself.

And yet because Renaissance scholars—like so many of their successors— emphasized the devastation of ancient Rome, they also tended to neglect less-conspicuous Renaissance efforts to preserve the ancient past. For example, in a fourteenth-century letter to Paolo Annibaldi, Petrarch affirmed that the contemporary Romans deserved to be considered the fiercest enemies of ancient Rome, worse than even the legendary marauding barbarians.[6] Written to a close friend who was equally concerned with the devastation of the ancient city, Petrarch probably intended this polemical generalization to stimulate greater controls in fourteenth-century Rome. And yet Petrarch's critique has left a lasting impact upon the literature, where later writers have simply taken him at his word. The idea that the Romans themselves destroyed ancient Rome has helped to disguise the deep-rooted interest in preservation issues among ordinary Romans.

By the same token, Renaissance writers also helped to disguise the important role of the church as an institution that supported the preservation of ancient remains in Rome. Lorenzo Ghiberti, in *I commentarii*, the first history of art in Italy to be written since antiquity, made no mention of the church as a protective institution. On the contrary, he affirmed that the church had conducted a relentless campaign to exterminate the material traces of the pagan past, "whitewashing" the temples to purge them of their tainted artifacts.[7] In this way, Ghiberti explained the apparent decline of art prior to his own time, thus setting the stage for the famous paradigm of the Italian Renaissance as a period of revival that brought new light to antiquity after centuries of neglect and abandonment.

And yet Ghiberti's explanation, although reasonable judged from the perspective of the practicing artist, ignored all evidence for papal preservation. Intent upon establishing the foundations for the modern history of Italian art, Ghiberti shifted the reader's attention away from the church in its historic role as guardian of Rome's surviving ancient remains. Instead, he portrayed the church as the implacable enemy of the classical tradition.

When Giorgio Vasari incorporated Ghiberti's argument into his phenomenally successful *Lives of the Artists*, the consequences were both profound and long lasting.[8] The negative judgment of the church with respect to the care of ancient remains at Rome, diffused and perpetuated by Vasari's text, soon acquired the status of incontrovertible truth.[9] As a result, the evidence for papal preservation efforts in Rome was effectively written out of the canonical history of Italian Renaissance art.

It is clear that such arguments were well intentioned, motivated by the ongoing and evident destruction of precious ancient remains in the papal capital. The turbulent archaeological conditions of Renaissance Rome, as a busy construction site that inevitably generated large-scale archaeological destruction, spurred intense anxieties among those who meditated upon the fate of the Eternal City. The grief-stricken words of Biondo Flavio, the most famous fifteenth-century antiquarian in Rome, epitomized the scholarly reaction to the ever-mounting scale of destruction: "we see so much devastation of antiquity every day that this alone can sometimes even make us weary of living at Rome."[10] Biondo's sensitivity to the constant erosion of the ancient past even pressured him to abandon his beloved city altogether.

Yet while fifteenth-century Rome witnessed the widespread destruction of antiquity, at the same time, the introduction of new preservation practices assumed new significance within this changing context. The preservation of antiquity was itself a historic and firmly established tradition in Rome, a tradition moreover with key political implications. The fifteenth-century popes, in consolidating their temporal rule over the city, could hardly be expected to cast this tradition aside.[11] The preservation of antiquity remained of paramount importance to the popes as a key element in their larger political strategy, which sought to extend and confirm their supreme legal jurisdiction over this complex physical environment. They recognized that the preservation of the past was in fact inseparable from the right to govern in Rome, and skillfully exploited this situation by strengthening the purview and power of existing preservation legislation at Rome, thereby reinforcing papal command over the city at this critical historical juncture.

This chapter considers how the Renaissance popes introduced key innovations in the administration and implementation of preservation practices in the ancient capital from the time of the arrival of Martin V in 1420 through the end of the century. From the beginning, the popes acted promptly to impose new restrictions upon the reuse and transformation of existing ancient remains. They proceeded in a logical way by targeting the existing bodies and agencies of the municipal government already charged with these duties. As we will see, papal reforms affected two agencies in particular, the *maestri di strade* and the Conservators. By directing these municipal officials to focus on the matter of preserving antiquity with greater severity, the fifteenth-century popes strengthened existing institutional controls and reinforced the regulatory system that had emerged over time in the ancient city. This in turn provided the essential foundations for the more effective regulation and control of ancient artifacts at Rome in the future.

At the same time, the fifteenth-century popes also recognized the essential importance of a coherent and comprehensive documentary record to ensure the effective preservation of ancient remains over time. The successful bureaucratic operation of the Renaissance papal administration depended upon the creation and maintenance of a carefully monitored archive. As we will see, the expansion of this archive to include matters of a distinctly archaeological nature was an essential step to improve the successful enforcement of new Renaissance preservation legislation.

Martin V, the Revival of Civic Institutions, and the *Maestri di Strade*

The fifteenth-century city was a far cry from the gleaming marble capital of Augustus. According to the famous lamentation of Poggio Bracciolini, the physical conditions of the city were pitiful. The seat of Roman authority and prestige, the Capitoline Hill, was reduced to a dung heap, while the Roman Forum itself, once echoing with the eloquence of ancient voices, was now known as the Campo Vaccino or "cow pasture," occupied by cattle and pigs, its earth plowed for humble vegetable gardens (figures 2.2 and 2.3).[12] Martin V and his successors immediately turned their attention to remedying these deplorable conditions, determined to improve the city's physical environment and the welfare of its people, and to transform this squalor into a setting suitable for the majesty of the Holy See.

The objectives of the fifteenth-century popes were of course explicitly political. Upon returning to the city after their prolonged absence, it was imperative to recover full command over this chaotic environment and its often recalcitrant citizenry. The reestablishment of the center of the church at Rome depended upon eliminating any possible danger of insurrection or other threats to papal security beforehand. Thus the need to gain mastery over the civic government of the capital, and specifically to control those particular components of the civic government that managed the physical territory of the capital itself, represented an issue of the greatest importance for the Renaissance

FIGURE 2.2. The Campo Vaccino as it appeared in the late fifteenth century. From left to right this view depicts the Arch of Septimius Severus, followed by the remains of the Temple of Saturn and the Temple of Vespasian. *Codex Escurialensis*, f. 20r.

popes. Through strategic manipulation of such preexisting civic elements the popes began to reshape the city itself to satisfy these goals and to conform to their needs.[13]

The urgency of fifteenth-century papal interests in reforming the city of Rome explains the particular papal attention to the civic office of the *maestri di strade e degli edifici*, the "masters of the streets and buildings" of Rome. The *maestri* were officers appointed by the medieval civic magistrates both to monitor building projects in the city and to maintain sufficient hygienic standards in the urban context.[14] The continued importance of this office over time in Rome suggests the Augustan legacy of the *cura urbis* persisted throughout the Middle Ages.[15]

Although the *maestri* originated as members of the civic magistracy, during the Renaissance they became the critical agents enabling the popes to implement their fundamental goals. The distinctive role of the *maestri* in their close personal supervision of the physical environment of Rome made them well suited to serve papal needs. They assisted the Renaissance popes in their objective of gaining strategic mastery over the public spaces of the city, controlling and thereby improving the physical conditions of the city itself. While the papal appropriation of civic powers in Renaissance Rome

FIGURE 2.3. Arch of Septimius Severus, photograph by Eugène Constant,
ca. 1848–55. Note the pedestals of the engaged columns on the triumphal arch are
now completely excavated. The columns of the Temple of Vespasian stand in the
foreground.

has been the study of considerable scholarly attention, the implications of
this process for preservation practices have been largely overlooked.[16] As we
will see, the papal takeover of the *maestri* launched by Martin V allowed for
more effective regulation and control over ancient remains in Rome to begin
right away.

The office of the *maestri*, which originated not long after the founding of
the medieval civic government, played a key role in determining how the preservation of antiquity occurred in Rome. There is evidence for this already in
the first known document to have been issued by the *maestri*, dated 1227,
which reported that they served as judges in a controversy regarding the construction of new walls upon existing structures and foundations in the Roman
Forum.[17] Empowered to make decisions "regarding all questions relating to
buildings, houses, walls, roads, squares, and property lines in Rome, both
inside and outside the city," as recorded in a later document dated 1255, the
maestri were the key representatives of the civic government entitled to decide
what could and—just as important—what could not be done to the existing
ancient remains.[18] In the context of postclassical Rome, filled to overflowing

with the ruins of imperial monuments, the global responsibilities of the *mae-stri* naturally also included the preservation of existing structures.

The first surviving statutes of the agency, dating to 1410, provide further, specific evidence for the ways that the *maestri* exercised control over the preservation of antiquity in early modern Rome.[19] Issued ten years before the return of Martin V and the papal court to the capital, these statutes specified how the *maestri* were expected not only to attend to the ongoing maintenance of the urban fabric but to intervene to preserve ancient structures. The active role of the *maestri* in the preservation of antiquity can be inferred by references in this legislation that described their role in caring for existing infrastructure of ancient Roman construction.

For example, chapter 8 of the statute declared that the *maestri* were charged with the maintenance of "buildings, fountains, bridges, and aqueducts."[20] In Rome, referring to these building types of necessity included ancient structures. The statutes stipulated that the *maestri* were authorized to repair and rebuild these structures when this became necessary, "providere super reparatione ac reformatione." Even if the statutes did not use either the term *instaurare* or *conservare*, the point was to ensure that the *maestri* maintained this ancient infrastructure in good repair—not only Rome's buildings in general, but those structures of special public utility, such as the city's water supply system as well as its bridges. Ongoing repairs by the *maestri* to the ancient bridges across the Tiber, as well as to the one ancient aqueduct and fountain that continued to function in the fifteenth-century city, the Acqua Vergine, were essential to their continued function. The survival of this vital infrastructure can at least in part be attributed to the active surveillance and regular supervision of these landmarks by the *maestri*.[21]

Chapter 24 of the same statutes specified that the *maestri* should ensure that all structures in the public way, including triumphal arches or *arcus triumphales*, remained unobstructed, to facilitate public access and traffic circulation throughout the city.[22] Here the statutes used the term *recuperare*, which implied returning these existing structures to their original functions or physical conditions, in case their passageways were blocked or otherwise altered. In early fifteenth-century Rome, where ancient triumphal arches spanned many of the key traffic arteries in the city, this ordinance also automatically translated into the active preservation of antiquity. It is clear that the *maestri* took a key role in guarding these distinctively Roman structures, ensuring that they remained accessible to the public and that no intruder should block their openings for private use. Surely the active surveillance by the *maestri* helped to ensure the extraordinary preservation of monuments such as the Arch of Constantine, where the *maestri* controlled continued public access and prohibited alterations by private individuals (figure 2.4).

FIGURE 2.4.   Arch of Constantine, printed by Nicolas Beatrizet, 1583.

Martin V and the Bull of 1425

When Martin V issued the famous Bull of 1425, he reinstated the civic officials of the *maestri* as his own appointments, thus investing them with explicit papal authority to correct and reform the intolerable urban conditions of the new papal capital.[23] This legislation is widely recognized as marking a watershed moment in the history of Renaissance Rome: Martin V's command to improve the city's public spaces, executed through the agency of the *maestri*, had profound ramifications for the future development of the city. This intervention established a vital precedent, anticipating the grandiose moves of later Renaissance popes who then continued to reshape the urban fabric of ancient Rome to suit their own expansive visions.

The Bull of 1425 awarded the *maestri* the right to monitor, regulate, and restore the entire built environment of Rome. The pope appended a long list of different kinds of structures and spaces that came under their jurisdiction, a comprehensive inventory implying that every possible type of building in the city was subject to their authority.[24] While the primary intent of the bull was to bring the dispersed and various parts of the city under stricter surveillance and greater control, this legislation also provided an efficient way to assume direct papal control over urban affairs. In short, with the Bull of 1425 Martin V transformed the *maestri* from the on-the-ground agents of the civic government into the on-the-ground agents of the papal administration.[25]

Scholars have regarded this legislation as inaugurating the progressive extension of papal authority over the affairs and responsibilities of the Capitoline magistrates and the civic government of Rome. As they have pointed out, this legislation signaled the direct interference by Martin V in the affairs of a once proudly independent civic institution. Even if the pope reiterated the historic authority of the *maestri* in carrying out their work in the papal capital, these officials now acted specifically upon papal command.[26]

But if this legislation represented an incipient papal infringement upon civic autonomy, as well as a critical move for the future urban development of Rome, we have overlooked the fact that the Bull of 1425 also signaled a vital turning point for the preservation of antiquity in the papal capital.

By appointing the *maestri* as papal officials, the pope sanctioned the existing system that had gradually taken form under the medieval civic government—based upon the Augustan legacy—which assumed as its duty the repair and maintenance of the ancient buildings and infrastructure of Rome. This merger of papal and civic power meant that the institutional memory of the preservation of antiquity was incorporated wholesale into the new papal administration as it prepared to tackle and transform the dilapidated urban conditions of the papal capital.

There are several indications in the Bull of 1425 that the preservation of antiquity was in fact at the top of Martin V's priorities. At one level, the bull represented an emergency action taken to remedy the rampant disregard for sanitary conditions at Rome, where artisans tossed their refuse into the public streets and squares.[27] Under Martin V such defilement was no longer tolerated; the *maestri* received full power to punish such abuses by issuing penalties and even imprisoning the offenders. The goal was to bring an end to these kinds of practices, as well as to bring the affected areas under direct papal control. Thus this legislation was intended to do more than merely encourage proper comportment in the city center: it was specifically intended to protect the most beautiful parts of Rome, where such anarchic and destructive behavior imperiled many of the surviving ancient monuments.

The degree to which Martin V was determined to reform chaotic existing conditions in the city becomes evident when we consider his decision to award the *maestri* immunity from all prosecution.[28] Under the medieval civic administration the *maestri* had been exempted from interference by higher-ranking civic magistrates as well. Martin V thus recalled and enhanced these sweeping privileges in the changed political context of the papal capital. Now the *maestri* were empowered to improve existing urban conditions in the city over the resistance of any private individual, including even that of the pope himself. By extension, Martin V awarded the *maestri* immense power in terms of the preservation of antiquity: in the context of implementing a vigorous new urban improvement program, the *maestri* were authorized to determine whether existing ancient structures would be either preserved or destroyed.

A Papal Excavation License of 1426

Key evidence for the management of the preservation and destruction of antiquity during the pontificate of Martin V survives in the form of a papal excavation license dated 1 July 1426 (see appendix, document 1).[29] Issued just one year after Martin V's Bull of 1425, the license attested to the improved bureaucratic practices of the papal administration, which required new levels of accountability from those who intervened upon ancient sites. Moreover, the excavation license also revealed how the papal preservation of antiquity translated into an expression of political power in the fifteenth-century city (figure 2.5).

When the nineteenth-century archaeologist Rodolfo Lanciani discussed this document in the *Storia degli scavi di Roma*, he minimized the possible impact of this excavation license in regulating the preservation of antiquity.[30] Lanciani's interpretation was already anticipated by the cataloguing system in the Vatican archives, where the document heading made no reference to preservation. Instead, this heading simply summarized the document as awarding permission "to the lime-kiln operators of Rome to extract stone from the foundations of the Templum Canapare to make lime and to provide half of their yield to Cardinal Jacopo Tusculano (also known as Cardinal Sant'Eustachio)."[31]

But such a characterization, while it noted such particulars as the removal of building stone from the ancient site, as well as the distinctive financial conditions imposed upon the excavators, failed to acknowledge the protective clauses that were also an integral part of this license. This papal license did not simply give the lime-kiln operators a free hand. On the contrary, it was clearly intended to govern, limit, and restrict the excavation process.

Even in 1426, when new work was just beginning on the papal capital, the archaeological remains were subject to explicit papal controls. As the license stipulated: "we grant to you and anyone among you authorization to break and extract from the foundations of the Templum Canapare those travertine stones that are not exposed to view." Excavation in fifteenth-century Rome was thus not a reckless free-for-all. On the contrary, the license explicitly prohibited the excavators from removing any stones that formed part of the visible ancient structure.

The license acknowledged that the removal of buried foundation stones might provoke further damage to the surviving remains: "if in extracting and

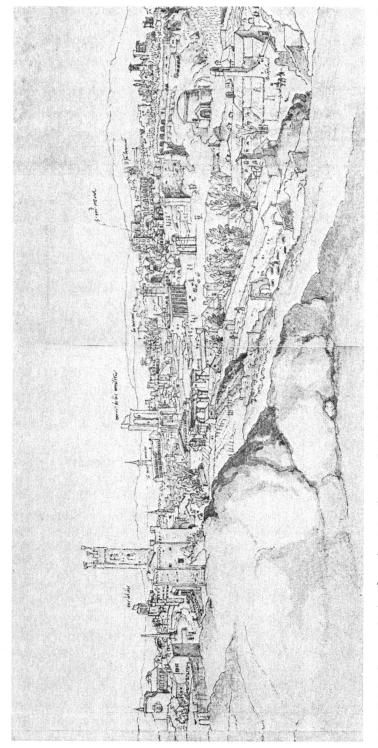

FIGURE 2.5. Panoramic view from the civic palaces on the Capitoline Hill, prior to their redesign by Michelangelo, to the ancient monuments of the valley of the Roman Forum, by Marten van Heemskerck, ca. 1532–36.

excavating stones of this sort the temple itself should come to ruin or if it even should be demolished, we grant, by this present tenor, the full and free reign for you to make lime from these said stones." The license thus recognized that greater destruction might be a consequence of this excavation activity on the ancient site, and affirmed that the excavators had full permission to burn all the stones generated by these interventions for lime.

A key condition of the license, as noted in the title assigned to the document, was that the yield was to be divided in two equal parts, with one part ceded to papal officials: "half of the lime of this sort to be made by you is to be handed over and granted to the Most Reverend Father and Lord in Christ, Lord Cardinal of Sant'Eustachio."

The document, however, imposed further conditions on this work by reiterating that not only were the excavators required to reserve half of their production for the cardinal, but explicitly forbidding them from collecting any more materials from the site: "it is our wish, however, that you should in no way sell or transfer the remaining half of the said lime without our investigation or special license, or that you should extract any more lime from the site." This condition was probably not so much intended to restrict further injury to the Templum Canapare as to prevent the excavators from defrauding the Camera Apostolica. They were not permitted to renew excavations at the site after setting aside the portion for the Camera Apostolica: if they were to continue such excavations, they would have made off with more than their fair share of the lime.

Finally, the license, issued on the first of July, also introduced an expiration date: "this permission will be valid for the entire present month." The excavators thus had a maximum of four weeks to collect travertine from the ancient site. This deadline also had a protective function. After the end of the month, unless the excavators received a special papal extension, they lost their access rights to the site and they were not allowed to continue further demolition.

Such limiting conditions, while not insignificant, have failed to attract the attention of scholars who have focused instead upon the destructive agency of this legislation. This preoccupation can be attributed in large part to the persuasive force of Lanciani's writing on the history of archaeology. Lanciani generally chose to overlook or otherwise downplay the evidence for preservation projects in Renaissance Rome. As his work remains one of our most important sources for the history of Roman archaeology, the idea of preservation has been largely overlooked in the archaeological literature.[32]

In Lanciani's view, the clauses that stipulated the preservation of the ancient site could be judged meaningless. Lanciani identified the Templum Canapare as the Basilica Julia in the Roman Forum and the evidence of a postclassical lime-kiln among these ruins as the same kiln established by the excavators in 1426. Thus he concluded that the lime-kiln workers proceeded to level the Basilica Julia to its foundations, ignoring the need for preservation completely.[33]

Lanciani also implied that Cardinal Sant'Eustachio, who collected an income from this work, had little incentive to rescue the ancient monument from further destruction. Naturally it was in the cardinal's best financial interests to encourage the excavation of as much ancient building stone from the site as possible rather than ensuring its protection. It was this kind of assessment that convinced modern archaeologists of the failure of Renaissance licenses to uphold the more rigorous principles of scientific archaeology and conservation theory.

The foundations of Lanciani's argument were shaky at best, however, both in terms of his critique of the cardinal's interests and in terms of the surviving archaeological evidence. The notion of dividing excavation proceeds between excavators and property owners was established custom in Rome since antiquity.[34] The presence of the financial clause in the 1426 license thus could not be used as conclusive proof one way or the other for the cardinal's attitudes toward the ancient remains on the site. On the contrary, such a clause merely testified to standard excavating procedure.

The identification of the Templum Canapare with the Basilica Julia has since also been thrown into doubt. The term *Canapare* or *Cannapara* served as a toponym that could refer to the entire western section of the Roman Forum, extending from the Capitoline Hill toward the Greek church of San Teodoro below the Palatine Hill.[35] Thus Lanciani's identification of the temple with the Basilica Julia cannot be sustained, and it is impossible to conclude that the lime-kiln operators leveled the structure to its foundations. Given the vigilance of the Camera Apostolica regarding the defense of its rights, it is quite likely the excavators were very careful to abide by the conditions of the license.

Rather than describing the 1426 papal excavation license as a kind of archaeological death warrant, it is more useful to consider how the papal administration issued such licenses to balance the need for regulation against the need for reuse in fifteenth-century Rome.[36] The license authorized the collection of valuable stone from this site for new construction. At the same time it sought to prevent the destruction of the ancient monument itself, within reasonable limits. Judged from the perspective of modern archaeology and conservation theory these may seem contradictory impulses, but from the perspective of the early fifteenth-century papal administration, confronted with a seemingly endless horizon of ancient ruins, such an approach clearly offered a pragmatic and reasonable solution.

While the Templum Canapare appears to have vanished, the survival of the 1426 excavation license itself as a documentary record explains how preservation measures became more effective under the papal administration. Although the civic magistrates had already attempted to institute similar legislation to regulate destruction and control the export of ancient remains in medieval Rome, the loss of the civic archives means that hardly any of these earlier licenses have survived.[37] The opening of such gaps in the documentary record, through either accident or negligence, made it more difficult to hold excavators accountable for their actions.

In contrast, the 1426 excavation license marked the advent of a highly organized record-keeping system under the bureaucratic papal administration.[38] The careful compilation of papal excavation licenses in standardized account books made a critical contribution to preservation practices in Renaissance Rome. Such licenses provided binding documentary evidence and incontrovertible proof to reinforce the regulation of various areas of the fifteenth-century city, evidence that was of course all the more important at a time when papal authority was often vigorously contested.

Thus the well-managed papal archive, critical to the successful administration of the affairs of the church, also provided the essential framework for the successful management of ancient Rome. Armed with a reliable paper trail, the papal administration wielded a powerful weapon: excavators dared to disregard the conditions outlined by excavation licenses at their own risk. The 1426 license represented legal proof, providing the Vatican with legal grounds to prosecute the lime burners if they failed to uphold their part of the bargain.

The regulation and control of ancient sites also served to make papal power manifest in the city. The active monitoring of ancient sites thus served a vital political function for the papacy itself. Such regulations reminded the Roman population—which of course continued to excavate in every part of this fabled landscape throughout its history—that the pope was supreme arbiter of physical conditions in Rome. Through excavation licenses the fifteenth-century papal administration inscribed its temporal authority upon the daily affairs of the city. Now papal mediation defined the relationship of the Roman populace not only to such individual ancient landmarks as the Templum Canapare but to the public spaces of the city, including the ancient Roman Forum itself.

The papal administration continued to issue excavation licenses with conditions not unlike that of the license issued in 1426 for the remainder of the fifteenth century. In certain cases these licenses awarded even more generous privileges to excavate across Rome, such as the license received by the builders of the Vatican Library under Sixtus IV in 1471.[39] Other licenses imposed more restrictive conditions, such as the license issued to "Bartolomeo il matto" under Innocent VIII in 1484, which not only limited this work to archaeological remains that were submerged below ground level and thus invisible, but also to those areas where there were no "public buildings."[40]

The surviving documentary evidence suggests that works of special significance to the papal capital, such as the construction of the Vatican Library, received excavation licenses offering more expansive terms and conditions than those excavations that were undertaken primarily for the benefit of a private individual or association. The discussion of sixteenth-century excavation licenses in chapter 3 will return to consider these distinctions at greater length, when these regulations became more numerous and more restrictive. Fifteenth-century papal excavation licenses, however, clearly attest to the sustained interest of the papal administration in controlling and regulating ancient sites in the context of a rapidly growing urban environment.[41]

Controlling Access to Ancient Remains under Nicholas V

Just as Martin V took key steps early in his pontificate to enforce and promote the preservation of antiquity in the papal capital, so was this tendency reinforced even more forcefully during the reigns of the two following popes, Eugenius IV and Nicholas V.

Eugenius IV faced serious challenges in his effort to achieve effective governance in Rome. Conciliar opposition continued to undermine papal authority, and in 1434 an uprising of the Roman populace forced the pope to abandon the city in disguise. The pope and the papal court, reluctant to return from exile without guarantee of stability in the Eternal City, spent the next ten years traveling between different locations in the Italian peninsula. Following a series of negotiations and concessions, Eugenius IV finally returned to the capital in triumph in 1443.[42]

Despite these highly unsettled political conditions, Eugenius IV nevertheless also managed to embark upon visionary preservation projects in Rome. As we will see in chapter 5, "The Pantheon," during his pontificate this prestigious monument became the focus of major preservation work. On papal command, the portico was cleared of later additions and market stalls to reveal its granite columns. This intervention appears to be among the very first attempts in the history of postclassical Rome to systematically restore an ancient building to an earlier presumed appearance by removing the evidence for subsequent changes over time.

But it was during the reign of Nicholas V that major regulations affecting the reuse of ancient remains were instituted on a citywide level, which most directly affected the way that ordinary Romans interacted with the surviving ancient remains in the city. Nicholas V built upon the precedent of Martin V, who had taken measures to regulate urban conditions and monitor preservation problems by issuing the Bull of 1425. Nicholas V, however, further restricted the kinds of interventions permitted at ancient sites and placed new limitations on public access to ancient remains.[43]

During the reign of Nicholas V, the political situation in Rome finally began to stabilize. The last troublesome reminder of the schism that had divided the fourteenth-century church disappeared in 1449 when Felix X, the last antipope, relinquished his claim to the papal throne. However, as Eugenius IV's expulsion from Rome was still a recent memory, Nicholas V remained vigilant for signs of possible insurrection and took steps to undermine lingering local resistance to papal power. In 1452 Nicholas V's agents uncovered the plot of Stefano Porcari and his associates, who intended to assassinate the pope and liberate Rome from the tyranny of papal rule. The execution of the ringleaders of the Porcari conspiracy marked the last significant attempt by the Roman populace to challenge the temporal supremacy of the pope.[44]

In the effort to amplify devotion, sustain the church, and reinforce papal power, Nicholas V also conceived a large-scale program of architectural and urban renewal for Rome, as recorded by his biographer Manetti.[45] Among other projects, this included the rebuilding of the third-century Constantinian basilica of Old St. Peter's, which was showing signs of progressive deterioration and even threatening to collapse. The grandiose urban program attributed to Nicholas V anticipated the plans later implemented by his successors, who also drew inspiration from the remains of imperial Rome to reinforce their own ambitions and ideals for the Renaissance papacy.

The many new construction sites opened during the reign of Nicholas V have long been blamed by scholars for the devastation of antiquity in Rome, and thus it is not surprising that we tend to overlook the fact that Nicholas V also supported and promoted preservation practices. Like his recent predecessor Martin V, and like Augustus centuries before, Nicholas V found the preservation of antiquity to be a strategic means to consolidate and reinforce autocratic rule in the ancient capital.

While we have tended to condemn the destruction of antiquity under Nicholas V as a glaring contradiction of the humanist values and ideals espoused by this erudite pope, such an approach does little to help advance our understanding of these demolitions as they were viewed at the time. In fifteenth-century papal Rome, such destruction was clearly considered to be justifiable. Moreover, it is clear that much of this demolition, although reviled by modern scholars, actually conformed to prevailing notions of preservation in fifteenth-century Rome.

The revised statutes of the *maestri*, issued in 1452 with the papal imprimatur, provide an ideal opportunity to reassess the approach to preservation problems during the reign of Nicholas V.[46] In the Bull of 1425, Martin V strengthened the autonomous power of these officials, authorizing them to take whatever actions they saw fit in undertaking the gigantic papal project of revitalizing the Eternal City. But in 1452, when Nicholas V issued a revision of the *maestri* statutes, he circumscribed their authority. This papal intervention in turn had far-reaching consequences for the preservation of antiquity.

When Martin V gave the *maestri* free rein to make decisions about the preservation and destruction of antiquity in the Bull of 1425, this included the right to authorize excavations on public land. This specific decision-making authority represented a vital means by which to regulate the way that the public interacted with ancient remains in public areas, those parts of the city that served as points of contact and exchange between individuals and the broader collective society.[47] Martin V allowed the *maestri* to determine the destiny of ancient remains on such sites.

The new statutes issued under Nicholas V, which defined the duties of the *maestri* with greater clarity and precision, targeted precisely this privilege. The rights of the *maestri* to authorize excavations on public land in Rome were specifically revoked in chapter 6: "the *maestri* may not grant a license to anyone to build walls, excavate, or install fences in any public place."[48] To prevent any possible equivocation, all previous building licenses granted by the *maestri* were retroactively invalidated.[49]

Where Martin V had allowed the *maestri* to decide the fate of Roman antiquity, under Nicholas V this was no longer the case. Instead, excavation licenses on public land now reverted to the responsibility of higher-level officials in the papal administration. In the future, subsequent excavation licenses awarded by the Vatican required the formal approval of the papal chamberlain, the highest office in the Camera Apostolica.[50] The revised structural procedures suggest that obtaining a license to excavate on public land now became significantly more difficult for the average individual in Rome.[51]

It may well be that these increased papal restrictions were not entirely altruistic in their effort to preserve ancient remains, as they could also be exploited to answer the demands of papal building sites. In this way, the revision of the *maestri* statutes also afforded an opportunity to create a papal monopoly on valuable ancient building stone in Rome. By restricting public access to the ruins, Nicholas V set aside a supply of ruined ancient remains—most notoriously the Colosseum—that could then be tapped to supply papal building sites in the ancient capital.[52]

Scholars have been quick to recognize this fact, but less quick to acknowledge that Nicholas V's excavations were not necessarily reckless. The award of an excavation license did not translate into an uncontrolled archaeological rampage. On the contrary, as in the example of the Templum Canapare, papal excavations conformed to precise notions about preservation that developed out of the difficult circumstances of building within the confines of an ancient and historic site. As such, they were consciously designed to meet two goals. One was obvious: to advance papal construction projects by facilitating the acquisition of building stone. The second goal, although less frequently noted, was just as essential as the first: to guarantee that the most important ancient architectural elements of this historic setting also survived into the future, despite the removal of building materials. The ongoing collaboration of the Conservators in the preservation of ancient remains provided a further check on preservation practices. While the 1426 excavation license at the Templum Canapare expressed some concern for the preservation of antiquity, the excavations at the Colosseum undertaken by Nicholas V were subject to much greater restrictions, as we will see in chapter 4.

One cannot fail to note the presence of Leon Battista Alberti, the preeminent humanist, theorist, and architect of fifteenth-century Italy, in the Rome of Nicholas V. A leading authority on the preservation and restoration of ancient remains, Alberti expressed his intense interest in the subject in his treatise *De re aedificatoria,* devoting the entire last book to the topic.[53] Certainly the preservation and restoration of antiquity attracted the attention of prominent humanists at the papal court.

The degree to which Alberti participated in the visionary plans of Nicholas V remains uncertain. One study suggests that Alberti may have viewed the pope's ambitious transformation of Rome in highly skeptical terms, if not condemning these interventions outright, precisely because they caused the reckless demolition of antiquity.[54] Such an interpretation implied that Nicholas V paid little heed to the urgent need for preserving antiquity in Rome.

And yet it is clear that Nicholas V also helped to prevent unregulated interventions upon ancient remains. After the *maestri* operated essentially as free agents under Martin V, papal revision of the *maestri* statutes subjected them to new standards set by the centralized authority of the papal bureaucracy itself. Such procedural changes had significant consequences for the future, in terms of both excavations and preservation practices in the papal capital. By prohibiting the *maestri* from making independent decisions about the fate of ancient artifacts, Nicholas V not only helped to eliminate unpredictable variables in the regulation of preservation practices in Rome, but also facilitated the adoption of more uniform preservation standards.[55]

Preservation in Fifteenth-Century Papal Urbanism

While the new road network that took form beginning in the Rome of Nicholas V may tempt comparisons with Baron Haussmann in nineteenth-century Paris or Robert Moses in twentieth-century New York, such comparisons tend to be misleading. The aggressive transformations of metropolitan areas launched by modern urban planners usually imposed a new circulation system upon a preexisting organism, often displaying complete disregard for circulation patterns that emerged over time. On the contrary, papal urban planning projects in fifteenth-century Rome suggested just the opposite: the development of these new arteries served both to reinforce and to preserve preexisting urban circulation systems.[56]

The need for circulation reform was urgent in fifteenth-century Rome, where certain parts of the inhabited city had become so dense that they were nearly impenetrable. Over the course of the century, papal improvements focused on three existing primary arteries: the Via del Pellegrino, the Via Papalis, and the Via Recta.[57] The Via Pellegrino snaked across the western edge of the Campus Martius toward the city market at the Campo de' Fiori; the Via

Papalis traversed the central section of the Campus Martius toward the Lateran Basilica; and the Via Recta crossed the northern Campus Martius, leading to the Via Flaminia and the pilgrimage routes to the north. All three roads converged upon the Ponte Sant'Angelo, as the all-important crossing between the *abitato* on one side and the Borgo and the Vatican on the other.[58]

Fifteenth-century urban planning thus focused less upon radical surgery than upon adapting the existing arterial system to suit changing current needs.[59] The incoherent thicket of dead ends in the *abitato* could be pruned and cleared, and existing narrow alleys widened, to serve as the backbone for a new arterial system for the papal capital.[60] The fifteenth-century tolerance for preexisting circulation patterns and road alignments in some ways recalled the approach sanctioned by Augustus, who chose to leave certain existing property lines undisturbed during the construction of his new Forum of Augustus. The history of archaeology has made notorious the Renaissance destruction of ancient artifacts to clear the way for new thoroughfares, such as Alexander VI's decision to clear away the remains of the Meta Romuli in 1499 for the new Via Alessandrina in the Borgo.[61] But by the same token, the literature's single-minded emphasis on archaeological destruction has also obscured the ways that the new "global vision of the city" of the Renaissance popes, as it imposed a new unifying order, also preserved ancient circulation patterns in its expansion and improvement of the existing road network of fifteenth-century Rome.[62]

Preservation Negotiations Between the Vatican and Campidoglio

Just as the fifteenth-century popes progressively redefined the powers and duties of the *maestri di strade* to limit the damage caused to antiquity in the ancient capital, so did the popes also encourage the highest office of the municipal government of Rome, the Conservators, to focus with increased energy and concentration upon the problem of preserving and defending ancient remains.

By the end of the fourteenth century, the Conservators had emerged as the leading magistrates of the civic government on the Capitoline Hill, or the Campidoglio.[63] Following the arrival of Martin V in Rome in 1420, the process of integrating the civic government as an apparatus of the papal administration accelerated, and increasing papal involvement in the temporal affairs of Rome had critical implications not just for the *maestri* but for the Conservators as well (figure 2.6).

Even if the Conservators rejoiced at the return of the pope to Rome in 1420, their relationship with the papal monarch was sometimes strained. Displaced from the center of power, the noble families that held the posts of the Conservators often felt lingering antagonism toward papal rule and objected to the perceived infringement of papal and curial power upon their own traditional

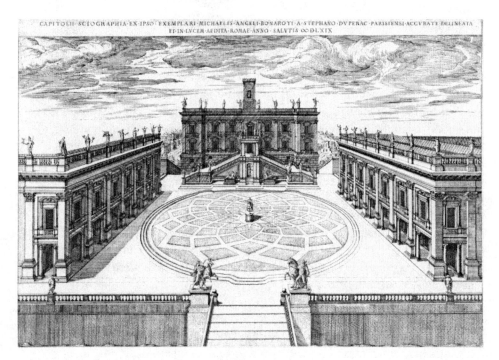

FIGURE 2.6. Palaces on the Capitoline Hill, ca. 1569. Paul III inaugurated the transformation of this venerable site by relocating the equestrian statue of Marcus Aurelius here in 1537. Michelangelo designed the facades for the Senators' palace at center and the Conservators' palace to the right, as well as the pendant "palazzo nuovo."

privileges. Occasional instances of civic revolt against papal power thus continued to flare up even after the suppression of the Porcari conspiracy.[64]

Sensitive to these pressures, the Renaissance popes recognized that it was in their best interest to transform the Conservators into collaborators, and throughout the Renaissance the Conservators thus served as the direct intermediaries between the papal ruler and his subjects. While the superior authority of the popes had to remain unquestioned, the Conservators also retained a voice in determining the affairs of the city, as the spokesmen for the collective *popolo romano*. The Conservators, in their palace on the Capitoline Hill, provided a key forum in which to discuss and negotiate the sometimes opposing wills of the pope and the *popolo romano*.[65]

The preservation of antiquity played a critical role in this shifting political situation.[66] While the powers of the Renaissance pontiff by definition were absolute, it was clear that preservation problems in Rome had the power to stir up the proverbial hornets' nest in a setting where the political value of preservation had become an anchor of civic identity. The civic government from the time of its founding in the twelfth century seized upon preservation as a battle cry, and its dedication to these matters was formally enshrined in the civic statutes.

Even as the popes appropriated most of the important executive powers from the civic administration during the Renaissance, they allowed the Conservators to retain their historic duty of preserving ancient Rome. For example, although Nicholas V revoked the authority of the *maestri* to issue excavation licenses, he did not prevent the Conservators from doing so. The Conservators enjoyed the historic privilege of issuing excavation licenses in Rome, and Nicholas V sanctioned the continued operation of this two-tier system. Thus excavation licenses throughout the Renaissance continued to be issued separately by both papal and civic officials. This overlap of jurisdictions, which meant that both papal and civic officials retained authority over the care of ancient remains, also ensured that this legislation remained open to negotiation and debate.

The Bull of 1462, issued by Pius II, marked a key moment in the confirmation of the Conservators' authority as the guardians of ancient Rome.[67] In this document, a noted landmark for preservation legislation, the pope conceded this traditional role of the Conservators and formally sanctioned these jealously guarded privileges in the context of the papal capital.

Nowhere prior to the Bull of 1462 was the preservation of antiquity in Rome advocated with such sophistication. Pius II, as a humanist scholar himself, took particular interest in the fate of antiquity in the city under his rule. The impassioned opening of the document presented the pope's own responsibility for enacting such legislation:

> Desirous that our venerable city be preserved in its dignity and splendor [conservari cupiamus], we must attend to its care with the greatest vigilance. Not only the basilicas, churches, and religious sites, in which many relics of the saints reside, but also the ancient buildings and their ruins should be handed down to posterity, as these confer upon the city its most beautiful adornment and its greatest charm; they attest to ancient virtues and encourage us to emulate their glorious example.[68]

The preservation of antiquity—both pagan and Christian remains—was a matter of the utmost importance to the pope, as the leader of the universal church, because these artifacts provided tangible evidence for ancient virtues. The study of antiquity offered a unique historical vantage point to the past, and at the same time a blueprint for a future to which all humanity should aspire.

Pius II was clearly sensitive to the beauty of the ancient buildings and their ruins. His description of these ancient remains as Rome's "most beautiful adornment and its greatest charm" reflected the impact of Renaissance humanist ideals, which viewed ruins in positive terms, as a vital source that could generate both new ideas and powerful aesthetic responses.[69]

In terms of urban legislation, however, this same passage marked a radical epistemological shift. According to long-established Roman legislative tradition, ruins were condemned outright as signs of decadence and decay. Municipal authorities, responsible for enforcing this legislation, thus had reason to regard the crumbling ruins under their jurisdiction with considerable antagonism. But now Pius II insisted that not just ancient buildings, but specifically ancient ruins, even those in the most decrepit and fragmentary condition, should be carefully preserved and "handed down to posterity." Pius II celebrated Rome's fractured, ruinous ancient remains because their signs of deterioration and collapse provided an essential moral reminder to the present:

> Even more important, these same buildings permit us to better
> perceive the fragility of human affairs. They remind us that in no way
> can we depend upon human affairs, when such structures, judged to
> be immortal by our ancestors for their great strength and for their
> tremendous cost, are instead, by antiquity and other sinister contin-
> gencies, injured and brought to the ground.[70]

Thus, ruined ancient remains provided a fundamental reminder of human mortality and the vanity of human ambition. It was precisely because they were ruins that these structures had such value. Pius II insisted that the careful preservation of these ruins into the future was essential—the solicitous preservation of even the most fragmentary and scattered ancient artifacts helped to communicate this vital message to posterity. The pope thus articulated an extremely ambitious notion of preservation, one that in its sweeping extent anticipated the ideals of modern conservation theory.

This echo of modern conservation theory was further reinforced by Pius II's specific choice of terminology for this legislation. By including the word *conservare* in the very first line of the bull, Pius II recalled Biondo's discussion of this term in *Roma instaurata*, a text with which the pope was certainly acquainted. This choice of words served to distinguish Pius II's preservation program for Rome from the more familiar Roman paradigm of the *instauratio*, which invoked restoration of past glories, but also the active transformation of material artifacts in the present. Instead, the conscious use of *conservare* suggested that Pius II wished to shift away from this traditional model of urban renewal to develop a new urban program that specifically privileged the value of Rome's ancient remains as historic artifacts.

The pope acknowledged the legacy of many important predecessors, not only earlier popes but also the Conservators, as well as the statutes of the civic government that had established important precedents by prohibiting the destruction of ancient buildings and imposing financial penalties for abuses and destruction. Then Pius II prohibited the destruction of antiquity with a sweeping edict:

> We forbid all persons without exception, religious or secular, regard-
> less of power, dignity, status, or rank, whether they bear ecclesiastical
> or even papal office, from demolishing, dismantling, damaging, or
> converting into lime, directly or indirectly, publicly or secretly, any

ancient building or vestige existing on the soil of Rome or its environs, either on public or on private property.[71]

This legislation thus outlawed the destruction of any ancient remains, for any reason, either inside or outside the city, by any person, of any rank. The prohibition extended to include even the occupants of the papal office.[72] It is clear that this was intended to be the most comprehensive preservation legislation ever issued in Rome.

The Bull of 1462 also outlined how this radical vision of preservation was to be implemented in the ancient city. Pius II charged the Conservators with the primary responsibility for preservation:

> We concede authority to our beloved sons, the Conservators of the civic administration of Rome. . . . [T]hey should conduct diligent investigations through their officials, imprisoning those builders or laborers who demolish or devastate, confiscating their beasts of burden, their instruments, and all the rest, and require them to pay the penalty immediately, in its entirety.[73]

Pius II thus awarded the Conservators their traditional jurisdictional authority within the administrative hierarchy of the papal capital. By reassigning them this duty the pope emphasized that he and the Conservators were bound by a sense of shared purpose: the full administrative apparatus of the papal state was bent upon ensuring the survival of ancient Rome.[74]

Such legislation was motivated by a shrewd sense of diplomacy as much as by a sense of tactful restraint. Pius II (like most Renaissance popes, not a Roman, which raised further delicate problems of rightful ownership) deliberately renewed the Conservators' historic privileges as the guardians of ancient Rome. Yet at the same time, the pope did not fully concede his own power in this domain either. Thus we see the official sanctioning of a de facto jurisdictional arrangement that has been described by one scholar as utterly characteristic of government in early modern Rome, where preservation was suspended within a network or "web of overlapping jurisdictions."[75] Both the pope and the Conservators had legal authority to intervene in matters regarding the preservation of ancient remains in Renaissance Rome.

It was chiefly for this reason, within the evolving constellation of authority in the papal capital, that preservation issues became among the Conservators' most effective bargaining chips in their negotiation for power. In matters concerning the preservation of antiquity, it could be advantageous and often even necessary for the Renaissance popes to negotiate with the Conservators.

In the years following the landmark legislation of 1462, there is evidence that the Conservators began to address preservation issues with renewed energy and urgency. For example, in 1469 and 1470, during the reign of Pius II's immediate successor Paul II, the Conservators supervised a series of restoration projects at various ancient landmarks in the city. This included work at the Arch of Septimius Severus, the statues of the Dioscuri on the Quirinal Hill, and the Baths of Diocletian.[76] Prior to this time, there is no evidence that the Conservators supervised repairs to ancient artifacts in this categorical way. Further payment for repairs made by the pope, issued at the same time for the same ancient sites, suggests this work was conducted in collaboration by civic and papal officials.[77]

The unprecedented outburst by one of the Conservators, Lorenzo Caffarelli, at the Colosseum, also recorded during the reign of Paul II, further suggests that the civic magistrates attended to these particular duties with great seriousness.[78] Caffarelli is reported to have attacked and even wounded excavators working to collect building stone from the Colosseum (figure 2.7).[79] While on the one hand this vexed reaction may be considered extreme, given that such excavations had continued interrupted at the ancient monument for centuries, it also suggests that preservation had acquired heightened symbolic significance by the second half of the fifteenth century. Caffarelli's apparent rage might even be justified by the Bull of 1462, where Pius II encouraged the Conservators to focus with renewed attention on preservation problems in Rome.

The Conservators' heightened anxiety regarding preservation problems. epitomized by Caffarelli's lashing out against excavators at the Colosseum, was clearly capable of causing increased tension between the pope and civic magistrates. The Colosseum, like many other important ancient monuments in Rome, represented a major source of building stone for papal building projects. But now the Conservators operated with official papal authority if they chose to condemn papal excavations at the site for causing wanton destruction.

In 1471 Sixtus IV asserted the permanent political subordination of the civic administration to supreme papal authority through the creation of the Capitoline Museum.[80] The pope donated a collection of valuable ancient sculptures to the Conservators to be kept in perpetuity in their palace on the Capitoline Hill. With this bequest, the pope managed to transform the symbolic and historic seat of civic authority in Rome into a museum. As Massimo Miglio has observed, Sixtus IV reduced this venerable stage for political power into a scenographic antiquarian setting.[81] This suggests that the papal donation marked a further humiliation for the Roman nobility, emblematic of their progressive disenfranchisement, where the Sistine gift of ancient sculpture signaled that the Conservators were no longer power brokers in Rome.[82]

Thus by the sixteenth century, the lavish ceremonials of the Conservators suggested only "a certain vain and ridiculous authority" to the historian Paolo Giovio, in his observations of life in the papal capital. Moreover, Giovio noted that the popes awarded positions of power to non-Romans, so that all that remained to the Romans were "the images of ancient honors."[83]

But if the bequest by Sixtus IV signaled the demotion of the Conservators, it also reaffirmed their new role as the custodians of the past in the papal

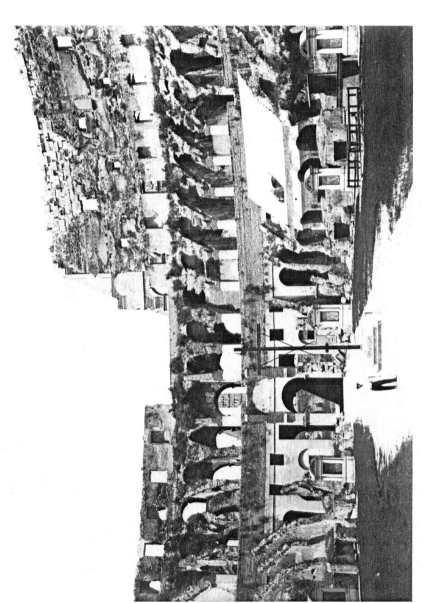

FIGURE 2.7. View of the Colosseum *cavea* with conspicuous modern restorations. Photograph by Robert Macpherson, ca. 1870. In the eighteenth century, after Benedict XIV consecrated the amphitheater to the Passion of Christ, a crucifix was erected at the center of the arena with fourteen tabernacles of the Passion placed around its perimeter.

state. In this capacity the Conservators discovered opportunities to exercise power that were hardly insignificant. Earlier in the century, the papal manipulation of the office of the *maestri* demonstrated how the authority to preserve the past offered a vital route to power. Ongoing construction activity meant that the papal capital remained a site of pressing and complex preservation problems. Now as the appointed defenders of antiquity, the Renaissance Conservators wielded a growing authority that enabled them to resist and at times—as discussed in the next chapter—even to defy the will of the pope himself (figure 2.8).[84]

The 1494 version of the civic statutes, issued with the approval of the reigning pope Alexander VI, formally enshrined the duty of preserving ancient Rome as the most important responsibility of the Conservators, second only to their obligation to support the papacy:

> The Conservators before all other things are responsible for the
> vigilant and attentive care for the pope and the Roman church, and
> they must always attend to the welfare of the city [pro urbis tutela]

FIGURE 2.8. Panorama of Rome and St. Peter's, taken from the campanile of the Senators' palace on the Capitoline Hill. Photograph by James Anderson, ca. 1850–70.

and the tranquility of its citizens. They must guard and protect all buildings and public works intact and undamaged [et quecumque edificia et opera publica inviolata et illesa custodire]. And they must remain vigilant, investigating and inflicting the most severe punishment against all those who destroy ancient things [rerum vetustarum], and those who remove or otherwise damage the stones or ornament of any temples or churches.[85]

This document confirmed a process that had been taking shape over the course of the century, where changing political conditions had caused the office of the Conservators to assume new contours. Thus the Conservators became the official guardians of ancient Rome, with the support and encouragement of the pope himself. At the same time that the Conservators were firmly subordinated to papal power, their historic political authority was renewed through the papal emphasis upon their responsibility to safeguard ancient Roman artifacts.[86]

A letter written by Isabella d'Este, the Mantuan marchesa famous for her avid collecting of antiquities, suggests the Conservators were in fact vigilant in discharging their duties as the protectors of ancient remains. Isabella, writing to her Roman agent, counseled him that "because of the Conservators, it is necessary to use art to bring [antiquities] out of Rome."[87] From the perspective of a wealthy collector of ancient art, the Conservators represented something of a nuisance: they threatened to prevent the removal of valuable ancient remains from the Eternal City if one did not proceed with due caution. Of course the Conservators could not secure the ancient remains of Rome from every possible act of pilfering or destruction. But Isabella's cautionary note reminds us that at some level, as the appointed guardians of Roman antiquity, the Conservators succeeded in imposing effective controls to prevent unauthorized meddling with the city's ancient remains.[88]

The enhanced attention of the Conservators to the practice of preservation, with their aggressive efforts to defend and protect all ancient artifacts as part of a notional ancient patrimony, moved in the direction of the humanist ideals outlined by Pius II and even toward the ideals of modern conservation theory. This same move also made the title of the Conservators increasingly available to the new meaning of *conservare*, with its specific archaeological inflection to which Pius II alluded in the Bull of 1462. The emerging shape of civic institutions in Renaissance Rome thus reflected not only a heightened urgency but also a new precision in pursuing the obligation to preserve the historic artifacts of ancient Rome.

3

A Sixteenth-Century Meteor in the Roman Forum

In the first decades of the sixteenth century, the Renaissance popes commemorated the imperial history of Rome with ever more superb flourishes. Not only were ambitious building campaigns styled after the classical monuments of antiquity, but even the newly elected pope, Giulio Della Rovere, styled himself after Julius Caesar with the choice of Julius II as his regnal name. Less than a century before, Martin V confronted a city on the brink of collapse: in the early sixteenth century the resurgent papal capital anticipated only the most auspicious future, where the promise of the Roman *instauratio* and *renovatio imperii* appeared imminent.[1] The successful relocation of the papal court infused Rome with new life and energy, transforming what had been a ruinous outpost into one of the greatest centers of European civilization. Merchants, scholars, and artists, drawn as if by centripetal force, converged in a stream of steady traffic upon the ancient roads leading to the metropolis. In and around the vast territory enclosed by the Aurelian Walls, the close examination of Rome's imperial remains, preserved over the centuries, provided inspiration and justification for papal claims to universal power.

The unparalleled archaeological setting of Rome also made it uniquely possible, in the context of the papal court, to envision a glorious reconciliation and synthesis of the remains of the pagan past with the triumphant Christian present. On the surface of a globe that had expanded to encompass the most distant lands of Asia as well as the still-uncharted territories of the New World, the possible realms of papal triumph seemed unlimited. A famous sermon delivered in 1507 by Egidio da Viterbo at St. Peter's evoked the fulfillment of scripture and the arrival of a Christian Golden Age, concepts that also animated the majestic forms of the Sistine Ceiling, completed by Michelangelo in 1512.[2]

In contrast to such splendid visions, the actual archaeological conditions of sixteenth-century Rome have long been depicted in much less flattering colors. The ongoing excavation of the ancient remains of Rome only became more vigorous at this time, driven by the urgent need to unearth new sources of building stone to supply immense and insatiable new construction sites, and further stimulated by the zeal of roving antiquarian treasure hunters. Such conditions suggest that while archaeological destruction was already a serious problem in the papal capital of the fifteenth century, this destruction intensified considerably at the dawn of the High Renaissance. The view of Rome in the *Nuremberg Chronicle* showed a city still dominated by ancient remains. With the construction of every new Renaissance palace and church, however, the balance slowly tipped further away from antiquity and toward modernity. By the early sixteenth century it was not so much the ancient landmarks as the modern monuments sponsored by the pope and the papal court that dominated the Roman landscape, concentrated above all at the Vatican.[3]

This energetic Renaissance building activity, within and among the venerable remains of ancient Rome, was taken to task by the prominent nineteenth-century archaeologist and historian Rodolfo Lanciani. Employed as a municipal archaeologist in Rome as the new capital of postunification Italy, Lanciani was in fact himself embroiled in contemporary controversies surrounding archaeological destruction caused during his own salvage operations.[4] Facing international disapproval, and pressured to justify his own actions, Lanciani discovered that pointing out the mistakes made by earlier excavators in the Eternal City, and particularly the egregious errors of the High Renaissance popes, could be used to help redeem his reputation.[5] In his voluminous writings on Roman archaeology he often returned to the theme of reckless Renaissance destruction, while choosing to sidestep the evidence for Renaissance preservation measures. Lanciani's argument proved to be highly influential for later historians and archaeologists, coming as it did at a formative moment for the creation of the discipline of archaeology.[6]

In his survey of the history of excavations at Rome from the eleventh century through the Renaissance, the *Storia degli scavi di Roma*, Lanciani reserved his most exasperated rhetoric for the sixteenth century. Examining the traces of earlier excavations in the Roman Forum, Lanciani concluded that sixteenth-century excavators had gone on an uncontrolled rampage. Only this could explain the violent disturbances he observed in the archaeological stratigraphy. Lanciani envisioned Renaissance work teams that "traversed the valley of the Roman Forum like a devastating meteor . . . destroying the monuments down to the level of the ground."[7] It was the thoroughness of these excavations that most horrified Lanciani: unlike the earlier sporadic pilfering and destruction that had taken place throughout history, he regarded the systematic sixteenth-century scouring of the Roman Forum as leaving only upturned devastation in its wake.

To be fair, this is how Lanciani imagined the destructive impact of excavations in sixteenth-century Rome. It is true that the imperial ambitions of sixteenth-century papal builders, combined with the increasing coordination and organization of sixteenth-century papal excavation campaigns, caused irreversible changes to the ancient landscape of Rome. Perhaps these deserve to be described as truly "meteoric" changes, to use Lanciani's phrase. But by the same token, the use of this polemical description has also distracted our attention from the continuing importance of ongoing Renaissance preservation practices in the papal capital.

In chapter 2 we investigated how the preservation of antiquity in the fifteenth-century papal capital was not of "merely antiquarian" concern, but an issue of intense political significance, as it represented a key access route to power.[8] Under the broad umbrella of papal authority, the preexisting institutional structures of the municipal government were gradually retooled to better govern the care of ancient remains in the papal capital, focusing renewed attention upon preservation problems and thereby also causing the political stock of preservation to rise. This chapter turns to consider the first half of the sixteenth century, from the election of Julius II in 1503 to the death of Paul III in 1549, encompassing the pontificates of two of the most active builders in Renaissance Rome and a period of prodigious change in the Eternal City. We will reexamine the premise made so compelling by Lanciani, which has since attained the status of a received truth: namely, that these High Renaissance builders pursued the ruthless and even exhibitionist destruction of ancient remains in the creation of the new papal capital. According to this paradigm, the material presence of antiquity in Rome represented something of a double-edged sword, where the renewed humanist study of ancient remains also caused their undoing.[9] Certainly the scale of construction in sixteenth-century Rome was in every sense spectacular, and it is not unreasonable to conclude that the level of concurrent archaeological destruction was no less grandiose.

But by concentrating upon this history of destruction, we overlook an essential if unexpected part of the story: there is no question that the archaeological upheaval of sixteenth-century Rome also forced preservation practices to become ever more focused and precise. This chapter examines how sixteenth-century excavation licenses issued by both the papal and civic administrations were carefully honed to improve their effectiveness. In particular, during the decade of the 1520s, a more accurate, scrupulous, and exacting vocabulary began to supplant the more elastic and potentially lenient language of earlier permissions. Sixteenth-century Rome was thus not simply a scene of archaeological carnage: on the contrary, heightened awareness of the precarious status of ancient remains generated excavation licenses of unprecedented specificity.

In this context, the ruling Roman authorities, both papal and civic, sought to close remaining loopholes and to take every possible precaution to ensure the survival of valuable and endangered ancient remains.

In 1534, Paul III appointed Latino Giovenale Manetti as the first papal commissioner of antiquity. This marked the culminating point in a process of more overt papal involvement in the preservation of antiquity that had been under way since the Bull of 1462, which conceived of the entire urban environment of Rome as worthy of protection. And yet protection was intimately connected to urban transformation and renewal, as in the preparations for the triumph of Charles V in 1536, where Manetti played a leading role in reconfiguring the ancient remains at the heart of the Eternal City. Moreover, although Manetti's appointment marked an incursion upon the Conservators' privileges as the guardians of the ancient past, these officials still retained preservation powers, and thereby political authority, in the papal capital. Their abiding interest in preservation, even as their actual power diminished, may seem to reinforce the conventional presumption that preservation agendas are aligned with conservative political ideologies. But the Conservators' continued role in monitoring the preservation of ancient remains also offered them exceptional political advantages in their negotiations with the supreme authority of the pope.

Preserving Antiquity at the New St. Peter's

In 1506, when Julius II made the momentous decision to move ahead with the plans of his architect Donato Bramante to rebuild the approximately twelve hundred-year-old basilica of Old St. Peter's, demolition began at the crossing (figure 3.1). Bramante's design featured a centralized plan crowned by an immense dome, to exalt the location of the tomb of St. Peter himself, the stable rock upon which the foundations of the church literally rested. More than any other surviving remains in the ancient city, it was the presence of this tomb that had recalled the Renaissance popes to Rome: it was from this surviving material evidence that the popes could trace their unbroken lineage back to Christ himself.[10] The tomb of St. Peter thus substantiated and justified the claims of the Renaissance popes to supreme authority in their command of the universal church.

For all the compelling power of Bramante's new design, it also required the demolition of an ancient and very sacred structure. Bramante, with the full support of Julius II, thus instigated the demolition of one of the most venerated landmarks of the Christian world. That the pope and his architect should have made this extraordinary decision, which obliged their successors for the remainder of the century to continue in their footsteps, has long been regarded as epitomizing the brutal disregard of Renaissance builders for the preservation of antiquity in Rome.

FIGURE 3.1.   New St. Peter's from the north, by Marten van Heemskerck,
ca. 1532–37. The remains of the fourth-century crossing of the Constantinian
basilica stand in the foreground.

And yet it is wrong to assume that Julius II and Bramante disregarded
or otherwise dismissed the urgent need for preservation. As the history of
preservation in Rome over the *longue durée* suggests, the issue of preserving
antiquity was charged with such loaded symbolic meaning, and the source
of such important political power, that it could scarcely be ignored in the
context of the sweeping urban transformations of early sixteenth-century
Rome. Rather, Julius II paid extremely sharp attention to the problem of
preserving ancient Rome, as we might surmise considering his papal name,
which registered an acute sensitivity to the power of recalling and preserving
ancient precedents. This hypothesis is further substantiated by documentary
evidence which indicates that papal excavations continued to become more
explicitly restrictive regarding their projected impact upon ancient artifacts
during his pontificate.

The notion of "building against time" is well suited to describe the heroic
efforts of Julius II and Bramante to transform the city of Rome.[11] Both men
were approaching the end of their careers, and they were both keenly aware of
the fact that they had only limited time to implement sweeping change. At the
same time, other comparable building projects in Italy provided clear cautionary evidence: although work at the cathedral of Milan had been inaugurated more than a century before, the structure was still far from complete,

while at Siena the project to rebuild the cathedral had come to an unexpected but permanent halt. The prospect of failure thus loomed large in Renaissance Rome: less than fifty years earlier, Nicholas V had also confronted the reality that he would never live to see ambitious urban transformations brought to completion.

Such evidence steeled the determination of Julius II and Bramante to take every measure to ensure the success of the new basilica, and this explains their decision to begin with the reconstruction of the crossing. By the time of Julius II's death in 1513, not only had the original crossing been demolished, but the four towering new piers had been built to delineate the location of the ancient tomb. The remarkable rapidity of this demolition and new construction, realized in less than a decade, anchored Bramante's domed design in permanent form at the basilica.[12]

Earlier construction projects in Rome provided important points of reference for the program of rebuilding Old St. Peter's from its foundations. The new Palazzo della Cancelleria, begun for Julius II's cousin Raffaele Riario in the last decades of the fifteenth century, had accomplished just such an objective, where its vast bulk had transformed a nearby section of the *abitato* nearly beyond recognition. In this project, the immense new cardinal's palace now dominated the site, completely absorbing and engulfing the adjacent historic titular church, the early Christian basilica of San Lorenzo in Damaso. Although the decision of the builders of the Cancelleria to level the early Christian basilica only to rebuild it behind the gleaming travertine facade of the new palace might suggest a defiant and uncompromising approach to the preservation of the past, in other ways these same builders also exhibited a more deferential attitude toward the preexisting church. As recent excavations have confirmed, the dimensions and even the original architectural layout of the original basilica of San Lorenzo in Damaso were closely echoed in the form of the new structure that replaced it.[13]

However, the imperial scale of construction envisioned by Julius II and Bramante quickly surpassed even the gigantic form of the Palazzo della Cancelleria. The new Belvedere Court at the Vatican, commissioned by Julius II shortly after his election in 1503, was emblematic of this new colossal grandeur, which reshaped the entire topography of the region north of St Peter's.[14] At the Belvedere Court, Bramante invented a new formal ceremonial space more adequate for a royal residence by enclosing the valley between the Vatican Palace and the Villa Belvedere to form a vast courtyard. The long wings of the court formed two parallel, superimposed galleries that spanned the irregular landscape like the arcades of an ancient aqueduct. Bramante regularized the enclosed hillside with a series of rising terraces connected by ramps and stairs, culminating at the top with a large exedra. In generating an entirely new landform, the Belvedere Court recalled the ambitious terracing projects of Hellenistic sites such as the Temple of Fortuna complex at Praeneste.

Subsequent papal interventions radiated outward from the palace and basilica of the Holy See into the ancient city itself.[15] A broad straight avenue, named the Via Giulia, modeled upon the *viae rectae* of antiquity, drove into the western edge of the *abitato*, parallel to the stretch of the Tiber below the Vatican. The Via Giulia was intended to put the Vatican into direct connection with a massive new building, the Palazzo dei Tribunali, also designed by Bramante, as a centralized location for the dispersed ecclesiastical courts of Rome.[16]

On the opposite bank of the Tiber, Julius II opened the Via della Lungara. This new *via recta* sliced through the open land south of the Vatican into Trastevere to join the Ponte Sisto, which in turn recrossed the Tiber to meet the Via Giulia. The Via della Lungara then continued straight on from the Ponte Sisto all the way to the Ripa Grande at the southern edge of Rome, forging a direct link between the main port of Rome and the Vatican. Such urban operations served to suture together the different corners of the city and created a network of radial axes that reoriented the existing ancient metropolis toward the ruling nucleus of the papal court.

Of all these ambitious and far-reaching interventions introduced to Rome by Julius II and Bramante, however, by far the most radical was the construction of the New Basilica of St. Peter's.[17] This titanic operation, the inauguration of the largest work site in the known world, exceeded all other building projects in its physical and symbolic magnitude as well as in its enduring and also unexpected consequences. Bramante's soaring new dome, intended to symbolize the triumph of the unified Roman church, also became a symbol of its fragmentation, as renewed efforts to fund the ongoing construction through the sale of indulgences in northern Europe helped to precipitate the Protestant Reformation.

If in 1506 this was still in the future, the launch of new construction at St. Peter's had immediate, tangible, and lasting impact in terms of the physical experience of this famous site. The implementation of Bramante's visionary new design meant that the tomb of St. Peter, the ultimate destination of all Christian pilgrims to Rome, would be submerged behind shrouds of scaffolding and clouds of dust for years to come. A view by the Dutch artist Marten van Heemskerck, resident at Rome between 1532 and 1537, showed the chaos of the simultaneous construction and destruction initiated by Julius II and Bramante, where the crumbling remains of the ancient nave in the foreground sank below the towering new crossing piers (figure 3.2).[18]

The same image, however, also suggests that Julius II and Bramante were aware of the need for preservation efforts in this sacred setting. At the center of the crossing rose a new structure, the *tiburio*, designed by Bramante and intended to serve as a temporary protective shell for the high altar and the tomb itself.[19] The creation of the *tiburio* guaranteed the safety of the tomb of St. Peter's, at the center of the construction maelstrom, as well as affording some degree of shelter for the papal liturgy, which had to continue without interruption

FIGURE 3.2.   New St. Peter's from the east, by Marten van Heemskerck,
ca. 1532–37. The pavilion structure against the wall of the nave toward the left
supported an organ and sheltered the fourteenth-century bronze statue of St. Peter.

at the center of this dangerous work site. The late date of this structure, begun
by Bramante for Leo X, shortly after the death of Julius II in 1513, indicates that
the protection of this site was perhaps overlooked in the frenetic launch of new
construction. However, Bramante's direct involvement in its design proves he
was mindful of the need for its careful preservation.

We are so accustomed to associating Bramante with destruction—in his
own lifetime he was referred to as *Bramante ruinante*—that it seems hard to
believe that this visionary architect, intent upon promoting a radical new vision
of the papal capital, could be at the same time deeply and personally invested
in the preservation of ancient remains.[20] But the fact is that Bramante was
involved in developing important preservation measures for ancient remains
at the Vatican at the same time that he also promoted extensive demolition
at St. Peter's.

It is well known that Bramante's designs for the New St. Peter's included the
Vatican obelisk as a key component. This familiar ancient Egyptian landmark,

rumored to contain the ashes of Julius Caesar in the bronze ball on its summit, still stood on its original foundations in the ancient circus of Nero on the south side of the Old St. Peter's.[21] The deteriorating condition of the adjacent basilica had long posed a conspicuous threat to the obelisk. More than fifty years earlier, Leon Battista Alberti, in his discussion of the nave walls of St. Peter's in the *De re aedificatoria*, observed that "the continual force of the wind has already displaced the wall more than six feet from the vertical; I have no doubt that eventually some gentle pressure or slight movement will make it collapse."[22] The prevailing wind from the north to which Alberti referred had tilted the nave toward the obelisk, and a fifteenth-century proposal to relocate the obelisk, which may be the work of Alberti himself, was probably inspired by the necessity to rescue this prestigious and venerable landmark from the looming threat of the adjacent basilica.[23]

If Alberti was concerned about the need to preserve the obelisk, Bramante was equally interested in the same problem. Conditions had not improved at St. Peter's in the intervening half-century. Although Nicholas V inaugurated repairs to the apse, there is no evidence to suggest the slant of the nave walls had been corrected. The nave walls were thus probably leaning even farther away from vertical, menacing the obelisk even more, when Bramante began work in 1506. Obviously Bramante's plan for large-scale new construction at the crossing of St. Peter's, in the immediate vicinity of the obelisk, further jeopardized its security. But according to a report by Egidio da Viterbo describing Bramante's proposal for the redevelopment of the Vatican from the ground up, it is clear that *Bramante ruinante* went out of his way to ensure the careful preservation of this ancient structure.

Egidio da Viterbo reported that Bramante's design for the Vatican overturned all expectations about appropriate preservation priorities on this sacred site. Bramante chose to privilege not the preservation of the ancient basilica built by the first Christian emperor of Rome but the preservation of the ancient obelisk, symbol of ancient Egypt and imperial might. To this end, Bramante encouraged Julius II to reorient the basilica, and to relocate the tomb of St. Peter to a more suitable location:

> Bramante, who was the first among architects at the time, tried to persuade Julius to shift the Apostle's tomb to a more convenient part of the church, and that the church facade should no longer be turned eastward as it now faces, but to the south, so that the obelisk would greet the people ascending into the church in the great church courtyard. Julius said no to this, declaring that sacred shrines should be stationary, and he prohibited moving what should not be moved. Bramante again pressed the point, promising that the result would be extremely beneficial if this most august church of Julius the Pope would have the monument of Julius Caesar (as the populace believe)

at the vestibule of the very entrance to the church itself. . . . He
himself would assume responsibility for transferring the tomb, he
would move nothing but promised that he would transfer the whole
tomb with its surrounding floor with the least stress possible.[24]

With this astonishing proposal, Bramante proposed to excavate and transport the tomb of St. Peter to bring it into axial alignment with the obelisk.
Thus Bramante's visionary plan for the new basilica literally pivoted around
the preservation of the obelisk, the monument of the Egyptian pharoahs,
while the rest of the complex of St. Peter's—including even the tomb and
sacred relics of St. Peter himself—could be adjusted around this fixed reference point.[25]

According to Egidio da Viterbo, Julius II refused to be swayed by Bramante's
magnificent visions, declaring "he [Julius II] would allow nothing of the old
church site to be turned, nothing taken from the old tomb of the first pope. . . .
he himself would decide what was appropriate for Caesar's obelisk, but he, for
one, was not going to put profane matters before sacred, splendor before religion, and ornaments before piety."[26] Julius II's obstinate refusal to relocate the
tomb of St. Peter provided impressive evidence for his passionate commitment
to the preservation of antiquity, even if this was not the particular antiquity that
Bramante wished to privilege. Today the tomb and high altar stand in a slightly
eccentric position relative to the dome, an asymmetry resulting from preexisting
conditions on the site that attests to the pope's determination to preserve the
tomb intact in its original location. Throughout the subsequent vicissitudes of
building the new basilica, it would be the tomb of St. Peter, not the Vatican obelisk, that attained the status of a timeless artifact, frozen in the eye of the storm.

Although Julius II rejected Bramante's design, the preservation of the
Vatican obelisk clearly remained an urgent priority as work began at St. Peter's.
Throughout the ensuing demolition and reconstruction, which happened with
great swiftness, the ancient landmark survived completely unscathed. The perfect preservation of this fragile artifact in the midst of a dangerous building
site—where the unexpected collapse of the destabilized nave would have shattered the obelisk beyond any hope of recovery—proves that Bramante as well as
his patron took special pains to provide for its careful protection.[27]

Our preoccupation with Julius II and Bramante as adamant and callous
destroyers has clearly prevented us from recognizing their evident interest in
preservation. While it is true that they instigated large-scale destruction at the
Vatican, it is just as true that they were alert to the urgent need for preservation,
and that they took key steps to introduce and enforce critical preservation
measures. Early in the seventeenth century, when the last surviving remains of
the Constantinian nave were dismantled and rebuilt, it was still possible to
claim that the reconstruction of the site had in fact preserved the entire ancient
structure, given that the entire plan of the original Constantinian basilica was

encompassed by the new building.[28] The enduring problem, of course, is that there has never been unanimous support for the way that preservation took place during this major rebuilding operation, or any consensus in terms of deciding which specific artifacts deserved to be preserved unchanged. As the early construction history of the New St. Peter's suggests, even Julius II and Bramante had diverging ideas on this complicated subject.[29]

Beyond the deeply contentious and high-profile example of the preservation of antiquity at St. Peter's, there is still further evidence for renewed attention to preservation problems during the pontificate of Julius II. Other ancient remains, even those that were peripheral to the mission and ideals of the Renaissance popes, were nevertheless also regulated and subject to external supervision. The mechanism of excavation licenses continued to serve a vital function in this regard.

For example, on 3 January 1506, four months before Julius II descended into the foundation trench of the New St. Peter's to place the foundation medal of the new basilica, a papal excavation license was issued by the builder of the Palazzo Cancelleria, Raffaele Riario, in his capacity as papal lord chamberlain, to the canons of the basilica of San Nicola in Carcere (see appendix, document 2).[30] This document reported that the *maestri di strade* were supervising road repair outside the church, and it authorized the canons to remove any building stone that might be unearthed during this construction activity. At the same time, the license explicitly prevented them from excavating or reusing any ancient stones from inside the church itself. Moreover, it also authorized the *maestri* "to excavate for us in those sites not belonging to the church, where the ground has already been disturbed."

This legislation, while it allowed the canons and the *maestri* to take advantage of those ancient remains that came to light during this road repair, was clearly conceived as a protective measure. The first component was its restriction upon the *maestri* to collect stones only "where the ground has already been disturbed." This indicated that undisturbed areas should remain so: the only archaeological artifacts that they were authorized to remove were those from places where digging had already occurred.

But the second, and even more important, component of this license in terms of the preservation of antiquity was its restriction upon the scope of excavations conducted by the canons. Embedded within the walls of the basilica and in the foundations of San Nicola were the remains of three different temples dating to the late Republican period. The canons, interested in augmenting their income, might have proceeded to sell off these invisible and presumably unimportant remains. The presence of a specific clause in the papal excavation license, however, prohibited all such tampering with these materials. Thus the 1506 license played a vital part in safeguarding the material remains of some of the most ancient temples to still survive today in Rome.[31]

Such an example might seem minor when we consider the scale of Julius II's building projects in Rome. Nevertheless, it provides an important reminder that the preservation of antiquity remained a key concern during his pontificate and that the destruction of ancient sites was not simply awarded papal sanction. The traditional legislative restrictions limiting the destruction of antiquity that had emerged over the centuries at Rome remained firmly in place. What is more, the existing system was further strengthened and improved for, as we will see, sixteenth-century papal excavation licenses now began to define the objectives and goals of preservation with a new and unprecedented clarity.

Preservation in the Rome of Leo X and Raphael

As the construction of the New St. Peter's continued to be a primary objective for the successors of Julius II, so did this enormous building project continue to direct the attention of the Renaissance popes to the preservation of antiquity. Above all, this was attested in the work of the artist Raphael, whose attentive and creative study of antiquity provided the formative background for his composition, in collaboration with Baldassare Castiglione, of the "Letter to Leo X." The "Letter to Leo X" remains the most famous manifesto on behalf of the preservation of antiquity to be produced in Renaissance Italy, providing powerful testimony for the contemporary desire to improve conditions for the preservation of antiquity in the papal capital. Yet it is critical to note that Raphael's privileged access to antiquity, which made this letter possible, was in turn made possible through his work as architect of the New St. Peter's.

Following Bramante's death in 1514, the newly elected Leo X appointed Raphael to the position of chief architect at St. Peter's.[32] Although the architectural profession had no set entry requirements in the early sixteenth century, most architects were expected to have had some experience on a building site. Prior experience would seem to be a concern of particular importance for the selection of a chief architect to head such a gargantuan building project, where the planning and construction of a basilica of unprecedented size raised all sorts of complex and unexpected problems. Although Raphael was known for his virtuoso accomplishments as a painter, he had very little experience in building. The fact that Leo X set this extraordinary charge upon Raphael, despite his relative youth and inexperience, paid tribute not only to his artistic talent and personal charisma but also to his remarkable managerial skills, as revealed in his recent work on the Vatican Stanze.[33]

The preservation of antiquity may have appeared less urgent during the reign of Leo X, as the rate of demolition and new construction slowed down considerably at the Vatican following the deaths of Julius II and Bramante. But Leo X was resolved to continue construction. In a papal brief issued in 1515, a year after appointing Raphael as the architect of St. Peter's, Leo X authorized

Raphael to collect building materials from within a ten-mile radius of Rome to supply ongoing construction at the site.[34] As this document attested, it was a papal priority of the utmost importance to continue work on the new Temple of the Apostles, and Leo X gave Raphael oversight for excavations throughout the city and its environs to ensure that construction at the New St. Peter's continued without delay.

While the papal brief insisted upon the need for new construction materials, it did not disregard the papal obligation to safeguard the ancient remains of Rome. Thus the brief acknowledged that not all of these ancient artifacts were appropriate for reuse, as some of them might be inscribed with "letters or other carvings" of special value for the ongoing humanist investigation of classical antiquity. For these reasons, the pope authorized Raphael to determine what artifacts had such antiquarian value. By conferring upon Raphael the right to decide which remains should be set aside and preserved for posterity, the papal brief acknowledged Raphael's preeminence as a leading connoisseur of classical antiquity.

Surely Raphael received this legislation with tremendous excitement. Leo X, by granting Raphael oversight over ancient remains gathered from within a ten-mile radius of Rome, provided him with extraordinary access to a vast quantity of ancient artifacts, including those which were just in the process of being extracted from the earth. Through this commission, Raphael received an unequalled opportunity to study antiquity in a comprehensive way that most antiquarians could only dream of, with the special privilege and benefit of first-hand experience. But at the same time, Raphael had reason to view this legislation as a terrible burden. The duty to select materials to supply the construction site at St. Peter's represented a kind of death warrant for the ancient remains, especially judged from the perspective of someone so enamored of classical antiquity. At the same moment that Leo X empowered Raphael to increase his knowledge of ancient Rome, he also made Raphael personally complicit in its destruction.

When we realize Raphael's difficult and paradoxical situation, where his work as the chief architect of St. Peter's was fractured by unresolvable tensions relating to preservation problems, we can better appreciate the particular and highly personal investment of this artist in the preservation of antiquity. Raphael's primary duty as papal builder was to raise a vast new building in early sixteenth-century Rome. His antiquarian concerns, however, prompted him to consider ways to mitigate the immense destruction caused by this new construction. Through his wide exposure to different ancient remains in various states of repair all over Rome, and by making decisions about what could be saved and what could be reused, Raphael also gained new insights into the many possible ways that ancient remains could be preserved. Raphael's unique position empowered him, perhaps more than anyone else in Rome, to understand the complex interdependence of preservation and destruction. This specialized knowledge in turn enabled him to conceive of precise, realistic solutions to balance the need for preservation against the ongoing urban development and transformation of Rome itself.

A close reading of the "Letter to Leo X," attributed to Raphael in collaboration with the humanist Baldassare Castiglione, invites us to consider how these figures envisioned implementing a new and more comprehensive preservation program in the expanding papal capital.[35] The letter was divided into two distinct parts, the first a humanist appeal calling for the pope to defend ancient remains with renewed vigilance, while the second presented a more technical proposal, involving a new plan to document the remains of ancient Rome. The following discussion concentrates upon the first part of the letter. Although the elegance of its language and humanist concepts has often been interpreted as evidence for Castiglione's authorship, Raphael's specialized knowledge and personal experience with the dilemma of balancing preservation against destruction suggests his contribution to this part of the letter was equally critical.[36]

The "Letter to Leo X" began by addressing the recent, escalating destruction of ancient remains in the papal capital, where ruins continued to supply building sites around the city. Worst of all was the Roman practice of burning marble for lime, which offered a quick and cost-efficient way to create mortar for brick construction, at the cost of annihilating irreplaceable fragments of classical antiquity. The appropriation of existing ancient materials for new construction was of course a long-established tradition at Rome, and the practice of burning ancient marble to produce lime was even reflected in the name of the Calcarario, the southern district of the Campus Martius, called after its many lime-kilns.[37] Raphael and Castiglione observed that even with the changed political, social, and economic conditions of the Renaissance capital, construction practices remained the same: "this new Rome which we see today, however great, however beautiful, however adorned with palaces, churches, and other buildings, all has been built with lime made from ancient marble."[38]

From the perspective of these writers, there was only one possible hope to remedy the ongoing destruction of antiquity: direct papal intervention. Only the pope himself could choose to correct this situation and to curb the interminable demolitions in the city. The letter was clearly conceived to bring the situation to the attention of Leo X, as the ruling pontiff who had appointed Raphael to oversee the escalating destruction of the ancient remains of Rome: "Most Holy Father, let it not be last in the thought of Your Holiness to have a care that the little which remains of the ancient mother of glory and of the Italian name . . . should not be altogether wiped out by the depredations of the evil and the ignorant."[39] Despite the oblique and deferential rhetoric used by Raphael and Castiglione in this missive to the Holy See, the urgency of the matter was all too apparent. This was a vehement appeal to Leo X to institute more

rigorous preservation practices in the papal capital and thereby interrupt the
ceaseless pattern of destruction.

While the "Letter to Leo X" is often cited as a landmark for the history of
architectural preservation, its very notoriety has also obscured the fact that the
notion of preserving antiquity was not a novel idea at Rome. One of the central
arguments of this book is that preservation itself was a vital and historic tradition in the Eternal City, and that both the papal administration and the civic
government were involved for centuries in regulating, controlling, and limiting
the destruction of ancient remains. Yet the letter of Raphael and Castiglione
made no reference to this tradition or to established protective systems. It is
likely that this oversight was a conscious choice, stemming from the perception
that existing measures to protect ancient remains in the papal capital were so
flawed as to be of negligible importance. Given the overpowering evidence for
ongoing demolition at Rome, especially when judged from Raphael's vanguard
position as the chief architect of the New St. Peter's, the existing procedures to
safeguard ancient remains in the papal capital appeared far too lax.

It is also possible that Raphael and Castiglione's decision to overlook, and
thereby to devalue, the tradition of preserving antiquity at Rome had further
political motivations. By asking Leo X to assume greater responsibility for the
preservation of antiquity, they encouraged him to take a more active role in an
area that also fell under the jurisdiction of the Conservators. They made no
mention of the historic role of these officials, or of their continuing interest in
preservation during the previous century. On the contrary, the letter implied
that the task of safeguarding antiquity in Renaissance Rome was exclusively a
papal preoccupation. This may not be surprising, as Raphael himself was a
papal official: the letter thus acknowledged the current political situation that
obtained in Rome, where supreme authority rested with the pope. And yet its
silence with regard to the Conservators' role in defending antiquity at Rome
was also significant. It implied that this role, given the new political conditions
of the papal capital, was not worth mentioning.

As we have seen, the emerging fifteenth-century definition of the Conservators' responsibilities in the papal capital laid increasing emphasis upon their
duty as the guardians of ancient Rome, beginning with the Bull of 1462 issued
by Pius II. But now the "Letter to Leo X" challenged the historic authority of the
Conservators in this field. The fact that Raphael and Castiglione invited Leo X
to attend more closely to the preservation of antiquity might in fact be perceived as a real threat to the Conservators' authority. From their point of view,
the letter could be seen as a scheme to persuade the pope to deprive the Conservators of their cherished responsibilities, transferring them instead to a
more efficient and effective papal functionary. In such a context the preservation of antiquity was even more freighted with political significance: papal
courtiers on one side and the Conservators on the other sought to deploy preservation as a tactic to consolidate their respective authorities.[40]

Just as the Conservators expressed renewed interest in the preservation of antiquity soon after Pius II issued the Bull of 1462, so did they also express vigorous interest in preservation around the time of the composition of the "Letter to Leo X." Although the dating of the letter remains controversial, it was probably completed by 1519.[41] Yet the Conservators' tenacious defense of their preservation prerogatives was already recorded in a legal case in July 1518, which in fact documented a dispute between the Conservators and Raphael himself. In this case, the Conservators accused Raphael of trying to gain custody by illegal means of a valuable collection of ancient statues that had belonged to the late Gabriele De' Rossi, of a prominent Roman family.[42] According to the Conservators, a clause in De' Rossi's will revealed that he had intended to bequeath the collection to the civic officials, in light of their sanctioned role as the custodians of the ancient sculpture collection on the Capitoline Hill. They charged Raphael with attempting to bypass this clause (and perhaps exploiting his enlarged authority over ancient remains in Rome as granted by Leo X), and they sued for restitution of these ancient artifacts, which were rightfully theirs. Following a verbal message received from the pope, the evidence suggests the case was settled in favor of the Conservators.

Not only does this legal case represent our only source regarding Raphael's direct involvement in the growing antiquities trade in the Eternal City, but it also provides key evidence for the Conservators' efforts to prevent papal incursions upon their historic prerogatives as the custodians of ancient Rome. It seems that the power the Conservators wielded with respect to the custody of ancient remains was still considerable, even if their other powers were diminished. Raphael himself, entitled to decide the fate of ancient remains by papal fiat, appears to have been rendered powerless by the civic magistrates: the Conservators' claim to superior legal authority over the De' Rossi antiquities was evidently acknowledged and confirmed. This quarrel in turn may have also given Raphael cause to de-emphasize the role of the Conservators in the "Letter to Leo X." But Leo X himself, as the supreme temporal authority in Rome, could hardly choose to ignore the Conservators' authority, as this was sanctioned by both history and papal precedent.

Improved Preservation Legislation after 1520

Preservation issues became only more urgent in the papal capital in the decade of the 1520s, as indicated by the growing number of excavation documents issued by both papal and civic authorities.[43] Raphael's death in April 1520 was described by contemporaries as a loss above all for the study of antiquity, and it may well be that this sudden and unexpected news helped to draw greater public attention to the urgent need to improve preservation practices in Rome.[44] But the evidence of surviving licenses also suggests that preservation had become very sharply contested political terrain during this period, and as such, the preservation of antiquity remained a point of recurring and persistent conflicts between high members of the papal court and the Conservators. One result of these ongoing conflicts was the gradual refinement of the specific language used in the excavation licenses.

On 10 March 1520, the first Conservator, Prospero Colonna, exhorted his colleagues to defend the ancient remains of Rome at all costs, and insisted that the Conservators should impose heavy punishments upon those who caused destruction (appendix, document 3).[45] The vehemence of Colonna's outburst must be gauged in response to an excavation license issued by Cardinal Francesco Armellini Medici in the previous month. Armellini Medici, an Umbrian transplant to Rome, was a favorite of the Medici pontiff, and much of his wealth derived from building speculation in the papal capital.[46] The cardinal had awarded a team of excavators the right to excavate "gold, silver, pearls, gems, stones, metals, and treasures of all kinds . . . in the hills, grottoes, and caves of Rome, and on all territories subject to ecclesiastical control."[47] Thus the angry defense of Roman antiquity by Prospero Colonna had a precise contemporary purpose: it allowed him a perfectly legal and orthodox means by which to chastise and upbraid the wealthy, influential, and non-Roman cardinal, without however explicitly naming names. The civic magistrates' anxious desire to protect ancient Rome thus translated into a veiled attack upon what they perceived to be an outrageous misuse of power by a papal courtier, whose excavation license clearly circumvented their authority.

Later that same year, on 10 September 1520, the Conservators approved the excavation of ancient building stone by the Senator of Rome, Pietro de Squarcialupi, adjacent to the Arch of Septimius Severus in the Roman Forum (appendix, document 4).[48] This license indicated that on occasion the Conservators could be persuaded to relax their vigorous defense of antiquity, at least when it suited their own purposes. Squarcialupi proposed to continue work on "the loggia begun by himself with travertine stone." This was a project clearly intended to benefit the Conservators themselves, as at least part of these archaeological finds were destined to become "the ornaments and decorations of the Capitoline Palace."

At the same time that the Conservators authorized these excavations, they were very aware of the need to protect the many historic landmarks in the immediate vicinity of these excavations in the Roman Forum. Thus the civic magistrates required that a committee consisting of "eight or ten citizens should be elected by the Magnificent Conservators, the chancellor, and the head of the *caporioni*, to go to the excavation site and supervise with diligence so that no further unearthing and tearing away of stones of any type whatsoever should take place." The presence of this supervisory committee during the excavation was obviously intended to guarantee that the ongoing work adhered to the Conservators' preservation standards.

In addition, the license specifically required Squarcialupi's excavations to avoid threatening the foundations of the adjacent Arch of Septimius Severus itself. It also placed limits on how many stones should be extracted, and how they should be used: "he may take only as many of the stones as necessary for the completion of the aforesaid task, and that the rest be used for the Palace of the Conservators; but let him [alone] be provided with the stones; these should not be ceded to others." The excavation was authorized to remove only that number needed to complete the necessary work. Finally, it insisted that the right to excavate was awarded exclusively to Squarcialupi: this was a privilege that was not in any way transferable.

As indicated by the legal case that the Conservators brought against Raphael in 1518, the civic magistrates reacted sharply to perceived encroachments by powerful papal officials upon their responsibilities. Another struggle of this kind ensued at the end of the same year, as reported on 1 December 1520, when the Conservators interrupted the excavation of the Forum of Nerva undertaken by Cardinal Agostino Trivulzio (figure 3.3; document 5).[49] According to the Conservators, stone workers employed by Trivulzio dismantled the foundations of an ancient structure identified as the "Arca di Noè," possibly

FIGURE 3.3. The Forum of Nerva as it appeared in the late fifteenth century, with the Temple of Minerva on the left (dismantled in the seventeenth century), the so-called *Colonnacce* along the perimeter wall of the forum on the right, and the medieval tower of the Torre dei Conti rising above at the rear. *Codex Escurialensis*, f. 58r.

referring to the arch in the southern end wall of the Forum of Nerva, adjacent
to the pair of engaged columns known as *Le Colonnacce*.[50] Because Trivulzio
failed to obtain the express permission of the Conservators to excavate at this
site, the Conservators, in due exercise of their rightful jurisdictional authority,
imprisoned Trivulzio's excavating team. Trivulzio in turn defied the authority
of the Conservators by then liberating his workers from prison.

The chief Conservator, Francesco De Brancis, vented his fury at this contra-
vention by declaring that nothing would remain of the ancient buildings that
ornamented the city, and that the pope needed to be reminded that these antiquities should be carefully preserved from the vindictive attacks of such "Goths
and Vandals." The documents did not record the final outcome of the conflict
between the Conservators and Trivulzio. It is clear, however, that even if Trivulzio
managed to evade the authority of the Conservators, this episode provided an
ideal opportunity for them to mount a patriotic campaign against these incursions and to denounce the shameful treatment of the venerable remains of
ancient Rome by a "barbarian" member of the papal court.[51] The developments
of the 1520s reveal how the Conservators regarded the preservation of antiquity
as a defining aspect of their official identity. These clashes encouraged the Conservators to uphold preservation ideals with new ardor and to investigate new
ways to curb the destructive impact of such interventions upon the ancient
environment.

In contrast to the restrictions imposed by the Conservators, the tradition of
papal excavation licenses tended to be more generous in scope and perhaps
also less rigorously monitored. While fifteenth-century papal excavation
licenses had already prohibited the demolition of ancient remains, such documents rarely approached the elaborate nature of the Conservators' excavation
license of September 1520, with its appointed supervisory committee. Moreover,
the Conservators generally refrained from granting sweeping powers to excavate throughout the city of Rome, which was an accepted practice in the papal
court, as indicated by the example of the license awarded by Cardinal Armellini
Medici.

The evidence of papal excavation licenses recorded during the decade
between 1520 and 1530 suggests, however, that there were renewed efforts to
improve this sometimes lax record of preservation legislation at the time. While
the excavation licenses issued from the Vatican during the first part of the decade
of the 1520s were still relatively open ended, by the end of the decade such
licenses were already much more restrictive. This shift can be traced through the
introduction of a more specific vocabulary, which served to anticipate as well as
to curtail the impact of interventions with unprecedented precision.

A papal excavation license issued in 1523 to Maddalena Brugmans, while
authorizing excavations across a broad expanse of the city, extending south
from the Colosseum to the Via Appia, also exhibited particular interest in
safeguarding the many existing ancient structures in this region.[52] Although

Brugmans was authorized to excavate throughout this area, the license stipulated that her activities should not cause any damage to anything that could be defined as "public buildings."[53] Thus Brugmans's right to excavate was intended to be circumscribed, although the ambiguous definition of what qualified as public buildings meant she would have enjoyed some interpretive leeway. But existing preservation boundaries already in place at prominent ancient sites such as the Colosseum, where excavations focused on the removal of stones from the "coscia Colisei," placed unmistakable restrictions upon the scope of her work.

Cardinal Santiquattro, like Cardinal Armellini Medici, was also an eminent figure in the papal court of the early sixteenth century as well as a long-standing supporter of the Medici family.[54] On 8 August 1524, Santiquattro received a generous papal excavation license, awarded on behalf of Clement VII (appendix, document 6).[55] The magnanimous terms of this document empowered the cardinal to excavate unlimited quantities of columns, marble, and other kinds of ancient stone from the Baths of Caracalla to supply building materials for the construction of a new palace.

And yet while the authorization of unlimited excavations suggest a strategic papal reward to a loyal ally, over the course of four years these licenses now applied new limitations. Unlike the global terms of Armellini Medici's license, which extended to all territories of Rome subject to ecclesiastical control, Santiquattro's excavations were focused on one particular ancient site. Moreover, unlike Armellini Medici, Santiquattro did not dictate the terms of his own license as an independent operator. Instead, this prominent member of the papal court received his permission like any other ordinary applicant for a papal excavation license, through the normative bureaucratic channels of the papal chamberlain.

Santiquattro's license also cited a specific purpose for the excavated materials: the cardinal intended to use the ancient building materials acquired at the Baths of Caracalla to create "a sublime and ornate palace built for the beautification of the city next to the basilica of the prince of the apostles, St. Peter."[56] This was clearly intended to be a spectacular structure: its prominent location on the south flank of St. Peter's was symmetrically opposite the papal palace itself. As further evidence for Santiquattro's ambitions, we know the cardinal even attempted to commission Michelangelo to produce its design.[57] The creation of this private palace could be seen as also serving a distinctly public purpose in exalting and embellishing the magnificence of the papal capital, and this in turn could be used to justify the excavations at the Baths of Caracalla.

In comparison, a license issued the next year, on 12 January 1525, to a much more modest applicant, described only as "Jacopo Romano, excavator of travertine and other marble stones," indicates how contemporary papal excavation licenses also introduced specific prohibitions to further control the destruction of ancient remains (appendix, document 7).[58] Jacopo received permission from the Vatican to excavate throughout Rome, "to search for and excavate every type of the aforesaid stones in Rome, in the mountains, caves, hollows, and in all places subject to the Holy Roman Church and the Camera Apostolica." He was given the duration of a year to exercise this privilege.

And yet this license also came with an explicit and binding limitation, as it prohibited him from causing "any ruin, especially near sites known as *antica-glie*." This clause revealed that papal legislation had become considerably more specific in its efforts to preserve ancient remains. Only two years earlier, in 1523, Maddalena Brugmans had received a similar wide-ranging excavation license, but where her license limited damage caused to "public buildings," Jacopo was expressly forbidden to cause any ruin or to damage any artifacts in Rome. The contrast between these two licenses suggests a new interest in locating the source of value precisely in the age and antiquity of Rome's historic artifacts.[59]

As the Vatican introduced new restrictions to control the fate of ancient sites, so did the Conservators on the Capitoline Hill also regulate interventions on ancient sites in Rome. Those alterations conducted by individuals connected to the papal court appear to have been subject to especially vigilant and strict attention on the part of the civic officials. On 3 March 1526, the Conservators reprimanded the *maestri di strade* for damaging the Arcus Traiani, probably the remains of an ancient triumphal arch that once linked the Forum of Nerva to the adjacent Forum of Trajan (appendix, document 8).[60] The Conservators appointed the *caporione* of Monti, charged with supervising the surrounding district, to prevent the *maestri* from causing further damage to this structure.

When the Conservators reconvened on 23 March, three weeks later, they agreed that they "should ensure by every possible way and means that these stones be returned by their destroyers to their original locations" (appendix, document 9).[61] Three days later, on 26 March, the Conservators decreed that "the demolished stones should be returned by whatever means to their original locations," after affirming that neither "the *maestri di strade*, nor should others dare to lay waste to the antiquities of the city, as it is in the process of being restored" (document 10).[62] Thus the Conservators insisted that the ongoing building activity of papal Rome needed to be conducted in a way that respected the integrity of the city's ancient monuments.

Although the preservation of antiquity represented a long-established institutional tradition for the office of the *maestri*, in 1526 the Conservators condemned the *maestri* for failing miserably to uphold normative preservation standards. Surely this critique was all the more pointed, given that the civic officials knew the *maestri* represented the direct dependencies of the papal administration. Thus the Conservators exploited their prerogative as the guardians of antiquity to interfere with the agents conducting urban operations for the papal court.

Yet even if the Conservators were sometimes suspicious of papal-sanctioned interventions upon ancient remains, the excavation licenses issued by the Vatican were also tending to become more stringent. On 21 February 1527, Giovanni Maria della Porta, a minister of the Duke of Urbino residing in Rome, received a license to excavate among the numerous ancient remains on the Quirinal Hill (appendix, document 11).[63] These included the imposing ruins of the Baths of Constantine, the last major thermal complex to be built in Rome. Della Porta had "discovered travertine marble and other kinds of stones" in this area, and the license authorized him to excavate, "provided first that the designated caves and sites in which you plan to dig are returned to the pristine and original form in which they are at present, and moreover . . . [that these excavations] cause no danger or indemnity."

With this license Della Porta was contractually obliged to return the site to its original appearance. It narrowed his possible activities on the site to a very limited range, requiring him to plan his excavations in a very cautious and methodical manner in the effort to make the impact of these interventions upon the historic setting completely reversible. The fundamental goal was clearly to minimize the visual impact of these excavations, making them all but imperceptible to a viewer who might return to see the site after they were completed. In closing, the license insisted that "no building or ancient artifact may be demolished on the Via Pontificia," reiterating the importance assigned to the preservation of the existing urban environment in the papal capital.[64]

The Sack of Rome in May 1527 made it very clear that the vaunted imperial aspirations of the Renaissance popes had very little to do with tangible reality. Although Clement VII hoped to free Italy from imperial domination by forging an alliance with the king of France, Francis I, against Charles V, the Holy Roman Emperor, the superior force of the imperial armies soon defeated the French. In the aftermath, mercenary soldiers hired by the imperial army descended the peninsula intent upon capturing the city of Rome, a tempting prize that had been further desacralized and anathematized by virulent Protestant rhetoric. While Clement VII and the papal court took refuge in the Castel Sant'Angelo, the troops plundered the city, thus bringing an abrupt and tragic end to the visionary ideals of Renaissance Rome.[65]

But in terms of the preservation of antiquity, the sack may have had a largely beneficial effect. As André Chastel has observed, such convulsions of cruelty sometimes also have a positive outcome, and even as it shattered ordinary Roman life, the spectacle of the Sack of Rome focused renewed attention upon the problem of safeguarding the surviving remains of the ancient city from enemies and predators.[66] Even if few of the ancient remains appear to have suffered directly from this disaster—the Swiss *lanzichenecchi* were more focused upon extracting portable wealth from the city than in leveling its monuments—this assault gave new visibility to the issue of stabilizing and securing the safety of antiquity. This impulse was readily translated into ever

more rigorous and painstaking efforts to limit and control the impact of excavations in Rome.

It is telling that the first excavation license to be recorded in the *Diversa
Cameralia* following the Sack, dated five years later on 6 April 1532, outlined a
comprehensive program for the preservation of antiquity of extraordinary
scope (appendix, document 12).[67] This license awarded Francesco Cochicio the
right to excavate marble and other treasures, but at the same time it also
imposed extremely strict conditions. Cochicio was not to cause damage to any
ancient or modern public building, or to any public or private place. In the
event that any such damage did occur, Cochicio was under obligation to remedy
the damage and to restore the site to its earlier condition.[68] This expansive and
all-embracing approach to preservation brought together the innovations of
earlier papal excavation licenses, requiring the protection of every kind of
existing structure, in every possible setting, imposing conditions for improvement and repair to counter the ill effects of any damage. Such a scrupulous
approach, which mandated the utmost reverence for existing conditions, drew
inspiration from the recent atrocities and destruction visited upon Rome
during the sack.

Paul III and the Triumph of Preservation

Paul III was elected in October 1534 on a platform of reform and recovery after
the humiliation of the Sack of Rome. Significantly, he was the first native
Roman pope to have been elected to the pontificate since Martin V. The preservation of antiquity in the papal capital remained an issue of the utmost importance throughout his long and active reign. Both in the years leading up to the
sack and in the years afterward, there were already important efforts to improve
the effective regulation and management of ancient sites in the papal capital,
and Paul III wasted no time capitalizing upon this momentum. Within a month
of his election, the pope appointed his friend and fellow humanist Latino
Giovenale Manetti as the first papal commissioner of antiquity.[69]

Manetti's appointment marked a critical turning point for the preservation
of antiquity in Rome. The creation of this new office was clearly intended to
streamline and clarify the complicated existing system, which from the perspective of the papal court appeared hampered by the overlapping jurisdiction
and authority exercised by the Conservators. The active role of the Conservators
in defending ancient remains in the papal capital had focused critical attention
upon these matters, but, by the same token, we have seen the Conservators
were also capable of manipulating preservation issues in ways that reflected
negatively upon members of the papal court. From the perspective of Paul III,
the diffused availability of preservation legislation at different levels of the
papal and civic administration represented a stumbling block both in terms of

the efficient governance of Rome, as well as the implementation of effective preservation practices.

The notion of a direct papal appointment also fulfilled a vision for Rome alluded to by Raphael and Castiglione in the "Letter to Leo X." Preservation practices were too important to be simply delegated by the pope to extraneous entities such as the *maestri* or the Conservators. Instead, Paul III formally entrusted the preservation of antiquity to an official within the ranks of the papal administration itself, making preservation the responsibility of a single, centralized papal office.[70]

The institutional commitment on behalf of the papacy to the preservation of antiquity also had historical implications, as Manetti's appointment ensured that preservation remained an official papal obligation throughout the remaining history of the papal government in Rome. Thus in 1534 Manetti became the first occupant of a post that remained staffed until 1870, or for an uninterrupted period of more than three hundred years. The perpetuation of preservation as a papal duty can be seen in this continuous chain of appointments, which in itself suggests the effectiveness of Paul III's solution to provide for the attentive supervision of the city's ancient remains.[71]

Yet if Manetti's appointment was intended to clarify and expedite the administration of papal preservation practices in Rome, Paul III still did not venture to revoke these powers from the Conservators.[72] Manetti, as the commissioner of antiquity, was thus placed at the apex of the existing administrative system, but his appointment did not resolve the complicated tangle of overlapping jurisdictions regarding preservation that had taken form in the Renaissance city. Clearly Paul III himself considered it problematic, if not impossible, to extricate this duty from the Conservators' sphere of power. Thus throughout the remainder of the sixteenth century the Conservators retained their illustrious and jealously guarded privileges over the preservation of ancient remains.[73]

The Triumph of Charles V in 1536

In 1536, less than two years after creating the new papal commissioner of antiquity, Paul III discovered a momentous and unexpected opportunity to put new preservation practices into effect. The event that triggered these interventions was the surprise arrival in the papal capital of Charles V, the Holy Roman Emperor and the most powerful ruler in Europe. Although Charles V had made every effort to distance himself from the Sack of 1527, as the head of the imperial armies that had ravaged the city he was often blamed for this dishonorable outrage. Charles V had never visited the city before, but following a battle against Islamic raiders in North Africa and the conquest of Tunis in 1535, his arrival became inevitable: the imperial cortege traveled first to Naples and then prepared to travel north through the Italian peninsula. This projected route put Charles V squarely on the road to Rome (figure 3.4 and 3.5).

Paul III, obliged to welcome the formidable and feared Holy Roman Emperor on his own turf of the Papal States, decided to make the best of a bad situation.[74] Not surprisingly, the Roman population reacted with horror to the

FIGURE 3.4. View through the Arch of Titus into the Roman Forum, by Marten van Heemskerck, ca. 1532–37.

FIGURE 3.5.   Arch of Titus, photograph by Giacomo Caneva, ca. 1850s.
The dark stone surfaces of the central bay, preserved as part of the medieval
fortifications belonging to the Frangipani, make a vivid contrast with the restored
piers, largely reconstructed in travertine by Valadier in 1822.

news of the impending arrival of the same troops who had caused the sack only
nine years before, and they immediately began making preparations to flee the
city. Paul III, however, refused to cave in to these pressures, and he decreed that
no one should abandon the papal capital. Instead, Paul III resolved to celebrate
the arrival of the emperor by staging a splendid ceremonial procession into the
heart of the city itself, scheduled to take place on 5 April 1536. The doubts of his
contemporaries regarding the virtues of this decision were manifested in the
account by the historian Paolo Giovio, who noted: "we await with public celebration and with private sorrow the arrival of His Imperial Highness."[75]

The preservation of antiquity played an essential role in Paul III's project
to honor and welcome the erstwhile conqueror of the Eternal City. In the four
intervening months between Charles V's acceptance of the pope's invitation
and his final entry into Rome, the physical appearance of the city was radically
transformed.[76] In consultation with the papal commissioner of antiquity
Manetti, a series of major demolition projects were organized to allow Charles
V to retrace the route by which the victorious processions of classical antiquity

wound their way into the Roman Forum. "Desiring that his majesty would see the marvels of antiquity," in the words of the contemporary Roman writer Marcello Alberini, Paul III and Manetti developed an elaborate ritual itinerary for the emperor.[77] The monumental ancient remains lining the route from the southern gate of the Porta San Sebastiano all the way into the Roman Forum were cleared for the admiration of the triumphal procession. The ultimate destination, of course, for Charles V and his retinue, after making their conspicuous detour through the Roman Forum, was the Vatican, where Paul III awaited them at the new Basilica of St. Peter.

In developing the choreography for this triumphal procession, Paul III and Manetti chose to place the preservation and display of ancient remains at center stage. This was a strategy conceived to answer two key goals. One was clearly related to the appointment of the papal commissioner of antiquity: the arrival of the Holy Roman Emperor served as a catalyst to jumpstart a program of urban renewal and to improve the physical conditions of the surviving ancient remains around the city.[78] As reported in the brief confirming Manetti's appointment, the noxious impact of invasive plants such as ivy and wild fig, coupled with ongoing excavations at ancient sites to provide materials for new construction, had accelerated the decay of the ancient remains.[79] By transforming the triumphal procession into an occasion to arrest this decay and to clean and restore the ancient remains, Paul III and Manetti introduced a major preservation program calculated to slow these natural and man-made destructive forces, and in some cases they even brought this ongoing degradation to a halt.

But perhaps even more important in terms of the political agenda of Paul III was the immense symbolic weight of this arduous preservation program. The execution of this work provided a unique opportunity to affirm in tangible, material terms the moral victory of the pope over the emperor who had tacitly approved of the Sack of Rome in 1527. By excavating, exhibiting, and preserving the ancient remains along the triumphal route, Paul III exalted the magnificence of ancient Rome as an abiding presence that had withstood numberless onslaughts, including the most recent depredations by Charles V's troops. The colossal history of ancient Rome could be thus deployed with great dexterity, in a manner that put the redoubtable forces of Charles V into useful historical perspective. At the same time, such interventions also afforded Paul III the opportunity to present the papacy as the benevolent custodian of Rome, in contrast to the uncouth behavior of the imperial forces nine years before. The calculated display of papal preservation in practice was thus designed as a timely and essential element in a papal propaganda campaign. The preservation of ancient Rome paid tribute to the attentive papal tutelage of antiquity, in vivid contrast to the offensive destruction visited by the imperial troops upon the city.

In a way, the choreographed display of the preservation of ancient Rome to the imperial cavalcade also enabled the pope to upstage the breathtaking

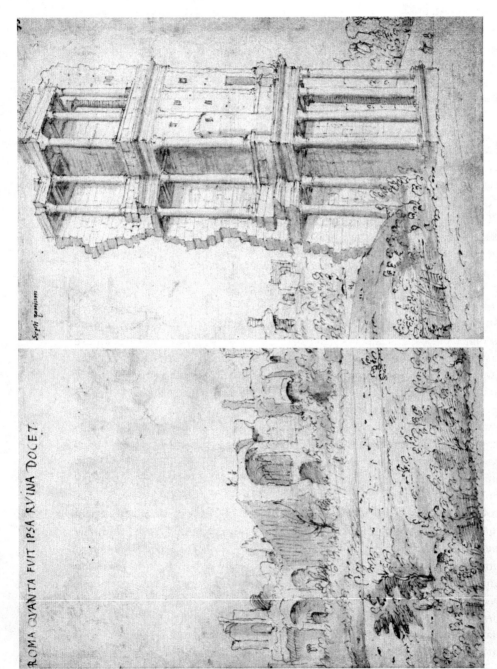

FIGURE 3.6. Septizodium in front of the Palatine Hill, by Marten van Heemskerck, ca. 1532–37.

spectacle of the imperial procession with the even more breathtaking spectacle of ancient Rome itself, newly revealed and laid open to the awestruck and appreciative antiquarian gaze. The systematic excavation and display of ancient Rome transformed a bedraggled, unkempt, and often unintelligible landscape of jumbled ruins into a panorama of preserved monuments standing in splendid isolation.[80] Charles V could claim a recent victory at Tunis, but the survival and preservation of Rome's ruins over the centuries attested to the eternal triumph of Rome.

From the beginning, the active preservation of ancient remains represented a fundamental component of these urban preparations. As reported in a surviving document dated 5 December 1535, while the Conservators were also enlisted in preparation for the triumph and required to share the burden of the expense with the Camera Apostolica, the permanent interventions involving ancient remains were administered solely by papal officials.[81] The papal program was designed to answer three fundamental objectives, all of which had to do with making the ancient monuments more visible: redesigning the existing topography of Rome to provide clear sightlines to the ancient remains from the processional route, clearing away brush and overgrowth that had encroached upon the ancient monuments, and, finally, demolishing those structures that had been built nearby or on top of the ancient remains. Given the short time available to conduct these works, it is not surprising that no mention was made of any attempts to restore or otherwise patch up the ancient structures to make them more presentable. The removal of surrounding plants and later buildings from these ancient sites, however, undoubtedly undermined the stability of some of these artifacts, and it is likely that some emergency repairs to shore up fragile or deteriorating ancient elements were also necessary.

Another mandate that has not been previously published, issued by the papal administration on 12 January 1536, provides us with more details regarding the radical nature of this ambitious project and its proposed transformation of the ancient landscape (appendix, document 13).[82] As reported in this document, Paul III and Manetti leaned heavily upon the assistance of the *maestri* to implement this all-encompassing transformation. The so-called Septizodium presented an astonishing display of the vagaries of preservation: built by the Severan emperors as a gigantic wall of superimposed colonnades to announce the imperial palaces at the southern edge of the Palatine Hill, in the ensuing centuries the monument had entirely collapsed except for one surviving bay (figure 3.6). This superb ruin, however, still stood to its original height, dominating the Circus Maximus and the triumphal route as it turned toward the Roman Forum. The papal mandate charged the *maestri* to slice open the vineyard below this ancient monument, thereby making it visible from its foundation to its highest cornice.[83]

At the venerable Arch of Constantine, standing at the opposite end of the Palatine Hill, the *maestri* were ordered to isolate the ancient monument by clearing a space around it that was again as big as the arch itself: "mettere in insula l'archo di Constantino quanto è largo."[84] The creation of an island of space around the Arch of Constantine thus provided the ancient structure with a suitably commodious and dignified setting. The opening of this sort of spatial breathing room also made it possible for the members of the triumphal cortege to examine the monument from all angles as they approached it on the Via Triumphalis and traveled through its central archway on their ascent toward the Roman Forum (figure 3.7). Moreover, the opening of a cleared perimeter

FIGURE 3.7. Arch of Constantine by Marten van Heemskerck, ca. 1532–37. The ancient landmarks became visible from new angles following the excavations of 1536.

around the ancient landmark also had the advantage of creating a kind of protective buffer zone between the ancient structure and its surrounding environment, thereby further defending it from possible damage.

These interventions help explain how Paul III and Manetti envisioned and understood the preservation of ancient remains in Rome. Centuries of decay and ongoing disintegration meant that many of the city's prominent ancient sites were slowly sinking into the surrounding landscape. Engulfed by flourishing undergrowth, altered and covered up by later additions, such structures risked gradually becoming invisible and eventually vanishing for good. The program implemented by Paul III and his commissioner of antiquity was conceived to counter this process of progressive entropy. They literally pulled the ancient monuments out of the context that had taken form around them over time, which had also served to integrate them into ordinary life in Rome. Now these structures were put on conscious display, where a sharp spatial boundary served to identify their value and prestige as much as their unusual designs and surviving marble veneers.

The same document of 1536 also reported that Paul III and Manetti planned the systematic demolition and removal of many later structures built near the ancient monuments, especially in the Roman Forum, otherwise called the Campo Vaccino or "cow pasture." Here medieval towers, churches, and workshops took shelter in the shadow of the towering columns and entablatures that survived from ancient Rome. The glorification of ancient Rome in this context meant glorifying the imperial Roman past. Thus the 1536 document ordered the demolition of the hostelry for the cattle drovers to better exhibit the Arch of Septimius Severus: "buttar in terra l'hostaria di Cavalier quasi incontro a Sant'Adriano tanto che si scopra l'archo di Septimio." A medieval tower standing in front of the same triumphal arch was also slated for destruction, along with a house and projecting roof occupied by a wagon repair business. Such humble and ordinary buildings only obscured the past that the pope and his commissioner were trying to make visible for Charles V, and thus they cleared them away in the effort to make the imperial past more legible.

François Rabelais recorded his impressions of these papal interventions later in the same month: on 28 January 1536 he observed, "they have demolished and knocked down more than two hundred houses, and three or four churches have been leveled to the ground. . . . [I]t is a pity to see the ruin of houses which have been demolished, and no payment or compensation has been made to any of their owners."[85] Papal payments made to reimburse owners for their losses, however, belie Rabelais's critique of these procedures.[86] But the revolutionary transformation of the Campo Vaccino could hardly have been welcomed by everyone. Such aggressive archaeological transformations could only have very serious consequences for the people who resided or otherwise made their daily living in proximity to these ancient artifacts.

The impact of Paul III and Manetti's preservation program was so wide-spread that it can be seen as even affecting the symbolic orientation of the Eternal City. For centuries the pilgrimage routes linking Rome to the Christian centers of northern Europe dominated the traffic patterns of the papal capital. The work executed by Paul III and Manetti, however, now reactivated the long-dormant Via Triumphalis, the route leading into the city from the south, by which the heroes of ancient Rome returning from their Mediterranean conquests entered the city. Thus the preservation program inaugurated by Paul III and Manetti recalled the orientation of imperial Rome, reconnecting the ancient capital to its historic Mediterranean empire.[87] By extension, this work also reconnected the remote and infrequented southern quadrant of the city with the expanding network of Renaissance roads that converged upon the Vatican.

These preservation efforts also had further symbolic significance in that they created a new way for visitors to physically experience ancient Rome in the present context of the papal capital. Although other triumphal celebrations had employed the ancient remains as scenographic staging elements, none came anywhere near the comprehensiveness of the interventions designed by Paul III and his commissioner of antiquity.[88] Their work made it possible for Charles V to reenact the ancient Roman triumph in the reality of the present, surrounded by and experiencing the very same material artifacts that had been known to the emperors of ancient Rome. Preserved visible and intact in their original positions, these monuments served as the material signs of historical continuity, forming an indissoluble bridge between the past and the present. The modern tourist who pauses to gaze on the ancient remains lining the Via Sacra in the Roman Forum can still relive the unforgettable experience of not just the ancient Roman emperors but also the Holy Roman Emperor Charles V.

In every way, the triumph orchestrated by Paul III and Manetti should also be described as a triumph of preservation. The enduring consequences of their work may be measured in their lasting impact upon contemporary visual culture. Marten van Heemskerck, sketching and drawing in Rome at the time that these massive demolitions and repairs were underway, discovered that exaggerated angles, including steep perspectives and wide-angle views taken at close range, were necessary to better approximate the magnificent vistas that were now being opened onto the ancient remains of Rome.[89] Foreshortened views served to emphasize the surprising enormity of these landmarks, aspects which suddenly became even more evident as they were excavated and became more accessible. Many of Heemskerck's views recorded the specific landmarks lining the processional route of Charles V, and thus his work served as a tribute to the work of Paul III and Manetti: they succeeded in making these ancient artifacts ever more dominant and visible in the papal capital.

By the same token, the transformation of Rome in 1536 continued to affect the way people saw the city in later centuries. Heemskerck produced a famous panorama of the Roman Forum that extended from the majestic surviving trio of columns from the Temple of Castor and Pollux on the left, across the broad expanse of the Campo Vaccino and its ancient landmarks, dominated by the Capitoline Hill and the Senator's Palace in the background, and culminating with the bulk of the Arch of Septimius Severus on the right (figure 3.8). Heemskerck even included workers laboring in the foreground with pickaxes, presumably leveling the processional route of the Via Sacra in preparation for the imperial triumph. In 1857, shortly before the transfer of the capital of the newly unified nation of Italy to Rome, the British photographer James Anderson captured the same view (figure 3.9). When we stand on the Via Sacra today and survey this preserved archaeological landscape, we are also surveying the invention of Paul III and his commissioner of antiquity Manetti.

By all accounts, this archaeological panorama had a profound impact upon Charles V, who decided to change his plans and to prolong his stay in the Eternal City, thereby allowing himself more time to become better acquainted with these unforgettable views. Yet the preservation program set into motion by Paul III and Manetti, which privileged the notion of the city as a static and unchanging archaeological environment, also marked a momentous conceptual shift. Up until this point, Rome had been above all a living city, even if this complex, layered urban environment also included many traces of the past. Following the implementation of the preservation program of 1536, much of

FIGURE 3.8. Panoramic view of the Roman Forum, by Marten van Heemskerck, ca. 1532–37.

FIGURE 3.9. Panoramic view of the Roman Forum, by James Anderson, ca. 1857.

the urban fabric of Rome itself increasingly became a historic site, one that was devoted above all to the memory of the past. The decision to efface the medieval and contemporary buildings in the Campo Vaccino, and the exaltation of the remains of imperial Rome, sacrificed the living present to commemorate the historic importance of the ancient Roman Forum.[90] Thus the interventions of Paul III and Manetti, intent upon better exposing the ancient contours of the Roman Forum, announced the beginning of the end for the Campo Vaccino: the scientific archaeological campaigns of the nineteenth century finally brought this chapter to a close by eliminating the last traces of this picturesque medieval landscape.

Toward a Contemporary Understanding of Preservation Practices

The excavation of the Campo Vaccino proves that preservation efforts are always inseparable from destruction, and it is useful to keep this close relationship in mind when we review the situation of the Roman Forum in 1540. Four years after the triumph of Charles V, Paul III revoked all prior excavation licenses in the Roman Forum and transferred authority to excavate these ancient remains to the deputies of the Fabbrica di San Pietro to collect building stone for the new basilica.[91] These excavations were sharply criticized by Rodolfo Lanciani, who compared the papal excavations that continued in the Forum over the course of the next ten years to a meteor strike.[92] Yet Paul III could not have found it reasonable or opportune to betray the preservation principles he believed in, and which he had carefully honed and perfected with his commissioner of antiquity. Of course, the actual situation on the ground was very complex, but it is clear that the excavations beginning in 1540 in the Roman Forum, just like the papal excavations that had occurred four years before, were always subject to conscientious and systematic Renaissance preservation practices.

Lanciani's litany of the ancient remains spoliated and destroyed by Paul III's excavations in itself demonstrates the critical influence of these Renaissance preservation practices: the destruction he described was hardly indiscriminate. None of the structures destroyed during these campaigns were represented in the canonical roster of ancient monuments in the Roman Forum. The excavations organized in 1536 for the triumph of Charles V were intended to showcase the greatest surviving monumental remains of ancient Rome and the papal excavations between 1540 and 1550, in the same way, made every effort to protect and preserve these same ancient structures intact. Avoiding the destruction of any existing landmarks, they concentrated instead upon foundation platforms and other anonymous ancient remains submerged below ground level. Prominent monuments such as the three columns of the Temple of Castor and Pollux, described by the Renaissance architect Baldassare Peruzzi as an example of the most beautiful and finely worked architecture in Rome, "la più bella e meglio lavorata opera di Roma," survived unscathed (figure 3.10).[93]

Rather than condemning these excavations as evidence for mindless Renaissance scavenging, they may be better understood as merely the long-term extension and continuation of the preservation program introduced in 1536. Moreover, in this context, the strenuous effort of clearing these structures of later accretions and making them more visible now offered an additional bonus, where the freshly unearthed materials collected during these operations were available to supply the building site at St. Peter's. Just as the excavation license of 1532 issued by the papal administration to Francesco Cochicio was concerned to reverse the impact of these excavations, so was the same principle at work in the papal excavations at the Roman Forum. After the excavations were completed, the earlier appearance of the Roman Forum soon could be restored by backfilling open excavation trenches.

Vocal complaints by contemporary antiquarian scholars such as Pirro Ligorio regarding these same excavations by Paul III in the Roman Forum reveal, however, that these papal preservation practices were already under attack. The humanist study of ancient artifacts made the historic Roman practice of reusing

FIGURE 3.10. View of the Roman Forum, photographed by Robert Macpherson,
ca. 1851–58. The remains of the Temple of Castor and Pollux stand at the right.
At left is the Temple of Antoninus and Faustina with the seventeenth-century
church of Santi Cosma e Damiano, and to the right rise the vaults of the Basilica
Maxentius.

ancient building stones for new construction extremely controversial. Thus
Ligorio described the decision to send an ancient capital and a column base
discovered in the Basilica of Maxentius to the work site at St. Peter's with open
repugnance: "Today excavations in this Temple unearthed a base of a column
and a capital . . . which were taken to St. Peter's surely to be destroyed; it is an
ugly thing to ruin ancient remains which are well made, only to ornament
something which does not deserve great praise, especially considering how
much they are spending on it."[94]

Ligorio's disgust with sixteenth-century excavations was appreciated by
Lanciani as evidence for a nascent archaeological sensibility that regarded the
destruction caused by Paul III in the Roman Forum with loathing.[95] But this
overlooked the reality of Renaissance preservation practices: in fact, excavation licenses issued in the Roman Forum during the 1540s continued to introduce new restrictions. For example, in a license issued in 1541, "Antonio
antiquario romano" was required to excavate at a distance of "tre canne,"
meaning he had to maintain a very wide berth (approximately twenty-one feet)

from any surviving ancient structures.[96] There is also evidence that in the 1540s some ancient structures deemed to be of exceptional value even had an official, salaried custodian resident on the premises to defend these priceless vestiges of antiquity from damage.[97]

But the continued development of important new Renaissance strategies to limit the destruction of ancient remains was of little interest to either Ligorio or Lanciani, who saw only meteors raining down upon the hallowed remains of the Roman Forum. Such innovations may have appeared pragmatic, reasonable, and effective when judged from the perspective of the Renaissance papal court, from the perspective of the Conservators and the other municipal officials of the civic government, and from the perspective of the vast majority of ordinary Romans. Ironically, however, these vital protective efforts were never rigorous enough to satisfy the standards of those who wrote the history of archaeology for Renaissance Rome.

PART II

Object Biographies

FIGURE 4.1. Colosseum, detail from map of Rome by Etienne Dupérac, 1577.

4

The Colosseum

More than any other landmark in Rome, the ruinous Colosseum epitomizes the everlasting endurance of the ancient city against all odds (figure 4.1). Despite the destruction caused by ongoing structural collapse and the gradual and inexorable wearing away of its stone, brick, and cement over time, nothing has been able to obliterate the gigantic structure. The mystery of its indomitable survival is at least as compelling as the slaughter known to have occurred in its arena. Thus does the Colosseum continue to hold every generation spellbound: its tough, serrated edge serves as an icon for the Eternal City itself.

Originally known as the Flavian Amphitheater, so called after the dynasty of emperors who constructed it directly on top of the remains of the Domus Aurea, the Colosseum was the largest amphitheater of the Roman world.[1] Although the enormity of this architectural undertaking was conceived to inspire awe from the beginning, if anything, its status as a marvel was only further realized and confirmed as the landmark slowly transitioned into a ruin. Gigantic sections of the superstructure disintegrated and tumbled to earth, tearing free from their companion arches which then dangled a hundred feet above the ground, suspended in the air. While the progressive exposure of the internal structures made it more and more difficult to decipher the original design of the interior, the clear geometry of its external oval plan, extruded into three dimensions by its pattern of repetitive, superimposed arcades, has always remained a prominent and easily intelligible landmark in the urban landscape of Rome.

The partial preservation of the Colosseum's severe geometry created a spectacular juxtaposition of two opposites within the same monument, highlighting the persistence of architectural form against the encroaching formlessness of a destroyed ruin. The process of decay could be traced at the amphitheater by comparing broken sections of the exterior arcades with the preserved sections that survived immediately adjacent to them. Thus the ordinary viewer not only could imagine how the monument might have collapsed but could also picture with relative ease how it must have appeared when it was still intact. The huge size and unusual clarity of the surviving remains of the Colosseum contributed to its mesmerizing allure over the millennia.

At the beginning of the nineteenth century, Lord Byron was overwhelmed by the epic forces of collapse and devastation that were in such conspicuous evidence at this famous site. In the fourth canto of *Childe Harold's Pilgrimage*, he described the shattered "skeleton" of the Colosseum in tragic terms:

> A ruin—yet what ruin! from its mass
> Walls, palaces, half-cities, have been rear'd;
> Yet oft the enormous skeleton ye pass,
> And marvel where the spoil could have appear'd.
> Hath it indeed been plunder'd, or but clear'd?
> Alas! developed, opens the decay,
> When the colossal fabric's form is near'd:
> It will not bear the brightness of the day,
> Which streams too much on all years, man, have reft away.[2]

This was more than just a ruined monument. A ruin implied something that was in the process of disintegrating or that had otherwise fallen apart. But as Byron remarked, the Colosseum was actually in the process of becoming something else: the material remains of the landmark furnished an endless stream of building stone for new construction over the centuries. With his reference to the "palaces" and "half-cities" built with the Colosseum's remains, he alluded to the architectural and urban creations of the Renaissance papal capital known to have ravaged the monument for its building stone.

Noting "oft the enormous skeleton ye pass," Byron observed that the Colosseum exercised a magnetic force on people: they returned again and again to gaze and reflect upon its mysterious remains. The contemplation of this gigantic structure generated endless and seemingly unanswerable questions: what were the original positions of the many fallen stones scattered around the foundations of the monument? What was the fate of those stones that had since vanished? Even more important, what had provoked the initial collapse? Was it simply great age that brought down the walls of the venerable Colosseum, or were other, darker forces of destruction at work in its continuing decay?

Byron was aware that the damaged Colosseum bore the traces of two different kinds of destruction, some natural, and some man-made. Although the

ongoing disintegration of the monument caused by natural forces was regret-
table, such a process was also understandable, and in a way, even reassuring.
Such a process supported the immutable order of the physical laws of the universe, which decreed that all things, even those things that were built for eternity, must eventually come to an end. But as Byron affirmed with anguish, the
discovery that much of the ongoing destruction was caused by human hands
was much more upsetting. Indeed, this realization could only provoke the
greatest distress, as it served to confirm the very worst suspicions about the
baseness of human nature: the same hands capable of conceiving such ingenious marvels were equally capable of violating and dismembering them.

In a subsequent stanza of *Childe Harold*, Byron incorporated the legendary
lines attributed to the Venerable Bede:

> While the Colosseum stands, Rome shall stand;
> When falls the Colosseum, Rome shall fall;
> And when Rome falls—the world.[3]

In contrast to Byron's melancholy reflections on the destructiveness of humanity
at the Colosseum, this famous medieval tercet exalted the monument's steadfast
resilience. The celebrated structure represented a human triumph over the forces
of decay and collapse, to the point where it could even be regarded as something
of a protective talisman. As long as the Colosseum endured, both the city of
Rome and even the world itself could be confident of surviving into the future.
Such ideas tapped into the abiding belief in the *Salvatio Romae*, or the myth that
the city of Rome itself would never perish.[4] The proverb also suggested there was
an analogy between the oval form of the amphitheater and the round vault of the
celestial cosmos. The Colosseum, like the sky above, was a permanent fixture in
the universe. From such a perspective, the ultimate collapse of the Colosseum
was clearly unthinkable, equivalent to the coming of the apocalypse.

Bede's famous proverb proclaimed the triumph of the Colosseum over
time, while Byron's poem identified the malevolence of later generations in the
ruinous condition of the present monument. Both Bede and Byron, however,
agreed that the rugged Colosseum was pitted against the ceaseless forces of
destruction. Neither made any reference or acknowledgment of the role of later
generations in preserving this venerable structure. While Bede's proverb side-
stepped this question, Byron emphasized that later generations had played only
a negative role in their remorseless plundering of its skeletal remains. Thus
from Bede to Byron, or for a trajectory of more than a thousand years, a pattern
of thinking took form that focused exclusively upon the Colosseum's destruction. The enthusiasm of these writers for the legendary monument's tenacious
hold in the face of such cataclysmic destruction ironically also helped efface the
evidence for ongoing preservation measures at the site.

The disappearance of this preservation record had especially serious
consequences for the Renaissance history of the monument. Unprecedented

large-scale organized quarrying took place at the site during the fifteenth- and sixteenth-century rebuilding of the papal capital. This period has thus long been notorious in the annals of Colosseum archaeology. According to the historian Eugène Müntz, sifting through the records of papal Rome, the fact that a noted Renaissance humanist such as Nicholas V could approve excavations at the Colosseum was baffling, if not completely incomprehensible.[5]

And yet the evidence for Renaissance pillaging was impossible to ignore. Papal excavation licenses issued throughout the early modern period provide irrefutable proof for the merciless quarrying of the Colosseum's ancient building stone by the Renaissance popes to build their "walls, palaces, half-cities." Even the fervent admiration of nineteenth-century critics for the achievements of the Renaissance was insufficient to quell their revulsion for such obvious and blatant hypocrisy. From the founding of the modern discipline of archaeology, the notion that the Colosseum was ravaged and plundered by these builders became taken for granted as a lamentable but incontrovertible truth about the history of archaeology in fifteenth- and sixteenth-century Rome.

Given that this way of thinking has been entrenched for so long, it comes as a shock to discover that the Colosseum actually represented a landmark in the development of Renaissance preservation practices. During the fifteenth and sixteenth centuries, new safeguards of unprecedented clarity were introduced at the site to regulate the ongoing extraction of ancient building stone and to control the loss of historic fabric. The careful regulation of excavations at the amphitheater at this time was critical for its long-term future survival. As anyone who visits Rome soon discovers, the Colosseum is usually sheathed by layers of workers' scaffolding. Although we tend to assume that such ongoing maintenance represents a singularly modern phenomenon, the survival of the Colosseum throughout history has depended upon ongoing supervision, regulation, and maintenance. Preservation practices were never more important than during the tumultuous urban expansion of the Renaissance papal capital.

This chapter explores how the careful regulation of excavations at the Colosseum reached a critical point in Renaissance Rome, with the exponential increase in demand for building stone to supply the new construction sites in the papal capital. Often in postclassical Rome, building stones for new construction were excavated from the nearest ancient site. The Colosseum, the largest ruin in the city, surrounded by mountainous stone piles formed by its collapsed arcades, was pillaged in this way throughout its history. And yet, although excavations continued throughout the fifteenth and sixteenth centuries, quarrying during the Renaissance was neither casual nor reckless. Instead, it was at this time that a specialized, on-site preservation program introducing strict controls over the course of excavations took shape, with the approval of both papal and civic leaders. Perhaps no other legislation in the history of the amphitheater did more to ensure its survival. Thus the semiruined form of the Colosseum, recognized around the world as a shorthand symbol of the Eternal City, can also be seen as the direct product of conscious Renaissance preservation practices.

This chapter also considers how the Passion plays staged at the Colosseum, as an expression of popular piety, can be understood in terms of changing Renaissance ideas about the adaptive reuse of ancient landmarks. To the fifteenth-century organizers of the Passion plays, the blood-stained Roman amphitheater, the legendary setting of Christian persecutions in antiquity, provided an ideal venue to stage these dramatic reenactments. And yet after a series of successful performances, Paul III canceled them permanently in 1539. As we will see, the papal interdict on the Passion plays suggests the emergence of a more restrictive approach to the adaptive reuse of the Colosseum in sixteenth-century Rome. When the Passion plays threatened to disintegrate into civil disorder, Paul III intervened to defend the ancient landmark from casual and reckless destruction.

From Flavian Amphitheater to a Quarry for Building Stone

The Amphitheatrum Flavium, built by Vespasian and completed by his son Titus in 80 A.D., was conceived along the lines of an enormous and robust machine, designed with a ruthless attention to detail. Massively overengineered, the amphitheater was built to withstand the brutal combats that took place within the arena, the tremendous pressures imposed by gigantic crowds funneling in and out of the complex, and the heavy lifting and lowering mechanisms required for its normal operation. Regular maintenance and operation of this landmark, however, was an extremely costly venture. When such an expense became unsustainable in the changing economic conditions of the late Roman Empire, deterioration soon set in. The eventual collapse of the external circuit of southern arcades created the astonishing image of a half-standing landmark juxtaposed against its own ruinous remains, by far one of the most memorable sights in the postclassical city.

The Colosseum represented the culmination of a Roman tradition of extensive building knowledge and sophisticated engineering experience. Its design provided a breathtaking display of technical virtuosity. A carefully planned circulation system, featuring a network of concentric annular corridors connected by dozens of staircases, made it possible for fifty thousand people to ascend from ground level to their individual seats in a manner of minutes. The amphitheater also made dramatic use of state-of-the-art technology. Fresh drinking water was available throughout the structure, delivered via an aqueduct from a cistern located on the neighboring Caelian Hill, which enabled water to be pumped even to the upper stories using only the force of gravity.[6] Transport elevators connected the *hypogea*, the network of subterranean galleries built below grade, to the arena through vertical shafts covered by trapdoors. Such technology ensured the swift movement of animals and gladiators from staging points into combat, as well as the expeditious evacuation and elimination of their remains.[7]

But even more than the ferocious efficiency of its planning and mechanical systems, the outlandish size of the Colosseum itself was unforgettable. When viewed either from afar or from immediately below, the superimposed tiers wrapped its shell in a rhythmic and infinite loop. The dizzying architectural repetition of this colossal structure rendered palpable the limitless political command and material resources of imperial Rome itself.

Despite the obvious intention of the designers of the Colosseum to make the building completely impervious to wear and decay, the structure's external shell was its Achilles heel. Unlike semicircular Greek theaters, carved into the natural landscape, Roman amphitheaters stood detached from their surrounding environment in superb isolation. But such a freestanding structure was also much more vulnerable to destruction. The lower levels of the Colosseum were supported by a system of vaulted corridors, further reinforced by a network of concentric and radial walls. Ascending to its higher levels, however, these reinforcing structures became both fewer and smaller. Thus the towering attic story was reinforced only on its inside surface by a single file of columns raised above the *maenianum summum in ligneis*, the highest tier of wooden seating.

While the superstructure gained some compressive strength when it was completed as a continuous ring of stone, this part of the Colosseum, more than any other, was still menaced with destruction. The lofty attic story, pierced only at every other bay by a square opening, was exposed to the force of the wind, and its resistance was further compromised by the *velarium*, the awning winched out to protect the spectators from the sun.[8] Wooden masts extending through stone sockets set into the exterior face of the attic story supported the *velarium* with its cantilever and rigging cables. These in turn allowed the *velarium* to be lowered over the arena far below. Not only did the wooden masts have to counter the deadweight of the canopy, but they also had to resist the additional pressure placed upon them whenever its billowing fabric was caught by wind gusts. And during lightning storms, the circuit of masts crowning the Colosseum parapet could turn its superstructure into a tinderbox.

Restorations were already necessary within a century of the Colosseum's completion in 80 A.D., perhaps following a fire ignited during a lightning storm.[9] The historian Dio Cassius described the devastating impact of another fire in the amphitheater touched off by lightning in the early third century:

> The hunting theater [as Dio referred to the Colosseum] was struck by thunderbolts on the very day of the Vulcanalia, and such a blaze followed that its entire upper circuit and everything in the arena was consumed, and thereupon the rest of the structure was ravaged by the flames and reduced to ruins. Neither human aid could avail against the conflagration, though practically every aqueduct was

emptied, nor could the downpour from the sky, which was most heavy and violent, accomplish anything—to such an extent was the water from both sources consumed by the power of the thunderbolts, and, in fact, actually contributed in a measure to the damage done. In consequence of this disaster the gladiatorial show was held in the stadium for many years.[10]

The catastrophic scale of the disaster as described by this ancient source has been confirmed by archaeological examination of the building fabric, which suggests that under the Severan dynasty perhaps the entire northwestern quadrant of the structure was completely rebuilt from the ground up.[11] A number of column capitals discovered in the substructures of the arena have been traced to the colonnade at the attic story, at the level of the *maenianum summum in ligneis*. The fact that these capitals are dated to different periods suggests the attic story also needed frequent restorations. The rigging of the *velarium*, constantly exposed to fire, would have brought down extensive portions of the colonnade and attic along with it when it collapsed.[12]

As long as the Roman Empire was flourishing, it was possible to conduct such extensive and expensive repairs on a regular basis. The high cost of maintenance, however, coupled with increasing political instability, began to make this kind of work cost prohibitive. The last recorded repairs at the Colosseum took place at the end of the fifth century, subsidized by the *praefectus urbi* Decius Marius Venantius Basilius, who funded the restoration of the arena and podium with his private income.[13] After the last *venationes* or animal fights recorded at the amphitheater in the sixth century, the structure was closed to public entry, and the arcades along its perimeter were sealed off with wooden barricades.[14] Archaeological evidence suggests that people in the vicinity soon began to appropriate the interior galleries of the Colosseum as a shelter for livestock. Holes cut into the walls supported vertical partitions, subdividing the annular corridors into stables, while the installation of horizontal platforms turned the vaulted arches into haylofts.[15] The warren of corridors in the lower levels of the structure lent themselves to adaptive reuse as a shelter and storage facility.

As early as the eighth century, or approximately two or three centuries of neglect since the last restorations of Venantius Basilius, the southern half of the Colosseum suffered a massive collapse that pulled down many of its external arcades. This transformed the southern perimeter of the landmark into a mountainous moonscape of rubble, collectively called the *coscia Colisei*.[16] While this name is of uncertain origin, it may have referred to the strange appearance of the newly exposed internal core of the monument following this collapse. Stripped of its classical travertine veneer, the coarse brick and concrete viscera of the monument now resembled an organic growth more than an architectural structure. Thus the name *coscia Colisei* may be derived from *coxae*, or the boreholes created by sea mollusks burrowing into stones (figure 4.2).[17]

The cause of the epic collapse, creating the trademark half-ruined appearance of the Colosseum as we know it today, has yet to be determined. Archaeologists have identified two different kinds of sedimentation under the monument, and perhaps these two kinds of earth settled at different rates under the immense weight of the structure resting upon them. Such different rates of settlement may have caused the two halves to pull apart from each other, thus accelerating the process of decay.[18] Further archaeological evidence suggests that scavengers were already collecting building stone from the southern half of the monument as early as the sixth century.[19] Perhaps the southern arcades had already suffered some significant damage or collapse, dislodging or otherwise facilitating the removal of building stone in this area.

Thanks to the eighth-century collapse, a startling distinction between the two surviving halves of the Flavian amphitheater became a permanent feature of the monument: from now on, the excellent condition of the Colosseum's northern half stood in marked contrast to that of its deteriorating southern half. As we will see, this fundamental contrast between the two parts of the Colosseum played an instrumental role in the later establishment of Renaissance preservation practices at the monument.

FIGURE 4.2. Colosseum, southern perimeter and *coscia Colisei*, by Marten van Heemskerck, ca. 1532–37.

Following the collapse of the southern arcades, which brought vast quantities of high-quality building stone to the ground, excavations at the Flavian amphitheater became only more frequent.[20] The *coscia Colisei* provided abundant materials for new construction throughout the city. Of course, collecting building stone from this rubble was easier than the perilous task of attempting to dismantle the structure itself. The removal of such stone also served to clear the terrain of ruins, which, according to the established tradition of late antique Roman legislation, were condemned as disfigured and ugly. Detached from the ancient amphitheater, individual building stones lost their architectural meaning and became mere debris or *spolia* available for reuse.

This does not mean, however, that there was no interest in the preservation of the ancient landmark at that time. On the contrary, the dramatic collapse of the southern part of the monument served to heighten the remarkable resilience of the northern arcades that managed to withstand this cataclysmic destruction. The ongoing endurance of this fragment of the Flavian amphitheater provided an apt symbol for the Eternal City. Moreover, it also played an important role in the life of the medieval city, as this half of the Colosseum faced the *abitato*, the center of Rome during the Middle Ages. From the *abitato*, the northern arcades were the most visible portion of the monument, and this particular orientation favored their survival. They stood directly above the Via

FIGURE 4.3. Colosseum, preserved north external wall as it appeared in the late fifteenth century. Figures stand silhouetted in the third-story arcades, admiring the view, while a stonemason labors in the right foreground. *Codex Escurialensis*, f. 41v.

Maggiore, the main processional route linking the major basilicas of St. Peter and the Lateran, providing a magnificent display of the grandeur of ancient Rome for important papal ceremonial processions conducted along this route, including the papal investiture itself.[21] Sensitive to the rich symbolic value of this splendid and scenographic backdrop to their processions, the medieval popes undoubtedly played an instrumental role in ensuring the careful preservation of the northern arcades (figure 4.3).

The History of Destruction at the Renaissance Colosseum

In a letter dated 1349, Petrarch reported that a great earthquake had shaken the city of Rome, causing the collapse of its famous but dilapidated and neglected ancient monuments:

> Massive ancient buildings, neglected by the citizenry but admired by foreigners, fell; that tower truly unique in the world, called the Torre dei Conti, weakened by huge cracks, crumbled and now looks down upon its head, once the proud decoration of its summit, which has tumbled to the ground. Finally, to cite still more testimony of divine wrath, the beauty of many churches was destroyed; in particular, the one dedicated to the apostle Paul had a good portion of its sanctuary tumble to the ground, and the top of St. John Lateran has crumbled.[22]

Citing Pliny as an authority, Petrarch affirmed with foreboding that the earthquake was a portent of some ominous future event.

It is not surprising that the history of archaeology has taken note of Petrarch's letter, with its reference to the destruction of important archaeological artifacts in Rome. But there has been a tendency in the scholarship to exaggerate the significance of Petrarch's generalized reference to the destruction of "massive ancient buildings."[23] Based upon the evident magnitude of the ancient buildings involved, and the scale of destruction implied by Petrarch's text, scholars have assumed that he was referring to the massive collapse of the Colosseum. In the absence of other archaeological evidence, we have long assumed that Petrarch in fact witnessed the collapse of the Colosseum's southern arcades (figure 4.4).[24]

The evidence of more recent archaeological investigations has since discredited this long-standing assumption by moving the date of the initial collapse of the southern arcades much further back in time, to the eighth century if not even earlier. Of course Petrarch saw the damaged Colosseum, and perhaps he even witnessed an earthquake at the site. It is clear, however, that his letter provided more particulars regarding earthquake damage at other late antique and medieval buildings, such as the fourth-century basilicas of St. Paul and the Lateran, and the thirteenth-century Torre dei Conti.

FIGURE 4.4.   Colosseum, profile of broken north external wall, facing the Roman
Forum. *Codex Escurialensis*, f. 24v.

It is also indisputable that later scholars jumped to the conclusion that Petrarch's earthquake caused apocalyptic destruction of the Colosseum at the dawn of the Italian Renaissance. It seems Petrarch's idea that the earthquake presaged some ominous future event struck a chord with those scholars studying the archaeological history of the Colosseum, who knew with the benefit of hindsight that excavations at the amphitheater increased exponentially in the coming centuries. Petrarch deplored the ongoing destruction of antiquity in Rome, and his sense that the earthquake was a terrible omen would be amply fulfilled at the Colosseum in the following years, as the number of excavations escalated at the site to build the churches and palaces of Renaissance Rome. The impulse to connect Petrarch's vague description of "massive ancient buildings" to the Colosseum, as the greatest ruin of the Eternal City, reminds us how accustomed we are to thinking of the Renaissance history of this monument in exclusively destructive terms.

Of course, this is not to minimize the damage caused at the Colosseum either by the fourteenth-century earthquake or by Renaissance excavations at the site. But as papal excavations proceeded to remove building stone from the monument with renewed energy in the fifteenth and sixteenth centuries, these same excavations also highlighted the tension between papal preservation ideals and preservation practices, a tension that was more evident at the Colosseum than at any other site in Renaissance Rome.

As we saw already with the reaction of Eugène Müntz, who despaired over the evidence for reckless destruction caused by Nicholas V at the Colosseum, scholars have concluded that the Renaissance popes must have betrayed their better ideals in plundering this venerable landmark to build the papal capital. The Renaissance popes issued legislation that attested, at least in theory, to a revolutionary new approach to preservation, endorsing a comprehensive notion of preservation to safeguard all ancient monuments from any kind of damage. But in practice, such ideals often seemed to fall far short. The presence of major papal-sponsored excavations at the Colosseum through the rest of the fifteenth century appeared perhaps the most flagrant contradiction of these preservation ideals.

For example, when Eugenius IV issued a papal bull in 1431 which decreed that ancient remains of Rome should not be destroyed, he pointed to the Colosseum itself, as a prized ancient artifact that needed to be protected and preserved for the future. As he declared, "to demolish the monuments of Rome is nothing other than to diminish the excellence of this same city, and that of the entire world. . . . [N]ot even the smallest stone of the Colosseum should be allowed to be destroyed."[25] And yet eight years later, in 1439, Eugenius IV himself approved the removal of stone from the Colosseum to conduct repairs at the Lateran Basilica.[26]

It was during the pontificate of Eugenius IV's successor, Nicholas V, famous for his passionate humanist interests, the founder of the Vatican Library, promoter of the cause of scholarship and the diffusion of knowledge, that some of the most extensive and notorious fifteenth-century excavations occurred at the Colosseum. As Müntz reported, in 1452 alone, 2,522 cartloads of ancient stone were extracted from the monument to supply papal work sites around the city.[27]

In the famous Bull of 1462, Pius II revived the concept of comprehensive preservation that Eugenius IV had conceived in his legislation of 1431 for the Colosseum. Pius II radically expanded this concept, however, by applying it to the entire city of Rome. Thus Pius II prohibited the demolition of "any ancient building or vestige existing on the soil of Rome or its environs."[28] The fact that the pope began to import marble to Rome from the ancient quarries at Carrara indicates his desire to make use of quarries other than the Colosseum.[29] Nevertheless, it is well known that during Pius II's pontificate, excavations still continued at ancient monuments, including the Colosseum, which provided building stone for the work site at St. Peter's.[30] Ancient building stone was collected to supply construction material for the square in front of the basilica, new steps, and the new Benediction Loggia.[31]

Stone quarried at the Colosseum was also delivered to the work site of the Palazzo Venezia between 1466 and 1467, the Roman residence of the Venetian cardinal Pietro Barbo who was elected Paul II in 1464.[32] Paul II also expressed interest in the preservation of ancient remains at Rome, as revealed in papal payments made during his reign for the restoration of prominent ancient monuments such as the Arch of Titus and the Pantheon.[33] Thus this pope exhibited the same apparently paradoxical and duplicitous behavior of his predecessors, where he "protected the classical edifices of the city with one hand and damaged them with the other."[34]

Considering the scale of ongoing papal-sponsored excavations at ancient Roman sites in the fifteenth century, and especially at the Colosseum, it is not surprising that the evident conflict between papal preservation ideals and the reality of papal interventions should have also registered upon the popular imagination in Renaissance Rome. The popes, as well as other important figures in the papal court, as the promoters of large-scale construction projects in the city, were often accused of pillaging the Colosseum to satisfy their own objectives. This was even true in those cases for which there was little evidence to substantiate such defamatory claims. Thus the humanist Evangelista Maddaleni Capodiferro accused Sixtus IV of destroying the Colosseum in a polemical epigram: "in order that the foundations of a little bridge be erected, must your hands bring down great amphitheaters?"[35] Although Capodiferro took aim at the pope for pilfering stone from the ancient monument to construct the new Ponte Sisto, there is no conclusive evidence to prove that Sixtus IV excavated materials for this work site from the Colosseum.[36]

In the same way, when Cardinal Alessandro Farnese, the future Paul III, began work on the vast Palazzo Farnese in the late fifteenth century, it was taken for granted that the cardinal had plundered the Colosseum to build his new palace. According to a common urban legend in Rome, the Farnese family secretly plundered the Colosseum in one night to build the Palazzo Farnese. And yet as Lanciani noted, although the construction of the Farnese palace did involve the collection of ancient materials from elsewhere in Rome, the pillaging of the Colosseum cannot be substantiated.[37] By the second half of the fifteenth century, excavating at the Colosseum had clearly become a provocative and inflammatory act, one that was likely to generate popular outrage.[38]

In the next section we rethink some of these conventional assumptions about the Renaissance Colosseum. Our preoccupation with its destruction has distracted us from a more important question: how were the infamous interventions of the Renaissance popes at the Colosseum in fact consonant with Renaissance conceptions of preservation practices? Further investigation suggests that papal excavations at the Colosseum throughout the fifteenth century adhered closely to normative preservation standards as they were outlined in fifteenth-century legislation.

The Boundaries of Preservation at the Renaissance Colosseum

In the fourteenth century, a prominent Roman civic confraternity, the Compagnia del Salvatore, began to acquire and occupy various sections of the Colosseum. The Salvatore was one of the most prestigious and influential religious sodalities in the city.[39] Its members included delegates of the civic administration as well as leading figures from the papal court. The confraternity was noted for playing a critical role in stabilizing mutual agreements and consensus between these sometimes rival constituencies.[40]

Both the Renaissance popes and the civic magistrates took sharp interest in the fate of the Colosseum, and both intervened to ensure its proper regulation.[41] Thus it is significant that the growing presence of the Salvatore confraternity at the Colosseum did not raise objections from either the papal court or the civic magistrates at any point during the Renaissance. Clearly both the reigning popes and the Conservators considered the confraternity to be a suitable and worthy occupant for this illustrious landmark.[42]

To accommodate their ritual and liturgical needs, as well as to mark their presence at the site, the members of the Salvatore confraternity constructed three new chapels at the Colosseum. These included San Salvatore de Rota Colisei inside the arena, San Salvatore in Insula set into the southeast arcades, on the side of the monument facing the Lateran basilica, and San Salvatore de Arcu de Trasi standing outside the Colosseum, toward the nearby Arch of Constantine.[43] The confraternity also carved their insignia, an image of the head of Christ flanked by two flaming candelabra, into the keystones over the major entrances into the arena on its eastern and western axes, where they are still visible today.

As the official occupant of the Colosseum during the fifteenth century, the Salvatore confraternity also exercised an important role in the preservation of the structure. The most significant innovation introduced under the confraternity involved the redistricting of its existing property lines. Different property owners over the centuries had partitioned the monument into various irregular subdivisions. Under the Salvatore, in consultation with the civic magistrates, these eccentric property lines were formally redrawn in conformity with a new master plan, outlining a new Renaissance preservation program of elegant simplicity and unprecedented clarity.

In 1435, a contract recording the redistricting of existing property lines at the Colosseum was issued, confirmed, and approved by the Compagnia del Salvatore and the civic magistrates.[44] The fact that the confirmation of Eugenius IV was not recorded in this document may be related to his absence from the papal capital, following the uprising that forced him to flee to Florence in the previous year.

The contract awarded the Compagnia del Salvatore "an undivided third part of the entire Colosseum, with the remaining two third parts belonging to the Camera Urbis."[45] The haphazard acquisition of property by the Salvatore confraternity over the past century at the Colosseum meant that their holdings were dispersed throughout the ancient monument. However, as the contract stipulated, these holdings were now redistributed to make them "undivided." To this end, the Salvatore relinquished certain properties while they acquired others, thereby consolidating their holdings in a single contiguous block.

Plaques affixed to the exterior piers of the ancient landmark rendered these boundary lines visible, and divided the Colosseum into two unequal segments.[46] One segment, marked by the plaques, began at the large archway at the end of the monument's east axis. This segment then extended all the way around to the far side of the structure, to a corresponding set of plaques placed on the sixth archway to the south of the opposite opening. This was the smaller segment of the Colosseum, the "undivided third part" assigned to the Salvatore confraternity. The remainder of the monument, including the full sweep of the surviving northern arcades, was transferred in its entirety to the jurisdiction of the civic magistrates.

The 1435 contract, by formally dividing the Colosseum into two separate jurisdictions, one corresponding to the ruinous southern section, and one the intact northern section, made official the archaeological distinctions observed prior to this time only by convenience and by chance. This division had immensely important consequences for the preservation of the monument throughout the remainder of the century, as the demand for building materials began to escalate in the papal capital.

Thus the overwhelming majority of excavations conducted at the Colosseum in subsequent decades concentrated upon the southern section, assigned to the jurisdiction of the Compagnia del Salvatore.[47] This focused especially on

the *coscia Colisei*, the mountain of stones shaken free from their original architectural setting and now piled in heaps along the perimeter of the monument.
As a permanent on-site occupant of the Colosseum, the confraternity was in an
ideal position to monitor and regulate these ongoing excavations and to ensure
that they did not cause unauthorized damage.[48] The income generated from
the sale of stone acquired at the *coscia Colisei* was channeled into the support of
the hospital maintained by the confraternity as well as their other charitable
works.[49]

The civic government, for its part, retained control over the best-preserved
northern quadrants of the Colosseum. Although archaeological investigations
reveal that excavations also took place in these parts of the structure, such work
was carefully limited to internal areas of the *cavea*. No excavations or demolitions were ever allowed in any places that would jeopardize the structural security of the soaring exterior arcades of the northern facade. Of course the careful
preservation of a broken fragment was not unheard of in the Renaissance. The
same approach was adopted for the equally famous Torso Belvedere, another
shattered ancient artifact preserved intact and unchanged from the time of its
earliest recorded appearance in the 1430s.[50]

When we recognize how the 1435 property lines introduced at the Colosseum functioned according to the fifteenth-century understanding of preservation practices, we can also begin to reevaluate the notorious excavations at the
site conducted by the Renaissance popes. The excavation of building stone that
took place at the Colosseum during the pontificates of Eugenius IV, Nicholas V,
Pius II, Paul II, and others converged upon its ruinous quadrants. Lanciani
himself affirmed that even the most exacting study of papal records failed to
prove the Quattrocento popes ever demolished any portion of the still-standing
Colosseum. Instead, they made exclusive use of those building stones on the
site that had fallen to the earth.[51] While these excavations involved the removal
of often significant quantities of archaeological materials from the ancient
monument, they were in full conformity with the preservation program outlined for the Colosseum by the contract of 1435.

As we have seen, scholars have been perplexed by the ostensible hypocrisy
of the Renaissance popes in their attitude toward the preservation of antiquity,
noting the apparent contradiction between their manifest interest in preservation and their actual interventions on ancient sites. This contradiction was
especially noticeable at a site like the Colosseum, which successive popes continued to excavate without interruption.[52]

Yet the real cause of this perplexity appears to be less indicative of the problematic behavior of the Renaissance popes than of the problematic nature of
our conventional approach to the topic. The prevalent scholarly assessment of
Renaissance interventions on ancient remains in Rome has always judged
them according to the principles of modern conservation theory. Not surprisingly, these interventions often contradicted the normative conservation ideals

established and developed since the eighteenth century. But rather than attempting to understand how these interventions by Renaissance builders on ancient sites might be valid for their own time, we have condemned them for causing inexplicable destruction and rebuked them for not meeting our own expectations.

This illogical condemnation becomes more understandable when we consider the revolutionary nature of the preservation ideals and ambitions outlined by Renaissance papal legislation itself. The parameters formulated by the fifteenth-century popes to guide the care of ancient remains in the papal capital were of such visionary breadth that scholars have inevitably focused upon the evident disjuncture that occurs when these ideals are measured against the actual physical interventions that took place on the ground. Thus scholars have repeatedly described Renaissance interventions on ancient sites such as the Colosseum with disappointment when they inevitably fail to meet our own standards. Viewed through the lenses of modern scientific archaeology and conservation theory, Renaissance interventions at the Colosseum have repeatedly been branded as monstrous and appalling. We have concluded that only destruction took place at this historic landmark in Renaissance Rome.

While we are accustomed to think of preservation and destruction as binary opposites, it is important to note that this conventional belief in fact rests upon a highly questionable assumption. Just as even the most attentive and comprehensive modern conservation measures cannot prevent inevitable material degradation, so is the opposite also true: in those cases that appear to be the most outrageous archaeological devastation there may also be evidence for attentive preservation.[53] Rather than thinking of preservation and destruction purely in terms of forces locked in irreconcilable conflict, preservation and destruction may be more properly characterized as two sides of the same coin.

When we acknowledge the intimate link between preservation and destruction, the common scholarly verdict judging Renaissance interventions at the Colosseum as preservation failures is rendered meaningless. Moreover, as this position makes no attempt to understand Renaissance preservation practices in the context of their own time, it also fails to recognize, a priori, that such legislation actually had significant impact.

Of all the critiques leveled at these fifteenth-century popes, we need in particular to reconsider our censure of Pius II, whose excavations at the Colosseum have been condemned as a flagrant contradiction of the ambitious preservation program that he outlined in the Bull of 1462. In the surviving payments made for building stone quarried at the Colosseum during his pontificate, the last payment to be recorded was made on 10 January 1462, or four months before the proclamation of his famous bull.[54] The fact that no similar subsequent payments have been located in the archives seems more than mere coincidence. It seems plausible that after issuing the Bull of 1462, Pius II in fact imposed rigorous restrictions upon the reuse of building stone from the

Colosseum, the most famous quarry of ancient Rome, throughout the remainder of his reign.

Our review of the documentary evidence suggests that preservation practices in Rome in general, and at the Colosseum in particular, were undergoing rapid change in the fifteenth century. Although papal excavations at the landmark did continue through the end of the century, it is clear that such interventions also carried a stigma, as the highly visible and scandalous depredation of the city's iconic symbol by its own rulers. The negative publicity of such work undoubtedly dissuaded more and more papal builders from exploiting the site, even if such work still conformed to the historic contract of 1435. By 1462, if not even before, it was clear there was urgent need for greater safeguarding measures to protect the famous amphitheater, including even its most ruined parts.

And yet, during this unsettled time, with preservation practices at the Colosseum still subject to debate, work began on two key papal building projects designed to recall the form of the Colosseum itself: the Benediction Loggia at the Vatican, begun by Pius II, and the complex of the Palazzo Venezia and the basilica of San Marco, inaugurated by Paul II (figure 4.5).[55] Both of these projects incorporated dignified loggias composed of superimposed arches and engaged pilasters.[56] In both cases, the use of stone quarried from the Colosseum was documented at the construction work sites.[57] Today the reuse of stone taken from the *coscia Colisei* runs counter to modern conservation theory. But in the context of fifteenth-century Rome, these projects served to literally resurrect the fallen arcades of the Colosseum in prominent new locations of the papal capital. Perhaps structures of this sort, built with material from the *coscia Colisei*, could also be conceived of as a kind of Renaissance preservation measure, as they helped to perpetuate and preserve the Colosseum in a way that transcended the physical properties of the actual building itself.

The conditions introduced to preserve the Colosseum by the contract of 1435 remained in force throughout the sixteenth century, as the Salvatore confraternity continued to manage ongoing excavations at the *coscia Colisei* and to collect income from the sale of its stones. But the reuse of building stone from this site, especially in large quantities, remained very controversial. At one point, in 1574, the Conservators debated exploiting the Colosseum as a quarry to furnish desperately needed building stone to the work site of the Ponte Santa Maria, but this suggestion was then decisively voted down.[58] Anxious to improve the viability and economic success of the modern capital city, even the Conservators, the guardians of ancient Rome, could entertain the idea of putting the ruinous remains of the Colosseum to better use.[59]

As for the sixteenth-century popes who inaugurated grandiose building operations in the papal capital, very few references to any excavations at the Colosseum to supply these construction sites have survived.[60] The increasing popular awareness of the need to defend the acclaimed ancient landmark,

FIGURE 4.5. Benediction Loggia at St. Peter's, printed by Claudio Duchetti and Antonio Lafréry, ca. 1581–82. Behind the four bays of the Benediction Loggia stands the gable end of the Old St. Peter's, while work continues on Michelangelo's drum.

which was of course advanced by papal legislation, probably made it difficult for the sixteenth-century popes to justify continued excavations at the site. This in itself may have been enough of a deterrent to cause them to renounce the famous quarry of the Colosseum, despite their constant need for high-quality building stone. For the most part, the actual interventions on the Colosseum approved by both the Conservators and the Renaissance popes during the sixteenth century thus conformed not just to the norms of the contract of 1435, but also to the even stricter preservation ideals outlined by the Bull of 1462 issued by Pius II.

Adapting the Colosseum for the Passion Play

The preservation of the Colosseum in Renaissance Rome not only was a matter of regulating the excavation of the existing ancient site, but also included adapting the surviving monument to serve new functions. The amphitheater provided a setting for animal and gladiatorial combat, its original primary purpose, for approximately five hundred years, but during subsequent centuries the Colosseum often lay dormant, aside from periodic quarrying of the deteriorating internal structures and the *coscia Colisei*. A bullfight staged in the structure in 1332 indicated that the memory of the monument as a setting for pageantry still survived.[61] It was only in the late fifteenth century, however, as excavations at the Colosseum supplied building stone to furnish construction sites in Renaissance Rome, that it again began to be used as a regular venue for public spectacles and performances.

Like the Compagnia del Salvatore, the Compagnia del Gonfalone was a Roman confraternity linked to the rise of the mendicant movement in thirteenth-century Italy.[62] They sought to promote popular piety through the reenactment of momentous religious events, in the manner of the members of the Franciscan order. The *sacre rappresentazioni*, or Passion plays, served this purpose by giving the remote and solemn story of the life of Christ a new immediacy and accessibility: the scene of the Crucifixion was performed on Good Friday, and the culminating scene of the Resurrection followed on Easter Sunday. In the mid-fifteenth century the *sacre rappresentazioni* met with critical success in Florence, where elaborate staging and costumes made them an even more vivid experience.[63]

In the late fifteenth century the Gonfalone confraternity played an instrumental role in bringing the Passion plays to Rome. The ruined amphitheater was infamous as the setting where the cruel Roman emperors presided over the butchery of Christian innocents, and the members of the confraternity realized that using this distinctive historic environment as their stage could bring the story of Christ to life in an extraordinary way. In particular, staging the climactic resurrection scene against the splendid panorama of the deteriorating arena also reinforced the idea of the enduring moral victory of Christianity over the errors of the pagan past.

In March 1490 the Compagnia del Gonfalone received permission from both the ruling pope Innocent VIII and the Conservators to stage Passion plays in the ancient structure.[64] The necessity for authorization from both papal and civic officials indicated that both of these entities claimed the responsibility of regulating the ancient landmark. The fact that the agreement was signed "in palatio Conservatorum," however, suggested that final authority perhaps rested with the Conservators.[65]

The fact that the Passion plays did not require significant transformations to the ancient amphitheater must have recommended this adaptive reuse to both the pope and the civic magistrates. According to the contract of 1490, the members of the Gonfalone confraternity acquired a number of existing houses in the structure from the Compagnia del Salvatore, "certas domos et accasamenta positas et posita in amphiteatro Colisei."[66] These served to store equipment for the performances, including costumes, props, musical instruments, and machinery, as well as to fulfill the statutory requirement that the confraternity members provide the actors in the Passion plays with "a decent meal" after their performances.[67] As the contract of 1435 relocated the holdings of the Compagnia del Salvatore at the Colosseum to the southern quadrants of the amphitheater, it is likely that these houses were also on the southern, more damaged side of the ancient arena.

The primary theatrical stage for the Passion plays was at the eastern end of the arena, as indicated by archaeological evidence which suggests that fifteen voids in this area were reconfigured to accommodate the needs of the performances.[68] A chapel standing in this part of the arena, dedicated to Santa Maria della Pietà, offered a convenient platform on which to perform the Passion plays. The primary stage was evidently situated on its roof but also extended onto adjacent structures.[69]

Similar performances staged at the Arena, the ancient amphitheater in Verona, used a portable system of collapsible tents and pavilions to frame the action and direct the audience's attention.[70] It is reasonable to assume the Passion plays at the Colosseum also employed lightweight, temporary devices that had minimal impact upon this archaeological environment.[71] Thus the Gonfalone confraternity demonstrated resourcefulness in configuring the Passion plays to existing conditions at the site, without causing significant alterations to the ancient structure.

The revival of the Colosseum as a performance venue also led to the reconstruction of certain original elements at the site. These included the building of a new circuit wall around the arena to replace the vanishing traces of the *murus podii* that encircled the arena in antiquity.[72] Moreover, some seating arrangement, such as the the construction of wooden stands, was also necessary to accommodate the audience. Even in an improvised or temporary way, the rebuilding of such elements helped to recall the original layout of the ancient amphitheater.

Thus the Passion plays revived the ruinous ancient landmark, giving it a new vitality as an occupied, living structure, and offering their audiences a unique opportunity to experience a version of the past in the present. Ten centuries after the collapse of ancient Rome, the Passion plays brought the classical world back to life, with actors playing Roman soldiers, wearing *all'antica* cuirasses and carrying standards emblazoned with the insignia SPQR, gathering again in the Colosseum arena.[73]

Arnolf von Harff, visiting Rome from Cologne, admired the setting of the 1497 performance of the Passion play:

> It is worth visiting the Colosseum, a magnificent ancient palace, round in shape, with various orders of arches and vaults, which contains within it a round piazza, surrounded by stone steps by which one may ascend to the top. They say that in antiquity the lords were seated on these steps to see the combats between gladiators and beasts. In contrast, we saw in the same piazza on Holy Thursday the performance of the Passion of Jesus Christ. Living men portrayed the flagellation, the crucifixion, the death of Judas, etc. They were all young men of rich families; thus the event proceeded with great order and decorum.[74]

Past and present overlapped in "the same piazza" where "gladiators and beasts" once fought, and which now served as the setting for the dramatic performance of the central Christian narrative. The sixteenth-century antiquarian Andrea Fulvio declared that the audiences that gathered for the Passion plays rivaled the size of the audiences that attended such spectacles in antiquity.[75] Although this statement indulged in some rhetorical exaggeration, it is clear the performances were very popular in Renaissance Rome.

While von Harff underscored the decorousness of the performance he witnessed in 1497, decorum was in fact a problematic topic. Renaissance Passion plays, by showcasing the vicious treatment of Christ and often incorporating anti-Semitic invective, had a dangerous tendency to spiral out of control. They were fully capable of inciting pious audiences to fury. In Florence, performances of the Passion plays were abruptly terminated in the mid-fifteenth century for precisely this reason.[76] At the end of the Colosseum performances, the members of the Compagnia del Gonfalone departed the amphitheater flagellating themselves with scourges, an aggressive display of penance that only added to the frenzy.

After nearly fifty years of performances at the Colosseum, Paul III terminated the Passion plays in 1539. No formal explanation for this papal decision has survived, but it seems certain that the pope was opposed to the civil disorder and violence spawned by these dramatic events.[77] And although few have noted this point, undoubtedly Paul III was also concerned for the safety of the Colosseum, as attested already at the beginning of his reign, when he appointed the first papal commissioner of antiquity in 1534. This suggests a changing approach to the preservation of the Colosseum between the Rome of the 1490s and the Rome of the 1530s. Paul III clearly considered the behavior of the audiences of the Passion plays far too unpredictable to permit their continued presence at this preeminent archaeological site.

The text of one of the Passion plays performed at the Colosseum provides key evidence to substantiate this point. In the final act, following an extended and emotional portrayal of the sufferings of Christ, the performers recited these lines:

> The Pharisees, enraged, pick up stones and say:
> Elijah, Abraham, Leon, Sabbatuccio,
> David, Isaac, Solomon, and Joseph,
> These will do to knock his block off.
> See how good he was at making fun of us.
> He has his fun and
> let every enraged person take up stones in his hands
> and let this liar be stoned.
> *finis*[78]

Such an exhortation had ominous implications in the context of the ruinous arena of the Colosseum. This archaeological setting provided more than enough stones for the audience of the Passion plays to seize upon if they were so inclined.

A Tabernacle for Michelangelo's *Pietà*

Building stone continued to be removed from the Colosseum through the sixteenth century, although on a much smaller scale than in the previous century.[79] Thus the continuing excavation of the *coscia Colisei* remained standard practice in Rome. This was the case even into the nineteenth century, when the Napoleonic administration in Rome imposed new regulations, informed by modern conservation ideals, which curtailed the excavation of these remains.[80]

The ongoing, systematic removal of the rubble along the southern perimeter of the monument profoundly transformed the ancient site. This is perhaps revealed most vividly when we compare a Renaissance drawing of the Colosseum's southern perimeter from the Codex Escurialensis with a nineteenth-century photograph taken from approximately the same angle by Robert Macpherson (figures 4.6 and 4.7). The comparison shows that while during the Renaissance

FIGURE 4.6. Colosseum and the Arch of Constantine. Cattle are being herded through the Arch of Constantine toward the Campo Vaccino. Between the Arch and the Colosseum stands the conical masonry core of an ancient fountain known as the Meta Sudans. *Codex Escurialensis*, f. 28v.

the piles of fallen building stone were still taller than a man mounted on horseback, nearly nothing remained of this rubble four centuries later. Today the site has been excavated down to the level of the Colosseum foundations.

But while the continued erosion of fallen stone from the *coscia Colisei* can be seen as a characteristically Roman kind of metabolizing urban monuments for new uses, at the same time, it is clear that the individual stone fragments of this rubble also began to acquire potent new meanings. In particular, the powerful link established between the Colosseum and Christianity, reinforced by the dramatic Renaissance spectacle of the Passion plays, invested the ruins with the special value of religious relics.

In 1577 the sacristan at the Basilica of St. Peter issued an order to acquire two blocks of high-quality marble, or *marmo gentile*, from the Colosseum for the construction of a new tabernacle to house Michelangelo's much-admired *Pietà*.[81] High-quality stone was of course available elsewhere, both in Rome and outside the city, but the sacristan's request for stone from this specific site suggests more than just a preoccupation with material quality.

Repeated performances of the Passion plays over the course of fifty years only reinforced the connection between this ancient monument and the story

FIGURE 4.7. Colosseum, by Robert Macpherson, ca. 1851–58. Note prominent
nineteenth-century restorations on the south perimeter as well as the addition of the
stepped buttress at the edge of the northern arcades. The Meta Sudans, which stood at
the point where the Via Sacra turned up into the Roman Forum, was removed in 1936.

of the life and trials of Christ in the popular imagination. The *Pietà* depicted
the Virgin Mary as she appeared at the moment when she confronted and
accepted the lacerated body of her son, and this same scene also figured
prominently in the final tableau of the Passion plays. Moreover, the Compagnia del Gonfalone itself was especially devoted to the Madonna della Miseri-
cordia, the Virgin of Mercy.[82] The rich connections between the Colosseum
and the *Pietà* suggest that the sacristan's specific request for marble from the
ancient amphitheater hinged upon the belief that its remains were in fact
also religious relics. Bearing traces of the trials of Christ, such stones were
imbued with special pathos that made them uniquely appropriate to house
Michelangelo's revered sculpture. Even the ruinous condition of the body of
Christ found a parallel in the shattered forms of the ancient amphitheater.
That the pious faith linked to the Passion plays could also extend a protective
aura over the scattered fragments of the *coscia Colisei* also enables us to interpret and assess another possible Renaissance understanding of preservation
practices.

   Portability was one of the distinctive feature of religious relics. The movement of relics could take place without harming either the original source
or the separated fragment, and this portable, fragmentary status extended the

efficacy of such artifacts, enabling them to transcend the limitations imposed by a fixed location.[83] In general, the static, permanent nature of most architecture tends to resist the mobility demanded of relics. However, unlike the Colosseum, the fragments of the *coscia Colisei* were available for transport and reuse. The sacristan's request for Colosseum marble to build the tabernacle for the *Pietà* suggests that this specific stone was uniquely suited to this exalted purpose: certainly from his perspective, such a project preserved the severed but venerated remains of the *coscia Colisei* in the form of a sacred reliquary.

Preservation and Destruction at the Colosseum over Time

The history of the Colosseum in Renaissance Rome reminds us that despite our ingrained belief that preservation and destruction are in fatal opposition, the implementation of preservation practices does not and cannot rule out the destruction of material remains. On the contrary, although preservation practices often become more stringent as the rate of archaeological destruction accelerates, even the most advanced preservation interventions have never been able to prevent destruction entirely. It is in the nature of physical objects to be susceptible to change: as Freud noted in his meditation on Rome in *Civilization and Its Discontents*, the perfect preservation of such artifacts is something that can be achieved only in the mind.

Although we have been trained to think of the Renaissance Colosseum as the site of wanton and heedless destruction, this gross generalization has obscured our ability to assess the accuracy and sensitivity of Renaissance preservation legislation and practices. Key regulatory advances set by the contract of 1435 clarified and reinforced official property lines at the site. These boundaries in turn guaranteed the survival of the northern arcades during this vigorous period of urban renewal. The fact that such protective measures were later judged insufficient at the iconic Colosseum reminds us that the boundaries of preservation are nothing if not fluid, and that preservation practices and ideals continue to be defined anew by successive generations.

Beginning in the early nineteenth century, under the Napoleonic administration, the construction of huge reinforcing buttresses at either end of the northern arcades served to shore up this increasingly brittle archaeological fragment. These buttresses are now the most visible evidence of the heroic efforts made by modern conservationists to preserve the venerable Colosseum. The elegant tiered design of the buttress facing the Roman Forum in particular represents the favored vantage point for photographs of the monument: it is this side of the Colosseum that is commemorated on the new Italian Euro five-cent coin.

Although the Colosseum buttresses are the most prominent sign of preservation interventions at the site today, it is important to remember that these are only the latest in a series of recurring efforts to preserve the ancient amphitheater over the centuries. The boundary lines of 1435 tend to be mostly invisible to the streams of visitors who flood the landmark every day. But upon closer examination, these boundaries are still very evident in the surviving structure. Just as much as the buttresses of the nineteenth century, so did fifteenth- and sixteenth-century preservation practices play a vital role in ensuring the Colosseum's survival.

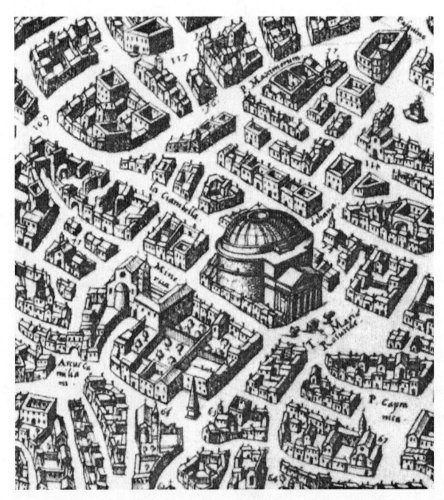

FIGURE 5.1. Pantheon, detail from map of Rome by Etienne Dupérac, 1577.

5

The Pantheon

The Pantheon is renowned for its extraordinary preservation.[1] Its enormous, buoyant dome, suspended in space and time, has hovered above the Campus Martius over the course of centuries, as if impervious to the vicissitudes of history (figure 5.1). The Pantheon has outlasted almost all the other buildings that once crowded around it in antiquity, and the miraculous completeness of its preservation—from foundations to crown—stands in especially vivid contrast to the half-leveled remains of the Colosseum. Yet the wonderful longevity of the landmark is not due only to chance, nor may it be attributed solely to its superb engineering. The sustained and vigilant attention of generations to the preservation of this jewel of antiquity has defended it from the corrosive effects of time and wear.

The exterior of the Pantheon is both arresting and awe inspiring. Its distinctive architectural composition, a vast rotunda surmounted by a hemispherical dome and fronted by a giant portico, has survived conflagrations, earthquakes, and the incursions of later builders, even as its surroundings have gone through radical changes. At present the building emerges from a depression sunk into the flat expanse of the Campus Martius. Modern archaeological investigations, however, reveal that in antiquity visitors ascended to the Pantheon portico by a flight of five marble steps. Moreover, its exposed brick exterior shell, unlike the travertine exterior of the Colosseum, was not originally intended to be visible. In antiquity, a decorative stucco veneer made to resemble the marble sheathing of the podium wrapped the monument in a luminous skin.[2]

Yet the absence of plaster on the battle-scarred and pock-marked Pantheon exterior exposes not just the corrugated brick of modern restorations but the brick relieving arches set into the rotunda wall. These arches offer a clue to the Pantheon's sophisticated engineering: the rotunda structure, formed of eight giant arches sealed with external curtain walls, is not unlike a much more compact version of the Colosseum arcades. The Pantheon's eight arches in turn distribute the weight of the dome onto eight colossal piers, while transverse walls and arches join the exterior and interior brick faces of the rotunda through its concrete core. Thus the structural design of the Pantheon may be characterized either as a series of arches carried on piers or as two concentric walls joined by transverse walls, creating a reinforced structural system offering the key advantages of comparatively little weight and exceptional stability.[3]

For all the lofty scale of the portico, gridded with monolithic granite columns, and the magnificence of the portal, flanked by towering bronze valves and with its threshold formed of a single gigantic block of striated black and red marble, the visitor is still unprepared for the overwhelming experience of the huge rotunda itself. Enclosing a perfect sphere, the rotunda rises uninterrupted to the wide opening of the oculus at its zenith. The circle of light cast through this opening onto the coffers of the vault and the faceted marble surfaces below is ever-changing and always in motion, not unlike the sky visible through the oculus itself.[4] Not just the architectural quality but also the physical integrity of this ancient space is unsurpassed among all the surviving ancient monuments of Rome. The dazzling array of marble and granite, drawn from every part of the Mediterranean, represents a catalogue of all the subject territories of the Roman Empire. More than any other building in the city, the material preservation of the Pantheon enables us to experience a palatial Roman interior as it appeared at the time of the emperors.

The superb preservation of the Pantheon offers obvious evidence to support a primary argument of this book, proving that the preservation of ancient remains has continued to be the subject of constant and focused attention in Rome since antiquity. Ensuring the regular upkeep of the Pantheon was always a preoccupation of the rulers of the Eternal City, who ranked this building among the city's greatest treasures from the time of its construction right up to the present. Closer examination of the history of successive interventions at the Pantheon, however, will enable us to explore a critical epistemological shift, where the understanding of preservation and restoration practices changed dramatically at this site during the Renaissance.

While viewers have always registered astonishment at the extraordinary shape and form of the Pantheon, the humanist and antiquarian studies of the fifteenth and sixteenth centuries drew new attention to its unique physical integrity. The Pantheon was not simply a church: it also represented a historic, material object that had persisted from antiquity. This enhanced appreciation for the material, even "archaeological" value of the Pantheon, in turn guided new ideas about what needed to be preserved on the site and how sub-sequent interventions to maintain and repair the monument should occur. As we will see, these Renaissance interventions had profound consequences for the later history of the monument. This chapter explores how Renaissance interventions upon the Pantheon established a critical notional benchmark for the preservation of ancient landmarks, both in Renaissance Rome and beyond.

Defending and Protecting the Pantheon in Postclassical Rome

The completion of the Pantheon around 125 A.D. during the reign of Hadrian marked not only a watershed for the history of Roman architecture, but also the inauguration of a program of periodic maintenance that has continued at the Pantheon ever since. It comes as no surprise that the Pantheon has the most complete maintenance log for any ancient building in Rome.

The restoration of a *templum Agrippae* was already recorded during the reign of Antoninus Pius, who succeeded Hadrian in 138 A.D.[5] This reference may have recalled the monument's original dedication to Marcus Agrippa, which was carried forward by Hadrianic restoration and immortalized by the splendid inscription set into the frieze over the portico.[6] Further work was evidently carried out in the early third century under the Severan emperors, as recorded in a subordinate inscription carved into the entablature below the Hadrianic inscription.[7] While neither of these restorations appears to have been of major structural significance, such early references to Pantheon repairs indicate that the monument benefited from the special attention and interest of the Roman emperors. The Pantheon was clearly considered to be one of the preeminent landmarks of the imperial capital.[8]

Papal interventions commenced in late antiquity with the intercession of Boniface IV, who appealed to the Byzantine emperor Phocas for permission to convert the Pantheon into a church in 608 A.D.[9] The consecration of the Pantheon and its effective acquisition by the papacy were events of immense significance for the future preservation of the structure. The conversion of this most prominent ancient monument into the church of Santa Maria ad Martyres set a vital precedent for the later adaptive reuse of other ancient structures by the church. But the papacy's appropriation of the Pantheon also meant that in the changing religious and cultural context of Christian Rome, this ancient structure now came under the direct protection of the emerging temporal and spiritual ruler of the city. Generations of successive popes assumed the protection of the Pantheon as one of their institutional traditions and responsibilities.[10]

In 663 A.D., less than sixty years after the conversion of the Pantheon into a church, the Byzantine emperor Constans II removed the bronze tiles that originally sheathed the Pantheon dome and shipped them to Byzantium.[11] The elimination of this protective layer exposed the shell of the dome to the elements and raised the risk of accelerated deterioration and collapse, until the intervention of Gregory III, an eighth-century pope, who replaced the missing bronze tiles with lead plates.[12] Thus Gregory III formally inaugurated the millennial papal practice of caring for the Pantheon's voluminous dome. More than any other factor, continuous papal repairs to the dome protected the Pantheon from decay throughout the following centuries.[13]

Of course the Pantheon also required alterations to accommodate its new liturgical functions as a church. Within the next century or so a new *schola cantorum* was installed in the rotunda, including a marble enclosure for the church choir, equipped with corresponding lecterns or *amboni*. Parts of this medieval structure have been recovered in excavations at the Pantheon, and the archaeological evidence suggests that some of its component materials were acquired by recarving marble slabs removed from the interior surfaces of the rotunda itself.[14]

In 1270, as recorded by an inscription placed in the Pantheon portico, a bell tower was constructed at the apex of the portico pediment (figure 5.2).[15]

FIGURE 5.2. View of the Piazza del Pantheon, with market stalls aligned in front of the Pantheon portico. The image records a restoration conducted late in the reign of Leo X (1513–21), when the porphyry sarcophagus in the square, flanked by recumbent Egyptian lions, was raised on two marble pedestals bearing commemorative inscriptions. In 1732 the sarcophagus was relocated to the Lateran as a papal tomb, and the pedestals were immured in the rear wall of the portico.

The use of bells appears to have been relatively circumscribed until the thirteenth century in Rome, and thus the Pantheon was properly endowed with a bell tower at a time when bell-ringing became increasingly important to its function as a church. The new brick belfry provided an indispensable service, its bells marking important ritual and ceremonial events as well as the daily passage of time.[16]

Also at this time the early Christian *schola cantorum* in the rotunda was replaced by a new high altar with a reliquary decorated with colored mosaics.[17] Both bell tower and high altar were thus part of an extensive thirteenth-century campaign to restore the interior and exterior of the Pantheon. That such restorations were launched at this particular time was remarkable: as recorded in the bell tower inscription, this restoration occurred during a prolonged interregnum between two pontificates. Clearly the Pantheon's care and upkeep had become a received institutional practice in Rome, one that could proceed even without direct papal involvement.[18]

Although the Pantheon was never intended to serve as a Christian liturgical space, adaptations made to allow such new functions rarely caused major damage to the original structure. Even when subsequent changes came at the expense of original elements, such as the reuse of marble stone panels to build the *schola cantorum*, the overall archaeological losses were quite limited. The relative caution of subsequent alterations probably attests to the ongoing supervisory role of church officials in monitoring such work. Above all, none of these interventions interfered with the primary experience of the soaring cupola of the rotunda.

The most significant changes to the Pantheon affected its exterior, where the collapse of many of the large imperial buildings in the area caused the surrounding terrain to rise up around the monument over time.[19] While the colonnaded forecourt that once opened in front of the building survived into the Middle Ages in the altered form of the Piazza del Pantheon, its stone pavement gradually sank below grade.[20] It was used as a marketplace, profiting from its strategic location on the pilgrimage route between St. Peter's and the northern gate to the city, the Porta del Popolo.[21]

The rising ground level also reversed the experience of ascending a flight of stairs to reach the podium of the Pantheon. Now visitors descended a flight of stairs to reach the level of the submerged portico.[22] Throughout the Renaissance, the portico thus functioned as a partly subterranean space, enclosed by retaining walls to keep out the accumulated earth (figure 5.3). In the square above, market vendors displayed their wares on the walls of the enclosure.

Despite the ongoing supervision of the popes, the immediate proximity of the surrounding city also meant that improvised additions continued to be made to the monument by its neighbors. Unlike the Colosseum, isolated in the *disabitato* through the Middle Ages and into the early modern period, the Pantheon stood in the densest part of the *abitato*. Houses crowded around the

FIGURE 5.3.   Interior of Pantheon portico, by Marten van Heemskerck, ca. 1532–37.

Pantheon rotunda and against the portico, and builders cut holes into its exterior walls and columns to support adjacent structures.

At some point a disaster involving a fire caused serious damage to the three columns and their entablature at the eastern corner of the portico.[23] The fact that the portico remained standing following this traumatic blow paid tribute to its rugged construction. In the absence of replacement columns, later restorers constructed a solid masonry wall to shore up the portico at this end, rescuing the building from further deterioration even as they sealed off the east end of the portico. Nevertheless, the restoration was clearly intended to preserve the original elements of the Pantheon. Renaissance drawings show pieces of a broken column carefully integrated into the brick masonry supporting the corner of the portico, in the conscious effort to preserve the traces of the original colonnade (figure 5.4).[24]

Thus although the imperial monument of Hadrian survived in remarkably good condition, actively maintained and preserved over time by the popes, by the beginning of the fifteenth century it also carried signs of the passage of time and the effects of change. Hemmed in on all sides by houses, its intercolumniations closed up by walls, a brick bell tower crowning its pediment, and fronted by a marketplace, the church of Santa Maria ad Martyres, or Santa Maria Rotonda as it was colloquially known, was fully absorbed into the life of the medieval city.

FIGURE 5.4.   Pantheon exterior, by Marten van Heemskerck, ca. 1532–37.

New Preservation Ideas for the Pantheon in
Fifteenth-Century Rome

As the fifteenth-century architect and theorist Leon Battista Alberti reported in his treatise *De re aedificatoria*, the importance of regular roof maintenance could not be underestimated for the survival and general well-being of an existing structure:

> Roofs are the most important elements. . . . [T]ake away the roof, and
> the woodwork rots, the walls totter and their sides crack; gradually
> the whole structure falls apart. Even the very foundations, though
> you may hardly believe it, rely on the protection of the roof for
> strength. Nor have as many buildings fallen into ruin by fire, sword,
> enemy hands, or by any other calamity, as have tumbled down for no
> other reason than human neglect, when left naked and deprived of
> the roof covering. Indeed, in buildings, the roofs are the weapons
> with which they defend themselves against the harmful onslaught of
> weather.[25]

Regular roof maintenance and repair was essential to the continuing health of every building, and this was especially true for a building with a roof the size of the Pantheon's. The remarkable astuteness of the popes in recognizing that the decay of the Pantheon's roof would lead to its collapse was attested by their ongoing and vigilant restoration of its lead tiles.

The roof of the Pantheon soon attracted the attention of Martin V following his return to Rome in 1420. The dome had suffered damage during a storm in 1405, and thus the pope had it "newly covered" with lead tiles, as reported by contemporary chroniclers.[26] With the reestablishment of the papacy at Rome, Martin V immediately resumed the traditional and time-honored responsibility of the pope as the self-appointed guardian of the structure.

Over the course of the fifteenth century, new ideas also began to emerge about preservation strategies for this prestigious landmark. As we have seen, with the Bull of 1425 Martin V charged the *maestri* with the responsibility of improving conditions in the city, attesting to his general interest in preserving Rome's historic urban environment. His successor Eugenius IV, however, focused specifically upon improving existing physical conditions at the Pantheon, as the best-preserved of the city's ancient structures.

As reported by Biondo Flavio in *Roma instaurata*, Eugenius IV's interventions at the Pantheon involved a two-pronged strategy. Not only did the pope conduct repairs to the cupola; at the same time he also introduced an unprecedented component to this traditional maintenance program in clearing away the obstructions that cluttered the portico:

> By your intervention, Pope Eugenius, and at your expense, the
> Pantheon's stupendous vault, torn in antiquity by earthquakes and
> threatened with ruin, was restored [instauratum]. The Curia rejoiced
> to see it covered with lead sheets where they were lacking. . . . That
> splendid church, clearly superior to all others, has had the lofty
> columns that support it hidden, for many centuries, by the squalid
> little market stalls [sordidissimis tabernis] surrounding it. These have
> now been completely cleaned off, and their bases and capitals laid bare
> [denudatae], to better reveal the beauty of this wonderful building.[27]

Biondo reported that the humanist members of the papal court "rejoiced" to see Eugenius IV resuming the long-standing papal responsibility of repairing the venerable Pantheon's lead roof tiles.

At the same time, Biondo also noted that the pope took measures to improve access to the monument, as well as improving the overall visibility and dignity of the ancient structure. This involved the elimination of the "squalid little market stalls" belonging to the merchants who had been gathering in the Piazza del Pantheon for centuries, which masked the lowest parts of the monument from view. Biondo was unequivocal in his assessment of this intervention: "cleaning off" the columns made them only more splendid.

The fact that Biondo bestowed equal praise upon the pope's decision to proceed with the repair of the dome and his decision to remove the market stalls helped to disguise the radical nature of the latter intervention.[28] After seven hundred years, the task of repairing the vault of the Pantheon had become a conventional papal duty. But the idea of stripping away the market stalls from the Pantheon facade was unheard of in postclassical Rome. This papal act attested to the implementation of an innovative, revolutionary notion of preservation at the Pantheon.[29]

Unlike the traditional papal program of regular roof maintenance at the Pantheon, which had relatively little impact upon the surrounding environment, Eugenius IV's decision to remove the Pantheon's market stalls extended the active preservation of the monument directly into the *abitato*. With this act, the pope decreed that the papal duty of preserving the monument required not only attending to the condition of the roof, but also regulating and controlling the customs and behavior of the people who surrounded the Pantheon itself. The proximity of this neighboring populace had eventually caused the dramatic transformation of the Pantheon's exterior over time. Perhaps nowhere were such changes more vivid than in the occupation of the portico by the local market. The aggressive display of goods obstructed the array of ancient monolithic granite columns, testimony to the engineering capacities of the ancient Romans. The interventions by Eugenius IV brought this adaptive reuse of the monument that had gradually emerged over time to an abrupt end.

Biondo exulted that the liberation of the columns was a magnificent revelation, restoring the historic form of the portico to view for the first time in living memory, but the vendors who used the portico as their marketplace had little reason to regard this intervention as a benevolent papal gesture. On the contrary, they had reason to regard it the undesirable interference of a harsh and autocratic papal ruler. This episode of fifteenth-century urban renewal at the Pantheon demonstrates how preservation practices, as a central component of the increased papal attention to the physical condition and environment of Rome, also provoked new tensions between the pope and the Roman populace.

Indeed, during Eugenius IV's pontificate the ongoing hostility between the Renaissance popes and the Romans reached its climax. It was Eugenius IV whom the Romans chased out of the city in 1434. The pope was able eventually to return to the papal capital in 1443, after ten years of exile. He ruled another four years in Rome before his death in 1447.

In 1442, before the pope finally returned to the city, another popular uprising against papal power occurred. The Romans rose up in revolt against the perceived injustice and abuse of power in the execution of two Roman citizens by papal authorities. As the Roman chronicler Stefano Infessura reported, the Romans chose to vent their fury by attacking the Pantheon:

> On that same day [when the executions took place] all the roofs of Santa Maria Rotonda were destroyed, and the piazza was ruined, and afterwards, all the market stalls alongside the columns of the portico were demolished.[30]

It is more than mere coincidence that the Roman populace directed their hatred against the Pantheon. The ancient monument was an obvious beneficiary of papal care, and its special treatment by the popes was especially obvious given its location in the *abitato*, surrounded by the houses of ordinary people. The focused destruction of the Pantheon's roof was all the more significant, as the particular object of constant papal attention. Destroying the Pantheon's roof offered a visceral means for the people of Rome to communicate their extreme dissatisfaction with papal authority.[31]

It seems that Eugenius IV's interventions on the Pantheon occurred after the popular uprising of 1442. Infessura's description suggests a sequence in which the popular uprising against the Pantheon came first, and then the market stalls in front of the portico were demolished.[32] This indicates that the pope, upon retaking control of the papal capital, intended to destroy the market stalls as a way to send an unmistakable message to the populace who dared to unleash their rage against the venerable structure. Eugenius IV's dismantling of the market stalls thus celebrated the Pantheon's antiquity but also reiterated that it was under the exclusive custody of the pope. Popular infringements of any sort on papal power—including even the presence of market stalls adjacent to the Pantheon portico—were not to be tolerated. In this context, the "cleaning off" of the Pantheon, celebrated by Biondo, also represented a definitive statement about the absolute and unquestioned authority of the pope in Renaissance Rome.

By the same token, the act of clearing the market stalls from the Pantheon portico also attested to an emerging Renaissance sensibility regarding the unique historic value of this structure. The papal tradition of protecting the Pantheon traditionally aimed at ensuring the continued survival of the building, and this of course continued to be a preoccupation for the Renaissance popes. Eugenius IV's interventions, however, also emphasized that this particular structure, as a unique ancient artifact, possessed extraordinary qualities that deserved special honor. Thus the pope gave the preservation of the Pantheon priority over the rights of its neighbors in the local community. While sustained papal attention signaled the privileged status of the Pantheon, the removal of its market stalls reinforced this status in unmistakable physical terms. The pope created a kind of protective boundary, a buffer zone, which highlighted its elite identity as well as isolating it from the risks posed by the surrounding city.[33]

Continuous repair and restoration activity at the Pantheon during the subsequent pontificates of Nicholas V, Pius II, and Paul II attested to ongoing papal vigilance for the care and preservation of this monument. At the same time, the intensity of this repair work may also indicate the extent of the damage inflicted by the popular riots of 1442. During the reign of Nicholas V, new lead roof tiles emblazoned with the papal shield and dated 1451 were installed (some of these Renaissance tiles are still on the dome today).[34] Considerable payments for repair work at the Pantheon were documented in papal accounts beginning in July 1453.[35] These continued through February 1454, when the roof repairs were reported to be complete.[36] The pope also continued to intervene in the effort to prevent the market in the piazza from encroaching upon the Pantheon. In 1457, on papal command, the *maestri di strade* once again removed the offending market stalls from the site.[37]

Pius II, noted for his concern regarding the preservation of ancient monuments in Rome, as attested by the Bull of 1462, conducted various interventions and repairs at the site. Two years after his election, and two years before issuing the famous bull, there was a papal payment in June 1460 for the provision of lime and pozzolana, presumably to make mortar, as well as the acquisition of some sort of metal locks. These last purchases suggested the intent to improve the existing security system at the monument.[38]

During the reign of Paul II, the focus of repairs expanded considerably to include many different areas of the structure. The first surviving records of payment, beginning in May 1468, or four years after the election of the new pope, involved some sort of masonry repairs.[39] Further payments made in June and July of the same year specified that the site for these repairs was the portico.[40] Also in May 1468, Paul II made payments to carpenters for expenses related to the repair of the portico roof.[41] Additional payments were made in June and July for planks and terracotta roof tiles to supply the same site.[42] Work resumed in August 1469 for further unspecified masonry repairs.[43] In 1470 payment was made for the restoration and repair of the portico, "instauratione seu reparatione porticalis ecclesie Sancte Marie Rotunde."[44] Another payment referred to the casting of six bronze keys as well as repairs to the lead plates on the Pantheon roof, as recorded in October of the same year.[45] These carefully documented repairs indicate Paul II's solicitous concern for the preservation of the ancient landmark.

Although papal repairs and maintenance of the Pantheon throughout the fifteenth century were clearly intended to stabilize the monument and extend its life, these repairs also generally respected the integrity of the historic Pantheon's original design. Another conscientious papal intervention of a different sort, however, was the construction of a new high altar at the Pantheon in 1491, built during the reign of Innocent VIII to replace the thirteenth-century altar that preceded it.[46]

Judging from a seventeenth-century view that recorded the appearance of Innocent VIII's altar prior to its removal during renovations conducted by Clement XI, the elaborate new structure was clearly intended to complement the magnificence of the rotunda.[47] The high altar itself was sheltered by a stepped marble canopy or ciborium standing on columns. In turn, this tabernacle was then raised aloft on a high-stepped podium base. By elevating the celebration of the Mass above the congregation, this architectural complex gave greater prominence to the presence of the Christian liturgy within the enormous rotunda.

In addition, the high altar was also moved to a more conspicuous location inside the Pantheon itself.[48] Previously the high altar had been contiguous with the rear wall of the main apse. Innocent VIII's altar complex, however, moved further out to take an unprecedented, dominating position within the main space of the rotunda. Freed from the confines of the main apse, the high altar assumed the character of a massive sculptural object occupying the center of the soaring space.[49] It was surrounded by a series of columns, set on top of a raised marble plinth and carrying a continuous entablature, that further marked off this sanctified enclosure as a three-dimensional volume within the rotunda.[50] Where the interventions by preceding fifteenth-century popes were primarily concerned with stabilizing the physical integrity of the ancient monument, Innocent VII's new high altar foregrounded its Christian identity.

Renaissance Interest in the Preserved
Material Fabric of the Pantheon

Despite the construction of the new high altar, Renaissance viewers of the Pantheon continued to be more struck by its character as a unique historic artifact surviving from the pagan world of antiquity than by its recently reinforced Christian identity. Bernardo Bembo, a Venetian dignitary attending the coronation of Julius II in 1504, recognized that the conscientious preservation of the Pantheon's fabric over time was in fact completely different from the kind of preservation that had taken place elsewhere in Rome:

> On 30 April, in the morning, we visited the church of Santa Maria Rotonda (as it is now called, but the structure was built by Marcus Agrippa, and it was originally called the Pantheon). This temple has a square portico as its vestibule, with very high columns made of costly stone; it is the only surviving example, I would argue, of the temples of antiquity. The temple of the Minerva [the church of Santa Maria sopra Minerva], which we saw the same day, only retains its original name, for it has been restored [instauratum], and in the process it has been significantly altered.[51]

By comparing the condition of the Pantheon to the condition of the nearby church of Santa Maria sopra Minerva, Bembo indicated that different approaches to preservation could yield very different results. The subsequent rebuilding campaigns at Santa Maria sopra Minerva had thoroughly erased all traces of the original building that once occupied the site; as he noted, of the ancient temple of Minerva the current building "only retains its original name."

Bembo thus pointed out the difference between restoration and preservation work. Restorations, while they might ensure the continued functioning of the structure, did not guarantee its survival in its original form. In the case of Santa Maria sopra Minerva, successive restorations over time meant that all physical traces of the ancient remains on the site had been completely absorbed by the modern church. In contrast, ongoing work at the Pantheon led to a very different outcome. Here, the efforts to repair and maintain the original building respected both the shape and materials of its original fabric. This scrupulous preservation allowed the ancient monument to endure in a way that conferred unique status upon it, as "the only surviving example . . . of the temples of antiquity."

Bembo's acute observations indicated a new Renaissance sensitivity to the need for careful calibration in preservation projects. While it was obviously necessary to conduct regular maintenance, it was also necessary to evaluate and monitor restoration and repair work with considerable care. Otherwise they were likely to lead to the progressive loss of valuable material evidence. Bembo's evident admiration for the survival of the Pantheon suggested that this monument provided an ideal standard for preservation practices, a classic exemplar against which to judge other restoration work.

Raphael, as an artist working in early sixteenth-century Rome, also had boundless admiration for the Pantheon. His energetic study of the monument extended far beyond Bembo's casual encounter, and his attentive interest in its preservation also had lasting implications for the future history of the monument itself. Raphael's interventions at the Pantheon not only revealed his ongoing fascination for the ancient monument, as a marvelous artifact preserved from the time of classical antiquity, but also helped to frame new approaches for the preservation of the structure, both in the present and in the future.

During the Renaissance, the Pantheon of course represented a primary model for architectural culture. According to tradition, Bramante conceived of the design for the New St. Peter's as the dome of the Pantheon raised upon the vaults of the Basilica of Maxentius.[52] As Bramante's successor as the chief architect on this work site, Raphael also examined the Pantheon as both source and inspiration for the great dome intended to crown the new basilica.

The evident lessons Raphael drew from the Pantheon, however, were even better articulated at the Chigi Chapel.[53] This small, centrally planned structure attached to the basilica of Santa Maria del Popolo, conceived as a funerary chapel for the Sienese banker Agostino Chigi, provided clear evidence for Raphael's passionate examination of even the smallest details of the Pantheon's design and execution.[54] With this design, Raphael created a miniature jewel-box version of the ancient Pantheon itself.

It is well known that Raphael was deeply impressed by the material qualities of ancient buildings. In the "Letter to Leo X," although Raphael and Castiglione admired the innovative architectural designs built in recent years in the papal capital, they reserved their greatest praise for the magnificent buildings of imperial Rome:

> [I]t is true that in our day architecture has very much revived and
> seems close to the style of the ancients, as one can see in the many

beautiful works of Bramante, but, all the same, the ornaments are
not of such precious material as was used by the ancients, who seem
with infinite expense to have been able to put into effect what was in
their imagination and by sheer will power overcome all difficulties.[55]

The "infinite expense" involved in the making of imperial Roman buildings,
and the superb, lasting quality of their building materials, made them infinitely superior to the new structures raised by Renaissance designers such
as Bramante.

Although Bramante's work approximated the beautiful appearance of
ancient structures, the ephemeral nature of much of his work was also considered to be problematic. *Bramante ruinante* was notorious for embarking upon
major architectural projects, including even the building piers of the New St.
Peter's, that later exhibited critical structural flaws and threatened to collapse.[56]
Although Bramante was also deeply interested in preservation, as we saw with
his efforts to protect the Vatican obelisk, his efforts to build immense projects at
great speed were sometimes jeopardized by his relatively lax quality control standards. Above all, Bramante's attitude toward building materials was epitomized
by his famous use of plaster casts or *getto* in early sixteenth-century Rome, which
enabled him to create convincing palace facades that looked as if they were fin-
ished in the *all'antica* manner, surfaced with ashlar or *bugnato* building stone.
However, while this technique facilitated rapid and cost-efficient construction, it
also meant his buildings soon risked transformation and disintegration.[57]

Raphael evidently regarded Bramante's building practices as inferior to the
ancient ones because Bramante's work had failed to hold up to the test of time.
Raphael's design for the Chigi Chapel demonstrated his intent to pursue an
opposite strategy, based upon the ancient practice of specifying the finest
building materials for new construction. Financed by Agostino Chigi, the rich-
est banker in sixteenth-century Rome, Raphael was able to acquire exquisite
building stone. The Egyptian granite threshold of the chapel, and the fine-
grained Carrara marble used for the pilaster capitals, were exactly the same
kinds of luxurious materials used at the Pantheon.

Of course, even for Raphael, access to such valuable stones was already
becoming more difficult in the early sixteenth century. The papal capital lacked
the direct access to the exotic quarries commanded by the builders of imperial
Rome. The builders of the Chigi Chapel had to resort to the conventional practice of plundering other ancient sites around the city to locate such precious
materials. And yet as Raphael himself knew through experience as the papal
inspector of ancient stones and as the chief architect of the New St. Peter's,
such quarrying was highly problematic, as it led to the extensive destruction of
archaeological sites.

Yet even the unlimited financial resources of a Renaissance patron like
Agostino Chigi yielded only the lapidary splendor of a small funerary chapel,

in contrast to the "infinite expense" borne by the ancient Roman builders of the Pantheon, who were "able to put into effect what was in their imagination and by sheer will power overcome all difficulties," as noted in the "Letter to Leo X." Such a project demonstrated that the achievements of ancient Rome were difficult if not impossible to reproduce in the context of Renaissance Rome. For Raphael, however, the sumptuous stone surfaces of the Pantheon represented the ultimate architectural ideal, built of materials that were both beautiful and enduring.

Raphael's Tomb and the Preservation of the Pantheon

When Raphael died on 7 April 1520, he specified in his will that he wished to be buried at the Pantheon.[58] This explicit choice made final tribute to Raphael's special veneration of the ancient monument, which exemplified the classical ideals he so admired, and which remained at the center of his life's work. But Raphael's decision to be buried at the Pantheon also had a lasting impact upon the ancient landmark itself, by forging an indissoluble link between the artist and the object of his study. From now on, the ancient landmark became known as the shrine of Raphael to all those who honored the artist's legacy. Raphael's tomb at the Pantheon thus gave rise to the modern definition of the word *pantheon*, meaning a final resting place that commemorated the lives of the most illustrious personages of a given nation.[59]

At the same time, Raphael's decision to erect his tomb at the Pantheon also revealed the artist's profound and explicit interest in the ongoing preservation of this ancient monument. His tomb was conceived from the outset to contribute to the ongoing project of improving the Pantheon's existing physical condition. Moreover, Raphael's final bequest at the Pantheon was also calculated to ensure that the structure continued to receive regular care and maintenance into the future.

Contemporary accounts reported that Raphael's unexpected death was the cause of universal grief, the premature passing of a dynamic artist who had played a leading role in creating the visual vocabulary of Renaissance Rome. And yet while Raphael was famous for the superb quality of so many frescoes and paintings, his death was mourned above all as a blow to the study of antiquity.[60] By the end of his life, this artist was recognized to be at the vanguard of Roman antiquarian studies. His proposed plan to catalogue and document the ancient city, discussed in the second half of the "Letter to Leo X," was eagerly anticipated by antiquarians and humanists. This project represented a comprehensive campaign to analyze and also preserve the surviving evidence of ancient Rome in graphic form.[61]

Death prevented Raphael from conducting these extended archaeological investigations. In the absence of another virtuoso architect-antiquarian capable of mastering both advanced analytical graphic skills and complex humanist knowledge about the classical world, this ambitious project was abruptly post-poned for the foreseeable future.[62] Yet Raphael's decision to place his tomb at the Pantheon also represented an enduring legacy for the preservation of antiquity.

At the time of his death in 1520, Raphael was at the height of his powers. He enjoyed the favor of the pope and some of the most powerful figures in the papal court, and he commanded a very sizable income, as is evident by his acquisition of the celebrated Palazzo Caprini designed by Bramante in the Borgo.[63] In deciding where to place his tomb, he could choose any church in the city of Rome. Raphael's selection of Santa Maria Rotonda thus came as a surprise: despite the fascination of Renaissance architects and antiquarians for this building, this was far from the most elite church in the city. Its dedication to the anonymous Christian martyrs was relatively obscure and insignificant. Although there were various medieval inhumations at the site, no other prominent secular figures or important members of the Roman clergy chose to be buried there in 1520.[64] Raphael's decision to erect his tomb at Santa Maria Rotonda defied current social expectations, further attesting to his devoted commitment to and admiration for this ancient monument.

Some of Raphael's innovative ideas about preservation may be deduced by considering the conditions that he stipulated for the creation of his tomb at the Pantheon. The first issue involved provision of sufficient funds. According to a letter written on 7 April 1520 by Pandolfo Pico, Raphael designated a thousand ducats in his last will and testament for the creation of a funerary chapel at Santa Maria Rotonda and established an endowment of another thousand ducats to provide for its regular maintenance and care.[65] This was an immense sum of money, equal to the cost of the tomb commissioned by a cardinal from Michelangelo over ten years later.[66] Although we cannot be sure of the exact sum, given that Raphael's will has not survived, the extent of his personal wealth suggests he was quite capable of making such a bequest.

Another issue was the nature of the work to be conducted at the Pantheon itself. As Giorgio Vasari reported, Raphael incorporated the restoration of an existing tabernacle inside the rotunda of the Pantheon in the creation of his tomb:

> He then ordered that they should restore [ordinò . . . che . . . si
> restaurasse] one of the ancient tabernacles in Santa Maria Rotonda at
> his expense, using new stones, and that an altar be created with a
> statue of Our Lady in marble; this was erected after his death for his
> sepulcher and place of repose.[67]

Vasari's choice of words offered suggestive indications about how Raphael intended to implement preservation practices at this venerable site. As Vasari indicated, Raphael wished to "restore" one of the ancient tabernacles. In the conventional Renaissance understanding of this term as established by Biondo Flavio in *Roma instaurata*, restoration involved the preservation but also active transformation and renewal of an existing ancient site. Vasari acknowledged that change was an integral part of this process in his reference to the "new stones" used to restore the altar, as well as to the addition of the "statue of Our Lady in marble." And yet, although these new elements altered the existing tabernacle, they did not completely transform its original character.

The statue commissioned for Raphael's tomb from his pupil Lorenzetto represented an intriguing example of the fusing of past and present made possible through simultaneous preservation and restoration work.[68] Other tabernacles in the rotunda had been adapted to serve as altars and framed depictions of the Madonna.[69] In this sense, the new statue thus followed established precedent. Portraying a tall, pivoting female figure wrapped in classicizing drapery, with a small child resting on her upper thigh, it could be readily identified as a Madonna and Child.

But at the same time, unlike more conventional iconic depictions of the haloed Virgin, Lorenzetto's statue made no overt reference to Christian iconography. On the contrary, her drapery and demeanor suggested the iconography of a classical pagan goddess. The inherent ambiguity of this design suggested the clever notion guiding Raphael's preservation program at the Pantheon. It was not intended as a philological or archaeological reconstruction of the ancient Pantheon. On the contrary, it allowed for the integration of new works that had no real archaeological precedent at the site. But these new works nevertheless were carefully designed to harmonize with their classical setting. The presence of Lorenzetto's sculpture at Raphael's tomb, set into the tabernacle immediately to the left of the main apse, blurred the visual distinctions separating the Pantheon as it had been in antiquity from Santa Maria Rotonda as it now appeared in the present.

At the same time, the ongoing restoration of the tabernacle itself suggested that the executors of Raphael's will respected the rich material qualities of the original structure. The report of the Venetian envoy Marino Sanuto, visiting the Pantheon in May 1523, three years after Raphael's death, revealed that significant work was then under way. Before commenting on the tomb, he described the monument itself:

> The church is a perfect circle, as if it were made with a compass, and it is full of altars all around; one of these is being worked upon as we speak, of serpentine, porphyry, and marble, and it will be very beautiful. This is the sepulcher of Raphael of Urbino.[70]

The stones Sanuto reported were all stones used by the ancient builders to decorate the interior surfaces of the rotunda. Thus the materials chosen for Raphael's tomb were carefully coordinated to correspond to the existing materials in the Pantheon itself.

Francisco de Holanda affirmed that the ongoing restoration work at the tabernacle had the effect of reviving its original appearance. He declared that

Raphael had received an honor not previously conceded to anyone in the creation of this tomb and then commented upon the work underway at the tabernacle, noting that "they polished the marble and the columns of [the tabernacle]
to appear as they did in antiquity."[71] De Holanda claimed that the restoration of
the tabernacle was not only a celebrated project, but also that it qualified as a
great honor. Moreover, the restoration of the tabernacle helped to revive the
earlier identity of the Pantheon: by polishing its ancient stone surfaces, with
the removal of accumulated layers of dirt and grime, this part of the rotunda
now began to look as it did at the time of the Roman emperors. The vision of
Raphael's restored, luminous tabernacle, gleaming among the shadows of the
rotunda, would make an unforgettable impact upon contemporary audiences
in Rome.

The publicity of Raphael's restoration of the tabernacle at the Pantheon
thus communicated the idea of restoring the classical aura and dignity of the
ancient monument to a broader public. Soon other artists in Rome began to
emulate his example. Baldassare Peruzzi, Raphael's close associate, requested
and received inhumation in the same tabernacle after his death in 1536. Peruzzi also followed Raphael's example by contributing to the ongoing restoration
of the tabernacle.[72] Others then followed suit. In the following years a series of
notable artists were interred at the Pantheon, including Perino del Vaga in
1547, Bartolomeo Baronino in 1554, Taddeo Zuccari in 1566, and Jacopo Baro-
zzi da Vignola in 1573.[73] These later individuals received permission for burial
alongside Raphael by joining the confraternity of the Compagnia di San
Giuseppe di Terrasanta, better known as the Virtuosi del Pantheon, granted
exclusive rights to authorize inhumations at the ancient landmark by Paul III
in 1545.[74] Raphael's tomb soon transformed the obscure church of Santa Maria
Rotonda into the most desirable place in Rome for an artist to receive burial.

The Virtuosi also institutionalized the tradition of preserving the Pantheon
by conveying funerary incomes to the monument, as established by Raphael.
Already in 1543, the confraternity requested permission to restore the chapel to
the left of the main portal, which "was not yet endowed with a perpetual ecclesiastical benefice."[75] The confraternity thus acknowledged that if Raphael set a
precedent by assigning an income to his tomb, not all the chapels in the Pantheon were yet the beneficiaries of such funds. The document indicated the
poor condition of the tabernacle itself, currently used as a place to store trash:
"si riponevano [in questa cappella] le immondizie della detta chiesa."[76] Thus
the confraternity proposed to restore the chapel, as Raphael had done previously at the tabernacle that served as his tomb, and also made provisions
for its future endowment. They declared that a fifth of all charity proceeds
would go to the general maintenance of the Pantheon, with the rest supporting the chapel.[77] The presence of the Virtuosi at the monument, following
the precedent established by Raphael with the endowment for his tomb, helped
to put the preservation of the Pantheon on more stable financial footing.

The Conservators and the
Preservation of the Pantheon after 1520

Throughout the fifteenth century and into the first part of the sixteenth century, the Conservators, as the official guardians of antiquity in Renaissance Rome, remained strangely silent regarding the Pantheon, the best-preserved of all of Rome's ancient buildings. While the popes continued their steady work on repairing and maintaining the monument over these years, no recorded evidence survives for the involvement of the Conservators at the site.

This situation, however, changed in 1520, the year of Raphael's death. In November of 1520, the Conservators reported that they intended to confer with Leo X, still reigning as pope, to ask him to conduct repairs to the roof of Santa Maria Rotonda as well as some necessary repairs for its doors.[78] The Conservators also reported that they planned to appeal to the pope to conduct similar restorations on behalf of the early Christian basilica of Sant'Agnese outside the city walls.

In the early sixteenth century, as stipulated in the civic statutes, the Conservators retained authority over the preservation of the ancient monuments of the city. It is unlikely, however, that the timing of this particular document was purely coincidental. The Conservators were fully aware of Raphael's passing seven months earlier, which had caused such a blow to antiquarian studies in the city. They were also fully aware of Raphael's decision to build a tomb inside the rotunda. It may be that prior to this time, the Conservators directed their attentions elsewhere simply because the preservation of the Pantheon was so clearly a papal priority. But Raphael's restorations of the tabernacle implied that the Pantheon required renewed attention, and for this reason the Conservators may have decided to intervene at the Pantheon as well.

As attested in the conflict recorded in 1518 regarding the De' Rossi collection of ancient statues, a problematic rivalry emerged between Raphael and the civic magistrates that centered specifically on the issue of determining who had superior jurisdiction in the care of ancient artifacts.[79] Both sides had reasonable claims to support their respective cases. As appointed by Leo X in 1515, Raphael was empowered to make important preservation decisions in the Eternal City. But on the other hand, the Conservators claimed the responsibility for preserving ancient Rome as their historic institutional prerogative. The evidence of the 1518 case suggests that even though Raphael had papal backing, the Conservators emerged as the victors.

Now Raphael, the primary exponent of the papal preservation program, was removed from the scene. The particular interest of the Conservators in the preservation of the Pantheon at just this time suggests they were seeking to take this opportunity to extend and further reinforce their time-honored duties as the custodians of Rome's ancient past. By advocating the care of the Pantheon, the final resting place of the papal official who had threatened to usurp their powers, the Conservators subtly asserted their successful retention of their historic right to govern the care of ancient remains in Renaissance Rome.

The documents of the Capitoline archives indicate that the Conservators turned their attention to the repair of the Pantheon with increasing frequency in later years. In a session dated 13 August 1524, the Conservators reported that Clement VII, the reigning pope, wished to assign a portion of available civic revenues for the restoration of the Pantheon, "restauretur templum Sancta Mariae Rotundae" (appendix, document 14).[80]

In Renaissance Rome, a key source of income available to support the ongoing preservation of ancient buildings included funds drawn from the *gabella studii*. These revenues, collected through a surcharge on imported wine sold in Roman taverns (*gabella vini forensis*), were so called because they were originally intended to finance the *studium urbis*, or the civic university of Rome. Ultimately, however, the funds were used to support a variety of needs.[81]

The Conservators, however, objected to Clement VII's proposal to assign these funds to the restoration of the Pantheon, on the grounds that the income was insufficient. As they affirmed, "neither this portion nor the funds available to the Roman people would be sufficient for this restoration." The Conservators thus proposed to intercede with the pope to identify additional revenues to provide for the preservation of the Pantheon.

The Pantheon again became a topic for debate among the Conservators on 29 October 1524, when they reported that the Pantheon required attention as part of the necessary preparations and improvements to prepare the city of Rome for the approaching Jubilee.[82] As pilgrims from all over Christendom turned toward the papal capital, the Conservators wished to receive these visitors with sufficient dignity. Again the Pantheon attracted the particular interest of the Conservators, and they announced that they had set aside the considerable sum of four hundred ducats to restore its roofing of lead tiles. The popes had been the official custodians of the Pantheon, and in particular the vigilant guardians of its roof, for over nine hundred years. With this legislation, however, the Conservators proposed to assume this responsibility themselves.

The Conservators' audacious if patriotic attempt to take over the care of the Pantheon met with sharp papal disapproval, as reported in a subsequent document, dated 12 January 1525 (appendix, document 15).[83] In this session, the first Conservator communicated to the assembly the evident displeasure of the pope regarding this proposed intervention. As he explained, "regarding the repairs that need to be done to the roof tiles of the temple of the Pantheon, it is improper that a deputy . . . appointed by the civic magistrates, repair the said temple." Despite the fact that the Conservators had allocated funding for this work, Clement VII refused to permit them to conduct this restoration work. The historic duty of preserving the ancient Pantheon did not belong to the civic officials, but instead belonged exclusively to the pope.[84]

In 1527 Rome was besieged by Swiss *lanzichenecchi* and imperial troops. Fueled by the promise of fabulous papal wealth as well as Protestant hostility, they plundered the helpless city. The devastating financial impact of this experience upon the papacy may also be measured in the records of the civic administration, when the Conservators reported on 12 September 1531 that Clement VII now appealed to the civic administration for assistance in finding funds to repair the Pantheon dome [appendix, document 16].[85] The Conservators reported that the pope had communicated to them that if additional funding was available from the *gabella studii*, it was the pope's wish that it be assigned to the repair of the Pantheon's lead tiles. The Conservators then agreed to create a dedicated fund to provide for this purpose.[86]

The Capitoline documents fall silent at this point, and there are no further reports of the Conservators' involvement with the ongoing restoration work at the Pantheon. This silence may perhaps be explained by the gradual financial recovery of the papal administration in subsequent years, which made such appeals to the Conservators for assistance unnecessary. At the same time, it may also be related to the appointment in 1534 of Latino Giovenale Manetti by Paul III as the official papal commissioner of antiquity. The preservation of the ancient remains of the papal capital was now officially assigned to a papal official, and although the Conservators continued to take an active role in preserving antiquity at Rome, the events of the preceding decade suggested that the popes still claimed the preservation of the Pantheon, more than any other ancient building in Rome, as their exclusive charge.[87]

The Double Identity of the Pantheon

Although the Pantheon was always regarded with fascination and awe over the course of the Middle Ages, during the Renaissance there was a radical shift in the appreciation and understanding of this famous landmark.[88] Medieval viewers tended to look askance on the structure as tainted with the pagan past. To them, its unsupported soaring dome was an unfathomable structural mystery, and quite possibly the work of the devil. Hermann of Fritzlar, visiting the Pantheon around 1350, related a famous legend of the *Mirabilia urbis* in which demons were reputed to have opened up the oculus in the dome as they scrambled to get out of the pagan temple at the moment of its consecration as a Christian church. He then described the structure by noting that it was "very large, and there is no column in it anywhere."[89] For a German viewer accustomed to hall churches with naves carried on arcades and columns, the Pantheon was a bizarre church indeed.

By the fifteenth century, however, the Pantheon was of course the revered architectural ideal of Italian Renaissance culture. As Tilmann Buddensieg has observed, Renaissance enthusiasm for the Pantheon was epitomized by Biondo

Flavio's evaluation of the Pantheon in the fifteenth century as "surpassing easily all the other churches in Rome."[90] Biondo's admiration for the Pantheon indicated the extraordinary about-face performed by Renaissance culture in relation to this monument. Antiquarians, humanists, and artists now embraced the Pantheon as a paragon of classical architecture and rejected the lingering medieval doubts and suspicions connected to it as spurious. By the same token, as Buddensieg noted, Biondo's admiration also represented a devastating critique of all the churches built in Rome during the intervening centuries. These later churches of course were specifically built for the celebration of the Christian liturgy, unlike the pagan Pantheon, and yet they came nowhere near the magnificence of this ancient building.

Yet Biondo's own fifteenth-century evaluation of the Pantheon also perpetuated long-established medieval traditions by describing the building as a church. By the sixteenth century, the historic Christian identity of the Pantheon as Santa Maria ad Martyres, or Santa Maria Rotonda, also began to be challenged by the advances made by Renaissance humanist studies. The extraordinary physical condition of the Pantheon, as an artifact that had miraculously survived from imperial Rome, prompted a new way of thinking about the ancient building that opened a gap between its archaeological and ecclesiastical identities.

Already in the fifteenth century Leon Battista Alberti chose to favor the use of the Latin *templum* rather than *ecclesia* when he discussed sacred buildings in his theoretical writings on architecture.[91] Alberti provided an important Renaissance precedent by privileging pagan rather than Christian associations in the discussion of religious buildings, and thus when Bernardo Bembo made reference to the Pantheon as a "temple" in his description of 1504, his choice of words conformed to received Albertian practice. Of course, according to the leading antiquarian authorities in Rome, the original function of the Pantheon was an ancient temple.[92] As Bembo emphasized in his description, it was precisely the ancient fabric of this building that had been so carefully preserved over time. By identifying the Pantheon not as a church but as a temple, Bembo was in fact also restoring the original word presumably used in antiquity to describe this ancient structure.

Raphael's tomb also marked an important advance in this process of shifting the identity of the Pantheon toward that of a pagan temple. As we have seen, the design of the tomb itself made no overt use of Christian iconography. On the contrary, the overt classicism of Lorenzetto's votive sculpture blurred the lines that separated pagan from Christian imagery. Further explicit evidence of Raphael's own tendency to actively efface the evidence for Christian presence at the Pantheon survives in his famous drawing of the interior of the rotunda (figure 5.5). In this drawing, Raphael provided meticulous and exquisitely rendered visual documentation of the interior of this best-preserved ancient structure in Rome. He included even the smallest details, such as the form of the acanthus leaves in the column capitals, the distinctive design of the

FIGURE 5.5. Raphael, interior of Pantheon rotunda, Uffizi 164 Ar.

marble paneling, and the alternating shapes of the tabernacles surrounding the rotunda.[93]

But for all of the precision of Raphael's exacting archaeological study, he was concerned only with recording the Pantheon's classical elements. The same drawing also obliterated all traces of Santa Maria Rotonda. Even though obviously it continued to serve its historic function as a church, Raphael's depiction recorded no evidence for Christian ritual or practice at the site. His detailed study of the main apse in particular indicated that this was a conscious, systematic decision, where his delicate shadowing flowed uninterrupted down from the invisible oculus above, around the curving recess, to the marble floor below.

It would have been impossible for Raphael to miss the newly restored high altar of Innocent VIII, installed approximately twenty years before, as it stood directly in front of this apse. Its restoration made its presence even more prominent and conspicuous. Raphael's decision to efface this structure, which so clearly attested to the sustained presence of Christianity at Santa Maria Rotonda, indicated that a by-product of his exaltation of the remains of classical antiquity at Rome was the conscious erasure of the material traces of Christianity from the Pantheon.[94]

The notion of privileging the Pantheon as a classical space rather than a Christian church met with consensus elsewhere in Renaissance Rome. For

FIGURE 5.6. Exterior of Pantheon, photograph by Eugène Constant, ca. 1848–55. Bernini replaced the 1270 belltower on the portico with a pair of belfries on the intermediary block, ca. 1626–27. Derided as the *orecchie d'asino* or asses' ears, the belfries were removed during the restorations of 1881–83.

instance, sixteenth-century Capitoline documents referred to the monument not just as Santa Maria Rotonda, but as a temple.[95] In addition, subsequent interventions on the site continued to privilege its ancient, pagan identity over its Christian identity. Innocent VIII's high altar itself was ultimately dismantled in the eighteenth century.[96] And yet the idea of favoring the classical identity of the Pantheon of course originated with the fifteenth-century interventions of Eugenius IV, who first removed the market stalls from the portico colonnade, as Biondo declared, "to better reveal the beauty of this wonderful building."

Renaissance Preservation Practices at the Pantheon

Although the Pantheon is a priceless archaeological artifact, it also functions much like any other ordinary building (figure 5.6). On wet days people gather inside the rotunda to watch the rain as it descends in a light, vertical plume from the oculus, falling in a column to pool on the porphyry and granite floor. Once the rain stops the guardian passes through with a mop to clean up the puddles. On very cold days in the winter, snowflakes spiral down from the illuminated opening above into the gloom of the rotunda. The giant valves of the entrance portal glide silently open and shut every day, and the tranquility of the guards as they push these massive bronze panels into place makes their operation seem perfectly normal. Yet when we reflect upon the fact that the Pantheon has been in continuous operation over millennia, these quotidian activities appear astonishing.

Diligent maintenance and constant repair were two of the essential ingredients that ensured the exceptional preservation of this building throughout its history. The careful attention of the popes in particular, as the devoted guardians of this extraordinary structure, was imperative for its continued well-being. Their attention helped to safeguard the Pantheon from the unexpected ruin suffered by substantial ancient Roman buildings such as the Colosseum, where creeping deterioration eventually led to critical structural failures, followed in turn by devastating collapse.[97]

Yet what may appear as the perfect preservation of the Pantheon is also to some degree a fiction. The Renaissance history of this famous landmark proves that the preservation of the Pantheon's ancient identity involved both the preservation but also the creative restoration of its historic form. Although this process continued uninterrupted from the time of the Pantheon's construction, the Renaissance interventions on the site adopted a distinctive approach by reducing the presence of later alterations deemed inconsistent with its original character. Such interventions, paradoxically, also diminished the ecclesiastical identity of Santa Maria Rotonda, which had ensured the Pantheon's survival since the seventh century.

The process of pruning away the perceived anachronistic accretions to the Pantheon that began in Renaissance thus generated the monument we see today.[98] In reality, the material fabric of the Pantheon continues to hold multiple temporalities in question: it is not always clear what parts survive from time of Hadrian and what have been substituted through the continuing process of repair. The concrete vault of the dome appears unchanged, but the exterior tiles protecting its shell have been repeatedly renewed over the centuries. Perhaps it is the convincing impression of the Pantheon's perfect material integrity that counts most: the ongoing, uninterrupted process of preservation and restoration that has taken place over the centuries at this site allows us, when we step into the rotunda, to experience a space that transcends time.

FIGURE 6.1.   Ponte Santa Maria, detail from map of Rome by Etienne Dupérac, 1577.

6

The Ponte Santa Maria

In *Dell'antichità di Roma*, a guidebook to Rome first printed in 1565, Bernardo Gamucci wrote his impressions of the recent collapse of the Ponte Santa Maria seven years earlier. Even in this cursory sketch, Gamucci indicated the essential importance of this bridge as a transportation corridor, both within the Roman urban network (figure 6.1), and for the movement of people and merchandise through central Italy:

> The bridge that today is called Santa Maria . . . from 1557 onward in large part has been ruined, causing great inconvenience to the inhabitants of Rome, as it is no longer possible to cross the river without traveling far out of the way to reach the Porta di San Pancrazio, which leads to the lands of Tuscany. And even if Julius III restored the bridge, and rebuilt one of its piers that was missing, the Romans have not had much time to enjoy it, as a new collapse caused it to break in part, and this is believed to have been provoked by nothing else other than by its own weight.[1]

The sixteenth-century history of the Ponte Santa Maria, punctuated by repeated structural failures and laborious restorations, caused mounting frustration for the rulers as well as the ordinary people of Renaissance Rome. Paul III organized a major restoration campaign in 1548 when the bridge began to show signs of imminent collapse, which allowed it to remain open during the Jubilee of 1550. As Gamucci reported, however, in 1557 a Tiber flood undermined one of its piers, bringing down part of the roadway and causing major traffic disruption in Rome. A temporary repair conceived under Pius IV ended in a fiasco. Finally, Gregory XIII sponsored another extensive rebuilding program in anticipation of the approaching Jubilee of 1575. But twenty-three years later, in 1598, one of the worst floods in the history of Rome carried away the eastern part of the Ponte Santa Maria, and after this catastrophe it was never again rebuilt.

Today only a stub of the mighty bridge known in antiquity as the Pons Aemilius survives, standing just downstream from the Tiber Island.[2] The nineteenth-century reconstruction of the Tiber embankments dismantled much of what still survived of the ancient structure after the flood of 1598, leaving only a short stretch of disintegrating roadbed in midriver, suspended above a single semicircular arch. The relic, best known as the Ponte Rotto, it is cut adrift from the surrounding metropolis, all but inaccessible from either bank. From the metal deck of its successor, the adjacent Ponte Palatino, it appears a leafy and romantic ruin. Caper plants cascade down its sides, grasses wave from its deck, and volunteer trees push up against its cutwaters.

Yet if the picturesque appearance of the Ponte Santa Maria seems not unlike the Colosseum in the era of Henry James, this uncelebrated ancient fragment has receded much further into obscurity than the ruins of the nearby ancient amphitheater. The occasional pedestrian on the Ponte Palatino may pause to examine the crumbling marble superstructure from above, and a curious tourist might scramble down to the southernmost tip of the Tiber Island to get a better view from below. But from the Tiber embankments, the typical angle from which one views the Ponte Santa Maria in the modern city, the one surviving arch is very hard to see. With the leafy bending branches of the plane trees along the Lungotevere in the way, it becomes nearly invisible.

Compared to the craggy ruins of the Colosseum and the breathtaking interior of the Pantheon, the prosaic Ponte Santa Maria seems scarcely worth a second glance. Yet this is to overlook the fact that this decaying relic was not only the first stone bridge to be built in Rome, but it is now the oldest bridge still standing in the Tiber. It was also one of the most important river crossings from antiquity into the Renaissance. Its present neglect belies its central importance in earlier centuries, when the Ponte Santa Maria was the object of intense repair operations. Indeed, the scale of work and expenses associated with its repair in the fifteenth and sixteenth centuries far surpassed that of contemporary work at either the Colosseum or the Pantheon. These intensive efforts to shore up the Ponte Santa Maria remind us that Renaissance preservation practices also focused upon workaday infrastructure in addition to the acclaimed monuments of antiquity. Regular maintenance of bridges, roads, aqueducts, and fortifications was essential to the well-being of the city. Nonetheless, even the most heroic Renaissance interventions at the Ponte Santa Maria were unable to prevent its eventual collapse.

This chapter considers how the Ponte Santa Maria became so important in the life of the postclassical city, and examines the causes that contributed to its eventual demise. The bridge was literally a lifeline for the papal capital, carrying local and long-distance traffic through the city. It was a critical artery for commerce and trade as well as for the pilgrimage network. The extensive repairs made in the effort to preserve the Ponte Santa Maria during the fifteenth and sixteenth centuries provide further evidence for the Renaissance understanding of preservation practices. Moreover, as we will see, the collapse of the Ponte Santa Maria may even encourage us to invert our received ideas about the reckless Renaissance disregard for antiquity. The 1551 collapse in particular, which may be considered the beginning of the end for the monument in terms of its history as a major Roman traffic artery, may be credited not so much to faulty Renaissance repairs as to overly cautious efforts to preserve the ancient structure intact and unchanged.

The Strategic Importance of the Ponte Santa Maria

From the earliest history of the city of Rome, the location of the Ponte Santa Maria marked one of the most important crossroads in the city (figure 6.2). The Tiber Island, with its adjacent rapids, created a natural obstacle to river traffic. The riverbank to the south of the island offered an ideal location for boats approaching Rome from the Tyrrhenian Sea to discharge their passengers and freight. By the time of the Republic this had become the *portus Tiberinus*, or the main port of Rome.[3] Both the Forum Boarium, the cattle market, and the Forum Holitorium, the vegetable market, were in the immediate vicinity of the port, attesting to its vital function as a crossroads for traffic by land and water. In later centuries, the main port relocated to the Ripa, slightly further downriver and on the other side of the Tiber. For centuries this remained the primary arrival point for travelers and cargo coming into Rome.[4]

The growing concentration of commercial activity made this area a hub for land traffic, both within the city itself and for the larger geographical region. Although the Tiber Island offered the narrowest crossing over the river, the first surviving evidence for a permanent bridge crossing was not here, but immediately to the south.[5] This was the wooden Pons Sublicius, which joined Trastevere with the area of the Forum Boarium.[6] The bridge that succeeded the Pons Sublicius and which eventually became the Ponte Santa Maria was the Pons Aemilius. The first stone bridge to be built in Rome, it may have taken its name from a Roman censor who contributed to its construction, M. Aemilius Lepidus.[7]

The Pons Aemilius was built in conjunction with the Via Aurelia, one of the consular highways that made up the expanding network of roads that radiated out of Rome in every direction.[8] The Via Aurelia provided an improved connection between Rome and Etruria to the northwest, corresponding to the

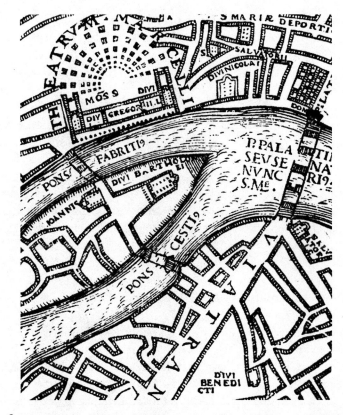

FIGURE 6.2. Ponte Santa Maria, detail from map of Rome by Leonardo Bufalini, 1551.

region of modern Tuscany. Descending the steep Janiculum ridge to the right bank of the river, the highway crossed the Tiber on the Pons Aemilius to arrive at the very center of Rome.

It is still possible today to retrace the route of the Via Aurelia from the Porta di San Pancrazio at the top of the Janiculum Hill, down the steps near San Pietro in Montorio and Bramante's Tempietto, to the Piazza di Santa Maria in Trastevere. From here one can travel across Trastevere in a straight line along the Via della Lungaretta, corresponding to the ancient Via Aurelia, to arrive at the bridgehead of the Pons Aemilius on the Tiber. It is more difficult to reconstruct the final section of the route, as the bridgehead was eliminated by the construction of the Lungotevere embankments in the nineteenth century. The Via della Lungaretta, however, leads directly to the vestige of the Ponte Santa Maria that still stands in the Tiber, better known today as the Ponte Rotto.

The ancient chronology for the Ponte Santa Maria is uncertain.[9] It is clear, however, that the bridge required regular reconstruction from the beginning of its history, and the surviving archaeological evidence in the Tiber riverbed is clearly the composite product of numerous different building campaigns. The

Roman historian Livy reported that the original bridge consisted of stone piers carrying a wooden deck.[10] This bridge, dating to around 179 B.C., was then completed in stone when the wooden deck was replaced in 142 B.C.

Under Augustus, a major overhaul of the Ponte Santa Maria may have taken place, including the construction of new embankments, ramps, and even a new triumphal arch.[11] The Augustan rebuilding probably introduced travertine stone facing. Refined architectural details that are still visible today, such as the sharp cutwaters orienting the piers toward the current, and the arched lunettes allowing floodwaters to pierce the superstructure, may also date from this time (figure 6.3).[12]

Later builders modified the structure while still making use of its preexisting footings, as indicated by the surviving Grotta Oscura tufa core visible in the eastern pier of the Ponte Rotto. The presence of this friable volcanic stone, often employed during the Republic but generally avoided in most later imperial architecture, substantiates this point, indicating that an earlier construction phase was absorbed into a successive reconstruction. While reuse of these footings offered a cost-effective way of reducing expenditures, such reuse may have also made a problematic design a permanent feature of the bridge. The Ponte Santa Maria rested on five piers, more than any other bridge in Rome, and during the frequent Tiber floods, these became a dangerous hazard. The history of constant repairs on the Ponte Santa Maria piers, and their eventual collapse in the sixteenth century, may be connected at least in part to the design of these piers.

DELLE ANTICHITA
Questo ponte già si diceua de' Senatori, altri lo diceuano ponte Palatino : ma al presente si dice ponte Santa Maria, & anco ponte Sisto.

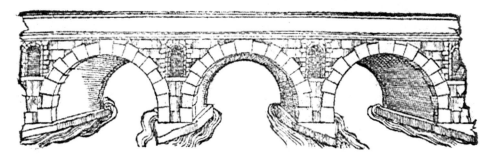

FIGURE 6.3. Elevation of Ponte Santa Maria, from Sebastiano Serlio, *Della antichità di Roma*, 1540.

In the postclassical city, the ancient bridge carried a number of different names: through a transliteration of Lepidus it was known as the Pons Lapideus, or the stone bridge; it was also known as the Pons Palatinus, from the nearby Palatine Hill; it was also simply called the Pons Maior, as the biggest bridge in the city.[13] Throughout it remained one of the most important Tiber crossings. It served as a key artery for commercial traffic, connecting the port to the center of the city.

A late fifteenth-century view of the bridge in the Codex Escurialensis recorded its function as a commercial conduit (figure 6.4). The artist depicted the Ponte Santa Maria from the perspective of travelers arriving in Rome from the sea. As the first bridge of the capital that they encountered, with its massive white masonry superstructure spanning the banks and reflected in the water below, the Ponte Santa Maria served as an appropriately monumental standard-bearer for the Eternal City. Travelers and cargo disembarked at the Ripa, shown in the left foreground, crowded with boats and barges. From here, merchandise destined for the center of Rome then traveled across the Ponte Santa Maria to reach the heart of the *abitato*, clustered around the dome of the Pantheon in the distance.

In addition to serving commercial traffic, the Ponte Santa Maria also provided the most direct route between two of the most important pilgrimage destinations in Rome, the basilica of St. Peter at the northern edge of the city, and the basilica of St. Paul to the south. Pilgrims traveling back and forth between these two sites frequently crossed the bridge. This only reinforced Rome's vital dependence upon the Ponte Santa Maria: the bridge facilitated the pilgrimage trade, one of the most important economic activities of the Christian capital.

As part of the series of prints known as the Speculum Romanae Magnificentiae, a map of Rome was issued for the Jubilee of 1575, soon after Gregory XIII completed large-scale repairs at the Ponte Santa Maria (figure 6.5).[14] Titled "Le sette chiese di Roma," the map was conceived more in symbolic terms than as an accurate topographical study. Privileging the locations of the seven primary pilgrimage churches, it reduced the city itself to a schematic diagram. But while the print exaggerated the size of the basilicas in relation to their context, it still indicated their relative positions with some accuracy. The map underscored the strategic siting of the Ponte Santa Maria in relation to the busy pilgrimage routes of the papal capital.[15]

At the bottom of the image stood the unfinished basilica of St. Peter, with the figure of St. Peter surrounded by reverent pilgrims. Other cowled pilgrims traveled in procession south from St. Peter's along the right bank of the Tiber, along the Via della Lungara, through the Porta Settimiana, and into the district of Trastevere. They passed two bridges, including the Ponte Sisto, omitted on this map, as well as the Ponte Cestio leading to the Tiber Island, to cross the river at the Ponte Santa Maria. This bridge offered a direct connection to the Porta San Paolo in the Aurelian Walls, next to the Pyramid of Cestius, and from there

FIGURE 6.4. View over the Tiber from the Aventine Hill. The Capitoline Hill, crowned by the bell tower of the Senators' palace and the church of Santa Maria degli Aracoeli, is visible at the upper right. *Codex Escurialensis*, 56v.

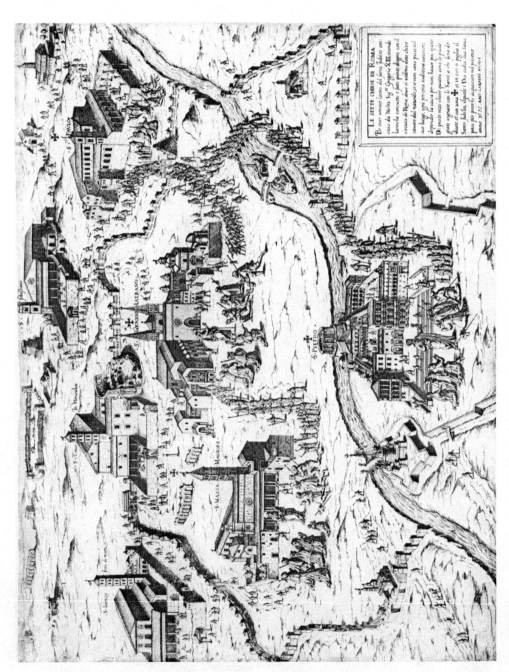

FIGURE 6.5. "Le sette chiese di Roma," printed by Antonio Lafréry, 1575.

to the basilica of St. Paul. Having reached their final destination, another group of pilgrims paid homage to St. Paul, the second of Rome's two patron saints. The Ponte Santa Maria, as shown in the print, stood at the exact midpoint between these two poles of Christian pilgrimage. A chapel dedicated to the Virgin built at midspan on the south parapet of the bridge itself further emphasized the vital importance of the Ponte Santa Maria to the ongoing religious life of the city.[16]

Hazards of the Tiber, and Medieval Repairs to the Ponte Santa Maria

The Tiber is known for its terrible floods, and the bridges built in the sinuous riverbed coursing through the city of Rome have always borne the brunt of this violence. Given the dangerous reputation of the river, the noted sixteenth-century inventor Fausto Veranzio was astonished that the ancient Roman builders chose to obstruct it with massive bridge piers:

> I marvel at the judgment of those ancient architects, whose practice
> was to establish and erect those bridges, without regard for the fact
> that their bridge piers occupied a third of the riverbed; it seems it
> would have been better that in those same places they should have at
> least widened the riverbed by the same amount.[17]

Instead the channel of the Tiber was hemmed in on both sides by steep banks. The grinding force of its constant and powerful current, further strengthened by the narrow channel, was capable of undermining even the sturdiest bridge foundations.

Above all, the recurring Tiber floods posed the most serious threat to the security of the ancient bridges.[18] The riverbanks were crowded with houses descending to the water level, and floodwaters could soon pull these buildings from their foundations. Houses and timber swept downstream by the flood could shatter a bridge upon impact. In the same way, an active milling industry based at the rapids around the Tiber Island placed additional ammunition in the way of the current. Mills on floating rafts, ripped from their anchors, became deadly projectiles when they slammed into bridges standing downstream.[19] As if this were not enough, the floodwaters sometimes even crested bridge superstructures. A major Tiber flood was perfectly capable of carrying an entire bridge away from its moorings.

The location of the Ponte Santa Maria along the Tiber was particularly hazardous. As the last bridge spanning the Tiber as it traveled downriver, the Ponte Santa Maria had to withstand the cumulative impact of the furious waters and everything they carried with them as they descended toward the sea. Moreover, the river itself swelled with renewed force just as it neared the Ponte Santa

Maria. After surging over the rapids at the Tiber Island, the floodwaters recon-
verged just as they careened into another major bend in the river. As Fausto
Veranzio observed, because the Ponte Santa Maria "stands in the current of two
water channels divided by the Tiber Island, it receives the force of the river
from the other side at an oblique and twisted angle."[20] The Ponte Santa Maria
stood in the direct line of fire of multiple changing currents that were so strong
and unpredictable they exposed the bridge to conditions that never could have
been anticipated by its builders. Even today, massive concrete blocks are stacked
along the inside curve of the river embankment in the effort to protect the modern embankments from the force of constant erosion.

As already noted, the design of the Ponte Santa Maria, with its five piers
blocking the Tiber riverbed, carried certain risks. Where the Colosseum's attic
story represented that monument's Achilles heel, so were the many piers of
the Ponte Santa Maria more vulnerable to collisions and thereby more prone
to destruction and collapse.[21] Close examination of the surviving archaeological evidence reveals that ingenious reconstructions took place at these piers.
Later builders sought to modify the pier profiles on an empirical basis, in the
effort to allow them to better divide the variable currents of the riverbed.[22]
Bridging this section of the river was clearly a very complex and troublesome
venture.[23]

Nevertheless, despite the inherent problems relating to these difficult site
conditions, regular repairs conducted at the Ponte Santa Maria over the years
enabled it to resist the Tiber currents. The periodic cycle of Tiber floods suggests the bridge required major rebuilding at least once a century.[24] The attentive ministrations of the rulers of Rome to the Ponte Santa Maria throughout
its history underscored the enduring and essential importance of this crossing.

The creation of the Roman civic government in the twelfth century
prompted renewed interest in the care and maintenance of urban infrastructure, including the walls, gates, and bridges of the city, where gaining control
over these key structures translated into gaining mastery over the city. The
medieval civic magistrates made efforts to restore the city bridges, as attested
by a prominent twelfth-century inscription still visible today on the parapet of
the neighboring Ponte Cestio.[25] The protection and strengthening of these
prominent transportation corridors also served to publicize the virtues of good
government as endorsed by the medieval civic magistrates.

The first set of surviving Roman civic statutes, dating from the fourteenth
century, gave additional evidence for the specific objectives of the civic government regarding the preservation of the city bridges. According to chapter 166,
titled "De curris et carrectis," or "On Wagons and Carts," the Tiber bridges
needed to be carefully protected from wagons carrying excessive loads:

[N]o wagon and no cart either carrying a load or empty, [drawn] by
buffaloes or oxen or horses, may cross on any bridge of the Urbs and

the Tiber River, except for the Ponte Mammolo, and no millstones may be transported without a sled. All offenders will be charged 100 soldi.[26]

With this legislation, the civic government banned all heavy wagon traffic from the Tiber bridges. The obvious aim was to preserve the bridges from undue wear and damage. The one exception was the Ponte Mammolo, standing outside the city, which carried the Via Tiburtina from Rome to Tivoli. Wagon traffic was still permitted across this bridge, perhaps because it provided a vital link between the travertine quarries at Tivoli and building sites at Rome. The history of sixteenth-century repairs at the Ponte Santa Maria will reveal that the Ponte Mammolo continued to be judged expendable in later years as well.

Another chapter in the same statutes indicated that civic government was also preoccupied with ensuring an unobstructed right-of-way on the bridges. In chapter 196, "De edificantibus in viis comunis et pontibus," or "On Building in Public Roadways and on Bridges," this duty was assigned to the Senator, as the leading official of the medieval administration:

> The Senator is obliged . . . to liberate and clear all the roadways and bridges, both inside and outside the Urbs, and if any structures, walls, entrances, porticoes, or any other structure is built . . . on these roadways and bridges . . . he must remove, destroy, and demolish them at the expense of those who have either built or caused buildings to be built on these roadways and bridges.[27]

It was established practice for merchants in medieval Italy, as elsewhere in Europe, to build their stalls on bridges. This setting offered an ideal opportunity to display their wares to a captive audience as it funneled past, and busy bridges became famous venues for the sale of various kinds of merchandise, such as the Ponte Vecchio in Florence and the Ponte Rialto in Venice. The Roman civic administration, however, was adamant in its intent to keep the city bridges free of these obstructions. The bridges across the Tiber were not to be impeded by shops or browsing customers: instead, traffic was to move across as smoothly and swiftly as possible. This distinctly Roman preoccupation with keeping the bridges clear may have derived in part from the experience of bridge congestion during Jubilee years.[28] To ensure proper enforcement, the *maestri di strade* were assigned the duty of policing the city bridges.[29]

The civic magistrates were not alone in their interest in maintaining these key Tiber crossings. The popes were also concerned regarding the upkeep of these structures as the essential means by which papal processions, diplomatic and commercial correspondence relating to the papal court, and pilgrims could get access to every part of Rome. The first surviving evidence for papal repairs at the Ponte Santa Maria occurred following the major flood of 1230, when

Gregory IX sponsored its reconstruction.[30] Further repairs took place less than a century later, following the epic flood of 1310.[31] The key role of the Ponte Santa Maria in the daily life of the city meant that it was in the best interests of the entire population to ensure its preservation.

Fifteenth-Century Restoration Politics at the Ponte Santa Maria

Beginning in the fifteenth century, with the return of Martin V to Rome, the ongoing restoration of the Ponte Santa Maria reflected the changing political conditions of the papal capital. The bridge was of indisputable importance for the well-being of Rome, and its continued repair was non-negotiable. When Martin V and the leading figures of the civic government collaborated in conducting repairs to the monument, this could be justified as a project of fundamental civic value. At the same time, the restoration of the Ponte Santa Maria offered useful opportunities to forge binding alliances between these sometimes reluctant political partners.[32]

On the last day of November in 1422, two years after the return of Martin V to the papal capital, the city was struck by a violent flood. The Roman chronicler Pietro dello Mastro reported that it left the Pantheon and the center of the *abitato* submerged:

> Santa Maria Rotonda remained full of water for more than a month, as its drain was obstructed; the flood caused great damage at Rome, because the surge of water was so sudden that no one had time to take any precautions. The rise and fall of the floodwaters lasted for three days.[33]

The Ponte Santa Maria appears to have been hard hit by this torrent, and the papal response to the situation was swift. The first surviving record of a papal payment, for 155 gold florins, made to Antonio Porcari, the appointed supervisor of restoration work to the bridge, shows that work began on 14 January 1423, when the floodwaters had scarcely receded from the Pantheon, and then continued through April.[34] During the dry summer months rebuilding accelerated, as recorded by the noteworthy payment of more than four thousand ducats to Porcari for the period between July and September.[35] The enormous expense of these repairs indicates that the bridge was indispensable, and the pressing demands of daily traffic made its restoration imperative.

During the winter flood season, building activity at the Ponte Santa Maria either slowed or came to a halt, but then took up again in the spring, as recorded in a payment made on 8 June 1424.[36] Although no payment records appear to have survived for 1425, payments were recorded in the late spring of 1426, beginning on 8 June when Antonio Porcari received 288 ducats for repair work at the bridge.[37] A change in the administration of the bridge project occurred in the next weeks, as a payment of 120 florins issued on 22 June was made not to Porcari but to Renzo Rienzolino, now identified as the supervisor of the project.[38] Porcari seems to have later resumed this position, as he received further payment of 126 ducats in August for ongoing work at the bridge.[39] Two more payments indicated that work at the site continued through 12 October, when payment reverted to Rienzolino.[40] The last payment recorded for this major reconstruction project, made more than four years after the flood of 1422 on 3 February 1427, was also made to Rienzolino.[41] Both the considerable expense and the extended time required for these repairs suggest that this overhaul of the ancient Ponte Santa Maria affected not only the piers and cutwaters but also much of the bridge superstructure.

Although Martin V followed papal tradition by taking steps to protect this important Tiber crossing, his interventions on this prominent Roman urban infrastructure answered both political and utilitarian objectives in the delicate political circumstances of early fifteenth-century Rome. Building and restoration contracts offered a vital means by which to build and strengthen political alliances with the leading families in Rome, whose collaboration assisted the pope in the project of reasserting papal control over the ancient city. Naturally, lucrative papal construction contracts could also bring in considerable revenues for the interested parties.

As it turns out, both Antonio Porcari and Renzo Rienzolino, the two primary supervisors of the restoration of the Ponte Santa Maria, also played important roles in the civic administration of Rome. Porcari was appointed Conservator in 1413.[42] Rienzolino served as head of the *caporioni* in 1424, and by 1430 he assumed the papal appointment of *maestro delle strade*.[43] In supervising the restoration of the Ponte Santa Maria, both of these civic officials thus benefited directly from papal patronage.[44] The ongoing close interaction of Porcari and Rienzolino with papal authorities indicates how the civic authorities and the papal administration collaborated in implementing repairs to prominent ancient remains in Rome. The rebuilding of the Ponte Santa Maria served as a vital infusion of papal wealth into the local community, serving to stimulate economic growth and thereby revive the faltering Roman economy. Civic officials implemented much of this work, and thus Martin V could expect to consolidate support for papal power among the leading members of the Roman oligarchy.

Further repairs to the Ponte Santa Maria took place during the reign of Nicholas V, perhaps continuing work begun under Martin V.[45] The same restoration was referred to in a 1551 contract issued during the reign of Julius III for the restoration of the Ponte Santa Maria, to be discussed in a subsequent section in greater detail. This document suggested that evidence for both of these repairs (presumably in the form of papal shields or inscriptions) was still visible on the structure in the mid-sixteenth century.[46] Clearly Nicholas V was anxious to ensure that this bridge, along with the other important Tiber crossings, remained open to traffic during the Jubilee of 1450. Such deadlines often required the opening of large-scale work sites to meet these very tight schedules.

At the same time, Nicholas V, like his predecessor Martin V, may have also taken the opportunity to use this major restoration project to strengthen papal partnerships with key Roman families. Such families continued to stand to benefit from the advantages offered by such papal interventions, as in the recent papal restoration of the Acqua Vergine and the Trevi Fountain.[47] Intent upon consolidating papal power in the city, Nicholas V could use the profitable contracts for the restoration of the Ponte Santa Maria as a means to favor key Roman constituents whose cooperation then helped him to overcome local resistance to papal power.

All physical evidence for work by Martin V and Nicholas V at the Ponte Santa Maria appears to have been effaced by later sixteenth-century restorations. It appears, however, that these fifteenth-century repairs met their objectives, for following the death of Nicholas V in 1455, no major maintenance work was recorded at the Ponte Santa Maria for nearly a century. The silence of the archive may of course be mere coincidence, but it also suggests that these restorations were in large part successful.[48]

Michelangelo at the Ponte Santa Maria, 1548–49

The first major intervention to take place on the Ponte Santa Maria in the sixteenth century was recorded in 1548.[49] That Michelangelo, the greatest artist of sixteenth-century Italy, also participated in this work is an indication of the importance Paul III, the reigning pope, assigned to the repair of the indispensable ancient bridge. By the same token, Michelangelo's involvement reminds us that the leading artists of the Italian Renaissance continued to take an active role in the urgent work of preserving the monumental ancient remains of Rome. Just as Raphael made a vital contribution to the preservation of the Pantheon, so Michelangelo was now called upon to protect the venerable Ponte Santa Maria.

After nearly a century when no repairs appear to have been recorded for the Ponte Santa Maria, it is not surprising that the bridge showed signs of advanced deterioration. A mammoth four-day flood in 1530 caused extensive damage to all the bridges in Rome, as reported by a contemporary anonymous account:

> The floodwater . . . dragged away both of the embankments of the
> Ponte Sant'Angelo, built of enormous marble blocks, and had the
> flood lasted much longer without doubt the entire bridge would have
> collapsed; it also destroyed the Ponte Sisto, and the Ponte Quattro
> Capi (the Ponte Fabricio).[50]

The author also reported that all the major Tiber crossings, including the Ponte Santa Maria, were entirely submerged by the floodwaters.[51] Even with the destabilizing deadweight of the medieval chapel built upon its parapet, the Ponte Santa Maria somehow managed to resist this onslaught. In the following years, however, the bridge did not benefit from necessary repairs, probably as a consequence of the difficult financial conditions of the papal administration following the Sack of Rome in 1527.

By 1548, eighteen years after the flood of 1530, the financial conditions of the Holy See had improved to the point that it was possible to take action to restore the Ponte Santa Maria. The impending Jubilee year of 1550 made such repairs even more urgent, and like his predecessor Nicholas V, Paul III spearheaded these restorations in the effort to prevent the disruption of Jubilee pilgrimage traffic.

Paul III communicated his restoration plan for the Ponte Santa Maria to the Conservators, as recorded in a session of the civic magistrates dated 28 July 1548. As the Conservator Battista Teodorico reported, the pope was intent upon assigning a share of the financial burden to the civic government for this work. As Teodorico admitted, given the Conservators' responsibilities as the guardians of ancient Rome, the pope's demands were not unexpected:

> As the restoration of the Ponte Santa Maria is of great importance, it
> should not seem strange if the *popolo romano* should be obliged to
> carry some of the cost that this will require. And let it be known, that
> we have not failed to act with all possible dexterity and diligence on our
> behalf, in beseeching His Holiness to go gently in exacting funds.[52]

Even following the appointment of Latino Giovenale Manetti as the papal commissioner of antiquity, the Conservators continued to contribute to the cost of caring for ancient remains in the papal capital. But although the Conservators were anxious to preserve ancient remains, they had limited financial resources at their disposal. Thus Teodorico acknowledged the understandable anxiety of the civic magistrates regarding Paul III's determination to impose this expense upon them.

Teodorico affirmed that the pope had responded favorably to his request by agreeing to allow the Conservators additional time to collect the necessary funds.[53] The Conservator then declared that the Ponte Santa Maria was in dire need of restoration work, and that if this did not happen swiftly, the bridge was sure to collapse:

> In awaiting the restoration of the bridge, we hope that with the help
> of God it will be delivered from that peril that will otherwise happen
> to it without doubt: that is the ruin of the two arches, which will
> cause even greater expense and inconvenience to the *popolo romano*.
> And to come to our conclusion, as we must ensure that the funds are

properly and honorably spent, with an eye to the wise, we have
thought to turn to Michelangelo Buonarroti, *homo singularissimo*,
whose virtue has been commended to us by His Holiness . . . as a
good Roman citizen known for his affection for Rome.[54]

Teodorico's reference to "the ruin of the two arches" indicated that one of the
piers showed signs of collapse, threatening to bring down the two arches which
it supported on either side. In response, the pope chose none other than
Michelangelo himself to direct this project. Teodorico applauded Paul III's appointment, noting that Michelangelo was admired not only for his sagacity but
also for his frugality—a point of special consideration for the Conservators.

Despite Paul III's insistence on the financial contribution by the Conservators, he also began to draw together other revenues to fund this hefty restoration work. Anticipating the economic difficulties of the Conservators, the papal
administration began to collect income from the wealthiest Roman guilds in
the previous week.[55] A series of extraordinary taxes imposed upon the guilds of
the goldsmiths as well as the bankers of Rome enabled the pope to amass the
necessary funds.[56]

Yet Paul III did not reduce the Conservators to a peripheral role in the
Ponte Santa Maria restoration. The surviving payment record for the work site
indicates that on the contrary the Conservators were actively involved in this
work.[57] They were responsible for approving the disbursement of funds to
cover expenses for materials and salaries, including even that of Michelangelo.[58] Thus the civic magistrates, in addition to making a financial contribution, assumed a supervisory role in managing the restoration of the Ponte
Santa Maria. Clearly the preservation of antiquity continued to be a collaborative venture in Rome of the mid-sixteenth century, where this duty was shared
by both the pope and the Conservators.

While the surviving evidence for Michelangelo's actual involvement on
the work site is only partial, it appears his role in overseeing this restoration
was limited. Michelangelo was charged with many pressing duties at this
time: the Ponte Santa Maria was only the latest entry on a growing list of responsibilities. In the previous year Paul III appointed him chief architect at
the New St. Peter's.[59] Michelangelo was also supervising the ongoing reconstruction of the civic palaces on the Capitoline Hill, as well the immense work
site of the new Palazzo Farnese.[60] He was also working on the frescoes of the
Pauline Chapel.[61] With such a heavy workload, and also because the repair of
the Ponte Santa Maria required specialized technical expertise, Michelangelo
may have been more willing to let his colleagues handle problems at the
bridge work site.[62] Also at around this time Michelangelo began to suffer from
a debilitating illness.[63] Given these extenuating circumstances, it seems likely
Michelangelo was often absent from the construction site, especially as
building activity neared its zenith.

But there is no reason to believe that Michelangelo was not very intrigued by this ambitious restoration project. Vasari reported that Michelangelo worked on a bridge design intended to link the Palazzo Farnese with the Villa Farnesina across the Tiber.[64] Even if this may have been just a passing fancy on the part of Paul III, the Ponte Santa Maria offered important and useful information about how to build (or not to build) in the Tiber riverbed.[65] Later, during the reign of Pius IV, Michelangelo's interventions on the ancient Baths of Diocletian revealed his continued interest in the challenges posed by the preservation of major ancient monuments in Rome.[66]

The restoration of the Ponte Santa Maria required a high degree of organization and efficiency to meet the approaching deadline of the 1550 Jubilee. The project was divided into two primary phases. The most urgent work involved rebuilding the pier showing signs of collapse. Once this pier was stabilized, the next phase involved repairing the damaged portions of the superstructure to provide a safe crossing for the public, including the arches, roadbed, and parapets. Payments issued to carpenters for timber construction indicate that parts of this restoration were realized in this lighter, more pliable, but also more temporary material.[67]

Ultimately the builders succeeded in meeting their deadline. For a stretch of time, teams of workers even labored on the site twenty-four hours a day, in the tremendous push to complete the project in just over a year.[68] The restored bridge opened to traffic right on schedule, only two months before the opening of the Jubilee of 1550, and only one month before the death of Paul III.[69] It was an unqualified success, at least in terms of a temporary stopgap measure. The bridge was sufficiently stabilized that no incidents were reported during the Jubilee, and traffic moved smoothly along the established pilgrimage route between the two major basilicas of St. Peter's and St. Paul's. Providing for the long-term preservation of the Ponte Santa Maria, however, proved to be an even more challenging and complicated problem.

Renaissance Preservation Practices and the Ponte Mammolo

As this book argues, preservation practices in Renaissance Rome did not always conform to the modern principles of scientific archaeology and conservation theory. A newly discovered document from the Vatican Archives invites us to explore this issue in greater detail. This document suggests that the need to preserve and restore the Ponte Santa Maria was deemed to be of such urgency that it was allowed to take precedence over the preservation of other significant archaeological artifacts.

On 22 June 1549, with restoration work at the Ponte Santa Maria already well under way, a papal excavation license was issued to Tommaso da Bologna, the head of the *scarpellini* or stoneworkers at the bridge work site (appendix,

document 17).[70] This license awarded Maestro da Bologna full authority to collect building stone at the Ponte Mammolo at Tivoli, to the east of Rome:

> We hereby command that Maestro Tommaso da Bologna, master of
> the stonemasons of Ponte Santa Maria in Rome, be allowed to
> excavate freely and without any impediment all those travertine
> stones from the Ponte Mammolo of the aforesaid provincial territory
> [of Tivoli] that are needed to provide for the restoration of the Ponte
> Santa Maria.

The Ponte Mammolo carried the Via Tiburtina, the Roman consular highway,
across the Aniene, an important tributary of the Tiber.[71] The Ponte Mammolo
was in fact a structure close in age to the Ponte Santa Maria: modern archaeologists have also dated this structure to the late Republic. It was of similar
design, as a pair of semicircular arches with a central pier framing a lunette, all
sheathed by a thick layer of massive travertine blocks. While considerably
smaller than the Ponte Santa Maria, in many ways the two bridges were clearly
very closely related.

The license issued to Maestro da Bologna indicated that the pope had
determined to sacrifice this venerable but provincial structure to rebuild the
Ponte Santa Maria. Addressed to "all and sundry, governor, officials, and individuals in the city and provincial territory of Tivoli," the language of the document was crafted to prevent any possible resistance by either local civic officials
or private individuals who might seek to obstruct or otherwise prevent the
dismantling of stones from taking place. Rome had requisitioned the Ponte
Mammolo for its own purposes, and the license warned the citizens of Tivoli
not to interfere with this decision.

At first glance, the papal command to strip building stone from the Ponte
Mammolo might appear to be just another example of the reckless Renaissance
plundering of antiquity. Judged by modern standards, such an intervention
seems an outrageous archaeological violation. The papal license proposed to
destroy a surviving ancient bridge and then, adding insult to injury, it approved
the removal of these ancient building stones to incorporate them into a completely different structure. Such an intervention suggests a primitive and un-
conscionable form of spoliation completely at odds with the objectives of
scientific archaeology and conservation theory.

But when we consider how it proposed to reuse this ancient building stone,
this papal license to demolish the Ponte Mammolo appears in very a different
light. The 1549 license was issued approximately four months before the work
site at the Ponte Santa Maria was brought to a close, a moment of maximum
effort with its builders working feverishly to finish in time for the Jubilee. With
this situation in mind, the pragmatic aims of this document become clearer.
The destruction of the Ponte Mammolo would furnish the necessary materials
to ensure the repair and preservation of the Ponte Santa Maria.

In a sense, the proposed strategy of extracting travertine from the Ponte Mammolo to integrate this material into the Ponte Santa Maria satisfied one of the primary goals of contemporary preservation theory, as it placed a premium upon maintaining the physical integrity of the original artifact. According to the twentieth-century Italian conservator Cesare Brandi, "restoration must aim to reestablish the potential unity of the work of art, as long as this is possible without producing an artistic or historical forgery, and without erasing every trace of the passage of time left on the work of art."[72] Brandi emphasized that a restoration should ensure the artistic coherence of an object. The restoration of the Ponte Santa Maria conformed to this principle of reestablishing the "potential unity" of the bridge by stitching together its fabric as an organic whole, even though it achieved this goal by robbing travertine from another ancient bridge. In addition, the fact that Maestro da Bologna was sent to Tivoli with the express aim of finding a perfect match for the existing stones of the Ponte Santa Maria suggests the sophistication of Renaissance preservation practices. These builders paid close attention to the specific quality of their building materials and identified a similar ancient structure to supply the exact needs of their work site.[73]

Other reasons could further justify this project. Not only was the building stone of the Ponte Mammolo a perfect match for the building stone of the Ponte Santa Maria, but these same materials could be transported to the work site in Rome via the Aniene itself. The individual blocks could be dismantled and shipped down to Rome by the same water route used by excavators at the Tivoli quarries to deliver travertine to the capital. The convenient location of the Ponte Mammolo on the Aniene thus eliminated the need for the more expensive and laborious transport of building stone by land.[74]

Finally, as we saw in the discussion of the fourteenth-century statutes, the Ponte Mammolo had long been exempted from the measures protecting all the other Tiber crossings from heavy wagon traffic. The Ponte Mammolo, alone of all the Roman bridges, remained open to this cumbersome and destructive kind of freight transportation. As a consequence it may have suffered more damage, and perhaps for this reason, the bridge was also considered to be more expendable.[75]

When we consider such factors, we realize that dismantling the Ponte Mammolo to restore the Ponte Santa Maria actually had much to recommend it to sixteenth-century audiences. Unlike the Ponte Mammolo, the Ponte Santa Maria was invaluable to the city of Rome. Paul III wanted to avoid disrupting the Jubilee at all costs, which could justify this sacrifice. Indeed, the 1549 license, at the same time that it might be judged a death warrant for the Ponte Mammolo, also revealed an innovative and imaginative approach to preservation problems, reinforcing yet again the key point that the forces of preservation and destruction are intimately bound together.

As it so happens, Maestro da Bologna did not end up using the powers granted him by the 1549 license. The superstructure of the Ponte Santa Maria was completed very quickly, within four months, and the rapid timeline of this work suggests that much of the remaining portions were executed using timber rather than masonry construction. It seems that the Renaissance builders decided at this point not only to forgo the destruction of the Ponte Mammolo but perhaps to forgo the use of stone entirely, and thus the Ponte Mammolo remained standing until the nineteenth century.[76]

It is quite possible that the decision not to demolish the Ponte Mammolo was also driven by changing Renaissance ideas about preservation. The notion of sacrificing this ancient bridge for its materials conflicted with the humanist concerns to preserve and defend all ancient and historic artifacts. We know that Michelangelo himself consciously decided against using ancient materials in other building projects.[77] Perhaps his involvement at the Ponte Santa Maria even contributed to the eventual decision to forgo this particular solution.

The 1551 Restoration of the Ponte Santa Maria

The story of the 1551 restoration of the Ponte Santa Maria has long been told from the perspective of Giorgio Vasari. In his *Life of Michelangelo,* Vasari related that Nanni di Baccio Bigio, a member of the *setta Sangallesca* and a notorious enemy of both Michelangelo and Vasari, forced Michelangelo to step down from overseeing the restoration of the Ponte Santa Maria. Vasari claimed that after the death of Paul III, Nanni's supporters in the papal court persuaded the newly elected Julius III to appoint Nanni to lead this project instead of Michelangelo.[78] Having attained this goal, Nanni then sold off much of the ancient building stone that protected the flanks of the Ponte Santa Maria, and replaced it with shoddy materials.[79] This work proved to be no match for the Tiber, and thus Vasari's narrative reached a triumphant climax with the collapse of the Ponte Santa Maria in 1557: the buckling of the ancient bridge not only served to vindicate Michelangelo, but also blacklisted Nanni forever in the canonical history of art. Vasari reported that Michelangelo foretold the ruin of the Ponte Santa Maria as they were crossing it together: "Giorgio, this bridge is trembling beneath us; let us spur our horses, so we are not on it when it falls."[80]

As Claudia Conforti has pointed out, for all of the anecdotal appeal of Vasari's narrative, it is not always consistent with other surviving evidence.[81] As we have seen, Michelangelo was already forced to scale back his involvement in the project because of other factors. Moreover, this first restoration project ended in October 1549, just in time for the Jubilee. Nanni on the other hand received a new contract for the restoration of the Ponte Santa Maria in July 1551. Vasari claimed Nanni's meddling caused Michelangelo to be demoted, and yet their interventions on the ancient bridge should be seen as unrelated. Nanni's restoration followed Michelangelo's after a fitting pause of two and a half years. Thus Vasari intentionally distorted the facts in order to assign Nanni full

responsibility for the disaster of 1557.[82] This enabled him to excoriate the work
of a contemporary competitor he despised, while also shielding Michelangelo
from criticism that the great artist could be in any way held responsible for this
terrible failure.

On 14 September 1557, when a powerful flood undermined the Ponte Santa
Maria, it ruptured the bridge deck for the first time in recorded history (figure
6.6). According to an account by Angelo Oldradi, "there has been an enormous
Tiber flood. . . . [I]t has taken away half of the Ponte Santa Maria, along with the
pretty little chapel built by Julius III which stood at the center of the structure,
which was built with great art and expense."[83] After centuries of resistance, the
bridge finally gave way. Oldradi exaggerated the impact of the flood on the
bridge, but its damage was still significant: it undermined the pier second from
Trastevere, pulled down the deck above, and made the bridge impassable.[84] In
addition, the flood carried away the historic and recently renovated chapel dedicated to the Virgin.

Yet while the restoration of 1551 was clearly insufficient, we still need to
reconsider the legacy of Vasari's account, which has perpetuated such a strong
bias in the literature against Nanni.[85] Nanni himself left an unfavorable record

FIGURE 6.6.   The collapse of Ponte Santa Maria in 1557, by Giovanni Antonio Dosio,
Uffizi 2582A. The upper image shows the pier as it was restored in 1575 by Matteo
da Castello for Gregory XIII.

in the form of a letter where he congratulated himself for his quick restoration of the bridge.[86] Despite this incriminating evidence, Nanni's engineering abilities may have been rather better than this episode would lead us to expect.[87] We may better evaluate Nanni's intervention by reviewing the conditions of the contract under which he worked.

Dated 3 July 1551, issued by Cardinal Giovanni Ricci and his representative Giulio Sauli, the new contract for the Ponte Santa Maria was intended to render permanent the restoration inaugurated by Paul III.[88] This was made clear in its opening paragraph, which declared "Maestro Nanni di Bartholameo Lippi agrees to rebuild the foundation of the pier of the Ponte Santa Maria which was rebuilt [in part] last year and which remains to be completed."[89] At the same time, the contract also introduced specific conditions to restrict Nanni's work. As we will see, these restrictions would have major implications for the future stability of the Ponte Santa Maria.

Throughout, the contract emphasized the importance of preserving the original design of the Ponte Santa Maria. To this end, it mandated the use of a uniform structural system: "[Nanni is] to raise the pier to the same height as the other piers constructed under Nicholas V and Martin V, using travertine for the exterior and good materials such as bricks or rubble in the same way that the others are built."[90] The contract was concerned with aesthetic issues as well, stipulating that there should be no visible differences between Nanni's restoration and the preceding work: "it should not be possible to distinguish any differences, either in the way the foundations are built, or in the way that the stones are replaced into the aforesaid vaults."[91] Not unlike what we have already seen in the Ponte Mammolo project, the point of this clause was to ensure a seamless connection between the new construction and the original structure.

The contract even outlined the exact process by which Nanni should conduct his restoration. After building a caisson or watertight retaining wall around the foundation, he was required to proceed as follows: "drain the water from around the footing, and then, exposing the cutwater at its lowest point, he will then begin to rebuild this foundation, replacing broken and ruined stones as he proceeds from here, moving upward toward the arches."[92] In this way Nanni was ordered to replace the critically damaged stones first at the lowest level near the waterline before moving upward.

As for the upper portions of the bridge that showed less damage, the contract imposed even stricter conditions upon his work: "it is of great consideration to the supervisors of the project that if Maestro Nanni should need to rebuild the pier from its foundations, he should only reinforce and restore the vaulted arches, and not rebuild these entirely."[93] The contract ordered Nanni to refrain from rebuilding the upper portion of the bridge in the way that he had rebuilt the piers. The papal officials who issued the contract were thus determined to leave as much of the bridge as possible in its original, unrestored condition.

Financial considerations may have played a part in shaping this agenda. Cardinal Ricci was renowned for his financial acuity, and thus he was likely to regard such thrifty measures with favor.[94] The history of the Ponte Santa Maria proved that costs for bridge repair had an alarming tendency to spiral swiftly upward, and such measures placed a cap upon these expenses. But funding was not the only consideration here. The contract placed particular emphasis on limiting the degree to which Nanni's restoration changed the original artifact, indicating that its writers were also motivated by a desire to preserve the Ponte Santa Maria intact. The contract expressed a restrictive, even rigid, notion of preservation practices, seeking to guarantee the survival of the original ancient fabric despite Nanni's interventions.[95]

Although historians have long assumed that the collapse of 1557 was Nanni's fault, this botched restoration was thus also the result of the conditions imposed by the contract itself, which deliberately restricted the scope of his rebuilding efforts. This could only hamper Nanni's efforts to restore the bridge and prevent him from conducting a more thorough repair. Yet if these meticulous restrictions prevented Nanni from destroying the ancient fabric of the Ponte Santa Maria, the Tiber itself had no inhibitions about such matters, as demonstrated decisively by the flood of 1557.

The Last Sixteenth-Century Restorations:
Pius IV and Gregory XIII

The collapse of the Ponte Santa Maria in 1557 caused turmoil in the papal capital. As Gamucci reported in the passage with which this chapter begins, the buckling of the bridge affected not only ordinary Romans but also merchants and traders who used the bridge every day to transport goods into the *abitato*. It also impeded the long-distance movement of passengers and freight on the Via Aurelia. But in addition, the collapse of the Ponte Santa Maria also forced sixteenth-century Romans to reconsider their ideas about how this ancient landmark should be preserved. In the twenty years following the failure of Nanni's restoration, two major restoration projects were organized to restore this vital Tiber crossing. Significantly, the meticulous preservation of the ancient fabric of the Ponte Santa Maria was not a primary consideration in either of these subsequent projects.

On 3 July 1561, the documents of the civic administration reported that Pius IV decided to repair this important traffic artery:

> We report to the assembly that Our Most Holy Father said yesterday
> that he had decided the Ponte Santa Maria should be restored in
> wood as it was not possible for the moment to rebuild it in stone,

and rebuilding it with a protective roofing would amount to around three thousand ducats, and without this roofing would come to around two thousand. And it would endure for twenty years with a roof, and ten without. And for all this he placed a deposit to launch this work.[96]

This project, like the project realized by Paul III in 1549, was from its inception a purely temporary measure.[97] Pius IV ruled out masonry construction from the beginning: "it was not possible for the moment to rebuild it in stone." This intervention was not intended in any way to approximate the ancient structure of the Ponte Santa Maria. Instead, it was a purely utilitarian solution to answer pressing Roman traffic needs until more permanent arrangements could be made.[98] Timber construction had the key advantage of being much easier to manipulate and less expensive than masonry. But it was also much more perishable, as indicated by the two proposed alternatives: the outside limit of the expected life span of a wooden bridge was set at twenty years. This structure would not be able to withstand constant and heavy traffic for long.

With immediate traffic needs taking priority over durability, preparations were made to build a wooden span across the broken pier. However, according to Girolamo Ferrucci's annotations in the 1588 edition of Andrea Fulvio's *Antiquitates urbis*, the restoration implemented by the civic magistrates soon met with disaster:

> [B]ecause it was very convenient for the traffic in merchandise that comes from the Ripa, which is the principal port of the Tiber in Rome, the *popolo romano* attempted in 1561 to rebuild the Ponte Santa Maria in wood as this was a less costly option, only for the convenience of bringing the aforesaid merchandise and wines from the Ripa; and having built a handsome structure, where they spent the sum of eight thousand ducats, while they sought to pull it from one extremity to the other of the bridge with pulleys and trusses, and having almost reached the other bank, the weight became too much, and the largest beams which were holding up the entire weight suddenly snapped, and it all fell precipitously into the Tiber, breaking everything up, and it all went to ruin and perdition, so that it was not possible to recuperate anything at all.[99]

Even if this wooden construction was designed to be only temporary, it was still conceived on an ambitious scale. Ferrucci indicated that its final cost was more than four times the anticipated costs proposed in 1561. Yet despite this major outlay of money and effort, it all came to nothing, and the Ponte Santa Maria remained impassable.

The final and most ambitious sixteenth-century restoration of the Ponte Santa Maria occurred in preparation for the Jubilee of 1575, sponsored by Gregory

XIII.[100] Following the recent failure of the temporary timber solution, a permanent masonry solution now seemed much preferable. Matteo da Castello was
hired to rebuild the second pier from Trastevere in the form of a masonry behe-
moth, thus presumably avoiding the mistakes made in both the 1551 and 1561
restorations.[101] The indomitable strength of this pier is still evident today,
where it supports the western end of the Ponte Rotto. Its gigantic stepped
footing resembles more a pyramid than a pier, with thick layers of reinforced
masonry rising in concentric bands from water level. This was a restoration
that was not taking any chances.[102]

As in earlier reconstruction phases of the Ponte Santa Maria, the Conservators again played an active role in this project. According to a document dated
1574, Conservator Giovanni Battista Cecchini even proposed the exceptional
step of authorizing the collection of ancient building stone from the *coscia Colisei* to facilitate its completion:

> *Magnifici signori*, because all works that are begun must come to their
> necessary end, for this reason it appears necessary to us, that as we
> are still lacking great quantities of travertine building stone with
> which to finish the restoration of the Ponte Santa Maria, and for now
> there are not any that can be brought to the work site; and it is said
> that at the Colosseum there is a great quantity of such stones lying
> under the ruins that have fallen, and they are not being used, and
> these stones could be excavated for this need.[103]

The fact that the Conservators entertained the notion of sacrificing stone from
the ruined *coscia Colisei* to hasten the completion of the Ponte Santa Maria suggested the gravity of the situation. The civic magistrates were the guardians of
ancient Rome, and yet this Conservator acknowledged that the ancient remains
of the Colosseum might be better used to restore the Ponte Santa Maria than
lying scattered on the earth. The desperate need for travertine stone prompted
this controversial step. It is telling, however, that when it came to a vote, this
pragmatic solution was rejected by a clear majority.[104]

The inscription commemorating the restoration of 1575, still visible today
on the parapet of the Ponte Santa Maria, declared that the preservation of antiquity remained the shared duty of both the pope and the Conservators in Renaissance Rome:

> By the will of Gregory XIII, Pontifex Maximus, and the Senate and
> People of Rome: The Pons Senatorum whose ancient arches col-
> lapsed and were then later rebuilt, when the impetus of the river
> again pulled them down, was restored to its original strength and
> beauty in the Jubilee Year 1575.[105]

Of course, Gregory XIII, like his predecessors, played a prominent role in this
restoration, as commemorated in many new decorative details added to the

Ponte Santa Maria. The Buoncompagni family insignia, the rampant dragon, was inserted in all the spandrels of the bridge as well as the sculpted shields placed over the lunettes, helping to cancel out the evidence for earlier papal efforts to shore up the ancient structure.[106]

At the same time, the inscription declared that the Conservators and all the people of Rome also participated in the ongoing effort to preserve this ancient bridge. Its formulation suggested that the preservation of antiquity in Renaissance Rome depended upon the close collaboration of these different constituencies. The decision to refer to the bridge as the Pons Senatorum rather than Ponte Santa Maria in the inscription may have been intended to evoke the august lineage of antiquity, but it seems more than pure coincidence that the name *Senatus* was also employed by the civic magistrates as well as by the college of cardinals to refer to their own assemblies.[107] This last Renaissance incarnation of the Ponte Santa Maria, or the Pons Senatorum, thus exalted the collaborative forces of the civic government and the papal court in their ongoing efforts to keep the Roman past alive.

Preservation, Destruction, and Experimentation

On Christmas Eve in 1598, the worst flood in the history of Rome destroyed the western half of the Ponte Santa Maria.[108] Although the pier restored by Matteo da Castello in 1575 held firm, it was now the two piers closest to the Forum Boarium that gave way. The Tiber finally gained the upper hand on this ancient bridge with its daring five-pier design, and the fallen piers were never again rebuilt (figure 6.7).

In later centuries the bridge assumed a new identity, as suggested by eighteenth-century descriptions which noted that the structure was accessible by a gate, and the surviving bridge deck that projected into midriver was covered with earth and planted with grass.[109] Thus the Ponte Santa Maria became a private garden oasis suspended off the Trastevere riverbank.

In 1853, the bridge was again opened to traffic when a new suspension bridge reconnected the broken stub to the opposite side of the river (figure 6.8).[110] But shortly afterward, the construction of the Lungotevere embankments led to the removal of this new addition as well as the demolition of the surviving ancient pier closest to Trastevere. An entirely new bridge, the Ponte Palatino, was built just downriver to replace the Ponte Santa Maria. This created the Ponte Rotto as we know it today, where the single surviving arch carried on two piers stands cut off from the surrounding city. Indeed, this curious isolation may well represent the most radical change the bridge has yet experienced throughout its history.[111]

The history of Renaissance interventions at the Ponte Santa Maria reminds us that not all such preservation projects meet with success, and that in fact

FIGURE 6.7. View of Ponte Santa Maria, early seventeenth century, by Gerard Ter Borch. Rijksmuseum, Amsterdam, RP-T-1887-A-871.

FIGURE 6.8. Ponte Santa Maria with metal suspension bridge, photographer unknown, ca. 1860.

many efforts to safeguard historic monuments meet with crushing defeat. Yet it is counterproductive to simply dismiss these efforts as misconceived or as failures. The vital importance of the Ponte Santa Maria to the daily life of the city, as a heavily used piece of urban infrastructure, transformed it into a test case for a remarkable range of innovative interventions. Each of these tackled the problem of preservation in very different ways. As we reach the end of this book, it is worth recalling that the preservation of antiquity remains an experimental venture, and there is always much to learn from the study of earlier preservation interventions. The surviving fragment of the Ponte Santa Maria may yet have more surprises for us in store.

Conclusion

Rethinking Preservation
Practices in Renaissance Rome

The title of this book, *The Ruin of the Eternal City*, can suggest two alternative interpretations, depending on our reading of the word *ruin*. Before we consider how these different interpretations may affect our understanding of the archaeological history of Rome, however, we should consider the significance of the famous appellation of Rome as the Eternal City. The word *eternal* in this title implies that Rome has existed for a period of time that is infinite and, in fact, immeasurable. Not only has the Eternal City always existed, but it will always exist. The Eternal City is eternal precisely because it transcends our normal chronological categories.[1]

The *Oxford English Dictionary* indicates that *ruin*, used as a noun, has two primary senses. One of these suggests "that which actively causes ruin." In this sense, the ruin of the Eternal City attests to the aggressive destruction and devastation of the city of Rome. The advent of ruin, according to this definition, signals the onset of damage, loss, dishonor, even the ultimate downfall of the city itself. This definition of ruin evokes an image of ancient Rome under siege.

According to the conventional perspective of modern scientific archaeology, such an image can well describe the conditions inflicted upon the archaeological remains of the imperial capital since antiquity itself. Age and neglect contributed to extensive decay, as have the people who have lived in Rome throughout postclassical history. Modern archaeologists, as Rodolfo Lanciani himself observed, might wish that like Pompei, Rome had been buried by some epic volcanic eruption at the height of its imperial power: this would have preserved its

FIGURE 7.1. Arch of Constantine with repair scaffolding suspended from the attic story, by Robert Macpherson, ca. 1870.

authentic ancient identity intact, without the messy alterations and depredations of later history, making it available for recuperation by modern science and technology.[2] One of the primary aims, of course, of modern scientific archaeology and conservation practices has been to slow the progressive disintegration of these archaeological artifacts over time.

Yet it is impossible to arrest this process entirely. The effects of age and pollution continue to wear away the ancient remains. Modern tourism does its share as well, when tourists brush accidentally against the monuments, or pick up pebbles as souvenirs to take home from the Roman Forum. Even modern archaeological practices themselves cause permanent disturbances to archaeological stratigraphy and contribute to the process of continuous degeneration and loss. Pursuing this argument to its extreme conclusions, the Eternal City itself can be seen as moving in the direction of eventual extinction.

But if the loss of archaeological evidence may be inevitable, there is still a problem with this formulation. While the idea of extinction contradicts by definition the very idea of the Eternal City, by the same token, the Eternal City did not become eternal by being fossilized for posterity. The city was never intended to be placed in a time capsule for safekeeping, to be set aside and then opened at some later date. In the words of Lanciani himself: "Rome instead has always lived, and has lived at the expense of the past: every generation has absorbed, one might say, and destroyed the works of preceding generations."[3] One might add that every generation in Rome has also preserved these historic works as well. But it is precisely Rome's identity as an inhabited archaeological site that has ensured its constant regeneration and continuing vitality.

For this reason it is important to consider the second sense of ruin, which gives the ruin of the Eternal City a different meaning. Ruin does not refer only to the active destruction of an artifact, but refers also to the state consequent upon collapse, to the condition of the surviving artifact itself. From this angle, the ruin of the Eternal City invites us to consider not so much the process of destruction as what remains, what survives, what still endures despite the disintegration that has of necessity taken place.

As this book has sought to demonstrate, thinking about the ruin of the Eternal City in terms of how the ancient ruins have survived, rather than concentrating only upon their destruction, is the key point. This provides a useful means by which to reconceptualize the history of archaeology in Rome, and the impact of the rebuilding of the Renaissance papal capital upon the ancient remains. At the same time, it also invites us to broaden our ideas about preservation practices: thinking more about how preservation takes place, why it is important, and what it can achieve, not just in terms of specific sites but also in terms of forging culture and identity.

The semantic and symbolic openness of ruins to interpretation has enabled them to be rich carriers of meanings from the Renaissance, often identified as the originating moment of the fascination of Western culture with such evident markings of decay, linked in turn to the emergence of a new historical consciousness.[4] Beginning in the fifteenth century, the study of ruins served as a means to recuperate lost knowledge, stimulating both zealous antiquarian research and imaginative, even fantastic reconstructions.[5] In the eighteenth century the ruin became an image of natural disaster and the catastrophes of human history, whereas the nineteenth-century Romantics valorized the ruin as a symbol of artistic creation. For modernity, the ruin embodies a palpable remnant of a failed future.[6] These multiple embedded meanings make it all the more difficult to see ruins with a fresh perspective.[7]

Yet we are not as used to thinking about ruins as material artifacts that always require meticulous attention and care over time. Ruins, if anything, are even more delicate than ordinary buildings.[8] Thus our tendency to see the ruins of Rome as the tough survivors of a meteoric blast is only partly true: while we are inclined to see ruins as the result of destruction, they are just as much the result of careful preservation practices. The ceaseless interventions of countless generations have consciously sculpted the archaeological landscape of Rome that we see today (figures 7.2 and 7.3).

FIGURE 7.2. Temple of Saturn in the Roman Forum, viewed from the east, by Giovanni Antonio Dosio, ca. 1569. The surviving fragment of the Temple of Vespasian stands at the right, in front of the Tabularium and the slope of the Capitoline Hill.

Rethinking our conventional assumptions about destruction and preservation, and reassessing how different cultures in different places have developed preservation solutions that were relevant and applicable for their own time, in a nonjudgmental way, can be a very beneficial process. It will be salutary in reshaping the conventional narrative of architectural history, which focuses primarily on the production of new buildings and related issues such as patronage, commission, design, and execution. Our emphasis on a building's origins, although this may be of great interest, tends to overlook the larger and more complex social and cultural questions of how buildings transform and evolve over time.

By the same token, thinking about the process of preservation and destruction will be helpful for architecture as it is taught as a professional discipline. Design schools are of course fixated obsessively upon design as a creative process. And yet the idea of thinking about how a building is transformed after its construction, both by the end user and by time, is also of great significance. While the issue has received some critical attention, it remains peripheral to the profession.[9] But a building continues to be a creative process long after it leaves the studio. A more balanced approach to design can take pleasure in this reality,

FIGURE 7.3. Temple of Saturn in the Roman Forum, viewed from the west, by James Anderson, ca. 1860–70s. A nineteenth-century viaduct traveled around this structure to reach the top of the Capitoline Hill.

rather than attempting to resist it or somehow cover it up. Architecture is a collaborative process both in terms of its realization and in terms of its ongoing life.

A heightened awareness of the intertwined relationship between preservation and destruction is also valuable in terms of thinking about the problem of managing limited resources, which of course remains a mantra as we begin the second decade of the twenty-first century. People have been thinking about these problems, and balancing preservation against destruction, for centuries.[10] We can benefit by thinking more carefully about these historic methods and solutions, taking them seriously, in the effort to brainstorm new and alternative approaches.[11]

Until we are literally able to do what Freud suggested can only happen in the mind, by superimposing different artifacts not only from different periods but in every possible successive state and condition, we need to be thinking realistically about what we can hope to accomplish through preservation. Embalming the past cannot be the answer, no matter how much we want to ensure that the extraordinary Roman skyline of domes and towers remains unchanged forever. We might wish the Renaissance popes had not caused the destruction of antiquity, and that they had preserved the city exactly as they found it. And yet had they done this, Renaissance Rome would not exist. The same could be said for antiquity. Imperial Rome itself was built only through immense destruction. But as we have seen, despite the pressures of destruction, the force of preservation remained a powerful current throughout.

In her discussion of the ritual practice of the classical Roman triumph, Mary Beard has explored the relation between conservatism and innovation, as an issue that lies at the very heart of Roman identity and culture.[12] The study of anthropology has long suggested that the performance of a ritual according to sanctioned ancestral tradition is of course never exactly that. On the contrary, tradition here offers a flexible kind of framework, in which scrupulous attention to precedent mixes with what Beard terms "convenient amnesia." The result is the active construction of precedent, or the invention of tradition, one of the essential ways in which change may be accepted and legitimated in any culture. New rituals are given authority not by their novelty, but through the claim that they mark a return to the venerable traditions of the past.[13]

Beard's analysis of the interpenetration of conservatism and innovation in Roman ritual practice is equally applicable to Roman preservation practices. Of course preservation is to some degree a conservative if not reactionary process, one that purports to arrest or at least slow the inevitable process of change. But by the same token, preservation can also be seen as highly innovative, and even as a radically progressive force, in terms of enabling historical and cultural change. The claim to preserve material artifacts from the past allows for the impression of continuity. At the same time, the flexibility of preservation as a concept and as a practice, where the degree of its implementation may vary widely from case to case, also enables the implementation of significant, even revolutionary, social, political, and cultural transformations. This gives new meaning to the notion of the Eternal City itself, as an urban environment that has managed to retain unbroken connections to the past while also fostering and promoting ongoing and extraordinary change.

Although Julius II inaugurated the New St. Peter's, promoting the construction of a monumental new structure at the heart of the Vatican that had no precedent in either Roman antiquity or Renaissance Italy, he also insisted upon leaving the tomb of St. Peter intact. The preservation of the sanctity and integrity of that site was literally at the core of his project. Throughout the process, the hallowed ground containing the relics of the first apostle remained inviolate and undefiled by new construction.

Yet the scrupulous preservation of this venerated tomb did not prevent Julius II from embarking upon the most phenomenal transformation of Rome to have occurred since antiquity. The scale of this transformation was so vast that later historians have generally tended to forget that the very act of preservation was what justified this herculean undertaking from the outset. The tomb

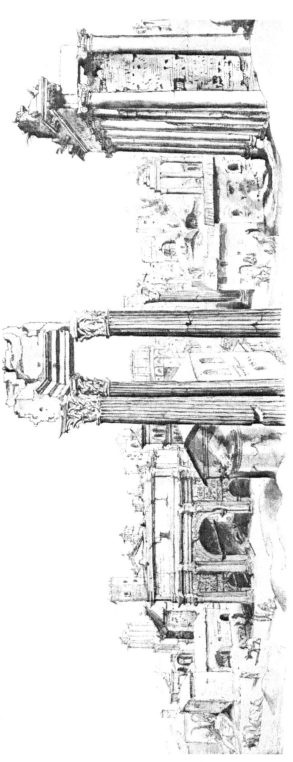

FIGURE 7.4. Roman Forum from Capitoline Hill, by Marten van Heemskerck, 1535. As noted by Hülsen and Egger (1931), 1.54. Heemskerck's panorama from the arcades of the Tabularium on the Capitoline Hill provided a remarkably comprehensive and precise record of this famous archaeological landscape. At the midpoint of the drawing, framed by the three colossal columns of the Temple of Vespasian, Heemskerck placed his signature and the date on the south wall of Santi Sergio e Bacco. Although this medieval church survived the demolitions for the triumph of 1536, it was eventually removed in 1562; see Hülsen (1927), 461–62.

of St. Peter was the touchstone of papal power, the ultimate source of papal legitimacy and authority for the Renaissance popes. Julius II was always profoundly aware of the reality that the enduring preservation of this artifact was
of the utmost importance not just as a way to exalt his own princely status but
for the power of the papacy as an institution, and for the history and future of
the church itself.

Culture, society, and history are dynamic entities in a state of constant flux.
Our material environment is also in a state of constant transformation, even if
our desire for stability and continuity with the past makes us often reluctant to
admit this fact. Our preservation strategies need to come to terms with these
dynamic forces while also preserving what mattered to others in the past, and
what also matters to us now in the present. This book reminds us that the continuing ruin of Rome is a tribute to its ongoing vitality as a living organism
(figure 7.4). Perhaps more than any other city in the world, Rome has flour-
ished for millennia by balancing the scrupulous preservation of the past against
the inevitable forces of change.

Appendix of
Archival Documents

Document 1

This papal license of 1426, the first dating from the reign of Martin V, authorized the excavation of travertine stones that were "not exposed to view" from the foundations of an ancient structure identified as the Templum Canapare. The license acknowledged that these excavations might provoke further destruction or even the collapse of the surviving remains. Yet it also imposed limitations intended to protect the site, such as explicitly prohibiting the removal of any additional archaeological material and limiting the validity of the license to the duration of one month.

Rome 1 iulii 1426
Benedictus de Guidalottis vicecam (nomi)
Calcarensibus Urbis extrahendi lapides ex fundamentis templi Canapare pro calce facienda et dandi medietatem calci Jacobo Tusculano card. licentiam concedit.
C. de Lombardis
Cam. Ap., Div. Cam. 9, 253r

[Transcribed by Cerasoli (1897), 141; Müntz (1884), 307–8; Wolf (2003), 73, note 49.]

Benedictus etc. providis viris Cole Machabeo, Paulo Mentabona, Iacobo Perlantis et Iacobo Thome, civibus et calcarensibus Romanis de regione Pinee, salutem etc.

De mandato Sanctissimi in Christo Patris et Domini Nostri Domini Martini, divina providentia pape quinti, super hoc vive vocis oraculo nobis facto, vobis et cuilibet vestrum frangendi et extrahendi nuperime ex fundamentis templi Canapare* lapides Tiburtinos non apparentes; ita tamen quod in extrahendo et fodiendo lapides huiusmodi templum ipsum ad ruinam devenire possit seu etiam demoliri, ac ex dictis lapidibus calcem per vos vel alios faciendi, et medietatem calcis huiusmodi per vos fiendi, tradendi et concedendi Reverendissimo in Christo Patri et Domino, Domino Cardinali Sancti Eustachii, aut alteri pro eo legitime recipienti plenam et liberam, tenore presentium, concedimus facultatem; volumus tamen quod reliquam medietatem dicte calcis absque requisitione nostra, aut nostra speciali licentia vendere vel alienare, aut alias distrahere nullatenus valeatis, presentibus per totum mensem presentem tantummodo valituris. Datum Rome apud Sanctosapostolos sub secreti etc., die prima mensis Iulii, indictione quarta pontificatus etc., anno nono.

*Although the Templum Canapare was long assumed to be the Basilica Aemilia, archaeologists are now less certain regarding its identity. This structure may have stood anywhere in the valley of the Forum between the eastern slope of the Capitoline Hill and the western slope of the Palatine Hill.

Document 1, *Translation*

Rome, 1 July 1426

From Benedictus de Guidalottis, Vice Chamberlain

License issued to the lime-kiln operators of Rome to extract stone from the foundations of the Templum Canapare to make lime and to provide half of their yield to Cardinal Jacopo Tusculano.

Cam. Ap., Div. Cam. 9, 253r

Benedetto etc. to the provident men: Cole Machabeo, Paulo Mentabona, Jacobo Prolantis, and Jacobo Thome, Roman citizens and lime-kiln operators in the rione of Pigna, greetings.

Regarding the mandate of His Most Holy Father and Lord in Christ, Our Lord Pope Martin V, by divine providence, with respect to the short speech relayed to us by word of mouth, we grant to you and anyone among you authorization to break and extract from the foundations of the Templum Canapare those travertine stones that are not exposed to view. If in extracting and excavating stones of this sort the temple itself should come to ruin or if it even should be demolished, we grant, by this present tenor, the full and free reign for you to make lime from these said stones. Half of the lime of this sort to be made by you is to be handed over and granted to the Most Reverend Father and Lord in Christ, Lord Cardinal of Sant'Eustachio, or to another man who accepts it legitimately on his behalf. It is our wish, however, that you should in no way sell or transfer the remaining half of the said lime without our investigation or special license, or that you should extract any more lime from the site. This permission will be valid for the entire present month.

Given in Rome at Santi Apostoli under [my] secret [seal] etc., on the first day of the month of July, in the fourth indiction* of the ninth year of the pontificate etc.

*Indiction refers to a medieval method of dating documents according to a fifteen-year cycle.

Document 2

Issued by Cardinal Raffaele Riario four months before the inauguration of the work site of the New St. Peter's, this papal license prohibited excavations from causing any damage to the church of San Nicola in Carcere.

Rome 3 ianuarii 1506
Declaratio cam. ap. super effodiendo tiburtino
Cam. Ap., Div. Cam. 57, 196v–97r

[Cf. partial transcriptions in Lanciani (1989), 1.185; Cerasoli (1897), 137.]

Declaratio Camerarii super effodientibus Tiburtinis.
Reverendissimus Epicopus Albanensis, Cardinalis Sancti Georgii, Dominus Pape Camerarius.
Venerabilibus viris dominis canonicis et capitulo Ecclesiae S. Nicolai in Carcere Tulliano de Urbe salutem in Domino . . . Hinc est quod cum nuper Sanctissimus Dominus Noster Iulius divina providentia papa II per suas literas subdatas Rome apud Sanctum Petrum VIII Kal. Novembris anno II vobis pro solutione silicatem Factas anno domos primus ecclesias . . . per spectabiles viros Dominos stratarum et edificiorum alme urbis magistros ac dominorum eiusdem dicte ecclesie pro amplianda via ante dictam ecclesiam demolicarum facultatem et licentiam effodiendi marmora et lapides tiburtinos in quibuslibet locis presentes ecclesiae dummodo non in ecclesia concesserit et nos presentam facultatem de mandato sue Sanctitatis approbaverimus ac per nostras patentes litteras prout in illis latius continetur concesserimus, quarum magistratorum . . . et spectabiles viri d. Iacobus de Alberinis et Hieronymus de Picchiis moderni magistri stratarum et edificorum eiusdem urbis asserentes effosionem per nos inchoatam non in pertientiis eiusdem ecclesie sed in presentis locis esse effodientes perturbarunt et terram iam inferri fecerunt . . .
Datum etc., die III Ianuarii MDVI Pontificatus anno tertio.
Reverendissimus Episcopus Alban . . . Cardinalis Sancti Georgii camerarius.

Document 2, *Translation*

Rome, 3 January 1506
Declaration from the Camera Apostolica regarding the excavation of travertine.
Cam. Ap., Div. Cam. 57, 196v–97r

The Most Reverend Bishop of Albano, Cardinal of San Giorgio, lord chamberlain of the Pope, to the venerable canons and chapter of the church of San Nicola in Carcere Tulliano in Rome, greetings.

From Pope Julius II, dated at Rome at St. Peter's on the eighth of November in the second year of his reign, regarding construction work at San Nicola in Carcere . . . to these honorable lords [of San Nicola]: while the *maestri di strade*, magistrates of Rome, are widening the road in front of the church, we award faculty and license to excavate marble and travertine stones at all these sites, however, in such a manner that these [excavations] are not undertaken in the church itself. Moreover we authorize the honorable magistrates Jacopo Alberini and Girolamo Picchi, *maestri di strade*, to excavate for us in those sites not belonging to the church, where the ground has already been disturbed . . .

Document 3

*This decree affirmed that the Conservators should take every precaution to prevent the demoli-
tion of antiquity in the expanding papal capital and punish those who committed reckless
destruction.*

ASC, Camera Capitolina, Credenza I, vol. 15, 55v (10 March 1520).

[Cf. partial transcription by Franceschini (1986), 144–45.]

Eodem die, mense, indictione, anno & Pontificatu & in eodem consilio idem Magnificus Dominus Prosper, primus conservator cum consensu etc., exposuit qualiter de
avitorum Romanorum gestis in amplitudine edificiorum & illorum decore nil aliud hiis
presentibus temporibus oculatim videtur, nisi ceu diruta palatia, terme, arcus, theatra &
amphiteatra ac balnea aquarumque latrine, que omnia si Romanorum facultas tanta
esset quod restaurari et conservari possent nulli dubium ad ostendendum illorum
animi ac potentie vires omnibus qui ex documentis ipsorum notitiam habent ex
locorum inspectione certiores redderentur. Quae omnia prae viribus illesa custodiri
debentur. Qua expositione audita beneque in huiusmodi senatus consulto cognita per
patres ibidem manentes decretum extitit quod si facultas restaurandi Romanis deest, a
devastantibus tueantur reique dum inveniuntur gravi pena puniantur; cum Magnificis
Dominis conservatoribus conservandi honus per summos pontifices in apostolicis
bubllis & aliis litteris impositum sit.

Document 3, *Translation*

ASC, Camera Capitolina, Credenza I, vol. 15, 55v (10 March 1520).

On this same day, and in the same month, indiction, year, and pontificate, and in this same council, Lord Prospero, chief Conservator with consent, etc., explained how none of the works of our Roman ancestors and the greatness of their buildings and decorations can be seen at these present times, except for ruined palaces, spas, arches, theaters and amphitheaters, baths, pools, and latrines, all of which, if the skill of the Romans were so great, could be restored and preserved. No doubt all those who are acquainted with their strength of spirit and power from documents of these very men might be made more certain from an inspection of these sites. All these [ancient remains] ought to be kept safe and unharmed at all cost. After this proposal was heard and well received by the council of the Senate, a decree was issued by the civic magistrates remaining there that if the Romans lacked the ability to restore [the ancient sites], that they be safeguarded from those who cause their destruction, and that if they [those who cause destruction] be found, they should be severely punished. May the responsibility of preservation fall upon the magnificent Conservators through the popes as affirmed in apostolic bulls and other letters.

Document 4

The following license issued by the civic government authorized Senator Squarcialupo to excavate on the Capitoline Hill under the close supervision of appointed civic officials.

ASC, Camera Capitolina, Credenza I, vol. 36, 84 (10 September 1520).

[Cf. partial transcription by Lanciani (1989), 1.257.]

In nomine Domini, Amen. Anno eiusdem MDXX, indictione nona, die vero XXII mensis Septembris, pontificatus etc., in mei scribe sacri senatus, etc., Magnificus et Egregius utriusque iuris Doctor, Dominus Prosper de Comitibus, primus Conservator cum consensu, etc., exposuit in concilio Domino Angelo de Cesis, Cancellario, Priori Capitum Regionum et capitibus Regionum consiliariis et aliis civibus ibidem manentibus, qualiter Illustris Dominus Petrus de Squarcialupis Senator ad presens urbis Almae, desiderat inceptum opus, id est, Iovium Tiburtino lapide per se inceptum perficere, intendatque Illos fodere prope Arcum Lucii Septimii, seu fodi facere ad perfectionem huiuscemodi operis, et id non sine licentia Magnificorum Dominorum Conservatorum et Magistratus. Qua prepositione audita et in concilio discussa ex senatus consulto decretum fuit quod pro ornatu et decore capitoline curie prefatus Illustris Dominus Senator discoperire possit seu detegere lapides et sua impensa et non alterius fodere volentis; quibus lapidibus detectis per Magnificos Dominos Conservatores, Cancellarium et Priorem capitum Regionum eligantur octo vel decem cives, qui se ad locum fossure conferant et diligenter videant, ne talis detectio et a[v]ulsio lapidum cuiuscumque generis existant; non preiudicare possit fundamentis dicti arcus et de illis tantum accipiat quantum se ad perfectionem operis predicti, residua vero sit ad utilitatem domus Dominorum Conservatorum, sed quod prius ad id provideatur, ne in alterius cedat utilitatem. Acta fuerunt hec in prima camera palacii Magnificorum Dominorum Conservatorum, presentibus Domino Luca de Mutianis et Domino Basilio de Tuncis testibus, etc.

Document 4, *Translation*

ASC, Camera Capitolina, Credenza I, vol. 36, 84 (10 September 1520).

In the name of our Lord, amen. In the same year of 1520, in the ninth indiction, on the twenty-second day of the month of September, [during the] pontificate [of Leo X] etc., in [the presence of me], the scribe of the sacred Senate, etc., the magnificent and distinguished doctor of both [canon and civil] laws, Lord Prospero de Conti, chief Conservator with consent, etc., explained in council to Lord Angelo de Cesi, the chancellor, the head of the *caporioni*, magistrates, and other citizens present, how the Illustrious Lord Pietro de Squarcialupi, Senator of the city of Rome, desires that the work that has begun, namely the loggia begun by himself with travertine stone, be completed, and proposes that they excavate or have people excavate near the Arch of Lucius Septimius [Severus] to the completion of this task, but not without the [excavation] license of the Magnificent Conservators and Magistrates. After this proposition had been heard and discussed in council, it was decreed by the Senate that as far as concerns the ornaments and decorations of the Capitoline Palace, the aforesaid Illustrious Lord Senator may discover or unearth stones and dig them up at his own expense and not according to any other person's will; [and that] after these stones have been unearthed, eight or ten citizens should be elected by the Magnificent Conservators, the chancellor, and the head of the *caporioni*, to go to the excavation site and supervise with diligence so that no further unearthing and tearing away of stones of any type whatsoever should take place; and that he [Senator Squarcialupi] may not threaten the foundations of the said arch, and that he may take only as many of the stones as necessary for the completion of the aforesaid task, and that the rest be used for the Palace of the Conservators; but let him [alone] be provided with the stones; these should not be ceded to others. Enacted in the main chamber of the palace of the Magnificent Conservators, with the witnesses, Lord Luca de Mutianis and Lord Basilio de Tuncis, [there] present.

Document 5

In the following decree the Conservators criticized the destructive intervention of Cardinal Trivulzio at the Forum of Nerva and appealed to the pope to assist them in preserving and defending the antiquities of Rome from damage.

ASC, Camera Capitolina, Credenza I, vol. 15, 67v (1 December 1520).

[Cf. partial transcription by Franceschini (1986), 145.]

Eodem die, mense, indictione, anno & Pontificatu idem Nobilis & Magnificus Dominus Franciscus in eodem concilio exposuit etc., qualiter aliqui lapidum fossores fundamenta Arcus Triumphalis Noè in foro divi Nerve foderunt & fossi eripuerunt, quorum unus de eius commissione carceratus nomine Francischinus dixit id fecisse de commissione et mandato Reverendissimi Domini Cardinalis Trivulsii; qui Reverendissimus Dominus Cardinalis de mandato S.D.N. captum liberare fecit; et nil aliud remansisse de avitorum memoria in urbe nisi permanentia edificia, que urbem illorum memoria decorant, que ab alienigenis non modica admiratione ac veneratione inspiciuntur; que quidem aedificia, et antiquitates omni virium conatu a Romanis civibus immunia & illesa conservari debent. Qua prepositione audita et permoleste discussa ex eodem senatus consulto decretum fuit quod Magnifici Domini Conservatores una cum Cancellariis, Priore & electis S.D.N. orent, ut ornamenta sue urbis a quibusvis Gotis & Vandalis illam devastantibus acerbissima vindicta conservet, & oportunis utatur remediis in aliorum exemplum.

Document 5, *Translation*

ASC, Camera Capitolina, Credenza I, vol. 15, 67v (1 December 1520).

On the same day, in the same month, indiction, year, and pontificate, the same noble and magnificent Lord Francesco [chief Conservator] explained in this same council how some stone excavators even excavated the foundations of the triumphal arch of Noè in the forum of the divine Nerva,* and when the stones were unearthed, they removed them; one of these men, named Francischinus, who was incarcerated for his action, said that he did so under the order and command of the Right Reverend Lord Cardinal Trivulzio; subsequently the Right Reverend Cardinal, under the order of our Most Holy Father, had the prisoner liberated; and [Lord Francesco said] that nothing else remained in the city of the memory of our ancestors, except for the permanent edifices, which grace the city with the memory of those men, [and] which are regarded by foreigners with much admiration, veneration, and praise; and every effort should be made by the citizens of Rome to preserve these buildings and antiquities safe and undamaged. After this proposal was heard and debated with great ardor by the same Senate, it was decreed that the Magnificent Conservators, together with the chancellors, prior, and elected officials, should ask our Most Holy Father to preserve the ornaments of their city from any Goths and Vandals, who lay waste to it with the most bitter vengeance, and to use the remedies at hand as an example for others.

* While the exact identification and location of the "Arca di Noè," or "Noah's Ark," in the Forum of Nerva is still debated, it seems to have included an arched opening into the southern end of the forum near the pair of engaged columns now known as *Le Colonnacce*.

Document 6

This excavation license authorized Cardinal Lorenzo Pucci, or Santiquattro, unrestricted access to excavate at the Baths of Caracalla for the construction of a new palace adjacent to the New St. Peter's.

>Rome 8 augusti 1524
>Patentes card. Laurentio Puccio fodiendi marmora pro constructione sui palatii.
>Cam. Ap., Div. Cam. 74, 131v
>
>Patentes pro Reverissimo Cardinali S Quattuor possit effodi lapides.
>F. Armellinus.
>Volentes Reverendissimum in Christo patrem Dominum Laurentium Puccium Ecclesie Sanctorum Quatuor Coronatorum presbyterum Cardinalem, qui Sanctae Romanae Ecclesiae membrum honorabile existit et in oneribus Romane Curie que iugiter de necessitate subire oportet diei pondus et estas substinet et pro ornatu urbis iuxta basilicam principis apostolorum Beati Petri pro eius habitatione sublime et ornatum palatium edifficari facit, favore prosequi generoso, ut prefatus Reverendissimus Cardinalis in loco urbis l'antoniana nuncupato pro fabrica dicti palatii, columnas, marmores et alia diversa lapidum genera absque aliquo impedimento effodi, et in dictam fabricam transportari facere posset et valeat, de mandato etc., sibi per presentes concedimus auctoritatem, licentiam et facultatem, mandantes prefectis stratarum Alme Urbis et aliis quibuscumque officialibus et deputatis ad quos spectat sub excommunicationis et alia nostri arbitrii pena quatenus effodientibus et transportantibus dictos lapides pro dicta fabrica et aliis agentibus pro prefato Reverendissimo Cardinali nullum impedimentum inferant aut inferri faciant molestiam, sed solum competum ferrant. Constitutione, ordinatione, statutis, consuetudinibus et stabiliminibus ceterisque contrariis non obstantibus quibuscumque. In quorum etc. Datum Rome in Camera apostolica die octava mensis Augusti 1524°, pontificatus D. Clementis anno primo.
>F. Cardinalis, camerarius.

Document 6, *Translation*

Rome, 8 August 1524

License to Cardinal Lorenzo Pucci to excavate marble for the construction of his palace.

Cam. Ap., Div. Cam. 74, 131v

Francesco Armellinus.

Wishing to bestow a generous favor upon the Right Reverend Father in Christ, Lorenzo Pucci, cardinal-priest of the church of Santi Quattro Coronati, who is an honorable member of the Holy Roman Church and bears the weight of work and the heat of the day in the burdens of the Roman Curia, which he out of necessity must continually endure, and who is having a sublime and ornate palace built for the beautification of the city next to the basilica of the prince of the apostles, St. Peter, for his home, we grant to him through the present statement, "De mandato etc.," the authority, license, and authorization that he, the aforesaid Right Reverend Cardinal, can and may have columns, marble, and other various stones excavated without any impediment at that site in Rome known as the Antoniana* for the construction of the said palace, and have them transported to the said construction [site], and we command under pain of excommunication and other penalties at our discretion that the street prefects of Rome [or the *maestri di strade*] and any other officials and deputees, to whom it befalls, that they cause no impediment or harassment to the excavators and transporters of the said stones for this construction site or to other men acting on behalf of the said Right Reverend Cardinal, but that they only render an account [regarding these excavations].

Issued by the Camera Apostolica in Rome on the eighth day of August 1524, in the first year of the pontificate of Clement VII.

F. Armellinus, chamberlain.

*The Thermae Antoninanae, better known as the Baths of Caracalla.

Document 7

This excavation license authorized Jacobo Romano the right to excavate in sites under ecclesiastical authority for the duration of a year in Rome. However, it prohibited him from causing any ruin, especially near sites known for their "anticaglie."

> Rome 12 ianuarii 1525
> Patentes jacopo fossori travertinorum
> Cam. Ap., Div. Cam. 74, 170v
>
> Patentes pro Iacobo Romano ut posset effodere in quibusque locis.
> F. Armellinus Medices etc.
> Dilecto nobis in Christo Iacobo Romano fossori tevertinorum aliorumque lapidum marmoreorumque salutem in Domino. Cum a nobis quispiam petit que iusta sunt et honesta et Camere apostolice proficua, tam rigor aequitatis quam ordo rationis exigit, ut ea diligentia nostra ad debitum perducantur effectum. Propterea eorum desiderio et iustis petitionibus graciam facere et Camere apostolice, ut par est, utilitati consulere volentes; de mandato et auctoritate etc., ut in urbe, montibus, speluncis, cavernis, ac omnibus locis Sancte Romane Ecclesie et Camere apostolice subiectis, et ubi de interesse privatorum non agatur, nec aliqua ruina presertim circa loca anticaglie nuncupata causetur, omnia genera lapidum predictorum perquirere et effodere valeas, tibi per presentes licentiam et facultatem concedimus per unum annum proxime duraturum; hac tamen conditione et conventione apposita quod de omnibus generibus lapidum predictorum, qui per vos inveniri contigerit eidem Camere apostolice tertiam partem applicare volumus, mandantes sub excommunicationis et arbitrii nostri pena omnibus et singulis ad quorum notitiam hec nostre litere pervenerint quavis auctoritate et dignitate fulgente te huiusmodi occasione non molestent neque molestari permittant, sed a quibuscumque molestantibus personis immediate defendant in contrarium, facientibus non obstantibus quibuscumque. In quorum fidem etc. Datum Rome in Camera apostolica die XII° Ianuarii M°DXXV° Pontificatus Sanctissimi Domini Nostri Clementis Pape, VII anno eius secundo. De Curia
> Visa in Camera apostolica A. Puccius.
> Hippolytus de Cesis.

Document 7, *Translation*

Rome, 12 January 1525
License authorizing excavations by travertine excavator Jacopo Romano.
Cam. Ap., Div. Cam. 74, 170v

F[rancesco] Armellino de' Medici, etc.

To our beloved in Christ, Jacopo Romano, excavator of travertine and other marble stones, greetings.

When someone asks of us what is just and advantageous to the Camera Apostolica, both the rigor of equity and the order of reason demand that such [petitions] be [answered]. Furthermore, wishing to satisfy their just petitions and to take into account their usefulness for the Camera Apostolica, as is only fair, regarding this mandate and authority, we grant you through this present letter the license and capacity for the duration of the next year to search for and excavate every type of the aforesaid stones in Rome, in the mountains, caves, hollows, and in all places subject to the Holy Roman Church and the Camera Apostolica, so long as it is not done in the interests of private individuals or causes any ruin, especially near sites known as *anticaglie*. Yet under the condition and agreement that we establish, a third of every kind of the aforesaid stones that you discover will go to the Camera Apostolica. We command each and every person (of whatever authority or illustrious dignity) who should come across our letter, under pain of excommunication and in conformity with our will, not to harass you or permit you to be harassed . . . but that on the contrary they immediately defend you from any such harassment . . .

Given at Rome in the Camera Apostolica, 12 January 1525, in the second year of the pontificate of Our Most Holy Lord, Pope Clement VII, from the Curia.

Approved in the Camera Apostolica by A. Pucci.

Ippolito de Cesi.

Documents for the Forum of Nerva (1526)

Document 8

The following three documents (8–10) record a controversy between the Conservators and the maestri di strade *regarding the appropriate means to preserve ancient remains at the Forum of Nerva.*

ASC, Camera Capitolina, Credenza I, vol. 15, 149–50 (3 March 1526).

[Cf. partial transcriptions by Lanciani (1989), 1.278; Franceschini (1986), 146, note 16.]

Eodem die, mense, indictione, anno et pontificatu, & in eodem consilio fuit data custodia Arcus Traiani Imperatoris Capiti Regionis Montium, qui sollicitus esse debeat habere curam, ne vulterius devastetur per Magistros Stratarum. Acta fuerunt hec in prima camera Palatii dominorum Conservatorum, presentibus Domino Angelo de Vallatis & Domino Hieronymo Castrono testibus, etc.

Document 8, *Translation*

ASC, Camera Capitolina, Credenza I, vol. 15, 149–50 (3 March 1526).

In this counsel custody of the Arch of Emperor Trajan was awarded to the *caporione* of Monti,* who ought to take solicitous care to ensure that the *maestri di strade* cause it no further damage. Enacted in the main chamber of the palace of the Lord Conservators, in the presence of Lord Angelo de Vallatis and Lord Girolamo Castrono, the witnesses, etc.

*The large district (*rione*) of Monti extended from the upper reaches of the Esquiline Hill down into the area of the imperial forums.

Document 9

ASC, Camera Capitolina, Credenza I, vol. 15, 150 (23 March 1526)

[Cf. partial transcription by Lanciani (1989), 1.278.]

Item super lapidibus peperignis amotis ab Arcu Traiani, quod Magnifici domini Conservatores curent omnibus melioribus via & modo quibus fieri potest quod destructores in esse pristinos illos reponant.

Document 9, *Translation*

ASC, Camera Capitolina, Credenza I, vol. 15, 150 (23 March 1526)

Also regarding the peperino stones removed from the Arch of Trajan:* the Magnificent Lord Conservators should ensure by every possible way and means that these stones be returned by their destroyers to their original locations.

* The Arch of Trajan or *Arcus Traiani* has been identified as the remains of a structure that once linked the Forum of Nerva with the Forum of Trajan.

Document 10

ASC, Camera Capitolina, Credenza I, vol. 15, 150 (26 March 1526).

Eodem die, mense, indictione, anno & pontificatu & in eodem consilio idem Dominus Franciscus Conservator et exposuit, quod sibi videtur, quod Arcus Traiani in parte per Magistros Stratarum dirutus, ne alii audeant antiquitates Urbis devastare quod restauretur; qua expositione audita decretum ex consulto senatus extitit quod diruti lapides meliori modo quo poterit in suo pristino esse reponantur.

Document 10, *Translation*

ASC, Camera Capitolina, Credenza I, vol. 15, 150 (26 March 1526).

On the same day, month, indiction, year, and pontificate, and in the same council, Lord Francesco, Conservator, etc., explained that, in his opinion, the Arch of Trajan was partly destroyed by the *maestri di strade*, nor should others dare to lay waste to the antiquities of the city, as it is in the process of being restored; after this explanation was heard, it was decreed by the Senate that the demolished stones should be returned by whatever means to their original locations.

Document 11

Giovanni Maria della Porta, minister of the Duke of Urbino and resident in Rome, acquired permission with this excavation license to excavate near the Baths of Constantine on the Quirinal Hill. The license required him to return the site to its original appearance.

Rome 21 februarii 1527

Mandatum Johanni Marie de la Porta ducis Urbini oratori effodiendi marmora in Quirinale.

Cam. Ap., Div. Cam. 76, 174r

Franciscus Armellinus camerarius.

Dilecto nobis in Christo Iohanni Marie de la Porta domini Ducis Urbini apud Sanctissimum Dominum Nostrum oratori salutem in Domino. Cum nemini infra terram abscondita et oculta co[m]modo et utilitati esse agnoscamus tuque prout nobis nuper exponi fecisti unicam quandam in monte Quirinali prope thermas . . . marmora trivertina ac alia lapidum genera inesse reperisti. Cupiens illa effodi et in tui vel aliquorum utilitatem converti nobis in permissis licentiam et facultatem tibi concedere dignimur humiliter [. . .] fecisti. Nos attentis permissis ac tuis in hac parte [. . .] inclinati. De mandato etc., tibi facultatem et potestatem, in quantum [. . .] tua unica se extendit, effodiendi et effodi faciendi; dummodo prius idonee caveas loca in quibus effodere designas in pristinum et eandem formam in quam ad presens sunt redigendi, nec ob id aliquid vienus periculi vel indemnitatis inferatur damus, concedimus et elargimur, mandantes universis almae urbis officialibus, ne te vel ministros pro deputante impediant vel molestent sub excommunicationis et aliis arbitrio nostro imponentibus penis. In quorum fidem etc. Datum Rome in Camera apostolica, die XXI Februarii MDXXVII, pontificatus Sanctissimi Domini Nostri, Domini Clementis VII, anno quarto et in via pontifica non tamen edificia etiam antiqua demoliendo.

Franciscus Cardinalis Camerarius.

B. de Alexandris.

Document 11, *Translation*

Rome, 21 February 1527

Mandate authorizing Johanni Marie de la Porta, orator of the Duke of Urbino, to excavate marble on the Quirinal Hill.

Cam. Ap., Div. Cam. 76, 174r

Francesco Armellinus, chamberlain, to our beloved in Christ, Giovanni Maria della Porta, orator of the Duke of Urbino at our Most Holy Lord, greetings in the Lord.

While we acknowledge that below the earth there are hidden secrets both suitable and useful to no one, and given that you have recently communicated to us that on the Quirinal Hill near the Baths . . . you have discovered travertine marble and other kinds of stones. We hereby give, grant, and bestow upon you the authorization and power, in so far as [you are capable], to excavate [this site] or have [it] excavated, provided first that the designated caves and sites in which you plan to dig are returned to the pristine and original form in which they are at present, and moreover, on that account, [that these excavations] cause no danger or indemnity. We command all the officials of Rome not to impede or harass you or your assistants . . . under pain of excommunication or other penalties at our disposal. In whose faith, etc.

Given at Rome in the Camera Apostolica on 21 January 1527 in the fourth year of the pontificate of our Most Holy Lord, Lord Clement VII: and no building or ancient artifact may be demolished on the Via Pontificia.

Cardinal Francesco, chamberlain.

B. de Alexandris.

Document 12

This excavation license, the first to be recorded in the Diversa Cameralia after the Sack of Rome in 1527, required Francesco Cochicio to obey strict preservation requirements. No damage to any ancient or modern public building was permitted, and following the excavations, the excavator was held responsible for restoring all sites to their original condition at his own expense.

> Rome 6 aprilis 1532
> Licentia fodiendi pro marmoribus et thesaurius Francisco Cochicio de Ameria.
> Cam. Ap., Div. Cam. 85, 201v–2v

Dilecto nobis in Christo, Francisco Cochicio de Ameria, Urbis habitatori, salutem etc. Exposuisti nobis in Camera Apostolica quod cum propter antiquas et modernas huius Alme Urbis miserabiles ruinas diversa argenti et auri bona et localia pecunieque atque gemmarum et forsan thesauri per homines tunc temporis absconditi quos morte tunc preventa effodere vel manifestare non poterunt necnon etiam quam plura alia una cum marmoreis porfireisque et alterius diversi generis lapidibus, ruinis huiusmodi forte oppressis, occulta remanserint, sperares si tibi effodiendi et detegendi illa a nobis licentia et facultas concederetur aliqua ex dictis bonis et thesauris saltem lapidibus reperire et lucrari, ideo nobis humiliter supplicasti ut licentiam et facultatem huiusmodi de speciali gracia tibi concedere dignimur. Nos igitur volentes tibi graciam facere specialem ac operepretium esse, existimantes ea que occulta et deperdita iacent usui et decori humano restituere benemerito ex auctoritate . . . tibi ut ubicumque locorum Sancte Romane Ecclesie et presertim Alme Urbis et illius Territorii libere et licite effodere et effodi facere possis et valeas dummodo antiqua vel moderna publica edificia et loca etiam publica seu privata nimium damnificentur vel si damnificari necesse fuerint in pristinum statum reponi possint a licentia, et facultatem concedimus, mandantes omnibus et singulis Alme Urbis et aliorum locorum Sancte Romane Ecclesie gubernatoribus locatum, trextibus barisciellis, executoribus et officialibus quibuscumque quovis nomine nuncupatis et quacumque auctoritate et dignitate fungentibus, ad quos spectat et quibus presentes ostense fuerint. Quantus in locis publicis . . . [et] in privatis . . . de licentia . . . effodere sinant et permittant ac etiam si opus fuerit auxilium et favorem quem duxeris necessarium et oportinum ad omnem tuam simplicem requisitionem prestent et concedant sub pena nostri arbitrii, volentes enim quod de hiisque per te in locis tuis propriis aut publicis invenientur Tertia Camere Apostolice et reliquas duas tibi in privatis vero locis unam Camera Apostolica alias tibi et alias pro nostri loci vel prout cum eo tradere et quod loca in quibus effoderis in pristinum statum tuis expensis reponere tenearis. Volumus quoque quod antequam effodere incipias ipsarum camera certi facere tenearis ad effectum, ut sibi . . . aliquem assistentem addere noluerit id non ignoret . . . Datum Rome in Camera apostolica die sexta mensis Aprilis MDXXXII.

Document 12, *Translation*

Rome, 6 April 1532
License to Francesco Cochicio de Ameria to excavate marble and other treasures.
Cam. Ap., Div. Cam. 85, 201v–2v

To our beloved in Christ, Francesco Cochicio de Ameria, resident of Rome, greetings etc. You have declared to us in the Camera Apostolica regarding the ancient and modern [and] miserable ruins of this city of Rome, where diverse goods [of] silver and gold and perhaps [even] treasures of money and gems were hidden by men in the past. Then, when prevented by death, they were unable to excavate these sites or make them known, not to mention countless other [riches], together with marble, porphyry, and other various types of stone that lie buried beneath the ruins, and which remain hidden to this day. You hoped, if license and faculty to excavate and uncover these [riches] were granted to you by us, to discover and profit from the said goods and treasures, or at least these buried stones, and so you humbly requested from us that we deign to grant to you the license and faculty of this sort by our special grace. Therefore, deeming [your plan] to be worthwhile, we grant you permission to excavate or have excavated, freely and licitly, those things that lie hidden or lost . . . in Rome and in the territories belonging to the Roman Church, provided that you restore these buildings and sites to their original condition should these excavations cause too much damage to any ancient or modern public buildings, or even to any public or private sites, even if it is necessary that these be damaged . . . all church officials and governors are obliged to respect the conditions of this license . . . a third of the materials you unearth will go to the Camera Apostolica . . . you are obliged to return those sites in which you excavate to their original condition at your own expense. Given at Rome in the Camera Apostolica on the sixth day of April 1532.

Document 13

This mandate, issued under Paul III, authorized excavations and demolitions to display ancient remains along the triumphal route for the entry of Charles V.

> Rome 12 Januarii 1536
> Mandatum magistris stratarum Urbis.
> Cam. Ap., Div. Cam. 98, 89v–90v

> Dat Rome apud Camera apostolica die xii Jan 1536
> In primis fare spianar et reimpir et levar le acque dove faccia de bisogno in la strada de la scola Greca per in sino alla chiesia di S. Paulo, et rassettare la strada con le segate tanto di drento quanto di fuore, et per quelle persone della vigna più vicino, et altri vicini, ad che ne resulti maggior commodità, et beneficio, nel modo che vi e stato ordinato.
>
> Item rassettare la strada da San Paolo fine al fino delli Prati ad canto all'ultime vigne della via Appia fuor de la porta di S. Sebastiano, et similmente segtare la spianata et rempiere li bassi dove sonno fanghi & alargar nelli luochi strecti decta via Appia max^e apresso alla porta di S. Sebastiano, ad fine si possa vederla fatta.
>
> Item far rasettare nel medesimo modo, & spianar la strata predetta dalla porta sopradetta fino che se ha da rivoltare a Septisolio facendo aprire la vigna di Maphfei, qual incomincia a dicta rivolta & che essa ad Septem Solio damnificandola quanto mancho si possa.
>
> Item mettere in insula l'archo di Constantino quanto e largo con farli le ali incominciando alla fine alla vigna di m. Alex.° Roffino che fu di Io. Vinches qual ha el muro merlato a cusi dall'altra banda fino alla pianta del Lauro che vi sta.
>
> Item sequitar, spianar alarghare detta strada procendo all'archo di Tito, & far aprire la Vigna all'incontro di detto archo, quello dello magdaleni dove si faccia transito, quale essa dinanzi al muro di macellar.
>
> Item far buttare in terra l'hostaria di Cavalier quasi incontro a s. Adriano tanto che si scopra l'archo di Septimio.
>
> Item far levar quella casaccia la quale e attaccata alla torre dinanzi al detto archo, & levare un pezzo di tecto quale è attaccato alla detta casa ove si fanno sett[are] le caroze.
>
> 90v
> Item levar la casaccia dishabitata quale sta avanti al tempio di bacco.
>
> Item far fornire de ruinar le ruine cominciate da marforio sino in cima la costa ad man sinistra et dicta costa far sbassar più che si può per agguagliare di qua et dilla la strada.
>
> Item far la strada per le case di m. Mariano Stalla et vicini in capo al palazzo de s. Marco secondo l'ordine dato et levare el portico, di m. Marco Magdaleni.
>
> Item far far la mattonata da casa de Cesarini sino in campo di fiore.
>
> Item al uscita di campo di fiore dove è la Ruina di Maximi per questa intrata della Cesarea maesta allargar la strada in tutto o in parte secondo la volontà et ordine dattaci N. S.
>
> Item comandar per tutte le stradi di Roma dove sta impedimento di monti di sterchi o stabii o di altre cose, si debiano levar et tenerle nette sotto pene gravissime.

Document 13, *Translation*

Rome, 12 January 1536
Mandate to the *maestri di strade.*
Cam. Ap., Div. Cam. 98, 89v–90v

Signed at Rome in the Camera Apostolica on 12 January 1536

First level, fill holes, and drain standing water wherever necessary, to improve the road running from the scuola Greca (Santa Maria in Cosmedin) to the basilica of San Paolo; order and clean the roadway by putting down mown hay, also for those people in the nearest vigna, and others nearby, so that this results in greater commodiousness and benefit, in the manner that has been ordered.

Also order and improve the road from San Paolo to the end of the fields next to the last vigna on the Via Appia, beyond the gate of San Sebastiano, and similarly strew hay over the clearing and fill in the lower areas where there is mud, and widen the narrow areas of the aforesaid Via Appia, most of all near the gate of San Sebastiano, so the gate is more visible and prominent.

Also order and improve in the same way, and level the aforesaid road from the above-mentioned gate up to the point where it turns in front of the Septisolio (Septizodium), opening the vigna of the Maffei at this turn, and from this vigna to the Septizodium, taking care to cause as little damage as possible.

Also separate the Arch of Constantine from its adjacencies by a space that is again as wide as the arch, and create a processional route leading up to it, beginning at the end of the Roffino vigna, which used to belong to Vinches, with the crenellated wall, and on the other side in the same way up to the laurel plant growing there.

Also level and enlarge the aforesaid street proceeding from the arch of Titus, and open the vigna in front of this arch, that of the magdaleni where one passes through, up to that which is in front of the butcher's wall.

Also pull down the Hostaria di Cavalier standing almost directly opposite Sant'Adriano (the Curia), so as to reveal the Arch of Septimius Severus.

Also remove that shanty which is attached to the tower in front of the aforesaid arch, and remove the overhang attached to the shanty where they repair wagons.

90v

Also remove the abandoned house which stands in front of the Temple of Bacchus.

Also provide for the removal of the ruins from the Marforio up to the top along the left-hand side of the route and lower it as much as possible to level the roadway.

Also create a road from the houses of Mariano Stalla up to the top, to the palace of San Marco, according to orders, and remove the portico of Marco Magdaleni.

Also pave the roadway from the Casa Cesarini to the Campo dei Fiori.

Also at the exit from the Campo dei Fiori, at the ruins of the Maximi, widen the street for the triumphal entry of the Holy Roman Emperor, either all or in part, according to the will and orders of the Pope.

Also command that in all the streets of Rome, impediments such as heaps of dung or other refuse must be removed and these areas must kept clean under the most serious penalties.

Documents for the Pantheon (1524–31) and the Ponte Santa Maria (1549)

Document 14

The following three documents (14–16) record preparations by the civic officials for repairs conducted at the Pantheon.

ASC, Camera Capitolina, Credenza I, vol. 15, 125–26 (13 August 1524)

[Cf. partial transcription by Cerasoli (1909), 282.]

Eodem die, indictione, mense, anno & pontificatu idem Dominus Conservator exposuit qualiter S.D.N. vult quod de pecuniis portionum restauretur templum Sancta Mariae Rotundae; qua expositione audita & bene cognita per patres conscriptos ex senatusconsulto decretum extitit, quod Magnifici Domini Conservatores Sanctissimum Dominum Nostrum alloquantur, Suae Sanctitatis memoriae tradendo quod felix recordia Leonis X[i] sui patrui tales portiones edidit ad effectum quod Romanus populus universaliter de pecuniis ipsarum portionum fruerentur, et si de pecuniis portionum antiquitates Urbis restaurari debent, non ipsae portiones neque quod habet Romanus populus pro illarum restauratione sufficerent.

Document 14, *Translation*

ASC, Camera Capitolina, Credenza I, vol. 15, 125–26 (13 August 1524)

On the same day, in the same indiction, month, year, and pontificate, the same Lord Conservator explained how our Most Holy Father wishes that a portion of the money [be set aside] to restore the temple of Santa Maria Rotunda [i.e., the Pantheon]; after this proposal was heard and well acknowledged by the Conservators, it was decreed by the Senate that the Magnificent Lord Conservators should address our Most Holy Father [Clement VII], reminding him of the precedent set by His Holiness of blessed memory Leo X, his family relation, who issued an edict to the effect that the people of Rome should enjoy the benefit from a portion of this income; and if funding is needed to restore the antiquities of Rome, neither this portion nor the funds available to the Roman people would be sufficient for this restoration.

Document 15

ASC, Camera Capitolina, Credenza I, vol. 15, 136 (12 January 1525)

[Cf. partial transcription by Cerasoli (1909), 282.]

Magnificus Dominus Iohannes Aloysius de Aragonia primus Conservator cum consensu exposuit . . . Super reparatione fienda tecminis templi Pantheonis, que per Magistrum deputatum, ut dicitur, non ut decet dictum templum reparat.

Document 15, *Translation*

ASC, Camera Capitolina, Credenza I, vol. 15, 136 (12 January 1525)

The magnificent Lord Giovanni Aloysius de Aragon, chief Conservator with consent, explained [that] . . . regarding the repairs that need to be done to the roof tiles of the temple of the Pantheon, it is improper that a deputy, as he is called, appointed by the civic magistrates, repair the said temple.

Document 16

ASC, Camera Capitolina, Credenza I, vol. 16, 25 (12 September 1531)

In nomine Domini, Amen. Anno eiusdem millesimo, quingentesimo, trigesimo primo, indictione quinta, die vero duodecima mensis Septembris, Pontificatus etc., in mei scribe sacri senatus etc., Magnificus Dominus Marianus de Riciis primus conservator cum consensu etc., exposuit qualiter Reverendissimus Dominus Gubernator ex commissione S.D.N. pape ipsis dominis Conservatoribus intelligere fecit quod sue Sanctitatis mens est, quod si alique pecunie supersunt de Gabella studii, quod vult & intendit Sanctitas sua quod exponantur in reparatione teginimis ecclesie Sancte Marie Rotunde; qua expositione audita ex Senatusconsulto optentum extitit, quod si alique pecunie supersunt, detractis legitime detrahendis de fructibus dicte Gabelle, quod exponantur ad reparationem dicte ecclesie omni meliori modo, etc.

Document 16, *Translation*

ASC, Camera Capitolina, Credenza I, vol. 16, 25 (12 September 1531)

In the name of our Lord, amen. In the one thousand, five hundred, and thirty-first year of our Lord, the fifth indiction, the twelfth day of the month of September, [in the eighth year] of the pontificate [of Clement VII] etc., in [the presence of me,] the scribe of the sacred Senate, etc., the Magnificent Lord Mariano de Ricci, chief Conservator with consent, etc., explained how the Right Reverend Lord Governor on orders of his Most Holy Father, the Pope, made the Conservators themselves understand what is the intention of His Holiness: that if there was any money left over from the *gabella studii*,* His Holiness wants and intends that [this income] be set aside for the repairs to the roof tiles of the church of Santa Maria Rotunda; after this proposal was heard, it was decreed that any remaining funds, minus the amounts legitimately subtracted from from the income of the said *gabella*, should always be set aside for the repair of the said church.

*The *gabella studii* was a surcharge on the tax on imported wine sold in Roman taverns (*gabella vini forensis*), so called as it supported the Studium Urbis or the civic university of Rome.

Document 17

The following license issued by the papal administration authorized Tommaso da Bologna to dismantle and remove building stone from the ancient Ponte Mammolo in Tivoli to supply the Ponte Santa Maria work site.

> Rome 22 iunii 1549
> Licentia extrahendi lapides Thome de Bononia.
> Cam. Ap., Div. Cam. 159, 21r

A tutti e singoli governatore Officiali et particulare persone della città e Contado di Tivoli de ordine expresso della Santità di Nostro Signore et per l'autorità del nostro officio camerlinghato sotto pena del nostro arbitrio Commandiamo che lassino cavar liberamente et senza impedimento veruno dal ponte mamolo del detto Contado a Mastro Thomaso da Bologna Capo mastro de' Scarpellini del Ponte Santa Maria di Roma tutti quelli trevertini che bisognavano per risarcimento de esso ponte Santa Maria.

Document 17, *Translation*

Rome, 22 June 1549

> License to Tommaso da Bologna to excavate stone.
> Cam. Ap., Div. Cam. 159, 21r

To all and sundry, governor, officials, and individuals in the city and provincial territory of Tivoli, following the express order of Our Most Holy Father and by the authority of the office of the papal chamberlain, and under penalty of our arbitration, we hereby command that Maestro Tommaso da Bologna, master of the stonemasons of Ponte Santa Maria in Rome, be allowed to excavate freely and without any impediment all those travertine stones from the Ponte Mammolo of the aforesaid provincial territory that are needed to provide for the restoration of the Ponte Santa Maria.

Photograph Credits

Notes

INTRODUCTION

1. Freud (2005), esp. 42–48.

2. As Google Earth allows the viewer to zoom in on sites in contemporary Rome, so does Google Ancient Rome allow viewers to perform the same function on a virtual reconstruction of the ancient city.

3. "Destructive influences . . . are never lacking in the history of a city, even if it has a less chequered past than Rome. . . . [D]emolitions and replacement of buildings occur in the course of the most peaceful development of a city. . . . [T]he fact remains that only in the mind is such a preservation of all the earlier stages alongside of the final form possible." Freud (2005), 45–46.

4. "It is possible also that preservation in general is dependent upon certain favorable conditions. It is possible, but we know nothing about it." Ibid., 46.

5. For further discussion of the notion of "the anxiety of loss" as a lens through which subsequent writers have interpreted Renaissance interventions upon ancient Roman sites, see Karmon (2011).

6. See Jokilehto (1999), 47–100; Choay (2001), 63–81.

7. Lanciani (1902; rev. ed. 1989). See also Lanciani (1899), based upon the premise that the history of Rome recorded the history of destruction and transformation but not preservation.

8. Bignamini (2004), 1.

9. See for example Partner (1976), 177–180; Riegl (1982), 26–28; Jokilehto (1999), 16–19; Franzoni (2001), 306. Even a sensitive observer such as Françoise Choay is forced to conclude that "neither the elevated moral tone of the texts [referring to Renaissance preservation legislation] nor the magnitude of conservational projects accomplished should conceal the

antithetical behavior that is, paradoxically, coextensive with them: the same protago-
nists that describe themselves, and indeed show themselves to be so deeply implicated
in the cause of conservation, participated no less steadfastly, clearsightedly, and
cheerfully in the devastation of Rome and its antiquities." Choay (2001), 36–37.
Nonetheless there have also been important studies of preservation efforts in Renaissance Rome; see for example Cerasoli (1897); Gloton (1962); Jestaz (1963); Leisching
(1979); Fancelli (1985); Campbell (2004).

10. The comparison of Renaissance drawings with nineteenth-century photographs of key archaeological sites in Rome will help to illuminate this argument
throughout. For the history of photography in Rome, with reference to important
Roman photographers such as James Anderson and Robert Macpherson, see Becchetti
(1978, 1983); Ritter (2005). See also Santoni (1998) for specific reference to Roman
archaeological photography.

11. This is vividly attested on the international level by the flood of legislation
issued since World War II in the effort to preserve or defend cultural heritage. For a
recent summary, see Schildgen (2008), 175–85.

12. The periodical dismantling and reconstruction of the Ise shrine in Japan
represents only one alternative cultural solution to this universal problem; see
Jokilehto (1999), 245–94.

13. In the words of Anthony Grafton, "for so long as we content ourselves with
condemning the past, we must also be content not to understand it." Grafton (1977), 176.

14. Scholars have already begun to correct this bias in the literature on the history of
archaeology; see in particular the collected essays in Bignamini (2004); Trigger (2006).

15. This passage from Frank Matero's "Letter from the Chair" now introduces the
historic preservation program at the University of Pennsylvania; see http://www.
design.upenn.edu/historic-preservation. See also Brand (1994); Lowenthal (1998);
Tung (2001). For parallels in conservation across different disciplines see Eggert
(2009).

16. Cuno (2008). See also Greenfield (1996); Cuno (2009); Choay (2009).

17. Such arguments are not only repeatedly raised in Italy, but are often the focus
of special attention by the American press. For instance, regarding the Ara Pacis see
Seabrook (2005); for the custody of ancient artifacts in Rome see Povoledo (2006); for
ongoing archaeological collapses in the city see Kimmelman (2010).

18. See the reflections by Settis (2002, 2004), as well as Hansen (2002). For
contemporary preservation issues in application see Semes (2009). For changing
approaches to enduring conservation problems, and the notion of how to inherit the
past "well," see Gagliardi (2010).

19. Important published drawing collections of ancient sites in Renaissance
Rome include Egger et al. (1906); Hülsen (1910; repr. 1984); Bartoli (1914); Hülsen
and Egger (1916; repr. 1975); Egger (1931); Frutaz (1962); Wurm (1984); Wittkower
(1990); Fernández Gómez (2000). See also Schudt (1930).

20. Biondo Flavio, *Roma instaurata*, in *Opera omnia* (1531). For the critical history
of this text and its successive editions see Valentini and Zucchetti (1953), 4.247–323.
See also the critical edition and French translation of book I by Raffarin-Dupuis (2005).

21. "Confirmavit etiam nostrum describendi praepositum . . . aedo illius
conservationi utilis atque necessaries." Valentini and Zucchetti (1953), 4.259.

22. "sed collapsa, deformataque edifitia multis in locis maximo *instauratos* reficisques impendio." Ibid., 4.260.

23. In the remainder of the preface, Biondo used *instaurare* interchangeably with *renovare* and *restaurare*, suggesting that for him all these terms were synonyms for "to restore."

24. For conservation theory and contemporary conservation terminology, see Berducou (1996); Jokilehto (1999), 295–317; Muños Viñas (2005).

25. "[T]he word *restoration* . . . means the most total destruction which a building can suffer . . . a destruction accompanied with false descriptions of the thing destroyed. . . . [I]t is *impossible*, as impossible as to raise the dead, to restore anything that has ever been great or beautiful in architecture. . . . [T]hat spirit which is given only by the hand and eye of the workman never can be recalled. . . . Do not let us talk then of restoration. The thing is a Lie from beginning to end." Ruskin (1998), 194–96.

26. "Ipse contendam, ut sic tu Romam per ingenioli mei literarum monumenta, sicuti cementariorum fabrorumque libnariorum opera pergas instaurare." Valentini and Zucchetti (1953), 4.260.

27. "utrum . . . calce, latericio, materia, lapide aut ere, an literis facta solidior diuturniorve maneat instauratio." Ibid. For comparisons between the material city of Rome as the creation of magistrates, generals, and emperors, and the written city as the creation of antiquarians, historians, and poets, see Edwards (1996), 6–9.

CHAPTER I

1. For further discussion see Schnapp (1997), 11–12, who cites examples of lasting markers preserved from the past from the Fertile Crescent to China and the Pacific islands. For another extended meditation upon humanity's relationship to historic artifacts see Lowenthal (1985); for the question of how societies think about and use their pasts more generally see Connerton (1989); Fentress and Wickham (1992).

2. Bacon (2000), 2.2.1.

3. Proverbs 22:28. For discussion of this passage with particular reference to contemporary ideas about landmark preservation see collected essays in Reynolds (1996).

4. According to the Donation of Constantine, the first Christian emperor transferred imperial power at Rome to the pope in gratitude for his cure from leprosy through baptism. Despite the fact that the Donation was demonstrated to be a forgery during the Renaissance, this supposed bequest continued to justify imperialistic, secular papal ambitions into the sixteenth century, providing persuasive evidence for the value of preserving the authority of an invented past. For discussion of the debates about the Donation raised by Renaissance humanists see Stinger (1998), 246–54.

5. For the political history surrounding the advent of Augustus see Crook (1996). For Augustan piety and attitudes toward Roman religious life, see Price (1996). For the classic discussion of visual culture under Augustus, with special attention to the persuasive power of the visual imagery employed by the princeps, see Zanker (1988). For discussion of the idea of preservation in antiquity, especially as formulated by ancient authors with regard to Rome, see Edwards (1996).

6. Dionysius of Halicarnassus, *Roman Antiquities*, 1.79.11.

7. According to Vitruvius 2.1.5, the Casa Romuli instead stood on the Capitoline Hill. The idea of two competing versions of the hut has been connected with the tendency of collective memory to split into parallel, competitive sacred sites, as noted in Nagel and Wood (2010), 379, note 7. For further discussion of the different accounts of the Casa Romuli in the ancient sources see Balland (1984); Edwards (1996), esp. 27–43.

8. According to Andrea Carandini, a symbolic royal residency occupied this site as early as the late eighth century, which was then preserved through oral accounts that then governed the later reconstruction on the site; see Carandini (2000), 130–31. For a reconstruction of the progressive phases of the Palatine hillside with its succession of archaic huts between approximately the tenth and second centuries B.C., see Brocato (2000). For problems associated with the preservation of the memory of the founding of Rome, see Grandazzi (1997), 177–211.

9. Price (1996), 815. Price cites the example of the Roman cult of Hercules at the Ara Maxima near the Forum Boarium, as exemplifying the focus of Roman myths on a particular place.

10. According to Price, "the Augustan stress on restoration need not be treated as a cunning obfuscation: the age was fundamentally concerned to relate the present to the past." See Price (1996), 813. Zanker (1988), however, provides persuasive argument regarding the Augustan reinvention of Roman traditions in terms of a skillful kind of cultural manipulation. For more on Augustus's pious interventions on the past as a means of achieving contemporary objectives, see McEwen (2003), especially 190–95.

11. Augustus himself made particular efforts to connect himself in the popular imagination with Romulus as the founder of Rome by building his own house near the site of the Casa Romuli. Coarelli (2001), 158. For Augustus as "the new Romulus," discussed in relation to the founding of the Pantheon, see Coarelli (1983), 41–46.

12. Gabba (1991), 1–22. Dionysus's writings catered to a growing antiquarian interest among Romans in the first century B.C.; see Rawson (1985), 233–49.

13. Of course there was considerable latitude in determining just how such "exacting preservation" should take place, but it was the numerous interpretive possibilities which such interventions provided that would have made them so appealing. The issue would be further highlighted by dedicatory inscriptions, frequently used to commemorate restorations and rebuilding projects in imperial Rome, and yet which only rarely corresponded in a literal way to the actual repairs that took place. For more on this problem see Thomas and Witschel (1992).

14. See Price (1996), for evidence of this Augustan appropriation and transformation of the past in all aspects of Roman religious and cultural practices, from the treatment of the religious boundaries of the Roman pomerium to the successive reshaping of priesthoods, secular games, and imperial rituals.

15. *Res Gestae* 20. The Augustan program for the restoration of these temples was deeply indebted to the work of the Roman antiquarian Varro; see Zanker (1988), 102–3.

16. Zanker describes the process of Augustus's interventions as follows:

> in principle all the old temples were to be restored, but in practice the expenditure allotted for the worship of each divinity varied considerably. The most lavish structures were not those in the oldest sanctuaries or for the principal gods of the old Republic, but rather for those most closely associated

with Augustus: Apollo on the Palatine and Mars Ultor in the new Forum of Augustus. . . . [M]uch further down the scale were the eighty-two temples and shrines of the old gods which had been restored in 28 B.C. They were for the most part only spruced up, and the tufa columns got a new coating of stucco, but the old-fashioned wooden roofs and terra-cotta roof tiles were retained. This of course made painfully obvious their status vis-à-vis the new marble buildings for the gods of the imperial house. . . . [T]he varying levels of expenditure in the building of so many temples created in the popular mind a vivid impression of the different status of each divinity. The dominant ones were clearly those to which Augustus felt the closest. (1988, 108–10)

17. As Zanker notes, this cultural program also represented a useful strategy to repress the new oriental cults that were of rising popularity at Rome, but which were regarded with suspicion by Augustus.

18. Dio Cassius, *Roman History*, 51.30.3.

19. Marble was a rarity in the Republic, but the supply increased exponentially under Augustus with the opening of the quarries at Luna and the expanding international marble trade; see Friedländer (1909), 2.187–93; Ward-Perkins (1992). Improved building techniques, access to plentiful building resources from around the Mediterranean, and a flood of imperial wealth contributed to a scale and quality of building in Rome unprecedented in the ancient world. For the architectural "Roman Revolution," linked to the Domus Aurea of Nero, see Boëthius and Ward-Perkins (1970), 250–62; for the imperial construction industry see Delaine (2000); for construction techniques, see Adam (1994); Gros (1996); Lancaster (2005).

20. Suetonius, *Augustus*, 52.2.

21. For the design of the Forum of Augustus see Kockel (1995).

22. The use of massive squared stones or *opus quadrata* in this wall could be seen as consciously echoing the design of the earlier Servian Walls of Rome. This strong visual parallel not only further underscored Augustus's identity as the new Romulus, but also suggested a strategic design that evoked the preservation of the past, even as it marked a sweeping urban transformation. Thanks to Indra McEwen for this intriguing idea.

23. The resounding success of the Augustan system was followed by recurring concern for its maintenance throughout the imperial period; deviating too far from the Augustan model meant courting disaster. See Price (1996), 849.

24. Legislation was issued as early as the fifth century B.C. at Rome to regulate building sites and maintain urban decorum. This continued to be a preoccupation through the Republic, when two *censors* were traditionally appointed to administer public works, with individual *curators* occasionally appointed by the Senate to execute particular projects. General maintenance of public buildings, streets, and waterworks, however, was delegated to the office of the *aediles*. However, the responsibilities of these appointments were often poorly defined and proved insufficient to maintain Rome's expanding infrastructure. The best study of Augustus's interest in caring for the capital city, and the progressive reworking of the municipal bureaucracy to answer these objectives, is Favro (1992). See also Favro (1996); Hornblower and Spawforth (2003), 15–16. For more on the transition of the *aediles* between the late Republic and Augustan Rome see Strong (1968). For early Roman legislation prohibiting the demolition of buildings see Phillips (1973).

25. In the words of Diane Favro, "Agrippa treated the aedileship as a triumphal duty." Favro (1992), 76.

26. For more on the progressive transformation of the imperial capital with the rise of Christianity, see the fundamental study of Krautheimer (1980), as well as Ward-Perkins (1984).

27. For discussion of these late antique laws and their objectives, see Alchermes (1994).

28. N. Maj. 4.1, cited in Pharr (1952).

29. Ibid.

30. Preservation may have also been strategically encouraged in less coercive ways. For example, from the end of the fourth century, a number of emperors issued edicts providing tax rebates to those who contributed to the preservation of public buildings; see Cecchi (2006), 11.

31. Aristotle explored the notion of unity in the *Metaphysics*. For discussion see Barnes (1995).

32. Cicero, *De finibus bonorum et malorum*, 3.74. Thanks to Indra McEwen for this reference.

33. Aquinas, *Summa theologica*, pt. 1, qt. 73, art. 1. For further discussion of this point, and useful comparison with Byzantine notions that tended to discuss ruins as if they were in pristine condition, see Smith (1992), 158.

34. For discussion of Ostrogothic attitudes toward preservation see Ward-Perkins (1984), 203–4, 212. Several surviving texts record Theodoric, like late antique Roman legislation, describing ruins as ugly and unsightly.

35. Procopius, *Gothic War*, 4.22.5–6.

36. See Cameron (1985), 6–8; Cameron (2000), 77–78. See also the editor's introduction in Procopius (1914).

37. Schildgen describes the advent of a "state-sponsored preservation and reconstruction movement [that] began when Emperor Constantine the Great admitted Christianity to the imperial court." Schildgen (2008), 15–16.

38. Choay (2001), 21. Although Gregory the Great was rebuked by Renaissance humanists for authorizing the iconoclastic destruction of ancient monuments and literary collections, there is little actual evidence to substantiate these accusations; see Buddensieg (1965). For reuse of ancient materials through the middle ages see Greenhalgh (1989, 2009). Late antique civic institutions responsible for the maintenance of key buildings and infrastructure in the capital such as the *praefectus urbi* appear to have survived at least into the sixth century thanks to the support of the papacy. See Ward-Perkins (1984), 47.

39. Already in the late eighth century there is evidence that the popes had begun to repair ancient infrastructure such as the aqueduct system as well as the Aurelian Walls; see Coates-Stephens (1998), 166–78.

40. The importance with which the civic government invested preservation is revealed in the civic statutes (although the first surviving statutes date from the fourteenth century, these most likely repeated the original statutes compiled in the twelfth century), which included a specific clause addressing the necessity to protect and safeguard the ancient buildings of Rome.

41. For uses of antiquity for the medieval civic government see especially Gramaccini (1989). For further discussion of medieval cultural context in Rome and

government structure see Rodocanachi (1901); Halphen (1907); Salimei (1935); Natale (1939); Brezzi (1947); Theseider (1952); Moscati (1980); Krautheimer (1980); Benson (1982); Brentano (1991); Miglio (1998); Maire-Vigueur (2001).

42. As Dale Kinney has observed, when Innocent II embarked upon this project in 1140, it may have represented a rare moment of undisputed papal control over the ancient site. For the twelfth-century excavations at the Baths of Caracalla see Kinney (1986).

43. "Nos senatores . . . audita controversia . . . ecclesia cum columpna, domibus, hortis, et omnibus ei pertinentibus eidem Abbatissa investimento et auctoritate Senatus ei et per eam monasterio Sancti Cyriaci in perpetuum restituimus salvo iure parochialis ecclesie SS Apostolorum Philippi et Iacobi et salvo onore publico urbis, eidem columpne ne unquam per aliquam personam obtentu investimenti huius restitutionis diruatur aut minuatur, sed ut est ad honorem ipsius ecclesie et totius populi romani integra et incorrupta permaneat, dum mundus durat, sic eius stante figura. Qui vero eam minuere temptaverit, persona eius ultimum patiatur suppliciuim et bona eius omnia fisco applicentur." See Cavallaro (1984), 80–81, note 18.

44. Kuttner (1982).

45. Gramaccini (1989), 42–43.

46. This office was probably founded soon after the creation of the new civic government; for overview of the office and bibliography see Verdi (1991).

47. "Ne ruynis civitas non deformetur et ut antiqua edificia decorem Urbis publice representent, statuimus quod nullus sit ausus aliquod antiquum edificium Urbis diruere vel dirui facere intra Urbem ad penam cento librarum prov., cuius pene medietas sit Camere et alia medietas sit accusantis." See Camillo Re, *Statuti della città di Roma* (1880), 188. See also Vendittelli (1993), 16.

48. Under Hadrian, regulations were implemented to divide income generated from excavating treasures in Rome between the discoverer and the owner of the property; see *Scriptores Historiae Augustae* 18.6; Wataghin (1984), 178–79. In the mid-twelfth century Henry of Blois, bishop of Winchester, obtained papal permission to export sculpture from Rome to England ("cum vero episcopus preter absolutionem se nichil optinere posse videret, accepta licentia rediens veteres statuas emit Rome, quas Wintoniam deferri fecit"); see Poole (1927), 81. See also Fedele (1909).

49. For these payments see Fumi (1891), 27–28; Borsari (1897); Lanciani (1989), 1.28.

50. De Boüard argued the civic government probably gained a good part of its operating revenues in this way; see De Boüard (1911), 241–44.

51. A prominent example of such medieval civic preservation projects is the so-called Casa di Crescenzio, dating from about 1100, and thus presumably anticipating the spirit that led to the formation of the new civic government; see Krautheimer (1980), 197–98.

52. For discussion see Weiss (1988), 38–42; see also Wright (1975); Maire-Vigueur (1982); Musto (2003), 112–17.

53. For overview of these conditions see Stinger (1998); Gill (2005); Rowland (2005). The evidence of fifteenth-century registries of papal imports further underscores the fundamental dependence of Rome upon papal wealth; see Esch (1981).

CHAPTER 2

1. For Vergerio's 1398 letter and context, see Smith (1934); Valentini and Zucchetti (1953), 4.98.

2. See for example Simoncini (2004). Fifteenth-century Roman economic and social conditions have been notably clarified thanks to the investigations of Arnold Esch; see Esch (1976, 1981, 1995, 2007).

3. "li conservatori et li caporioni con molti cittadini di Roma parecchie sere si givano colle torcie in mano accese, la sera sempre dicendo Viva Papa Martino, Viva Papa Martino." Infessura (1890), 23.

4. For critical orientation to political and cultural issues during the reign of Martin V see collected essays in Chiabò (1992); for overview of this period in Rome's history see also Pastor (1925); Partner (1958, 1972); Caravale and Caracciolo (1978); Thomson (1980); Prodi (1987); Stinger (1998).

5. Claridge (2010), 67. See also Watkin (2009), 142–43.

6. Petrarch (1831), 2.330–37. Petrarch famously pointed out Roman ignorance in a letter addressed to Cardinal Giovanni Colonna, where he reported "nusquam minus Roma cognoscitur quam Romae," nowhere else is Rome known less than at Rome; see Valentini and Zucchetti (1953), 4.10. Petrarch's notion that the local inhabitants of Rome were its greatest enemies was not unprecedented. On the contrary, it recalled the anxieties voiced already by the Roman antiquarian Varro, as cited from a lost passage in the *Antiquitates rerum divinarum* by Augustine: "He [Varro] writes in that very work that he is afraid that they [ancient Roman customs and traditions] may disappear not through some enemy attack, but through the carelessness of Rome's citizens." Aug. *De civ. D.* 6.2, cited in Edwards (1996), 5. Petrarch's critique of fourteenth-century Romans may have further incorporated the prevailing Italian bias toward Florentine culture as well, although Petrarch also expressed ambivalence toward the capital city of his native Tuscany; see Wilkins (1961), 99–102; Bergin (1970), 81–84, Kleinhenz (1999).

7. "Adunque al tempo di Costantino imperatore e di Silvestro papa sormontò su la fede cristiana. Ebbe la idolatria grandissima persecuzione in modo tale, tutte le statue e le pitture furono disfatte e lacerate di tanta nobilità ed. antica e perfetta dignità . . . E poi, [per] levare via ogni antico costume di idolatria, costituirono i templi tutti essere bianchi. In questo tempo ordinorono grandissima pena a chi facesse alcuna statua o alcuna pittura, e così finì l'arte statuaria e la pittura ed. ogni dottrina che in essa fosse fatta. Finita che fu l'arte, stettero i templi bianchi circa d'anni 600." Ghiberti (1947), 32. For Ghiberti's preoccupation with the threat of artistic destruction, see Gilbert (1995), 137–38.

8. Vasari cited further examples of Christian iconoclasm to flesh out Ghiberti's basic point:

> Ma quello che sopra tutte le cose dette fu di perdita e danno infinitamente
> alle predette professioni, fu il fervente zelo della nuova religione cristiana . . .
> mentrechè ardentissimamente attendeva con ogni diligenza a levar via ed. a
> stirpare in tutto ogni minima occasione, donde poteva nascere errore; non
> guastò solamente o gettò per terra tutte le statue maravigliose, e le sculture,
> pitture, musaici ed. ornamenti de' fallaci Dii de' gentili; ma le memorie

ancora e gli onori d'infinite persone egregie, alle quali per gli eccellenti
meriti loro dalla virtuosissima antichità erano state poste in pubblico le
statue e l'altre memorie. Inoltre, per edificare le chiese all'usanza cristiana,
non solamente distrusse i più onorati tempj degli'idoli; ma per fare diventare
più nobile e per adornare San Pietro . . . spogliò di colonne di pietra la mole
d'Adriano, oggi detto Castello Sant'Agnolo, e molte altre, le quali veggiamo
oggi guaste. (Vasari 1906, 1.230–31)

9. Vasari's negative judgment of the safeguarding activities of the church was
later recalled by the negative assessments of archaeologists working in postunification
Rome, a context noted for its strong anticurial sentiment.

10. "cuius rei tanta per singulos dies videmus exempla, ut ea solum modo causa
nos aliquando Romae fastidiat habitatio." Biondo, *Roma instaurata*, in Valentini and
Zucchetti (1953), 4.310. For further discussion of Biondo's archaeological activities
see Weiss (1963, 1988); Mazzocco (1975). For recent bibliography see McCuaig
(1999).

11. Even the growth of private collections of ancient sculpture points to the rising
attention to preservation issues in Renaissance Rome; on these collections see
Christian (2010). For the development of the new monarchical model of the papacy
after the conciliarist crisis, and the exercise of temporal power by the early modern
popes, see the classic treatment by Prodi (1987).

12. "Hunc Capitolii collem, caput quondam Romani Imperii, atque orbis
terrarum arcem . . . stercorum ac purgamentorum receptaculum factum . . . Forum
iure dicundo . . . deserta squalent malignitate fortunae, alterum porcorum bubalo-
rumque diversorium, alterum serendis oleribus cultum." Poggio Bracciolini, "De
varietate fortunae," in Valentini and Zucchetti (1953), 4.241. Poggio's notion of the
Capitoline Hill as reverting to inchoate wilderness inverted the famous passage from
Virgil in the *Aeneid* 8, which contrasted the rustic origins of the Capitoline Hill with its
future imperial grandeur.

13. It is, however, also important to note that the popes were not simply imposing
a new order upon helpless or unwilling subjects. On the contrary, the leading civic
classes of Rome, having experienced at first hand the dire consequences of the
absence of the papal court from Rome during the previous century, realized that they
stood to benefit from papal involvement in the management of the city. Despite later
conflicting efforts to resist the growth of papal power, the civic classes under Martin V
were complicit in assisting the pope in his task of reasserting papal control. In reward
for their collaboration, members of these leading Roman families acquired important
posts in the reformed municipal government under Martin V and lucrative contracts
to implement major papal repairs to deteriorated urban infrastructure, such as the
work at Ponte Santa Maria, as discussed in chapter 6. For further discussion of social
and economic dimensions of papal-civic relations during the reign of Martin V see
especially Caravale (1992); Palermo (1992); Pavan (1992). See also the valuable
introduction in Verdi (1997).

14. For historic overview of the *maestri di strade e degli edifici*, or *magistri stratarum
aedificiorum urbis*, see Verdi (1991), 54–62. For more on the office and its statutes see
Schiaparelli (1902); Re (1920); Scarafoni (1927); Delumeau (1957-59), 1.230–46;

Westfall (1974), 77–84; Verdi (1997). For discussion of the the *maestri* in the urban reshaping of Renaissance Rome, see Ceen (1977), 89–103.

15. The notion of the *maestri* as the heirs of the Augustan legacy was already current by the sixteenth century, when historians of the office of the *maestri* referred to the *aediles* as their direct predecessors. See Bardi (1565).

16. For the powerful political objectives implicit in Renaissance architecture and urbanism, the fundamental reference remains the work of Manfredo Tafuri; for example see Tafuri (1992).

17. Fedele (1908), 147–55.

18. "super omnibus questionibus Urbis aedificiorum, domorum, murorum, viarum, platearum, divisionum tam intus quam extra." Cited from a legal decision issued on 8 July 1255; see Schiaparelli (1902), 30.

19. For the statutes of 1410 (known through a copy of 1480), see Scarafoni (1927), 240–308. The statutes indicated the *maestri* enjoyed considerable power in the hierarchy of the Capitoline government, as neither the Senator nor the Conservators were permitted to interfere with their decisions; see chapter 22, *Quod senator et conservators teneantur exequi sententias magistrorum*.

20. Chapter 8, *De cura habenda per magistros in reparatione locorum urbis et eius districtis*. "Item quod dicti domini magistri possint et valeant ex eorum officio providere super reparatione ac reformatione viarum et stratarum publicarum et aliorum locorum ac etiam edificiorum, fontium, pontium, et cursuum aquarum tam in Urbe quam extra Urbem." Ibid., 273.

21. For the history of civic interventions at the Acqua Vergine see Karmon (2005b).

22. Chapter 24, *Quod magistri teneantur recuperare loca publica occupata*. "Item quod dicti magistri teneantur recuperare suo posse omnia loca terrena, possessiones ypothecarias, vineas, ortos, arcus triumphales et pontes, edificia et muros quomodolibet occupatos, ad rem publicam urbis de iure vel de facto spectantes vel in publico existentes, et contra detentores et occupatores ac usurpatores et inobedientes ex eorum officio procedere summarie et de plano, sine strepitu et figura iudicii, omni iuris solemnitate omissa et quod de omni exequutione quam propter ea fecerint ad penam et scindicatum perpetuo non teneantur." Scarafoni (1927), 279.

23. *Etsi de cunctarum* (31 March 1425). For the text of the bull and commentary, see Müntz (1878), 335–36; D'Onofrio (1989), 17–21; Simoncini (2004), 2.248–51.

24. According to the bull, Martin V reestablished the office of the *maestri*: "pro viarum, stratarum, platearum et locorum aliorum tam publicorum quam privatorum, necnon aedificiorum lapideorum et ligneorum, parietum tignorum, banchorum, tectorum, tabulatuum, mignanorum, apothecarum et pontium, portarum, passorum, aquarum decursuum, canalium et meatuum, necnon urbanorum et rusticorum praediorum, pratorum, hortorum atque vinearum, finium, restaurationum, servitutum et libertatum administratione."

25. The bull—perhaps making an oblique criticism of the insufficient management of Rome by the Capitoline magistrates—indicated that prior to the moment of its issue, the office of the *maestri* had remained unstaffed, thus causing considerable civic upheaval and disruption: "Cum itaque Urbs districtusque praedicti . . . ex defectu officii magistrorum . . . institutum et ordinatum extitit, in praemissis et eorum singulis grandem deformitatem seu ruinam potius abhominabilem patiantur et iacturam."

26. As noted for example in Cherubini et al. (1984), 57; Verdi (1991), 55. For an important alternative argument, suggesting the persistence of civic autonomy in the context of papal Rome, see Nussdorfer (1992, 2000).

27. The bull condemned the practices of butchers and tanners whose by-products were then flung into the public spaces of the city: "viscera, intestina, capita, pedes, ossa, crurores, necnon pelles, carnes et pisces corruptos, resque alias foetidas atque corruptas in viis, stratis, plateis et locis publicis atque privatis."

28. For the immunity of the *maestri*, see section 4 of the bull, "Qualis eorum sit iurisdictio." The same section clearly gave the *maestri* authority to take whatever measures were necessary to improve the condition of failing structures in the city, either repairing them or demolishing them if necessary: "etiam per demolitionem quorumcumque aedificiorum aut rerum aliarum, seu modum alium, quaecumque reparandi, corrigendi et commendandi . . . mandatum damus ac etiam potestatem."

29. ASV, Camera Apostolica, *Diversa Cameralia* 9, 253, "Calcarensibus urbis extrahendi lapides ex fundamentis temple Canapare pro calce facienda" (1 July 1426). For discussion of the history and function of licenses governing excavations in Rome, as well as the officers responsible for supervising this legislative system, with particular reference to eighteenth-century Rome, see Bignamini and Hornsby (2010), 1.17–29.

30. Lanciani (1989), 1.55.

31. "Calcarensibus Urbis extrahendi lapides ex fundamentis templi Canapare pro calce facienda et dandi medietatem calci Jacobo Tusculano card. licentiam concedit."

32. Cerasoli (1897) published a number of papal excavation licenses as evidence for papal efforts to preserve antiquity in Renaissance Rome. However, Cerasoli's argument made little impact upon the contemporary literature, given that the notion of the Renaissance popes causing the destruction of antiquity carried the full weight of history. On the other hand, Lanciani, a prolific author and the municipal commissioner for archaeology in Rome, had pressing motives to efface the evidence for Renaissance preservation. Seeking to defend his own archaeological practices from attack by outraged critics, Lanciani discovered that a critique of Renaissance practices provided him with an invaluable scapegoat, one that enabled him to present the results of his own urgent salvage operations in a much more positive light. Lanciani's critique of Renaissance interventions upon ancient remains of Rome may have been all the more compelling because it also capitalized upon the prevailing anticurial sentiment in postunification Rome. For further discussion of Lanciani's motives see chapter 3.

33. According to Lanciani, "i pilastri furono invece smantellati sino alla terza fila dei travertini sotto il pavimento." Lanciani (1989), 1.55.

34. As noted in the previous chapter, the practice of dividing proceeds between the discoverer of ancient treasures and the property owner in Rome was already regulated by legislation under Hadrian, as reported in *Scriptores Historiae Augustae* 18.6. For further discussion see Wataghin (1984), 1.178–79.

35. Gnoli (1939), 56.

36. Another license survives for the same site, awarded to "Paulo de Ursinis" and dated 2 January 1413, during the reign of the preceding pope John XIII; for a transcription see Theiner (1862), 3.204. In contrast to the license of 1426, this document made no attempt to restrict the demolition of the monument; probably the high social status of Paulo de Ursinis, identifed as an officer in papal employ—"ad nostra et Romane ecclesie stipendia militancium Capitaneo"—guaranteed these generous terms. But it

may also suggest that the election of Martin V, as the new Roman pontiff, coincided with the taking of greater precautions for the preservation of antiquity.

37. For the losses suffered by the Roman civic archives see Guasco (1919, 1946).

38. As is well known, the creation and meticulous maintenance of a state archive run by an efficient bureaucratic administration represented a fundamental preoccupation of the early modern papacy. See Prodi (1987), 102–10. The vital importance of bureaucratic record keeping for the Renaissance papacy—highlighted by the laborious transportation of the papal archives around fifteenth-century Europe—is explored in Corbo (1999), 39–46.

39. ASV, Cam. Ap., *Div. Cam.* 36, 83r–83v, "Licentia vehendi lapides pro constructione bibliothecarum in palatio apostolico" (17 December 1471). For partial transcription see Lanciani (1989), 1.93.

40. ASV, Cam. Ap., *Div. Cam.* 44, 34r–34v, "Bartholomeo alias Matto effodiendi lapides marmoreos licentiam concedit" (17 November 1484). According to this license, "Bartholomeo alias il matto . . . facultas effodiendi lapides subterraneos in urbe, dummodo super eos aedificia publica non existant." For partial transcription see Cerasoli (1897), 133.

41. My research of fifteenth-century papal excavation licenses at the ASV, Camera Apostolica, *Diversa Cameralia*, has identified the following legislation as evidence for ongoing papal interest in controlling access to ancient remains: *Div. Cam.* 13, 88r–88v, "Oddo de Varris locumtenens Ludovico Antonii Phylippitti civi Spoletano effodiendi tesauros licentiam concedit" (8 July 1430); *Div. Cam.* 32, 250v, "Bannum de non vendendo calcem in Urbe sine incusura" (12 May 1466); *Div. Cam.* 36, 22r, "Antonello de Rocapriora castellano Ostie mandat ne marmora extrahantur, idem dohanerio Ripe et Ripette Urbis" (11 August 1471); *Div. Cam.* 51, 189, "Salvus conductus Stephano Fridicino magistro fodiendarum lapidum alcune viarum" (14 April 1497); *Div. Cam.* 51, 210v–211r, "Dominico Stephanelli de Urbe extrahendi lapides exc lapidicinia concedit" (22 May 1497).

42. Caravale and Caracciolo (1978), 49–65; Stinger (1998), 96–97.

43. This process of restricting access to ancient sites can be seen as part of the progressive affirmation of absolute papal control over the city. For the notion of Renaissance papal primacy as expounded in the 1439 bull *Laetantur Coeli*, see Westfall (1974), 2–5. For further discussion of Nicholas V and the expression of absolute papal power during his reign see Burroughs (1990); Tafuri (1992), 23–58; Grafton (2000), 293–315.

44. For the Porcari conspiracy see Cessi (1956), 65–128; see also Miglio (1974); Modigliani (1986, 1994).

45. For the work of Giannozzo Manetti see Smith and O'Connor (2006), including a transcription of the biography with commentary, 361–470. This volume treats all aspects of the so-called Plan of Nicholas V, including the reconstruction of the Vatican palace and the proposed rebuilding of St. Peter's. For a summary of extensive building activity conducted by Nicholas V in the Rome of 1451 by a contemporary chronicler, see Infessura (1890), 49–50.

46. For the text of the 1452 statutes, see Re (1920), 86–102; see also Verdi (1997), 44–59.

47. Porticoes in particular, as liminal public spaces vulnerable to takeover by private property owners, came under renewed attack in fifteenth-century papal urban

legislation. For discussion of notions of private and public space in medieval Rome see Broise and Maire-Vigueur (1983), 156–60.

48. "Che li detti maestri non possano . . . dare licentia ad veruna persona che possa murare, fabricare, fare nè fossa nè fratta nè stecchato in niuno luocho publico." Chapter 6, "Che li detti maestri non possano dare licentia de occupare niuno luecho publico." Re, (1920), 90. The 1452 statutes were also clearly intended to be more accessible to the general public, as they were now issued in Italian instead of Latin.

49. "se avessero dato licentia, ipso facto sia nullo et de niuno valore." Ibid.

50. As revealed by my examination of the series of excavation licenses recorded in the *Diversa Cameralia* (ASV) issued between 1420 and 1550.

51. While Verdi attributes this modification to papal intent to control new construction in Rome, it is important to emphasize that this legislation also enabled the pope to gain much greater control over the process of excavating in the papal capital. See Verdi (1997), 50–57.

52. Excavations documented at ancient building sites supplied major papal building projects during the reign of Nicholas V. For documentation of major excavations at the Colosseum see Müntz (1878), 170; Lanciani (1989), 1.62. For destruction at other sites see Lanciani (1989), 61–68; also Satzinger (1996), 251–54. Stone was collected for the New St. Peter's building site; for this project, and the new choir attributed by Vasari to the Florentine architect Bernardo Rossellino, see Thoenes (2005), 64–71.

53. Alberti presented *De re aedificatoria* (at least in part) to Nicholas V around 1450. The last book concluded with a proposed restoration for the Old St. Peter's; see Alberti (1988), 362. For more on this restoration see discussion in Burns (1998), esp. 116–20, and Burns (2005), 35. Alberti recorded his anxiety about the loss of antiquity in book 6: "examples of ancient temples and theaters have survived that may teach us as much as any professor, but I see—not without sorrow—these very buildings being despoiled more each day . . . nobody would deny that as a result of all this a whole section of our life and learning could disappear altogether." Alberti (1988), 155.

54. Alberti's criticism of the unnecessary destruction of buildings in the *De re aedificatoria* perhaps also reflected negatively upon Nicholas V's urban interventions; for further discussion see Smith and O'Connor (2006), 212–16.

55. Based on the evidence of the prescriptions recorded in the 1452 statutes—and in contrast to the argument advanced by Smith and O'Connor—Luigi Spezzaferro concludes that Nicholas V's intention was to preserve the ancient city, even more than to stimulate the construction of a new one. See Spezzaferro (1973), 18.

56. Allan Ceen describes planning in Rome prior to Sixtus V as "planning by accretion over time." This discussion draws upon Ceen (1977); see also Ackerman (1982) for discussion of planning in Renaissance Rome as a "coherent evolutionary process."

57. Chapter 32 of the 1452 statutes of the *maestri di strade*, which stipulated that it was necessary to clean the streets of the papal capital during the hot summer months to maintain sufficient standards of urban hygiene, noted that in those cases when it was not possible to clean every street in Rome, at least these three major axes across Rome should be properly maintained: "quando non si potesse fare per tutta la terra, almeno si faccia per queste tre strade principali: cioè dallo Canale de Ponte in sino ad

Sancto Angilo Piscivendolo, dallo Canale de Ponte per via Papale in sino ad Campitoglio, dallo Canale de Ponte per la via ritta in sino alla Magdalena." For the statute see Re (1920), 98–99.

58. The area identified as the Canale de Ponte in the 1452 statutes was the area immediately to the south of the Ponte Sant'Angelo, a vital transit hub in the papal capital and noted for its concentration of Florentine bankers and merchants. For urban interventions at this site during the reign of Nicholas V see Burroughs (1982).

59. This is still evident in Rome today, where the Via de' Coronari preserves the route of the ancient Via Recta across the Campus Martius, while the Via del Corso corresponds to the Via Lata, connecting to the Roman consular highway known as the Via Flaminia.

60. As Ceen points out in his discussion of the Trivium, rather than rectifying existing street alignments, Renaissance planners instead incorporated existing street alignments into new formal patterns; see Ceen (1977), 66–88.

61. For the destruction of the Meta Romuli see Weiss (1988), 100–101.

62. Nicholas V in particular may be credited for promoting this new "global vision of the city" in the Renaissance papal capital. See Broise and Maire-Vigueur (1983), esp. 156–59.

63. The origin of the title of the Conservators is uncertain, but perhaps can be traced to their duty as custodians of the public treasury; of course the creation of an appointed body to represent the *popolo romano* was the fundamental objective of the civic government from its inception. The Conservators officially shared governance duties with the Senator, a position of leading importance in the earlier history of the civic government, as reflected in the architectural preeminence of the Senators' palace on the Capitoline Hill. However, over the course of the fourteenth century the Senator's effective responsibilities had been steadily appropriated by the Conservators. By the early fifteenth century the Conservators consisted of one nobleman and two commoners, although the nobility soon gained a monopoly over these prestigious positions. The *caporioni* served as their subordinates, each representing the different districts of the city. The most succinct history of the office of the Conservators is Franceschini (1991, 1997). For the history of this magistracy in the context of the papal capital see also Rodocanachi (1901); Nussdorfer (1992); Tittoni (1997).

64. For instance, the famous antipapal uprising against Julius II in 1511; see Gennaro (1967). For more on lingering antipapal sentiment see Miglio (1983); for particular emerging political and social conditions in the papal capital between the later fifteenth century and the first quarter of the sixteenth century see the collected essays in Gensini (1994).

65. For the mutual dependence of the pope and Conservators in Renaissance Rome see Nussdorfer (2000).

66. Other authors discussing the role of the Conservators in regulating ancient remains in Renaissance Rome include Rodocanachi (1913); Franceschini (1986).

67. *Cum almam nostram Urbem* (28 April 1462). See Fea (1802), 82–83; D'Onofrio (1989), 25–26; Jokilehto (1999), 29; Choay (2001), 35–36; Schildgen (2008), 172–73.

68. "Cum Almam Nostram Urbem in sua dignitate, et splendore conservari cupiamus, potissime ad ea curam vigilem adhibere debemus, ut non solum Basilicae, ac Ecclesiae eiusdem Urbis, et pia, ac religiosa loca, in quibus plurimae Sanctorum

reliquiae resident, in eorum miris aedificiis manuteneantur, et praeserventur; verum etiam antiqua, et prisca aedificia, et illorum reliquiae ad posteros maneant, cum eadem aedificia ornamentum, et decorem maximum afferant dictae Urbi, et monimenta veterum virtutum, et incitamenta ad illarum laudes assequendas, existant." Cited from D'Onofrio (1989), 25.

69. The meditative and productive function of ancient ruins for Renaissance culture has been discussed by Greene (1982), 233; see also Settis (1985), 3.375–488. On the pleasure of ruins more generally see also Macaulay (1953); Zucker (1968); Roth et al. (1997); Woodward (2001). For depictions of ruins in Renaissance pictures, as an index of new interest in such matters, see Makarius (2004), 17–41. For more on the notional value of the fragment to Renaissance culture see Barkan (1999), 199–207.

70. "et quod etiam magis considerandum est, ex ipsis aedificiis, ac aedificiorum reliquiis rectius intueri licet rerum humanarum fragilitatem, et quod nullo modo in illis sit confidendum, cum eadem aedificia, quae maiores nostri cum eorum ingenti potentia, et sumptibus maximis, cum immortalitate certatura arbitrarentur, vetustate, et aliis sinistris casibus diminuta, et collapsa etiam esse cernantur." *Cum almam nostram Urbem* (28 April 1462), cited from D'Onofrio (1989), 25.

71. "[O]mnibus, et singulis, tam Ecclesiasticis, quam Saecularibus cuius-cumque praeminentiae, dignitatis, status, ordinis, vel conditionis existant, etiamsi Pontificali, aut alia quavis Ecclesiastica, vel mundana dignitate praefulgeant, auctoritate, et scientia praedictis districtius inhibemus, ne quis eorum directe, vel indirecte, publice, vel occulte, aliquod aedificium publicum antiquum, seu aedificii antiqui reliquias supra terram in dicta Urbe, vel eius districtu existens, seu existentes, etiam si in eorum praediis rusticis, vel urbanis fuerint, demoliri, destruere, seu comminuere, aut rumpere, seu in calcem convertere, quoquo modo praesumant." Ibid, 26.

72. The bull, however, concluded by making an important exception; no one except for the pope himself ("praeter Romanum Pontificem") was authorized to permit the demolition of ancient remains.

73. "Quod si quis fuerit, qui contra prohibitionem huiusmodi venire praesump-serit, dilectis filiis modernis, et pro tempore existentibus Conservatoribus Camerae dictae Urbis, qui pro praemissis per eorum officials diligenter inquiri faciant, artifices, seu laboratores in opere demolitionis, seu devastationis huiusmodi inventos, carcerari, eorumque animalia, instrumenta, et res alias capi, et arrestari, confiscari faciendi, eosque, nec non illos, quorum nominee id egerint, ad multae solutionem compellendi plenam, et liberam auctoritate, et scientia praedictis, earumdem tenore praesentium concedimus facultatem."

74. The text of the bull also noted that the Conservators had entreated Pius II on behalf of the preservation of antiquity.

75. This apt description of government in early modern Rome is that of Nussdor-fer (1992), 45.

76. Lanciani (1989), 1.90. Payments for these repairs were recorded between 22 December 1469 and 26 January 1470.

77. For the papal payment dated 26 January 1470, see Müntz (1879), 95.

78. This instance was recorded by Lanciani (1989), 1.132.

79. Caffarelli's pugnacious character is elsewhere attested by the report that in 1464 he attacked and wounded Giovanni Alberini in connection with an ongoing family vendetta; see Bartolini (1973), 244.

80. For discussion and summary of the extensive bibligraphy treating the Sistine foundations of the Capitoline Museum see Presicce (2000).

81. Miglio (1982), 177–86; Miglio (1984), 1.94–102. As Miglio points out, the decision by Sixtus IV to elevate the famous Capitoline Wolf as the paradigmatic symbol of Rome thus had ulterior motivations, as it strategically displaced another ancient marble sculpture depicting a lion devouring a horse that had served as the emblem of the medieval civic government. The resentment of the Roman civic nobility toward Sixtus IV was captured by the chronicler Stefano Infessura, who described the pope as a second Nero: "Gaude, prisce Nero, superat te crimine Xystus / hic scelus omne simul clauditur et vitium." Infessura (1890), 158.

82. However, it is important to note that the Conservators may have actively encouraged Sixtus IV to make this donation; see Presicce (2000), 194.

83. "lo scettro del senatore vestito di broccato d'oro, e i tre Conservatori di Roma, a fasci verdi, insegne dilettevoli da vedere fra le pompe e i giuochi d'Agone, rappresen-tavano una certa vana et ridicola autorità . . . che veramente la deliberatione di tutti i papi era . . . di concedere tutta Roma in preda a huomini forastieri et mezzo barbari, diradicando l'antica stirpe del sangue romano . . . et gli erano solamente restate le immagini de gli honor antichi." Paolo Giovio, "La vita del cardinal Colonna," in *Le vite di Leone Decimo et d'Adriano Sesto sommi pontefici, et del Cardinal Pompeo Colonna* (Florence, 1529), 498; cited in Miglio (1984), 111.

84. Legislation issued in 1476 by Sixtus IV again reconfirmed the jurisdiction of the Conservators over the preservation of ancient remains in Rome; see Rodocanachi (1901), 197–98.

85. "Ad officium conservatorum ante omnia spectat vigilem ac precipuam curam pro statu S. D. N. pape ac sante Romane ecclesie et pro urbis tutela et pro civium quiete semper habere. Et quecumque edificia et opera publica inviolata et illesa custodire. Et contra quoscumque interceptors aut violators rerum vetustarum et contra omnes templorum, ecclesiarum ornamenta aut lapides subripere aut corrumpere non verentes acerrime insurgere et inquirere et ut severeissime animadvertatur insistere." Cited from "De officio Conservatorum," in ASC, Camera Capitolina, Cred. 14, vol. 165, 10v; transcribed by Franceschini (1997), 22–24. As Franceschini notes, this is the first explicit codification of the Conservators' duties to survive.

86. In addition, the Conservators retained other various responsibilities of judiciary and inspectional nature, including civil and criminal authority in legal cases assigned to the *Camera Urbis* and the supervision and regulation of commerce in foodstuffs.

87. "bisogna usar arte in condurle fora de Roma per respecto a li Conservatori." Transcribed by D'Arco (1857), 2.44. For discussion of further efforts to overcome the restrictions imposed by late fifteenth-century legislation that rendered exportation of ancient remains from Rome illegal, see Fusco and Corti (2006), 187–89.

88. The Conservators also continued to supervise ongoing repairs and work on ancient monuments at the end of the fifteenth century, as recorded in a surviving payment for the repair of "certain marble heads" at the Arch of Constantine in 1498; see Müntz (1886), 154.

CHAPTER 3

1. For the *renovatio imperii* and the *renovatio Romae*, the ideology of papal continuity with the Roman Empire in the rebuilding of Renaissance Rome, see Miglio (1989); Stinger (1998), 235–54, with bibliography.

2. For the 1507 paean by Egidio da Viterbo celebrating the fulfillment of a Christian golden age see O'Malley (1969); for more on the theological significance of the Sistine Ceiling see O'Malley (1986). For an overview of artistic production during this period see Hall (2005).

3. New construction in the early sixteenth century was concentrated primarily in the areas of the *abitato*; urban expansion into the *disabitato* took place toward the end of the century, as suggested by the comparison of the Dosio map of 1562 with the Tempesta map of 1593.

4. In January 1886 the Italian Renaissance scholar Hermann Grimm published a letter titled "The Destruction of Rome" in the international press, which concluded with the pointed accusation: "the world knows that the Italians themselves destroyed Rome at the close of the nineteenth century;" see Grimm (1886). Three months after Grimm's blistering accusation, Lanciani delivered a spirited defense of the current state of the preservation of antiquity to the power brokers of modern Rome (including the king and queen of Italy), in which he pointed out that far greater atrocities had been committed during the sixteenth century in Rome. Lanciani insisted that although demolition was inevitable, infinite progress had been made since the Renaissance, given that excavations now benefited from the aid of modern science and modern conservation theory. The transcription of Lanciani's speech was published as Lanciani (1886). For Lanciani's biography see Palombi (2006).

5. The anticlerical bias of postunification Rome probably also played a role here. For the harsh judgment of archaeologists upon the misrule and stagnation of papal Rome see Purcell (1992), 449–50; Casciato (2002).

6. Lanciani's excellent command of English made it possible for him to reach a large Anglophone audience.

7. Lanciani (1882), 217. Lanciani used this formula to characterize the excavations authorized by Paul III in the Roman Forum beginning in 1540. The "meteor" metaphor surfaced in successive works, including Lanciani (1886), 360; Lanciani (1888), xvi-xvii, 154–55. For the relevant passage in the *Storia degli scavi*; see Lanciani (1989), 2.203–51.

8. Robert Gaston has rightly challenged the historiographic tendency to denigrate the value of antiquarian contributions; see Gaston (2003).

9. Roberto Weiss invoked this paradox when he noted that "the Renaissance passion for building on classical lines was the main cause for much of the destruction of what still remained of ancient Rome." Weiss (1988), 104; see also Barkan (1999), 33.

10. Based upon the exchange between Christ and Peter in Matthew 16:18 (inscribed in the frieze below the dome of the New St. Peter's): "Tu es Petrus, et super hanc petram aedificabo Ecclesiam meam." For further discussion of Renaissance notions of papal primacy in relation to the threats posed by conciliarism, see Stinger (1998), 158–66.

11. For the idea of "building against time" I refer to Burns (1995). In his lectures on the history of the New St. Peter's, John Shearman was fond of characterizing Julius II and Bramante as "two old men in a hurry."

12. Later in the sixteenth century Michelangelo would be equally preoccupied to advance work on the dome to ensure the faithful completion of his own design; Burns (1995), 115–23.

13. The new configuration of the Palazzo della Cancelleria meant that the position of the new basilica of San Damaso in Lorenzo was relocated away from its original location to the northern section of the site. However, as Frommel indicates, this relocation was carefully calculated to allow for uninterrupted access during construction. The designer (perhaps Baccio Pontelli, at least through 1492) conceived of the work in sequence, so that the ancient basilica remained accessible while the new basilica was built immediately adjacent to it. For the history of the complex transformation of this site see Frommel and Pentiricci (2009), esp. 411–28.

14. Ackerman (1951, 1954); Bruschi (1969), 291–434 and 865–82. See also Frommel (2002), 82–87.

15. Key discussion remains Spezzaferro (1973); Tafuri (1973, 1984). For a recent overview see Pellecchia (2005).

16. Bruschi (1994); Pagliara and Butters (1997); Frommel (2002), esp. 90–94. Pagliara and Butters moderate Tafuri's argument that Julius II intended the new palace as a direct challenge to the authority of the Capitoline government, suggesting that the increased efficiency of the new papal courts would have weakened the Capitoline government enough by comparison. Despite significant expenses recorded for this new project, only the mammoth foundations were completed, perhaps because of unstable soil conditions. A new bridge was planned to link the Via Giulia across the Tiber to the Vatican at its north end, raised upon the surviving foundations of an ancient Neronian bridge.

17. For useful orientation to the immense literature on the New St. Peter's see Francia (1977); Frommel (1994); Bruschi (1996); Bredekamp (2000); Frommel (2002), 87–90. The best succinct account of the early stages of the basilica's construction is Thoenes (2005), 64–92. For intriguing discussion of Heemskerck's depiction of New St. Peter's as a ruin see Thoenes (1986), translated into Italian with abbreviated notes in Thoenes (1998), 134–49.

18. Heemskerck is known to have arrived in Rome before mid-July 1532, when he met Vasari. The date of his departure from Rome is uncertain, but the commission of paintings for an altarpiece in Amsterdam from Heemskerck dating to November 1537 serves as a terminus post quem. For Heemskerck's activities in Rome, along with other contemporary artists from the Netherlands, see Dacos (2001).

19. The *tiburio* or *tegurium* was built in 1513 and stood until 1592. See Shearman (1974); Tronzo (1997).

20. The first known reference to Bramante by this rhyming epithet was made in 1511 by Paris de Grassis, master of ceremonies for Julius II, who implied that in a week Bramante had caused widespread destruction in Rome. See Ackerman (1974), 347.

21. For the obelisk, see Iversen (1968); D'Onofrio (1992); Curran et al. (2009).

22. Alberti (1988), 26.

23. Curran and Grafton (1995), 238.

24. "est ille persuadere Julio apostoli sepulcrum ut commodiorum in templi transferetur, templi frons, non ad orientem solem, ut nunc vergit, set uti in meridiem nothumque converteretur, ut obeliscus magna in templi area templum ascensuris

occurreret . . . rem omnium accommodatissimum futurum pollicere, si Julii pont[ificis] is templum, augustissimum Julii Caesaris monumentum, [quod] vulgo putant, in vestibulo et ipso templi aditu haberet." Egidio da Viterbo, *Historia viginti saeculorum*, Rome, Biblioteca Angelica, MS 351, 245r. Translated in Rowland (1998), 172–73; for Latin text see note 103. For hypothetical reconstruction of Bramante's plan see Frommel (1994), 400–401.

25. For the intense interest stirred by the survival of ancient Egyptian artifacts in early modern Italy see Curran (2007).

26. "quod Caesaris obeliscum deceat, ipse viderit, se sacra prophanis, religionem splendori, pietatem ornamentis esse praepositurum." Egidio da Viterbo, *Historia viginti saeculorum*, Rome, Biblioteca Angelica, MS 351, 245r.

27. Sixtus V, a pope perhaps even more notorious than Julius II for causing the destruction of ancient remains in Rome, devoted enormous energy to the meticulous preservation of this obelisk as a single monolithic stone during its laborious removal to its new location in the Piazza di San Pietro. The relocation was commemorated by Sixtus V's architect Domenico Fontana in the *Della trasportatione* (1590).

28. For changing interpretations of New St. Peter's over time see Thoenes (1998), 237–51.

29. For growing hostility to the destruction of Old St. Peter's see De Maio (1981), 307–28.

30. ASV, *Div. Cam.* 57, 196v–197, "Declaration cam. ap. super effodiendo tiburtino" (3 January 1506).

31. For archaeological discussion of these temples collectively known as the Republican victory temples, located in the ancient *Forum Holitorium* or vegetable market, see Coarelli (2001), 376–78; Claridge (2010), 279–82.

32. For the appointment document see Golzio (1936), 33; Shearman (2003), 1.186–89.

33. For Raphael's rapid maturity as an architect see collected essays in Frommel et al. (1984).

34. Golzio (1936), 38–40; Shearman (2003), 1.207–11.

35. For the critical edition of the three surviving versions of the "Letter to Leo X" see Di Teodoro (2003); see also Shearman (2003), 1.500–45. Its dating has long been a vexed question, although Di Teodoro persuasively argues (based upon internal evidence derived from the surviving manuscript at Mantua) that the draft was produced "between mid-September and the first days of November 1519." See Di Teodoro (2003), 44–56.

36. For discussion of sources for the first half of the Letter, see Di Teodoro (2003), 189–206.

37. Marchetti-Longhi (1919); Cortonesi (1986); Vaquero-Piñiero (2002). See also Manacorda (2003), 52.

38. "tutta questa Roma nova che hor si vede, quanto grande ch'ella si sia, quanto bella, quanto ornata di palaggi, chiese et altri aedificii, tutta è fabricata di calce di marmi antichi!" Di Teodoro (2003), 68.

39. "Non debe adonque, Padre Santissimo, esser tra gli ultimi pensieri di Vostra Santità lo haver cura che quello poco che resta di questa anticha madre de la gloria et grandezza italiana . . . non sii estirpato e guasto." Ibid.

40. For the notion that preservation of the past served as a means for the civic nobility to revenge themselves against powerful papal courtiers in early sixteenth-century Rome, as attested in the rhetoric of "native Romans" defending the remains of antiquity from invading barbaric "foreigners," see Franceschini (1986).

41. For the dating of the letter between September and November 1519 see Di Teodoro (2003), 44–56; for the argument that initial work on the letter began by 1516 or even earlier, see Shearman (2003), 1.543.

42. For the relative documents see Golzio (1936), 72–73; Shearman (2003), 1.355–57. For further discussion of the case see also Christian (2002), 151–65.

43. The Capitoline archives have been preserved only from the beginning of the sixteenth century; for the misfortunes of this collection see Guasco (1919, 1946). The increase in the number of papal excavation licenses for this period is most evident in surveying the records of the *Diversa Cameralia* in the Vatican archives.

44. Nesselrath (1983), 357; Perini (1995), 114. For Raphael's antiquarian investigations see also Müntz (1880), 453–64; Castagnoli (1968); Ray (1974), 265–71; Burns (1984); Morolli (1984); Nesselrath (1984); Biermann (1988).

45. ASC, Cred. I, vol. 36, 73 (10 March 1520).

46. Pastor describes Armellini Medici and Santiquattro as confidants of Leo X and blames them for pursuing ruinous economic policies; see Pastor (1898), 8.97–102. For the biography of the cardinal see De Caro (1962).

47. ASV, *Div. Cam.* 74, 74r; reported in part by Lanciani (1989), 1.254. According to the license, Armellini Medici authorized the excavation of "auri argenti margaritar. gemmar. lapillor. metallorum omniunq. thesauror. generis . . . in urbe montibus speluncis cavernis ac omnibus terris et locis S.R.E. subiectis."

48. ASC, Cred. I, vol. 36, 84(10 September 1520).

49. ASC, Cred. I, vol. 15, 67v (1 December 1520).

50. While the exact location of the Arca di Noè remains uncertain, it appears to have spanned the important thoroughfare passing through the Forum of Nerva, also known as the *Fundicus Macellorum de Archanoè*, that connected the area of the Roman Forum with that of the Suburra. See Hülsen (1927), 311; Platner and Ashby (1929), 228–29; Lalle (2005), 230.

51. Of a noble Milanese family, Cardinal Trivulzio was also a transplant to Rome. This attack by civic leaders upon the barbarity of the Curia resonated with the xenophobic complaint of the historian Paolo Giovio: "veramente la deliberatione di tutti i papi era . . . di concedere tutta Roma in preda a huomini forastieri et mezzo barbari, diradicando l'antica stirpe del sangue romano . . . et gli erano solamente restate le immagini degli honori antichi." Paolo Giovio, *Le vite di Leone X et d'Adriano Sesto sommi pontefici, et del Cardinal Pompeo Colonna* (1557), cited by Miglio (1984), 1.111.

52. ASV, *Div. Cam.* 73, 109v, "Licentia Marie Magdalene Brugmans Bremens fodiendi in Via Appia" (29 July 1523). For transcription see Cerasoli (1897), 141–42.

53. "sine alicuius etiam edificiorum publicorum preiudicio vel deterioratione." Ibid.

54. Cardinal Santiquattro, so called after his titular church of Santi Quattro Coronati, was the first cardinal appointed by Leo X in 1513; for much of his career he lived at the papal palace in the Vatican. For the history of the Pucci family—all devoted

Medici supporters—see Ciaconio (1677), 3.522–23; Ughelli (1717), 3.308–10. See also Chambers (1987).

55. ASV, *Div. Cam.* 74, 131v, "Patentes card. Laurentio Puccio fodiendi marmora pro constructione sui palatii" (8 August 1524).

56. "pro ornatu urbis iuxta basilicam principis apostolorum beati Petri." Ibid.

57. Barocchi and Ristori (1973), 3.133; Ackerman (1961), 2.142. Santiquattro did not live to see the completion of his palace. Standing immediately outside the southern colonnade of St. Peter's Square, it was occupied around 1566 and served as the seat for the Inquisition; see Frommel (1973), 1.146–47.

58. ASV, *Div. Cam.* 74, 170v, "Patentes jacopo fossori travertinorum" (12 January 1525).

59. This corresponds to what Alois Riegl later defined as age-value; see Riegl (1982), 31–34.

60. ASC, Cred. I, vol. 15, 149–50 (3 March 1526). For the Arcus Traiani see De Maria (1988), 296–97.

61. ASC, Cred. I, vol. 15, 150 (23 March 1526).

62. ASC, Cred. I, vol. 15, 150 (26 March 1526).

63. ASV, *Div. Cam.* 76, 174r, "Mandatum Johanni Marie de la Porta ducis Urbini oratori effodiendi marmora in Quirinale" (21 February 1527).

64. The maintenance of the Via Pontificia or the Via Papalis, which skirted the Quirinal Hill as it traversed the Campus Martius between St. Peter's and the Lateran, was the object of continued papal attention throughout the Renaissance, along with the Via Recta and the Via del Pellegrino. For the maintenance of these streets by the *maestri* see discussion in Re (1920), 17–24, and 98–99 for the 1452 *maestri* statutes, chapter 32.

65. The best treatment of the Sack of Rome is by Chastel (1977).

66. Ibid., 7.

67. ASV, *Div. Cam.*, 85, 201v–202v, "Licentia fodiendi pro marmoribus et thesaurius Francisco Cochicio de Amelia" (6 April 1532).

68. "valeas dummodo antiqua vel moderna publica edificia et loca at publica seu privata nimium damnificentur vel si damnificari necesse fuerint in pristinum statum reponi possint." Ibid.

69. *Inter ceteras Romani Pontificis curas* (8 November 1534). For the text of the appointment brief, which enumerated an exhaustive list of monuments that fell to Manetti's jurisdiction, see Fea (1784), 375–76; Fea (1802), 94–95; for a partial Italian translation see D'Onofrio (1973), 138–39. According to Lanciani, these were "belle e sante parole, ma nulla più: conciossiaché non possiamo dimenticare che colui medesimo il quale le ha scritte e le ha indirizzate a Manetti, sei anni dopo ordinava la distruzione atroce, implacabile, completa di tutti i monumenti del foro." Lanciani (1989), 2.39.

70. For Manetti's career and noted humanist interests, see Marini (1784), 384–85; Reumont (1870), 3.353; Orano (1896), 43, note 4; Dorez (1932), 1.115–40; D'Onofrio (1973), 138–42; Ridley (1992b), 117–18.

71. Ridley (1992b).

72. Manetti's own service as both *maestro di strade* and as a Conservator (he was elected to these positions both before and after his appointment as the commissioner

of antiquity) suggests that he himself would have been sympathetic to the idea of leaving preservation duties in the hands of the civic officials. For more on the erosion of the power of the civic government under Paul III see Caravale and Caracciolo (1978), 267–70.

73. Later evidence suggests that the Conservators' continued jurisdiction over preservation enabled them to bend the will of even the most dynamic and forceful popes. Demolition began on the ancient Mausoleum of Cecelia Metella in 1588, condemned by Sixtus V as an obstruction to his proposed rebuilding of the Via Appia and also because it provided problematic cover for brigands. However, the brothers Giovanni Battista Motino and Girolamo Leni, owners of the property and spearheading its demolition, were compelled to request formal permission from the pope, and also to request that the Conservators should not oppose the project, citing numerous extenuating conditions: "per essere fuori di Roma, et non in luoco pubblico, et altre ne siano state spogliate, una per la strada di Tivoli, un'altra di marmo al ponte dell'Arco, un'altra al Casal Ritonno, e molte altre." Sixtus V granted their request, and it seems he also pressured the Conservators to acquiesce, for on 5 June 1589 they voted by a large majority to allow destruction to continue. But on 18 July 1589 the Conservators declared this decision null and void. Citing the authority granted by Pius II in the Bull of 1462, the Conservators insisted that they were obliged by papal command to preserve the ancient structure, and only by an equivalent and contrary papal order could they authorize its destruction. Although we do not know the final outcome of the case, the aborted demolition of the mausoleum suggests that even the iron will of Sixtus V quailed at the thought of being branded the destroyer of ancient Roman remains. For this episode along with transcriptions of relevant documents see Antinori (1989).

74. For the tensions between the emperor and the pope in the months leading up to the triumph, see Pastor (1898), 11.233–41; Caravale and Caracciolo (1978), 244–46, 268–70; Visceglia (2001). See also collected essays in Fantoni (2000).

75. "Noi aspettiamo qua in publica letitia e privatu luctu Sua Cesarea Maestà." Giovio (1560), 16v.

76. Lanciani (1902), 229–55; Lanciani (1906), 101–12; Lanciani (1989), 2.63–74; Madonna (1980), 63–68; Madonna (1997), 50–67; Visceglia (2000, 2001); ibid. (2002), 53–197; Dacos (2001), 77–107; for review of earlier bibliography see Mitchell (1979), 125–28. Sixteenth-century accounts making special reference to the ancient remains include Podestà (1878), 303–44; Orano (1896), 43–74. For the enduring postclassical fascination for the classical triumph see Pinelli (1984). For more on the phenomenon of the classical Roman triumph see Beard (2007).

77. "volendo che sua maestate vedesse la meraviglia della antiquitate." Cited from Orano (1896), 45.

78. Manetti also served as *maestro di strade* in 1536, thus exercising a double mandate of both preservation and urban design. See Podestà (1878), 326; Orano (1896), 43.

79. "plenissimam tibi facultatem auctoritate Apostolica tenore praesentium concedimus, intendendi, incumbendi, et curandi, ut omnia dictae Urbis, et Districtus eius Monimenta, Arcus, Templa, Trophaea, Theatra, Amphitheatra, Circi, Nau-machiae, Porticus, Columnae, Sepulchra, Epitaphia, Eulogia [*sic*], Moles, Aquaeductus,

Statuae, Signa, Tabulae, Lapides, Marmora, et denique quicquid nomine Antiquitatum, vel Monimentorum comprehendi potest, quantum fieri poterit, conserventur,
atque a vepribus, virgultis, arboribus, praecipue hederis, et caprificis, omnino
liberentur: neve his novae domus, aut parietes applicentur, neu ipsa diruantur,
comminuantur, confringantur, in calcem coquantur, aut extra urbem asportentur."
Inter ceteras Romani Pontificis curas (8 November 1534). The brief of 1534 indicated that
just as wild plants destroyed ancient structures with their roots, so did the construction of new buildings destroy ancient buildings through the collection of ancient stone
that was then burned for lime.

80. The implementation of this preservation program under Paul III and Manetti
can thus be seen as a key step in the direction of the manicured ruins that confront
visitors to the Roman Forum today.

81. The document issued by the Conservators on 5 December 1535 was published
by Lanciani (1902), 231–33.

82. ASV, *Div. Cam.* 98, 89v–90v, "Mandatum magistris stratarum Urbis" (12
January 1536).

83. Ibid. "facendo aprire la vigna di Maphei . . . ad Septem Solio." For further
discussion of the Vigna Maffei, and the affected section adjacent to the basilica of San
Gregorio, see Lanciani (1989), 2.44.

84. ASV, *Div. Cam.* 98, 89v–90v (12 January 1536). "mettere in insula l'archo di
Constantino quanto è largo, con farlo le ali." The reference to "farlo le ali," suggesting
that the structure should have some sort of "wings," may have referred to the construction of new walls along the length of the approach from the Circus Maximus, visible in
the 1577 Dupérac map of Rome.

85. "on a desmoly et abattu plus de deux cens maisons, et trois ou quatre eglises
raz terre . . . c'est pityé de veoir la ruine des maisons qui ont esté démollyez, et n'est
faict payement ny récompense aulcune ès seigneurs d'ycelles." Transcribed in Dorez
(1932), 2.257–58.

86. Ibid. It is worth noting that demolitions to liberate ancient Roman structures
also occurred in sixteenth-century France; see Karmon (2010b).

87. For further discussion see especially Madonna (1997).

88. During the *possesso* of Leo X in 1513, ancient sculptures from private collections had been temporarily placed along the processional route; see Fagiolo and
Madonna (1997), 48.

89. For Heemskerck in 1536 see Dacos (2001), 77–107.

90. I refer to Pierre Nora's notion of the *milieu de mémoire*, the living environment of memory, as opposed to the *lieu de mémoire*, or the commemorative place of
memory; see Nora (1996-98). Thanks to Hilary Ballon for directing me to Nora's
fundamental work. See also Halbwachs (1992); Nelson (2003).

91. *Ut fabrica basilica principis apostolorum alme urbis nostre* (22 July 1540). For
transcription see Müntz (1884), 307–10. A fair copy with minor variations is at the
Archivio della Fabbrica di San Pietro, Armadio 1, Ripiano A, vol. 10, 44.

92. "Gli effetti disastrosi di questo infausto Breve appariranno chiari nella storia
del prossimo decennio. Ad esso dobbiamo la distruzione dei monumenti della valle del
foro, i quali, se avevano sofferto danni nella parte sporgente dal suolo moderno,
rimanevano presso che intatti nella parte protetta dallo strato dei ruderi." Thus

Lanciani blamed Paul III for causing the destruction of ancient foundations that would otherwise survived intact; Lanciani (1989), 2.203. For discussion of the individual affected monuments between 1540 and 1549 see ibid., 2.203–51.

93. Peruzzi recorded his praise for the Temple of Castor and Pollux on his detailed drawing of the monument (UA631r); see Wurm 1984, 459. See also Burns (1988a), 212.

94. "Hoggi in questo Tempio si è cavato una dele base delle colonne è un capitello . . . quali sono stati portati in San Pietro per guastarsi certamente; è pur cosa brutta à guastare le memorie antiche et ben fatte per ornare una cosa non molto lodata, con tutto che vi si spenda assai." Cited from Cod. Canonici Ital., 138, f. 191, in Burns (1988b), 42–43; see also Lanciani (1989), 2.236. As Burns notes, Ligorio's contempt for the design of the New St. Peter's suggests he probably wrote this passage after 1546, when his competitor Michelangelo had assumed the responsibility of chief architect.

95. In his discussion of excavations conducted at the Arch of Augustus beginning in 1542, Lanciani affirmed "tutte queste insigni memorie istoriche . . . furono o bruciati, o trasformati, o distrutti nel giro di poche settimane. Tra gli inni sciolti dal Panvinio al 'felicissimus principatus Pauli III' e i gridi d'orrore del Ligorio, mi sembra che la scelta non possa esser dubbia." Lanciani (1989), 2.227.

96. Archivio della Fabbrica di San Pietro, Armadio 53, Ripiano B, vol. 127, 92v–93, "Lettera patente con la facoltà e condizioni per scavare marmi, travertine, colonne, ecc. per loca publica etiam ecclesiae huius almae Urbis . . . per servizio della Fabbrica di S Pietro di Roma" (1 March 1546). Similar licenses have been published by Cascioli (1921).

97. On 14 April 1546 Vincenzo Veteri, "civi Romano," was deputized the custodian of the Column of Trajan, "custodiendam columnam Troianam in Regionem Montium," by the *maestri di strade*, with a regular monthly salary: "ducatos auri viginti quatuor de paulis X pro ducato pro eius sex mensium inceptorum die prima praesentis mensis aprilis et ut sequitur finiendorum ordinaria provisione." See Müntz (1884), 53. For a survey of subsequent protective legislation in Italy see Emiliani (1996).

CHAPTER 4

1. The Colosseum was raised by Vespasian directly on top of the palace, gardens, and artificial lake built by Nero, known as the Domus Aurea or the Golden House, as a spectacular act of imperial *damnatio memoriae*. The origin of the name "Colosseum" is disputed, but the general consensus is that by the eleventh century this name (also "Amphitheatrum-Coliseum") had been transferred to the monument from an adjacent statue of Nero known as the Colossus; Rea (1993), 30. The bibliography on the monument is immense but other studies paying particular attention to the afterlife of the monument include Colagrossi (1913); Lugli (1946), 344–46; Di Macco (1971); Moccheggiani-Carpano and Luciani (1981); Sear (1982); Golvin (1988), 1.173–80; Croci (1990); Richardson (1992), 7–10; Coarelli (2001), 196–204; La Regina (2001); Rea (2001); Rea (2002); Taylor (2003), 133–73; Beard and Hopkins (2005); Denker Nesselrath (2005); Karmon (2005); Claridge (2010), 312–19; Karmon (2010a). For the evolution of the Roman amphitheater as a structural form see Welch (2007).

2. Byron, *Childe Harold's Pilgrimage* (London, 1818), canto 4, stanza 143. For Byron's famous moonlit meditations on the ruins of the Colosseum see *Manfred* (London, 1817), Act 3, scene 4, lines 1–41.

3. Ibid., stanza 145. The original lines attributed to the Venerable Bede are "Quamdiu stat Colysaeum stat et Roma, quando cadet Colysaeum cadet et Roma, quando cadet et Roma cadet et mundus." Bede, *Collectanea*, 1.3.

4. For the myth of the *Salvatio Romae*, see Cilento (1983).

5. As Müntz observed while documenting Renaissance archaeological demolitions at the Colosseum, "éxplique qui pourra cette flagrante contradiction dans la conduite de Nicolas V; pour nous, notre tâche se borne à enregistrer le douloureux détail de ces mutilations sans nombre." Müntz (1878), 4.107.

6. Archaeological evidence that may be related to the water distribution system has been identified even at the highest stories of the Colosseum. However, the height of the Celian Hill limited the height to which water could be pumped. The water supply network certainly provided water to the level of the *maenianum secundum*, just below the uppermost level of the *maenianum secundum in ligneis*. See Corazza and Lombardi (2002), 46–65.

7. The question of whether *naumachiae* or naval battles were actually staged in the arena is uncertain; see Rea (1993), 34.

8. For the *velarium* see Graefe (1979), esp. 1.56–61; Goldman (1982); Coleman (2000), 233–34.

9. Restorations were reported at the Colosseum in the second century during the reign of Antoninus Pius; see *Scriptores Historia Augusta*, Ant. Pius 8.2.

10. Dio Cassius, 79.25.2. The gladiatorial spectacles of the Colosseum were transferred to the Stadium of Domitian, better known today as the Piazza Navona; see Coleman (2000), 242.

11. Lancaster (1998).

12. Mocchegiani-Carpano and Luciani (1981).

13. *CIL* 6.32094 b–c.

14. Antonetti and Rea (2002b), 287–90. For the last *venationes*, see Orlandi (1999); La Regina (2001), 24–25; Antonetti and Rea (2002b), 288.

15. Antonetti and Rea (2002a), 218–27.

16. For archaeological dating of the major collapse of the southern arcades to the eighth century, see Antonetti and Rea (2002b), 302.

17. Ibid., 333, note 128.

18. For sedimentation patterns see Funiciello et al. (2002), 161–67.

19. For discussion of sixth-century excavations see Rea and Pani (2002), 159.

20. It is likely, however, that the Colosseum was already exploited as a quarry even in antiquity. The ongoing maintenance of the Flavian amphitheater required extensive quantities of building stone to be available on hand to provide for ongoing repairs, and this ready supply of building stone could always then be pilfered for other projects.

21. For the medieval Via Maggiore as papal processional route see Adinolfi (1857), 91–93.

22. Petrarch (1975–85), vol. 2, 11.7.

23. In Petrarch's original Latin text: "cecidit aedificiorum veterum neglecta civibus stupenda peregrinis moles." Ibid.

24. Colagrossi observed this deductive reasoning met with common consensus; Colagrossi (1913), 164. This reasoning was still cited, although with perhaps greater caution, by Di Macco (1971), 41.

25. "Non potuimus non turbari audientes . . . ut quaedam Colisei pars . . . pro restauratione quorumdam domorum deiciatur. Nam demoliri Urbis monumenta nihil aliud est quam ipsius Urbis et totius orbis excellentiam diminuere . . . nec quovis modo permittatis ut et minimus dicti Colisei lapis seu aliorum edificiorum antiquorum deiiciatur." Lanciani (1989), 1.58–59.

26. "a dì 21 uno tedesco portò le tivertini da Coliseo a Sancto Johanni." For this payment see Müntz (1878), 48.

27. Payment recorded by Müntz (1876), 170.

28. For the Bull of 1462 see discussion in chapter 2.

29. For marble quarried at Carrara and brought to Rome under Pius II, see Müntz (1876), 172.

30. Müntz (1876), 172; Lanciani (1989), 1.79–81.

31. Lanciani reported that marble banks of seating stripped from the Colosseum were used to build the stairs at St. Peter's at this time; Lanciani (1989), 1.80.

32. For payment dated 31 December 1467 for stone quarried at the Colosseum to supply the work site of the Palazzo Venezia, see Müntz (1876), 174. For other payments made for excavations at the Colosseum beginning in November 1466 and continuing through December 1467, see Lanciani (1989), 1.87. Lanciani also records a payment made 30 April 1467 for a wagon to transport these materials: "Maestro Bartolomeo da Perosa che habita ascto Baxilio per un caro che a fato fare maestro Francesco da Borgo per tirare tivertine marmore et altre cosse."

33. For papal payments for work at the Arch of Titus, dated 21 May 1466, see Müntz (1876), 175. For papal payments for restorations to the Pantheon, documented from May 1468 to August 1470, see ibid., 163–64.

34. Choay (2001), 37.

35. "Ut parvi starent fondamina pontis, ampla tuae quatinant amphitheatra manus?" Cited in Müntz (1882), 133.

36. Perhaps this new construction employed travertine from the Theater of Marcellus, although this remains to be verified; see Cardilli (2000), 442, note 8. For further demolitions conducted during the pontificate of Sixtus IV see Vattuone (2000).

37. "Gli astigrafi ripetono vagamente, copiandosi l'un l'altro, come il palazzo fosse edificato coi marmi cavati . . . dal Colosseo. Assai popolare è in Roma l'aneddoto dell'astuzia usata dal card. Alessandro per ispogliare il Colosseo, perché, avendogli lo zio pontefice concesso di toglierne tante pietre quante avrebbe potuto trasportare alla sua fabbrica in una notte sola, egli raccolse a tale scopo più centinaia di carri, anche dai dintorni di Roma, e poté così compiere in poche ore il lavoro di più settimane. La verità è tutt'altra." Lanciani (1989), 2.165.

38. The Roman civic magistrate Lorenzo Caffarelli was reported to have attacked and wounded workers excavating travertine from the foundations of the Colosseum at some point already during the reign of Paul II (1464–71); see Lanciani (1989), 1.132, as well as discussion in chapter 2.

39. For the Compagnia del Salvatore see Marangoni (1746), 55; Adinolfi (1881), 1.325; Cerasoli (1902), 302; Pavan (1978, 1984).

40. As discussed by Burroughs (1990), 30.

41. Colagrossi affirms that the papal legates formally assigned the jurisdiction of the Colosseum to the civic magistrates in the fourteenth century, without however making it clear what sources substantiate this point; Colagrossi (1913), 155. Further evidence confirms his argument that throughout the Middle Ages both the popes and the civic magistrates participated in controlling this ancient site.

42. The magistrates of the civic government traditionally objected to the appropriation of ancient monuments by powerful Roman families, evident as early as 1162 in their decree for the preservation of the Column of Trajan. Thus the civic magistrates sought to expel the powerful Roman noble families from the Colosseum who built their fortified strongholds within its shell during the Middle Ages. For medieval interventions at the Colosseum see Marangoni (1746), 49–55; Adinolfi (1881), 1.356–89; Cerasoli (1902), 300–15; Colagrossi (1913), 147–69; Rodocanachi (1914); Di Macco (1971), 31–32. In particular, for the twelfth-century letter from the Senate recording the confiscation of the Colosseum from the Frangipani see Adinolfi (1881), 365. For the location of the Frangipani fortress in radial corridors 16–32 at the northeastern side of the monument see Antonetti and Rea (2002b), 313–14.

43. For the history and locations of these vanished churches see Armellini (1942), 1.636–38.

44. ASR, catasto Santi Sanctorum 1435, 59; transcribed in Cerasoli (1902), 303.

45. "tertia pars totius Colisei iuncta pro indiviso cum aliis duabus tertiis partibus Camere Urbis." Ibid.

46. See Rea (2002), 231–39; Antonetti and Rea (2002b), 333, note 129. The use of property markers was typical practice for the confraternity; see Guidoni (1983), 5.377.

47. Antonetti and Rea (2002b), 320–22.

48. Archaeological evidence suggests that the excavations conducted within the structural core of the Colosseum were in fact managed with considerable skill and dexterity. The removal of stone from the existing structure was a delicate operation, as the accidental removal of too much masonry could cause catastrophic collapse. Aided by the efficient system of the Colosseum staircases, which provided access to all parts of the structure, excavators dismantled the internal walls of the Colosseum from the top down. These walls were built with squared blocks of travertine as the carrying structure, with infill of equally carefully cut blocks of tufa, and they systematically removed the more valuable travertine while leaving the tufa in place. For discussion see Antonetti and Rea (2002b), 321; Taylor (2003), 146–47.

49. The confraternity maintained a hospital for women adjacent to the Colosseum, "Hospitale San Jacobi iuxta Coliseum . . . deputatum ad usum mulierum"; Cerasoli (1902), 303. See also Adinolfi (1857), 156–57, for a license to expand the hospital, issued by the *maestri di strade* on 19 November 1472: "Venerabilis hospitalis sacratissime Imaginis Salvatori Domini Nostri Jesu Christi ad Sancta Sanctor . . . apud Coliseum cum domibus in ea existentibus in quibus nonullas pauperes mulieres ab eodem hospitali receptas." The explicit use of income from the sale of building stone to benefit charitable activities was recorded in the property records of the confraternity in 1525: "la Compagnia del Salvatore domina e custode del Colosseo; il che per assai chiar si mantiene, havendo potesta de tutte tevertine de quello ruinassi posserne fare si come ali guardiani li paresse par darne allo hospitale miglio luchro et proficto." Gregorovius (1900), 7.677, note 2.

50. For the preservation of the Torso Belvedere, as well as discussion of Renaissance approaches to preserving and restoring sculpture fragments, see Barkan (1999), 186–207.

51. "pare certo che i papi del quattrocento non abbiano mai demolito espressamente alcuna parte del Colosseo, ma . . . si sieno largamente approfittati dei materiali caduti per ispontanea rovina, per terremoto, o per iscalzamento delle radici delle piante arborescenti." Lanciani (1989), 1.79.

52. Notes composed by a disciple of Pomponio Leto and later published by Francesco Albertini in the *Opusculum de mirabilibus novae urbis Romae* (1510) reported continuing excavations at the Colosseum during the reign of Sixtus IV (1471–84); see Lanciani (1989), 1.101. The area of the Colosseum as well as the Roman Forum also supplied building stone for the new Palazzo Cancelleria of Cardinal Riario between 1496 and 1497; see Bentivoglio (1982), 29. For papal payments for stone excavated "in nella cava de Coliseo," dating to 1499, during the reign of Alexander VI, see Müntz (1876), 175.

53. See for instance the example of Bramante and Julius II at St. Peter's as discussed in chapter 3.

54. Lanciani (1989), 1.81.

55. The architect Francesco del Borgo contributed to both of these projects, although his exact role at San Marco remains uncertain. See Frommel (1983, 1984), ibid. (1998), 382–90.

56. The loggias at Palazzo Venezia included the Benediction Loggia fronting the basilica of San Marco as well as the loggias of the palace courtyards, which inverted the exterior colonnades of the Colosseum by setting them around an internal rectangular court.

57. For the use of stone from the Colosseum to supply the St. Peter's work site under Pius II and for the Palazzo Venezia under Paul II, see notes 30 and 32 above.

58. For this episode, see discussion in chapter 6.

59. Thus in 1703 the Conservators approved the reuse of Colosseum travertine to construct the Porto Ripetta. See ASC, Cred. VI, vol. 59, 154–55, transcribed by Cesare D'Onofrio (1980), 284–85.

60. For example, for 1540 to 1550, a decade of energetic citywide excavations authorized by Paul III, only six documents have been found referring to excavations in the vicinity of the Colosseum, none of which appear to have been conducted within the structure itself. See Cascioli (1921), 374–76, notes 3–4.

61. Marangoni (1746), 54; Adinolfi (1881), 1.367–74; Colagrossi (1913), 158–61.

62. For the Gonfalone confraternity see Ruggieri (1866); Vattasso (1903); De Bartholomaeis (1943); Esposito (1984); Wisch (1991, 1992); Newbigin (2000).

63. Newbigin (1990).

64. *Recognitio facta per Guardianos Gonfalonis domorum de Coliseo* (17 March 1490). For transcription see Adinolfi (1857), 158–59. See also Marangoni (1746), 54; Adinolfi (1881), 1.367–74.

65. As argued by Colagrossi (1913), 172; Rodocanachi (1914), 170.

66. Adinolfi (1857), 158. The document states that these properties once belonged to the Annibaldi family: "que fuerunt quondam nobilium de Aniballis de Coliseo, qui illas Guardianis dicti hospitalis vendiderunt ut constat publico instrumento."

67. As noted in the original text of the statutes of the Gonfalone confraternity; for the transcription see Esposito (1984), 126.

68. Antonetti and Rea (2002b), 322.

69. For more on the chapel of Santa Maria della Pietà, rebuilt circa 1517–19, see Ruggieri (1866), 147; Adinolfi (1881), 379; Armellini (1942), 1.638–39.

70. For the performances in Verona, see Wisch (1992), 96.

71. Payment records for the first performance held at the Colosseum on Good Friday in 1490 show both the construction and dismantling of several stage settings, including the manger at Nazareth and the Temple at Jerusalem: "a mastro Pietro de Stefano da Firenze, legnaiulo, karolini 36 [e] i suoi lavoranti . . . quali hanno lavorato al Cholisseo a fare lo tempio et altre cose per l'ultimate devozione, et per disfar el castello, nazare et disfare el ditto tempio." See Vattasso (1903), 75–76.

72. Antonetti and Rea (2002b), 322.

73. Renewed interest in classical literature and theater in Renaissance Rome also stimulated this revival of the Colosseum as performance space; see Newbigin (2000), 188; also De Bartholomaeis (1943), 120; Di Macco (1971), 64–67; Stinger (1998), 288–89; Rowland (1998), 21–22, 151–57.

74. Von Harff (1876); partially transcribed in Cruciani (1983), 266.

75. Fulvio (1527), 53r.

76. Newbigin (2000), 173. Newbigin notes that the Passion plays at the Colosseum, perhaps not unexpectedly, emphasized the wrongdoing of the Jews while exonerating the Romans; ibid., 187.

77. Ibid., 187; Adinolfi (1881), 3.387–88. The Passion plays had already been suspended in 1522 for causing political disorder. According to the nineteenth-century historian Fabio Francesco Montani, after the performances angry crowds poured out of the Colosseum, attacking both the Jewish population and the city watch; Montani (1861), 53.

78. For this text and translation see Newbigin (2000), 180, and 195, note 49.

79. The papal administration continued to authorize the removal of stone from the Colosseum for the payment of debts; for example, in 1576, a creditor of the papal court, Agostino Paloni, requested and received payment in travertine and marble extracted from the *coscia Colisei*. ASV, Divers. X, p. 251, c. 205; cited in Lanciani (1989), 4.89.

80. Cerasoli (1902), 306–15. See also Ridley (1992).

81. "Reverendo ms. Giovanni Battista pagarete . . . Iuli dodeci ad Ambrogio carrettere per haver portati doi pezzi di marmo gentile per uso di detto ornamento dal Culiseo sino a San Pietro." ASV, Exit mandati sacr., p. 219 (31 July 1577); transcribed by Cascioli (1921), 376, note 5. For the embellishments of the chapel, commissioned for the Jubilee of 1575, see Brandt (1987), 88.

82. Wisch (2000), 206. The chapel in the arena of the Colosseum, rebuilt by the Gonfalone in 1517, was dedicated to the Madonna Santissima della Pietà.

83. For discussion of the *translatio* and the circulation of fragmentary relics see Geary (1990), 9–15.

CHAPTER 5

1. The *Lexicon Topographicum Urbis Romae* describes the Pantheon simply as "the best-preserved ancient edifice in Rome." Ziolkowski (1999), 54. For further discussion of the survival and preservation of the Pantheon across time, see Eroli (1895); Müntz (1876); Cerasoli (1909); Muñoz (1912); Rodocanachi (1914); De Fine

Licht (1968); Buddensieg (1971); Macdonald (1976); Coarelli (1983); Godfrey and Hemsoll (1986); Davies et al. (1987); Loercke (1982, 1990); Mark and Hutchinson (1986); Lanciani (1989), esp. 2.264–69; Martines (1991); Richardson (1992), 283–86; Moore (1995); Pasquali (1996); Ziolkowski (1999); Coarelli (2001), 346–51; Wilson-Jones (2001), esp. 176–213; Taylor (2003), esp. 190–211; Nesselrath (2005); Karmon (2008b), 41–42; Claridge (2010), 226–34.

2. Marble also sheathed the circular ledge around the cupola's stepped rings, and marble slabs also covered the lowest of these steps, which are still intact today. Ziolkowski (1999), 59.

3. Ibid.

4. The evident celestial analogy of the architecture has led to extensive speculation over the centuries about its possible cosmic significance. For discussion of the mathematical and astronomical significance of the Pantheon see Martines (1991, 2000).

5. *Hist. August Pius* 8.2.

6. The inscription, M. AGRIPPA L. F. COS TERTIUM FECIT (Marcus Agrippa, son of Lucius, erected this structure during his third consulship), reflected Hadrian's decision that restored structures should be reassigned to their original dedicants ("eaque omnia propriis auctorum nominibus consecravit"). The first iteration of the Pantheon, built by Augustus's close ally Marcus Agrippa in 27–25 B.C., was destroyed in a fire in 80 A.D.; the second iteration, built by Domitian, was then destroyed by fire in 110 A.D. Not surprisingly, for centuries the rotunda was believed to have been built by Agrippa.

7. PANTHEUM VETUSTATE CORRUPTUM CUM OMNI CULTU RESTITU-ERUNT (The Pantheon, worn by age, was restored with every refinement). The extent of this work is unknown but is believed to have been relatively minor.

8. Thus the fourth-century Roman historian Ammianus Marcellinus, reporting the visit of the emperor Constantius II to Rome in 357 A.D., described the emperor's admiration for both the Colosseum and the Pantheon as architectural achievements: "So then he entered Rome, the home of empire and of every virtue. . . . Then, as he surveyed the sections of the city and its suburbs, lying within the summits of the seven hills, along their slopes, or on level ground, he thought that whatever first met his gaze towered above all the rest . . . the huge bulk of the amphitheater, strengthened by its framework of Tiburtine stone, to whose top human eyesight barely ascends; the Pantheon like a rounded city-district, vaulted over in lofty beauty." *Roman History* 16.10.13–14.

9. As reported in the *Liber pontificalis*; see Duchesne (1886), 1.317.

10. Round-plan temples dedicated to the Virgin were already characteristic of early Christian martyria as early as the fourth century, and thus the design of the Pantheon resonated with Christian symbolism; see Krautheimer (1969), 107–9.

11. Reported in the *Liber pontificalis*; Duchesne (1886), 1.342; see also De Fine Licht (1968), 184. Constans II refrained from removing the original bronze plates around the oculus, which are still in situ today; Ziolkowski (1999), 59.

12. Duchesne (1886), 1.419. It is of course possible that work to protect the cupola began even before this date.

13. For discussion of later repairs by subsequent popes during the Middle Ages see Eroli (1895), 253–64.

14. As noted by Muñoz (1912), 27.

15. For transcription of the inscription see Eroli (1895), 360.

16. The late diffusion of the practice of ringing bells in Rome may in fact be linked to the enduring survival of ancient prohibitions on bells connected to the persecution of Christians. For the history of bells and bell towers at Rome see De Blaauw (1993). Thanks to Niall Atkinson for this reference.

17. For the inscription dating the altar to 1270 see Muñoz (1912), 31. The spiral colonnettes now framing the icon in the apse are *spolia* reused from this thirteenth-century altar.

18. Conflict between different rival factions of cardinals following the death of Clement IV in 1268 extended the interregnum for a period of three years prior to the election of Gregory X in 1271. For the altered political reality represented by the Vacant See in early modern Rome see Nussdorfer (1987).

19. For the progressive inhumation of the Pantheon, also caused by detritus carried into the area by repeated flooding of the Tiber, see Virgili (2000).

20. A document of 1368 reported that the square was used as a cemetery, suggesting that the Pantheon portico had been engulfed by the rising terrain; Modigliani (1998), 49.

21. For further discussion see ibid.

22. The sixteenth-century antiquarian Andrea Fulvio speculated that one now descended the same number of steps to reach the portico that in antiquity one climbed to reach the height of the podium: "Nam Pantheon totidem gradibus prius ascendebatur quot nunc descenditur." Fulvio (1527), 94v.

23. In his description of the Pantheon portico, the sixteenth-century antiquarian Bartolomeo Marliano indicated that its columns appeared to bear the signs of fire damage: "testudo xvi olim ingentibus columnis sustentabatur: nunc vero xiii: nam deest una, et duae incendio corruptae vidētur." Marliano (1544), 102; see also Lanciani (1989), 2.269.

24. The presence of papal shields on this wall, also recorded in these same later views of the restored corner of the Pantheon portico, suggests that this restoration was funded by the pope.

25. Alberti (1988), 26.

26. Duchesne (1886), 2.544. For the storm of 1405, see Infessura (1890), 14–15.

27. "Eius stupendum fornicem vetustate ipsa terraemotibus scissum ruinamque minantem tua pontifex Eugeni opera impensaque instauratum, et chartis plumbeius alicubi deficientibus coopertum laeta inspicit curia. Et cum ipsa insignis ecclesia ceteras facile superans multis ante saeculis celsas quibus attollitur columnas habuisset sordidissimis diversorum quaestuum tabernis a quibus obsidebantur occultatas, emundatae nunc in circuitu bases et capita denudatae mirabilis aedificii pulchritudinem ostendunt." Biondo (1531), 3.64–66. My translation is based upon that of Grafton (2000), 254–55.

28. As noted by Grafton (2000), 255, "these emollient words of praise smoothed over what must have been a controversial restoration process." Grafton further argues that Alberti may have played a strategic role along with Biondo in encouraging Eugenius IV to conduct these restorations for the benefit of antiquarian knowledge.

29. In the nineteenth century the architect Viollet-le-Duc removed later additions and reconstructed missing elements at historic structures in the effort to enable viewers to see them in their presumed pristine condition. See discussion in Jokilehto (1999); for further reference to Viollet-le-Duc's restoration strategies at Notre Dame, see Camille (2009). Eugenius IV's intervention was clearly of a more circumscribed scope than the restorations of Viollet-le-Duc, as this fifteenth-century operation did not involve any fictive re-creation, but merely the removal of offensive later additions.

30. "a esso li fu tagliato lo capo . . . et in tal dì foro guaste tutte le tetta di Santa Maria Rotonna, perché guastavano tutta la piazza, et dopo foro gittati tutti li portichi che stavano allo lato alle colonne dallo ditto portico." Infessura (1890), 42.

31. For acts of political aggression staged in the urban landscape of early modern Rome see Nussdorfer (1997).

32. This sequence is further confirmed by Adinolfi's dating of Eugenius IV's interventions to 15 December 1442; see Adinolfi (1881), 406, note 1.

33. The creation of a buffer zone around the Pantheon thus anticipated the later sixteenth-century interventions of Paul III and Manetti upon the ancient remains along the triumphal route for Charles V; for discussion see chapter 3.

34. For a photograph of these tiles carrying the papal insignia see De Fine Licht (1968), figure 236.

35. As Müntz reports, the payment for this work, made to "Renzo d'Altieri da Roma," on 31 December 1453, came to over 275 ducats. Müntz (1876), 162.

36. According to a payment dated 7 February 1454: "A Verone di Angelo Belferdino da Firenze . . . duc. quaranta tre bol. 36 di cam. Conti per opera date lui e suoi guar-giuni (garzoni) e per spese fatte per finire da conciare lo tetto di Santa Maria Ritonda da dì II di genaro insino a questo dì." See Müntz (1876), 163. For the contemporary excavation sponsored by Nicholas V of columns from the adjacent Baths of Agrippa, presumably intended for the new choir at St. Peter's, see Satzinger (1996), 251–53.

37. See Cugnoni (1885), 582–83; Verdi (1997), 36; Modigliani (1998), 100–103.

38. As reported in a payment of 72 florins to "maestro Galasso de Bononia pro reparatione Sanctae Mariae Rotundae." Another payment of 43 ducats was recorded on 16 June 1463 to "maestro Franciescho dal Borgo per fare aconciare a Sancta Maria Ritondo." Müntz (1876), 163. The occupation of the Pantheon by Stefano Porcari's nephew Tiburzio, who terrorized the city during the papal absence of 1459–60, gave the pope further reason to prevent unauthorized entry to the monument. For Pius II's reference to Tiburzio at the Pantheon, see Meserve and Simonetta (2003), 2.307.

39. Dated 25 May 1468, this payment for 40 "auri de camera" was made to "Magistro Gilio Andree de Tocco muratori." Müntz (1876), 163.

40. As noted for 10 June 1468, "Fabrica per eum sub certa conventione facta et facienda in ecclesia Sancte Marie Rotunde seu ejus proticali." Ibid.

41. From a payment dated 10 May 1468: "Magistro Matheo Jacobelli Greco carpentario flor. auri de camera viginti septem et bon. sex pro valore ccc [300] ligno-rum plane nuncupatorum ab eo emptorum et habitorum pro cohoperiendo tectum porticalis ecclesie Sancte Marie Rotunde alme urbis." Ibid.

42. A payment made on 20 June 1468 reported 14 ducats disbursed for "planellae de curro nuncupatae" for the same site. Another payment on 18 July 1468 recorded expenses for planking and terracotta roof tiles: "Provido viro Francisco Lori de

Florentia fornasario flor. auri de camera novem et bon. XXXVI pro residuo et complemento solutionis decem millium planellarum et tredecim millium centum canalium ab eo habitarum et emptarum pro coperiendo tectum porticalis ecclesie beate Marie Rotunde alme urbis." Ibid.

43. For a payment dated 19 August 1469: "Magistro Andree de Arce muratori florenos auri de camera quinquaginta pro complemento solutionis sue ratione laborerii per eum facti in claudendo certa foramina murorum alme urbis nec non pro reparatione facienda in Sancta Maria Rotunda." Ibid.

44. This payment, dated 13 August 1470 to various laborers, amounted to over 177 florins. Ibid, 164.

45. The payment was dated 19 October 1470: "Dominico Benedicti de urbe de Regione Pinee flor. auri de camera quinque bon. LXIIII, pro valore libr. sex clavorum de ere nec non stagni et aliarum rerum per eum datarum in certa reparatione tabularum plumbi ecclesie beate Marie Rotunde nec non manufacture ejusdem reparationis." Ibid.

46. As discussed in Ugonio (1588), 315; Marder (1980), 30. See also Lanciani (1989), I.III; Muñoz (1912), 29–30.

47. For this print, dated 1692, by G. Tiburtio Vergelli da Recanati, titled "Antico tempio romano detto Pantheon dedicato a tutti li santi," see Pasquali (1996), figures 16–17.

48. Lanciani (1989), I.III.

49. The fact that the oculus remained open to the weather, exposing the center of the rotunda to rainfall (as marked by the drainage holes set in the floor), ensured that the high altar did not occupy the precise center of the rotunda.

50. The project also involved the reinterment of the relics of the saints from which the Pantheon derived its name as Santa Maria ad Martyres near the high altar; see Marder (1980), 30.

51. "Trigesimo aprilis die, mane, templum divae Mariae Rotundae spectavimus (sic enim adpelatur nunc quod olim Marcus Agrippa qui id fieri fecerat, Pantheon adpelarat); habet autem id templum pro vestibulo quadratam porticum, nonullis columnis altissimis simul et crassissimis suffultam, unicum nunc, ut arbitror, testimonium antiquorum templorum, nam Minervae templum, quod eodem die vidimus, solum nomen retinet, etenim adeo instauratum ut verius immutatum fatearis." Cited in Müntz (1884), 304–5.

52. The source for this famous tradition associated with Bramante is unknown. As Thoenes observes, however, the architectural masses of the Basilica of Maxentius are in fact organized in a way that is quite different from Bramante's design for the New St. Peter's. Thoenes (2005), 81.

53. For the Chigi Chapel see Shearman (1961); Buddensieg (1968), 60–68; Ray (1974), 128–47; Bentivoglio (1976, 1984); Brandt (1986); Magnusson (1987).

54. For Agostino Chigi see Dante (1980); see also Rowland (1986).

55. "Che avegna che a' dì nostri l'architectura sia molto svegliata et ridutta assai proxima alla maniera delli antichi, come si vede per molte belle opere di Bramante, niente di meno, li ornamenti non sono di materia tanto pretiosa come li antichi che con infinita spesa par che metessero ad effetto ciò che imaginarno et che solo el lor volere rompesse ogni difficultate." For this passage, cited from the Munich version of the "Letter to Leo X," see Di Teodoro (2003), 136.

56. For *Bramante ruinante* see Ackerman (1974).

57. For example, Bramante's famous Roman residential palace, Palazzo Caprini, was irreparably transformed within several decades of its completion, precisely because it was made of such lightweight and malleable materials; Pagliara (2002), 526.

58. For relevant sources see Golzio (1936); see also Buddensieg (1968); Shearman (2003); Pasquali (2004). Letters dated 7 April 1520, one by Pandolfo Pico to Isabella d'Este and one by Alfonso Paolucci to Alfonso d'Este, report that Raphael was buried that same day in the Pantheon; see Shearman (2003), 1.575, 1.578.

59. On the process of this transformation see Pasquali (2004).

60. As Marcantonio Michiel observed in a letter of circa 6 April 1520, "dolse la morte sua precipue alli litterati, per non haver potuto fornire la escrittione e pittura di Roma antiqua che'l faceva, che era cosa bellissima, pro perfettione della quale haveva ottenuto un breve dal Papa che niuno potesse cavare in Roma, che non lo facesse intravenire." Shearman (2003), 1.572–74.

61. For discussion of the technical methods outlined in the second half of the "Letter to Leo X" to achieve these goals, which included the use of the compass and the coordinated production of architectural plans, elevations, and section drawings, as well as possibly perspectival views, see Di Teodoro (2003), 222–32.

62. For Fabio Calvo's *Antiquae urbis Romae cum regionibus simulachrum* of 1527 as a belated tribute to the efforts of Raphael, see Jacks (1993), 191–204. Lanciani's *Forma Urbis Romae* and the *plastico di Roma*, the model reconstruction of imperial Rome at EUR, may also be considered the latter-day heirs of Raphael's legacy.

63. Marcantonio Michiel reported on Raphael's properties and legacies in a letter to Antonio di Marsilio in Venice, dated 11 April 1520; for transcription and discussion see Shearman (2003), 1.581–82.

64. For a reproduction of a thirteenth-century inscribed tomb panel from the Pantheon see Muñoz (1912), 32.

65. Pandolfo Pico, reporting Raphael's death to Isabella d'Este in Mantua, noted that "detto Raphaello honoratissimamente è stato sepulto a la Rottunda ove lui ha ordinato che'l se glie fazi a sua memoria una sepultura de milli ducati, et altri tanti ha lassato per dottare la capella ove serà detta sepultura." Shearman (2003), 1.575. The assignation of a specific income for the perpetual benefit of a chapel or tomb was of course standard funerary practice in medieval and early modern Italy. See Norman (1995).

66. When Cardinal Innocenzo Cibo asked Michelangelo to design a tomb for him in 1531, he budgeted 1,500–2,000 ducats; Cardinal Enckevoert's budget for the tomb of Adrian VI was 1,000 ducats. See Shearman (2003), 1.577.

67. "Ordinò poi che delle sue facultà in Santa Maria Ritonda si restaurasse un tabernacolo di quegli antichi di pietre nuove, ed. un altare si facesse con una statua di Nostra Donna di marmo; la quale per sua sepoltura e riposo dopo la morte s'elesse." Vasari (1568), cited in Golzio (1936), 229.

68. "Dovendosi poi esseguire il testamento di Raffaello, gli [Lorenzetto] fu fatta fare una statua di marmo alta quattro braccia d'una Nostra Donna per lo sepolcro di esso Raffaello nel tempio di Santa Maria Ritonda, dove per ordine suo fu restaurato qual tabernacolo." Vasari, cited in Golzio (1936), 229. For discussion of the syncretistic aspect of Raphael's tomb design, see Buddensieg (1968).

69. Among these was the icon known as the Madonna del Pantheon; see Bertelli (1961).

70. "È la chiesa rotunda, come si la fosse stata fatta col compasso; et intorno tutta piena d'altari: tra i quali uno si lavora, di serpentini porfidi et marmi, che sarà molto bello; ed. è la sepoltura di Raffaello da Urbino." Albèri (1846), 109; Sanuto (1892), vol. 34, c. 220–21.

71. "y le mandó polir los jaspes y las colunas de aquel lugar como estaban antiguamente." De Holanda (1921), 35.

72. As reported by Pirro Ligorio: "et uno di essi sendo stato ristaurato da M. Baldassar Perruzzo Architetto Senese, et da Raphael d'Urbino Pittore miracoloso in natura, e stata cagione si fatta rinovatione, che alcuni altri hanno fatto il simile. Et nelli fianchi dell'Altare (prima) ristaurato, dov'è la bella figura di Marmo della santissima Vergine col figliuolo in braccio Bambino, sotto le Intitulationi delli sudetti ristauratori quivi appiedi sepolti, di Raphael et di Baldassar." Pirro Ligorio, *Libro XV delle antichità di Roma*, BAV Ottob. lat. 3372, 46v.

73. For these inhumations see Pasquali (2004), 38.

74. The Compagnia di San Giuseppe di Terrasanta was originally founded by Desiderio di Adiutorio, a canon at Santa Maria Rotonda, to commemorate pilgrimage relics brought from the Holy Land. The first statutes, dated 20 December 1545, report that Desiderio was also motivated by the desire to found "una Confraternita di huominj excellentiss. itanto in Architettura, scoltura, et pittura" at the Pantheon. For transcription of the statutes see Tiberia (1999), 225–42. See also pasquali (2004), 35–39.

75. "dalla parte sinistra di quell'ingresso era una delle cappelle più grandi della medesima chiesa non ancora eretta a titolo di perpetuo beneficio ecclesiastico." *Supplica di Desiderio d'Adiutorio a Paolo III* (1543), transcribed in Tiberia (1999), 225.

76. Ibid.

77. "per le elemosine da raccogliere nella stessa Cappella, delle quali assegnata la quinta parte alla menzionata chiesa il resto fosse a quelli della stessa cappella." Ibid., 225–26.

78. "quod supplicetur SDN pro reparatione testudinis sancta Marie Rotunde et illius porte . . . similiter pro restitutione monasterii sancta agnetis extra urbem" (9 November 1520); transcribed by Lanciani (1989), 1.270. As further evidence of the Conservators' ongoing attention to the preservation of antiquity, Lanciani observed that in a following session dated 23 March 1521 these officials agreed to elect two citizens every year who would be assigned the duty of monitoring the condition of the ancient Aurelian Walls.

79. For further references to the De' Rossi case see discussion in chapter 3.

80. ASC, Cred. I, vol. 15, 125–26 (13 August 1524). See partial transcription by Cerasoli (1909), 282; see also reference in Rodocanachi (1914), 112.

81. For discussion of the taxes used to fund the *studium urbis* see Chambers (1976).

82. "Et quia approprinquatur annus sanctus in quo omnes seu maior pars christianorum ad urbem venit ne videatur locus ille imperfectus et ita deformis quod cum fuerint depositati ducati quatringenti auri in bancho pro tegmine Sancte Marie Rotunde restaurando." ASC, Cred. I, vol. 36, 173 (29 October 1524); see transcription by Lanciani (1989), 1.265. Clement VII declared the ninth Jubilee on 24 December

1524, as an extraordinary measure intended to counter the rising pressures of the Protestant Reformation.

83. ASC, Cred. I, vol. 15, 136 (12 January 1525); see partial transcription by Cerasoli (1909), 282.

84. For additional work conducted in the Piazza del Pantheon by Clement VII in 1526, see Rodocanachi (1914), 112.

85. ASC Cred. I, vol. 16, 25v (12 September 1531). "S.D.N. pape ipsis dominis Conservatoribus intelligere fecit quod sue Sanctitatis mens est, quod si alique pecunie supersunt de Gabella studii, quod vult et intendit Sanctitas sua quod exponantur in reparatione teginimis ecclesie Sancte Marie Rotunde." According to one source, to commemorate this collaborative restoration, the papal arms of Clement VII were placed side by side with the arms of the Capitoline administration over the main portal of the Pantheon; see Baracconi (1884), 55.

86. In addition the flood of 1530 also caused extensive damage to the interior of the Pantheon, requiring further papal expenses for its restoration. For the observations of a contemporary witness of the 1530 flood see Gasparoni (1865), 90.

87. For subsequent papal restorations and repair at the Pantheon see Eroli (1895), 262–83; Krautheimer (1985); Marder (1991).

88. See especially Buddensieg (1971).

89. Ibid., 260.

90. "insignis ecclesia, ceteras facile superans." Cited from Biondo Flavio, *Roma instaurata*, in ibid., 261. As Buddensieg notes, Petrarch anticipated Biondo's reappraisal of the Pantheon when he affirmed that the Pantheon had been saved from destruction because of "Maria, quae antiquissimam illam domum sui nominis virtute sustentat."

91. For Alberti's discussion of sacred buildings see *De re aedificatoria*, book 7.

92. Biondo Flavio in *Roma instaurata* identified the Pantheon as a temple: "Pantheon quod templu[m] descry ere supra polliciti fuimus a Marco Agrippa aedificatum fuisse titulus in frontispicio adhuc ostendit." Biondo (1531), 62. Modern scholars are much more circumspect on this point, noting the Pantheon bears closer resemblance to imperial Roman secular structures. According to the *Lexicon Topographicum Urbis Romae*, "the best, or safest definition of Hadrian's Pantheon is thus: a free-standing imperial aula." Ziolkowski (1999), 60.

93. As Shearman notes, the extraordinary archaeological precision of Raphael's drawing was later altered, not only in copies executed by other artists, but by a revisionist hand working on Raphael's drawing itself. These alterations suggest that Raphael's successors were less concerned with archaeological accuracy than with the need to create a satisfying *veduta*. See Shearman (1977).

94. The project of conducting "virtual restorations" of major ancient monuments in Rome was of course widespread practice in Renaissance Rome, as a mental exercise of reconstruction that also had the advantage of being much easier to execute than any kind of actual restoration on the ground. For related virtual restorations of the Renaissance Pantheon see De Fine Licht (1968), 314, note 2.

95. Of the three documents in the appendix relating to the Pantheon (14–16), only the last (dated 1531) referred to the Pantheon as "ecclesia" rather than "templum."

96. These restorations relocated the altar to a less conspicuous position within the main apse. For interventions at the Pantheon conducted under Clement XI after 1710 see Pasquali (1996), 37–45.

97. The attentive preservation of the Pantheon by the early modern popes prompts us to reconsider the most infamous episode in the building's early modern history, when Urban VIII chose to remove the bronze beams and coffered ceiling from the portico in the early seventeenth century. This was of course the origin of the famous pasquinade: "Quod non fecerunt barbari fecerunt Barberini." And yet Urban VIII also continued the ongoing restoration project inaugurated by Eugenius IV by importing a monolithic granite column from the ruins of an ancient villa at Castelgandolfo to repair the front corner of the portico. If this incursion encouraged the development of more stringent preservation practices, Urban VIII undoubtedly considered this part of his larger restoration project, where he substituted the bronze beams of the portico with the present wooden structure. Thus preservation and destruction, rather than being binary opposites, are better described as inseparable.

98. For the operational substitution of artifacts in late medieval and Renaissance culture see Nagel and Wood (2010).

CHAPTER 6

1. "Il ponte oggi detto di Santa Maria . . . hora si vede dal LVII [1557] in qua con grandissimo incomodo de gli habitatori in gran parte rovinato, non si potendo passar più senza allungar la strada dall'una all'altra riva per andare alla porta di San Pancrazio, che guida alle terre Toscane. Et se ben pochi anni sono Iulio III lo restaurò et vi rifece una pila che vi mancava, non hanno però potuto i romani habitatori lungo tempo a goderlo che da nuova rovina si vede spezzato in parte, et questo non per altro si può credere che venisse se non per essere stato dal proprio peso aggravato." Gamucci (1565), 182.

2. Sources for the Pons Aemilius include Jordan (1871–1907), 1.1.420–21; Delbrück (1907–12), 1.12–22; Platner and Ashby (1929), 397–98; Le Gall (1953), 74–80; Lugli (1953); Gazzola (1963), 2.28–33; Nash (1968), 2.182–83; D'Onofrio (1980), 141–65; Coarelli (1988), 139–47; Richardson (1992), 296–97; Galliazzo (1994), 2.18–20; Coarelli (1999a); De Spirito (1999); Taylor (2002); Claridge (2010), 258, 285–86.

3. For the *portus Tiberinus*, see Buzzetti (1999).

4. Likewise, boats traveling down the Tiber from central Italy toward the sea unloaded at the other side of the island. The eventual descendant of this smaller port was the Ripetta, located upriver around the bend of the Tiber beyond the Ponte Sant'Angelo.

5. The Tiber Island was considered sacred; in the third century B.C. it was dedicated to the healing cult of Aesculapius. Its special status may have initially discouraged the construction of a direct crossing. For the island, see Degrassi (1996). In addition, the route of the Pons Sublicius and the later Pons Aemilius offered a more direct connection to the valley of the Circus Maximus, and from there to Campania and other destinations in southern Italy.

6. The name of the Pons Sublicius referred to its supporting wooden piles. The bridge was built without iron fastenings of any kind, in accordance with religious taboos and also as a defensive tactic to permit its rapid demolition. For this structure see Coarelli (1999b), 4.112–13.

7. Livy, 40.41.4, names only M. Fulvius Nobilior as responsible for the 179 B.C. rebuilding. Coarelli proposes that an earlier version of the bridge was built by a different Aemilius and then retained its original name; see Coarelli (1999a), 4.106.

8. For the Via Aurelia see Patterson (1999); Mari (2008).

9. Delbrück (1907–12), 1.12–22; Frank (1924), 129–41; Le Gall (1953), 79; Lugli (1953), 2.298–90; Gazzola (1963), 2.33; Galliazzo (1994), 2.18–20; Coarelli (1999a), 4.106–7; Taylor (2002).

10. Livy, 40.41.4. This bridge may have supported a wooden roof structure that later collapsed into the Tiber, as attested by a passage in Obsequens 16: "Pontis maximi tectum cum columnis in Tiberim deiectum."

11. The only evidence for an Augustan intervention is the report of an inscription that is now lost, from the triumphal arch at the adjoining bridgehead (IMP. CAESAR DIVI F. AUGUSTUS PONT[IFEX] MAX[IMUS] EX S[ENATUS] C[ONSULTU] REFECIT; CIL 6.878). The intervention would thus date after 12 B.C., when Augustus became Pontifex Maximus. Archaeological evidence at the site, including travertine and concrete construction, suggests typical construction of Augustan structures; see Frank (1924), 139–41. Rapid urban expansion in Trastevere, encouraged by Augustus, as well as a number of major floods, may have further justified such rebuilding; see Taylor (2002), 6. For an alternative argument that claims the surviving archaeological remains date exclusively from the earlier period of the Republic see Le Gall (1953), 79.

12. For the attribution of these details to the Augustan rebuilding, see Galliazzo (1994), 2.20.

13. For these later alternative names, see Gnoli (1939), 223; De Spirito (1999), 4.110.

14. For further discussion of the Speculum Romanae, see essays in Zorach (2008).

15. The Ponte Santa Maria (identified as the Pons Maior) was included in the Eisiedeln itinerary, dated around the early ninth century, as a key landmark on the pilgrimage route traversing the city from the Porta Aurelia (Porta San Pancrazio) to the Porta Praenestina (Porta Maggiore). See Valentini and Zucchetti (1942), 2.191.

16. The name Pons Sanctae Mariae itself further underscored the religious significance of the bridge, suggesting the presence of the chapel, but also the adjacent church of Santa Maria Egiziaca in the ancient Temple of Portunus, which stood at the eastern bridgehead. For the construction of the chapel on the Ponte Santa Maria, recorded as early as 1005 A.D., see De Spirito (1999), 4.110.

17. "mi nasce non picciola occasione di maravigliarmi, del giudicio di quelli Architetti antichi, c'hanno usato nel piantare et erigere quelli Ponti, non avertendo, che con li Pilastri de li Ponti, si viene ad occupare la terza parte del suo letto: e perciò sarebbe stato di bisogno, che in quelli medesimi luoghi, si fosse almeno dilatato altrettanto esso letto." Veranzio (ca. 1599), 2.

18. For discussion see Aldrete (2007), 115.

19. For a discussion of milling activity on the early modern Tiber, see D'Onofrio (1980), 38–64.

20. "posto nel concorso di due aque, cagionato dall'Isola superiore, riceve l'altra parte del fiume obliqua è torta." Veranzio (ca. 1599), 2.

21. The design of the Ponte Santa Maria piers was also unusually narrow in section; the surviving pier in the Tiber measures only 5.36 meters, narrower than any other pier on the Tiber. The piers of a contemporary Augustan bridge, the Pons Agrippae, were more than 2 meters wider. The more attenuated piers of the Ponte Santa Maria were thus necessarily more fragile. For comparative dimensions of these Tiber bridge piers see Galliazzo (1994), 2.7 and 2.19.

22. The Ponte Sant'Angelo, in contrast to the Ponte Santa Maria, was built on an axis perpendicular to the current. This meant the cutwaters on the bridge piers divided the current head-on. However, not only did the roadway of the Ponte Santa Maria cross the river at an oblique angle, but the two branches of the river itself converged upon the bridge from different directions. The design of the surviving ancient cutwater on the east end of the Ponte Rotto as it stands today shows an attempt to resolve this problem, where the point is not placed on axis with the pier, but instead is angled slightly in the direction of the current. See Galliazzo (1994), 2.18–19.

23. The current struck the piers at the most oblique angle on the Trastevere side of the bridge, and it was this side of the bridge that collapsed first, in 1557. For the conflict between the prevailing current and the position of this pier (the second from Trastevere) see Lanciani (1826). The piers of the modern Ponte Palatino are not perpendicular to the deck at all, but are instead oriented entirely to the current of the Tiber.

24. For a comparison of recorded floods on the Tiber see Aldrete (2007), 86.

25. The inscription recorded the restorations conducted by Senator Benedetto Carushomo to the Ponte Cestio between 1191 and 1193. For a reproduction of this inscription see D'Onofrio (1980), 113.

26. Chapter 166. "De curris et carrectis. Nullus currus honeratus carrecta honerata vel sine honere vel cum bubalis seu bovibus vel equis transeat per aliquem pontem de Urbe et etiam supra flumen tyburis salvo ponte mambulo et nulla prata molaria deferatur sine traglione et qui contrafecerit puniatur in 100 sollidis prov. quotiens contrafecerit, de quibus quilibet accusare vel denumptiare possit eni cum probatione unius testis de predictis creddatur." Re (1880), 177.

27. Chapter 196. "De edificantibus in viis comunis et pontibus. Senator teneatur vinculo sacramenti ad penam 100 librarum prov. precise omni exceptione et dilatione remota cum effectu expediri et excommorari omnes vias publicas et pontes, infra Urbem et extra, et si qua edificia opera hostia porticalia seu quecumque alia apparamenta facta sint vel facta apparent in hiis viis et pontibus, per quascumque personas cum effectu, omni exceptione et dilatione remota faciat tolli destrui et demoliri expensis illorum qui in predictis viis et pontibus edificaverunt seu edificari fecerunt et de dicta edificatione vel occupatione facta dictarum rerum et ponteium per quem seu per quos predicta edificatio seu occupatio fuerit facta stetur sacramento conquerentis de predictis seu denumptiantis predicta cum probatione publice fame. Et hoc semper inquirere teneatur." Ibid., 190.

28. The crush of people attempting to cross city bridges was especially problematic at Rome when pilgrims descended upon the city from every direction for the Jubilee. The infamous stampede on the Ponte Sant'Angelo during the reign of Nicholas V in 1450 indicated that this continued to be a serious problem into the fifteenth century. For a contemporary account of this disaster see Infessura (1890), 49.

29. See chapter 8, "De cura habenda per magistros in reparatione locorum urbis et eius districtis," and chapter 24, "Quod magistri teneantur recuperare loca publica occupata," of the first surviving statutes of the *maestri di strade*. The statutes are transcribed in Scarafoni (1927), 273, 279.

30. A passage in Gregory IX's biography reports: "Pontem autem Sanctae Mariae gravibus refeci impensis alluvione Tiberis demolitum." Cited by Adinolfi (1881), 1.25–26.

31. These repairs appear to have been sponsored by the civic government, based upon the report of a document dated 3 May 1311 that diverted civic tax income "pro reparatione pontis S. Mariae." Ibid., 1.26, note 2. For an anonymous account of the 1310 flood, recorded in BAV Cod. Vat. lat. 6880, 59–60, see the transcription by D'Onofrio (1980), 305.

32. For mutual benefits achieved through papal-civic interactions during the reign of Martin V see Caravale (1992); Palermo (1992); Pavan (1992); Verdi (1997); see also discussion in chapter 2.

33. "in Santa Maria Retonna rimase piena più de uno mese, perche se aparao la chiavica che è dentro; e fece molto danno per Roma, perche la crescenza fu si subita che l'omo non ve poteo reparare. Lo crescere ello decrescere durao tre die." Dello Mastro (1875), 6.

34. As reported in a payment dated 8 April 1423: "Antonio de Porcariis anteposito reparationis pontis S. Marie Urbis a die 14 january ad 8 april is flor. centum quinquaginta quinque auri similes [de camera]." Transcribed in Müntz (1886), 150; reprinted in Müntz (1887), 59.

35. For July through September 1423, the following payments were recorded: "Duc. quattro milia docento tredici e bol. vinticinque e mezzo paghammo a Antonio Porcaro deputato sopra la fabrica de ponte Sancte Marie." Ibid.

36. The payment dated September 1424 recorded an expense of more than 360 florins, made again to Porcari: "Antonio de Porcariis anteposito pontis sancte Marie Urbis flor. trecentos sexaginta duos de bon. quinquaginta ut supra et bon. triginta sex pro reparatione pontis predicti." Another payment recorded for 150 florins was made to Renzo Renzolini on 12 October 1426: "Renzio Renzolini civi romano anteposito pontis S. marie Urbis pro reparatione eiusdem pontis flor. centum quinquaginta, ad rationem bolognenorum quinquaginta quinque pro quolibet ducato." Ibid.

37. The payment of 8 June 1426 recorded: "Nobili viro Antonio de Porcariis civi romano anteposto pontis sanctae Mariae Urbis florenos 288 auri d.c. pro reparatione pontis praedicti." Müntz (1878), 175.

38. Recorded on 22 June 1426: "Renzio Renzolini civi romano anteposito pontis Sanctae Mariae urbis fl. 120 auri de camera in deductionem salarii magistrorum et aliorum laborantium in reparatione pontis praedicti." Ibid.

39. For 3 August 1426: "Nobili viro Juliano Antonii de Porcariis de Urbe olim anteposito pontis sanctae Mariae de Urbe pro expensis factis per eum in reparatione dicti pontis ducatos 126 ad rationem 55 bon. pro quolibet ducato." Ibid.

40. For 24 September 1426: "Magistri Honofrius della Cava et Peracrinus [?] de Prato capita magistrorum aliorumque laborantium in reparatione pontis Sanctae Mariae urbis." Another payment was also made on 12 October 1426: "Renzio Renzolini civi romano anteposito pontis S. marie Urbis pro reparatione eiusdem pontis flor. centum quinquaginta, ad rationem bolognenorum quinquaginta quinque pro quolibet ducato." For the first payment, see ibid.; for the last see Müntz (1887), 59.

41. For 3 February 1427: "Renzio Renzolini . . . olim anteposito pontis Sanctae Mariae Urbis florenos 62 de bon. 55 pro quolibet floreno et bon. 40 et denarios 3 pro residuo reparationis pontis praedicti." Müntz (1878), 175.

42. Porcari also was in close contact with Ludovico Colonna, a member of Martin V's own family, as well as Giovanni Astalli, the papal treasurer, as indicated by the

marriage license dated December 1421 issued for his daughter in the presence of both of these individuals. See Modigliani (1986), 329.

43. For Rienzolino's service as the head of the *caporioni*, see Verdi (1997), 32, note 41. For his appointment on 9 March 1430 as *maestro delle strade*, see ibid., 95.

44. In a similar process, Giovanni Astalli, Martin V's papal treasurer, also acquired significant rank in both papal and civic circles in his coordinating roles between these two administrations. See Palermo (1992), 512–14.

45. Although D'Onofrio cited Müntz for a surviving payment recording expenses for the *siligatura* or the paving of the roadbed under Nicholas V, I have been unable to locate this document. See D'Onofrio (1980), 145.

46. For the notion that shields and inscriptions during the pontificate of Nicholas V offered a strategic means by which to inscribe papal power upon the visual environment of fifteenth-century Rome, see Burroughs (1990).

47. For Nicholas V's rebuilding of the Trevi Fountain in 1453, as a project that directly benefited the essential papal allies of the Colonna family, see ibid., 95–96. See also discussion in Gargano (1988).

48. The Roman city bridges, offering key access to the heart of the city, required special defenses in the fifteenth century, and a fortified tower stood on the Trastevere bridgehead of the Ponte Santa Maria, as recorded in the 1474 Strozzi plan of Rome. Another tower belonging to the medieval Roman family of Nicolaus Crescens guarded the bridgehead on the opposite bank. According to one document, Renzo Magliano, a member of the Roman nobility, was appointed custodian of the bridge; see Adinolfi (1881), 1.28. Although the primary duty of such a civic officer was to prevent banditry, this official presence also undoubtedly contributed to the preservation of the ancient structure.

49. For discussion of this intervention see Ackerman (1986), 334; Vasari (1962), 4.1589–94; D'Onofrio (1980), 144–45; Contardi (1990); Conforti (2002).

50. "Lacqua . . . ha tolte entrambe le sponde che erano di marmore grossissimo a ponte Santo Angelo e poco piu che durava la furia dell'acqua sanza dubbio tuttolponte rovinava: ruppe ancora ponte Sisto: e ponte quattro Capora." Gasparoni (1865), 89.

51. "tutti li quattro Ponti di mirabile altezza erano coperti dacqua: cioe Ponte Santo Angelo: Ponte Santa Maria: Ponte Sisto: e Ponte quattro Capora." Ibid., 90.

52. "Perché la fabrica dell'instauratione del Ponte Santa Maria è di grande importanza, non pare strano alle S. V. se il Popolo alquanto è gravato per la sovventione alla spesa che in essa si fa. Et ne si fa intendere, che per noi non si è mancato con quella desterità et diligentia che si è potuto di operare appresso sua Santità che s'andasse con modestia nel esigere il dinaro." ASC, Cred. I, vol. 36, 625 (27 July 1548); for transcription see Lanciani (1989), 2.27, as well as D'Onofrio (1980), 144–45.

53. "Et ne hà data bona risposta con dire che Sua Santità in questo con currarebbe à furia, ma haverebbe rispetto al tempo in darne qual che dilateione nel esigere il denaro." ASC, Cred. I, vol. 36, 625 (27 July 1548).

54. "Donde s'attenderà à questa instauratione del ponte, che speramo con l'aiuto de Dio soccurrere à tal periglio che non facendosi, ne succederia senza dubbio, [cioè] la ruina delli doi archi con maggior spesa et incomodo del Popolo. Et per venire alla conclusione dovemo considerare, et provedere che il dinaro si spenda bene et honorevolmente, con l'occhio del sapiente che in ciò soprastia, come pensamo in messer

Michael Angelo Bonarota homo singularissimo la cui virtù n'è stata commendata da Sua Santità . . . como bono cittadino et affettionato a questa patria." Ibid.

55. Payments were documented beginning on 19 July 1548 for this purpose, as reported in ASR, *Camerale* I, busta 1514; for partial transcription see Conforti (2002), 86, note 11.

56. For the thrifty economic policies of Paul III during a pontificate that faced ongoing financial difficulties see Caravale and Carracciolo (1978), 237–73.

57. See payments transcribed by Podestà (1875), 130–33.

58. See for example the payment dated 13 October 1548, whereby the banker Bindo Altoviti released funds pending approval by the Conservators: "Magnifico M. Bindo Altoviti et Compagni depositari della taxa sopra il ponte S. M. pagati a Marco Ricio in scontro delli Sri Conservatori." Ibid., 130.

59. For Michelangelo's work at St. Peter's see discussion in Ackerman (1986); Argan and Contardi (1990). In addition see also Millon (2005); Zöllner et al. (2007), 361–70, 480–83.

60. For both of these projects see Ackerman (1986) and Argan and Contardi (1990). In addition, for Michelangelo's work at the Capitoline Hill see Morrogh (1994); Zöllner et al. (2007), 356–61, 476–79; for the reconstruction of the summer villa built by Paul III on the north side of the Capitoline Hill that helped trigger the initial project see also Di Apricena (1997–98). For Michelangelo at the Palazzo Farnese see Zöllner et al. (2007), 370–71, 483–84.

61. Michelangelo completed the frescoes of the Pauline Chapel in 1550; see Zöllner et al. (2007), 388–90; 464–67; also Wallace (2010), 253–53.

62. Iacopo Ermolao served as co-commissioner with Michelangelo; documents issued by the Camera Capitolina were signed by both commissioners. For reconstruction of the work site administration, see Conforti (2002), 80.

63. Michelangelo reported in a letter to his nephew Leonardo, dated 15 March 1549, that he was suffering and in poor health, as a result of problems caused by kidney stones. See Barocchi and Ristori (1973), 4.315 (Lettera MCXXIII).

64. "Et allora Michelagnolo ordinò che si dovessi a quella dirittura fare un ponte che attraversassi il fiume del Tevere, acciò si potessi andare da quel palazzo in Trastevere a un altro lor giardino e palazzo, perché, per la dirittura della porta principale che volta in Campo di Fiore, si vedessi a una occhiata il cortile, la fonte, strada Giulia et il ponte e la bellezza dell'altro giardino, fino all'altra porta che riusciva nella strada di Trastevere; cosa rara e degna di quel Pontefice e della virtù, giudizio e disegno di Michelagnolo." Vasari (1962), 1.87.

65. For discussion of the proposed bridge, see Spezzaferro and Tuttle (1981), 119–21.

66. For Michelangelo's work on the new basilica of Santa Maria degli Angeli, and discussion of his sustained interest in the preservation of antiquity, see Karmon (2008a, 2009). On Michelangelo's complex attitude toward the classical tradition see Brothers (2008), 45–83.

67. Four payments for work at the Ponte Santa Maria, including those dated 13, 20, and 27 October 1548, as well as that of 3 December 1548, all included considerable expenses for carpentry work by *falegnami* and *segatori*.

68. As reported by a document dated 13 October 1548: "ànno lavorato de dì et di notte cominciando dominica adì 7 de ottobre 1548 per insino oggi in questo dì 13 del

presente mese." See Podestà (1875), 131. The definitive closure of the project in October 1549 was confirmed by the closing of the small house occupied by the supervisors of the building project, adjacent to the Ponte Santa Maria; see Conforti (2002), 81.

69. It has been speculated that the Ponte Santa Maria suffered damage due to ongoing excavations authorized by Paul III for building materials to supply the building site at St. Peter's, thus ostensibly confirming the worst tendencies of the Renaissance popes to destroy and plunder ancient remains; see Francia (1977), 111; Ramieri (2003), 183. This claim for reckless Renaissance destruction, however, is also unfounded. While a number of excavation documents referred to the Ponte Santa Maria, especially in 1539–40 (see for example AFSP, Armadio 1, Ripiano A, vol. 45, *Liste e conti degli artisti di 1539*, 25, 102, 106, 111, 152), this reference was merely a convenient topographical reference for excavations in the adjacent Forum Boarium.

70. ASV, Cam. Ap., *Div. Cam.* 159, 21r, "Licentia extrahendi lapides Thome de Bononia" (22 June 1549).

71. For the Ponte Mammolo, originally formed of two equal arches separated by a smaller arch, see Gazzola (1963), 2.55–57; Mari (2008), 5.166.

72. "Il restauro deve mirare al ristabilimento della unità potenziale dell'opera d'arte, purché ciò sia possibile senza commettere un falso artistico o un falso storico, e senza cancellare ogni traccia del passaggio dell'opera d'arte nel tempo." Brandi (2000), 8; for translation see Brandi (1996), 231.

73. Of course the proposed Renaissance restoration of the Ponte Santa Maria was not conceived to introduce clear distinctions between authentic original materials and new additions. This was a principle that formed the backbone of Brandi's conservation theory, guiding prominent twentieth-century restorations such as that for the Sistine Ceiling, where restorers painted in lacunae using hatched surfaces that may be easily distinguished from the original sixteenth-century fresco. Far from establishing such clear distinctions between new and old, the use of Ponte Mammolo stone for the Ponte Santa Maria restoration intentionally blurred these distinctions, where the Ponte Mammolo travertine provided a near-perfect match for the Ponte Santa Maria stone. This was a project that disguised the disjuncture between new and old, and for this reason, Brandi might well have deprecated the proposed Renaissance restoration of the Ponte Santa Maria as the creation of an "artistic or historical forgery."

74. The use of the Aniene as a convenient water route to transport stone from Tivoli to Rome was an ancient practice that continued into the Renaissance. For the use of this route in antiquity see Lancaster (2005), 16–18.

75. Dismantling the Ponte Mammolo would not have caused insurmountable difficulties to Rome-Tivoli traffic, as the Ponte Lucano nearer to Tivoli also afforded a crossing over the Aniene. Transit by barge on the Aniene was obviously still an option, one that was in fact favored by Paul III for the delivery of building stone to Rome. A *motu proprio* issued on 23 August 1538 reaffirmed the authority of the papal administration over the length of the Aniene from Ponte Lucano to its juncture with the Tiber, with the purpose of facilitating the transport of travertine from these quarries to supply the building site of the New St. Peter's. For this reference see Cascioli (1923), 12.

76. The bridge was dynamited for defensive reasons by the French military in 1849; Gazzola (1963), 2.56; Mari (2008), 5.166.

77. Michelangelo expressed interest in preservation problems over the course of his long career, beginning as early as 1510 with his meticulous reconstruction of the

main portal of San Petronio in Bologna by Jacopo della Quercia, and culminating with his famous transformation of the Baths of Diocletian as Santa Maria degli Angeli, still under way at the time of his death in 1564. For further discussion see Karmon (2008a), 146–48.

78. "Venendosi nel tempo di Giulio terzo in congregazione coi cherici di camera in pratica di dargli fine [al Ponte Santa Maria], fu proposto fra loro da Nanni di Baccio Bigio architetto, che con poco tempo e somma di danari si sarebbe finito allogando in cottimo a lui; e con certo modo allegavano sotto spezie di bene per isgravar Michelagnolo, perché era vecchio e che non se ne curava; e stando così la cosa non se ne verrebbe mai a fine. Il papa, che voleva poche brighe, non pensando a quel che poteva nascere, diede autorità a' chierici di camera, che, come cosa loro, n'avessino cura; i quali lo dettono poi, senza che Michelagnolo ne sapessi altro, con tutte quelle materie, con patto libero a Nanni." Vasari (1962), 1.93–94.

79. "lo scaricò di peso per vendere gran numero di trevertini di che era rifiancato e solicato anticamente il ponte, che venivano a gravarlo e facevanlo più forte e sicuro e più gagliardo, mettendovi in quel cambio materia di ghiaie e altri getti, che non si vedeva alcun difetto di drento." Ibid., 1.94.

80. "Giorgio, questo ponte ci triema sotto; sollecitiamo il cavalcare, che non rovini in mentre ci siàn su." Ibid.

81. Conforti (2002), 78–81.

82. As Conforti notes, Vasari's insider knowledge of the project for the Ponte Santa Maria (he served briefly as manager of the project's financial accounts) indicates he consciously chose to distort the facts. For a diagram showing the financial management of the project, see ibid., 79.

83. "il Tevere haveva fatto una grossissima piena . . . hà portato via metà del ponte di Santa Maria insieme con quella bella cappelletta di Giulio III che vi era nel mezzo con tanta arte e spesa fabricata." Cited from Oldradi (1557) by Podestà (1875), 135–36; D'Onofrio (1980), 147.

84. The identification of the pier affected by the collapse of 1557 as the second pier from Trastevere is derived from the evidence of the drawing by Giovanni Antonio Dosio; see Conforti (2002), 77–78. It is unlikely that much of either Michelangelo or Nanni's restorations survived this collapse.

85. In addition to Conforti (2002), see also the reappraisal of Nanni in Wittkower (1968).

86. In a letter to Cardinal Ottavio Farnese dated 17 March 1553, Nanni boasted: "Questo anno qui in Roma io mi ho guadagnato dui milia scudi in quindici dì, e questo sì è, come sa V. Ecc.a, quanti danari si spesono a Ponte Santo da Michelagelo e dal Boccaccio; tale che questo anno saranno tutti isbigottiti. È lasciorno l'opra per disperata, e io la presi, e con altri modi in 15 giorni la spedii, che se ne stupì tutta Roma: di sorte che li errori fatti mi feciono bene." See Vasari (1962), 4.1592.

87. As noted by Wittkower (1968), 248.

88. The contract of 1551 is in ASR, *Notai capitolini*, Notaio Ceccholus Hieronimus de Tarano, vol. 458, 560. The contract was transcribed by Podestà (1875), 134–35; D'Onofrio (1980), 338.

89. "ms Nanni di bartholameo Lippi sia tenuto rifare il fundamento del pontone del pilastro del ponte di S.ta Maria quale fu refondato l'anno passato e mancò a

refondarsi e finire detto pontone." ASR, *Notai capitolini,* Notaio Ceccholus Hieronimus de Tarano, vol. 458, 560.

90. "sia tenuto murare detto pontone allaltezza de gl'altri fatti da papa Nicola [V] e Martino [V] di travertino di fuori e dentro di buona materia di mattoni o pezzami como ancora sonno fatti gl'altri gia fatti a detto ponte." Ibid.

91. "E perche in tale opera non possi nasciere alcuna diferentia sì per rifondare come per remetere pietre in detti archi a volta." Ibid.

92. "detto Maestro Nanni promette contentarvi che cavato l'acqua, e scoperto el piano del puntone inanzi, cominci a rinfondare e così inanzi rimeter agli archi le pietre già rotte e guaste." Ibid.

93. "havendo però detti Signori grande consideratione che Maestro Nanni a preso a rifare il puntone di nuovo e gli archi a volta raconciare e risarcire e non rifare di nuovo." Ibid.

94. For Cardinal Giovanni Ricci, see Deswarte Rosa (1991). A letter dated 26 October 1550 from Hieronimo Dandino to nuncio Sebastiano Pighino praised Cardinal Ricci's valuable financial work on behalf of the church: "per esser huomo che particolarmente ha molta pratica in queste cose pecuniarie dello Stato Ecclesiastico." See ibid., 114, note 8.

95. Perhaps Giulio Sauli, Cardinal Ricci's representative, contributed to the emphatically protective dimension of this contract. Sauli's approval is repeatedly recorded in documents relating to the Ponte Santa Maria work site in ASR, *Camerale I,* busta 1514.

96. "Le Signorie Vostre hanno anco a sapere che Nostro Signore ne disse hieri che la mente sua era che si acconciasse il Ponte Santa Maria di legname poi che non si posseva per hora rifare di pietra e rifacendosi di legname coperto ci andarebbe di spese tre mila scudi vel circa et domila incirca scoperto. Et durarebbe coperto vent'anni, et scoperto dieci. Et di tutto ciò se ne darrà sigurtà da chi pigliarà questa impresa." ASC, Cred. I, vol. 37, 83v (3 July 1561); transcribed in D' Onofrio (1980), 148.

97. For Pius IV's proposed restoration of the Ponte Santa Maria see D'Onofrio (1980), 147–50.

98. This episode attests to the continued collaboration of the Conservators and the pope in the ongoing preservation of the ancient bridge. As noted in the same document of 3 July 1561, the Conservators continued to seek to avoid the heavy financial burdens this work involved: "pensino e discurrino in che modo con minor danno del Popolo si po sodisfare alla mente di Sua Santità."

99. "perche suol esser molto commodo al condursi delle mercantie che vengono nella Ripa, che è il principal porto del Tevere in Roma, si tentò dal Popolo Romano l'anno 1561 di rifarlo di legno per minor spesa, solo per la commodità di condurre dette merca ntie, et vini da la Ripa; et essendosi fabricato un'assai bella machina, ove si era speso la somma di otto mila scudi, mentre cercano di tirarla da una estremità all'altra del ponte con argani et canapi, et essendo preso che ridotto all'altra sponda, aggravò tanto il peso di detta machina, che rompendosi à un tratto i più grossi capi, che sostenevano tutto detto peso, cadde precipitosamente nel Tevere, fracassandosi tutto et andando talmente in rovina, et perditione, che non se ne puote ricuperare cosa alcuna." Fulvio (1588), 74v–75.

100. Gregory XIII's renovation of the Ponte Santa Maria was an immensely expensive venture. As Girolamo Ferrucci reported in 1588, based upon communication

from Matteo da Castello, the total cost for this repair amounted to nearly four times the cost of the new bell tower for the Senators' palace on the Capitoline Hill: "la spesa, che vi andò in tutta la ristauratione di esso ponte ascese alla somma di scudi cinquantaquattro mila, si come intesi da esso M. Mattheo principale di detta opera. Si fabricò ancora pochi anni dopo la bella torre del Campidoglio, che fu finita l'anno 1583, opera tutta di mattoni, et di lavoro di scarpello, essendo quella antica di prima stata percossa del fulmine l'anno 1579, la spesa della quale arrivò alla somma di quattordici mila scudi si come intesa dal capo maestro di detta opera." Fulvio (1588), 74v. For further discussion of Gregory XIII's renovation see D'Onofrio (1980), 151–55.

101. Matteo da Castello was elected unanimously by the civic magistrates in 1573: "unitamente han decretato et risoluto che l'opera del ponte di quest'anno sia liberamente di Mastro Matteo da Castello, il quale à questo ed effetto sia deputato nominato et eletto." ASC, Cred. IV, vol. 95, 492 (4 June 1573), transcribed in D' Onofrio (1980), 152.

102. Matteo da Castello's bulky design, as it stands today in the Tiber, makes a vivid contrast with the surviving companion pier to its east, apparently of ancient construction, and presumably analogous to the form of the other ancient piers that have since been destroyed. The eastern pier features a much narrower, slimmer profile, rising from a flared, shallow escarpment sited just above the water level.

103. "Magnifici Signori perché tutte le opere cominciate devono havere il suo debito fine, però ci par necessario che mancando ancora molta quantità de tevertini per finire la restaurazione del Ponte di Santa Maria et per adesso non se ne possono far venire, et per questo essendoce detto che nel Coliseo ve ne è gran quantità sotto le ruvine che sono cascati, et non sono in opera quali si potrebbono far cavare per questo bisogno." ASC, Cred. IV, vol. 95, 548 (15 October 1574); transcribed in D'Onofrio (1980), 152–53. A Latin version of this text (ASC, Cred. I, vol. 26, 198) is transcribed by Lanciani (1989), 2.31.

104. The motion was rejected thirty-four to twenty-four. ASC, Cred. IV, vol. 95, 548 (15 October 1574).

105. EX AVCTORITATE GREGORII XIII. PONT. MAX./S.P.Q.R./PONTEM SENATORIVM CVIVS FORNICES VETVSTATE/COLLAPSOS ET IAMPRIDEM REFECTOS FLVMINIS/IMPETVS DENVO DEIECERAT IN PRISTINAM/FIRMI-TATEM AC PVLCHRITVDINEM RESTITVIT/ANNO IVBILEI M.D.LXXV. The text was transcribed in Fulvio (1588), 75.

106. Gregory XIII's restoration involved the refacing of the entire ancient structure in a new travertine skin, which effaced earlier papal insignias, including those of Martin V and Nicholas V. As Ferrucci noted, in 1588 the papal shields of Julius III, who had sponsored the 1551 restoration of the Ponte Santa Maria, were also visible on the structure prior to this restoration: "[il ponte Santa Maria] fu ristaurato in gran parte da Papa Giulio III circa l'anno 1551, come ancor hoggi vi si veggono le sue armi nei pilastri da' capi de le sponde di detto ponte." Ibid., 74.

107. Just as the civic magistrates consciously evoked the Roman Senate in their sessions on the Capitoline Hill, so did the college of Roman cardinals also regard themselves as the Sacred Senate. As Stinger writes, "Renaissance cardinals viewed themselves as Senators of the *respublica Christiana* with an obligation to emulate the secular splendor of their classical forebears." Stinger (1998), 28.

108. For a contemporary account of the flood of 1598 by Giacomo Castiglione see D'Onofrio (1980), 159–60. For comparison with other historic Tiber floods, see Aldrete (2007), 86.

109. Lanciani reported that the Conservators rented the bridge deck for three-year terms. For this, as well as a 1723 description of the Ponte Santa Maria as a "hanging garden," see Lanciani (1989), 1.254.

110. The concrete pilings for this structure are still visible on the eastern end of the Ponte Rotto. For the nineteenth-century afterlife of the bridge see D'Onofrio (1980), 164; Ramieri (2003), esp. 191–96.

111. As Lanciani noted, "il ponte durò in piedi sino alla inondazione del 24 dicembre 1598. Da quell'epoca non è stato mai più ricostruito in muratura. La generazione vivente ha finito di spiantarlo." Lanciani (1989), 2.31.

CONCLUSION

1. The first references to Rome as the Eternal City appear to date from the age of Augustus. See Edwards (1996), 86–88.

2. "Per coloro che professano culto per le antiche cose spinto oltre i limiti del buon senso, per coloro che, discutendo questioni d'arte e d'archeologia, sdegnano tenere a calcolo l'ambiente in cui si vive, lo spirito dei tempi, le necessità materiali della vita e del consorzio umano, sarebbe stato desiderabile che Roma fosse perita di morte violenta insieme all'impero; che ogni vita, ogni attività fosse rimasta in lei spenta dal secolo V in poi, affinchè noi, scavandola oggi secondo i più sani criteri scientifici, l'avessimo fatta risorgere da quel giaciglio di cenere nella pienezza del suo antico splendore, come avviene o è avvenuto appunto per Pompei, per Ostia, per Olimpia." Lanciani (1886), 355.

3. "Roma invece ha sempre vissuto, ed ha vissuto a spese del passato; ogni generazione ha assorbito, per cosi dire, e distrutte le opere della generazione precedente." Ibid.

4. For the many different symbolic meanings of the ruin for Renaissance culture see Forero-Mendoza (2002). More broadly see also Macaulay (1953); Roth et al. (1997); Woodward (2001); Makarius (2004).

5. The fifteenth-century work known as the *Hypnerotomachia Poliphili* illuminated the charged, emotional, erotic dimension of ruins as a source of knowledge for Renaissance culture; for the close relationship between sensory perception and knowledge as presented in this text see Smick (2003).

6. For the significance of ruins in the nineteenth-century United States see Yablon (2009). For ruins and fragments in modern and postmodern culture see Edwards (1999); Bergdoll and Oechslin (2006).

7. As noted by Hell and Schönle (2010).

8. For discussion of the challenges involved in preserving archaeological ruins see Ashurst 2007.

9. See for example Mostafavi and Leatherbarrow (1993); Brand (1994); Otero-Pailos (2009). Unfortunately the idea of the future history of a building goes against the grain of the profession in the United States, where built-in obsolescence has become integral to the value of real estate investments. See Duany et al. (2000), especially 220–21.

10. Rome was not the only place attuned to preservation problems in Renaissance Italy. The history of Renaissance Venice offers intriguing evidence for attentive interest in forest management and environmental protection issues. See Appuhn (2009).

11. For further discussion of ruins as an intermingling of preservation and destruction, see also *Cabinet Magazine* 20 (2005–06), available online at http://www.cabinetmagazine.org/. This issue includes correspondence between the artist Gordon Matta-Clark and a prominent demolition firm regarding Matta-Clark's 1970s "deconstruction" projects.

12. Beard (2007), esp. 93–100, also 292.

13. For further discussion of the way that ancient societies used memory to structure history, making selective choices about what to retain and emphasize from the past, see Price and Thonemann (2010).

Bibliography

ABBREVIATIONS

ARFSP: Archivio della Reverenda Fabbrica di San Pietro
ASC: Archivio Storico Capitolino
ASR: Archivio di Stato di Roma
ASV: Archivio Segreto Vaticano
BAV: Biblioteca Apostolica Vaticana

WORKS CITED

Ackerman, James S. "The Belvedere as a Classical Villa." *Journal of the Warburg and Courtauld Institutes* 14 (1951), 70–91; repr. in *Distance Points: Essays in Theory and Renaissance Architecture* (Cambridge, 1991), 325–59.
———. *The Cortile del Belvedere*. Vatican City, 1954.
———. *The Architecture of Michelangelo*. 2 vols. London, 1961; 2nd ed., Chicago, 1986.
———. "Notes on Bramante's Bad Reputation." In *Studi bramanteschi: atti del congresso internazionale*, 339–50. Rome, 1974.
———. "The Planning of Renaissance Rome, 1450–1580." In *Rome in the Renaissance: The City and the Myth*, ed. P. A. Ramsey, 3–18. Binghamton, 1982.
Adam, Jean-Pierre. *Roman Building: Materials and Techniques*. Trans. Anthony Mathews. London, 1994.
Adinolfi, Pasquale. *Laterano e via Maggiore: saggio della topografia di Roma nell'età di mezzo*. Rome, 1857.
———. *Roma nell'età di mezzo*. 3 vols. Rome, 1881.
Albèri, Eugenio. *Relazioni degli ambasciatori veneti al Senato*. Vols. 3–4. Rome, 1846.

Alberti, Leon Battista. *On the Art of Building in Ten Books.* Eds. Joseph Rykwert, Robert Tavernor, and Neil Leach. Cambridge, 1988.

Alchermes, Joseph. "Spolia in Roman Cities of the Late Empire: Legislative Rationales and Architectural Reuse." *Dumbarton Oaks Papers* 48 (1994): 167–78.

Aldrete, Gregory. *Floods of the Tiber in Ancient Rome.* Baltimore, 2007.

Antinori, Aloisio. "Il rapporto con l'antico nella Roma di Sisto V: la controversia sulla demolizione della tomba di Cecilia Metella." *Architettura Storia e Documenti* 1–2 (1989): 55–63.

Antonetti, Stefano, and Rossella Rea. "Soppalchi (contignationes, tabulati)." In *Rota Colisei: la valle del Colosseo attraverso i secoli,* ed. Rossella Rea, 218–27. Milan, 2002a.

——. "Inquadramento cronologico delle tracce del riuso." In *Rota Colisei: la valle del Colosseo attraverso i secoli,* ed. Rossella Rea, 283–333. Milan, 2002b.

Appuhn, Karl. *A Forest on the Sea: Environmental Expertise in Renaissance Venice.* Baltimore, 2009.

Argan, Giulio Carlo, and Bruno Contardi. *Michelangelo architetto.* Milan, 1990.

Armellini, Mariano. *Le chiese di Roma dal secolo IV al XIX.* 2 vols. Rome, 1942.

Ashurst, Gregory. *Conservation of Ruins.* Amsterdam, 2007.

Bacon, Francis. *The Advancement of Learning.* Ed. Michael Kiernan. Oxford, 2000.

Balland, André. "La Casa Romuli au Palatin et au Capitole." *Revue des études latines* (1984): 57–80.

Baracconi, Giuseppe. *Il Pantheon: ricordi, fantasie, attualità.* Rome, 1884.

Bardi, Marcantonio. *Facultates magistratus curatorum viarum aedificiorumque publicorum et privatorum Almae urbis.* Rome, 1565.

Barkan, Leonard. *Unearthing the Past: Archaeology and Aesthetics in the Making of Renaissance Culture.* New Haven and London, 1999.

Barnes, Jonathan. "Metaphysics." In *The Cambridge Companion to Aristotle,* ed. Jonathan Barnes, 66–108. Cambridge, 1995.

Barocchi, Paola, and Renzo Ristori. *Il carteggio di Michelangelo.* 5 vols. Florence, 1973.

Bartoli, Alfonso, ed. *I monumenti antichi di Roma negli disegni degli Uffizi di Firenze.* 5 vols. Florence, 1914.

Bartolini, Gabriella. "Antonio Caffarelli." In *Dizionario biografico degli italiani,* ed. Alberto Ghisalberti, 16.243–44. Rome, 1973.

Beard, Mary. *The Roman Triumph.* Cambridge, 2007.

Beard, Mary, and Keith Hopkins. *The Colosseum.* Cambridge, 2005.

Becchetti, Piero. *Fotografi e fotografia in Italia: 1839–1880.* Rome, 1978.

——. *La fotografia a Roma dalle origini al 1915.* Rome, 1983.

Benson, Robert. "Political Renovatio: Two Models from Roman Antiquity." In *Renaissance and Renewal in the Twelfth Century,* eds. Robert Benson and Giles Constable, 339–86. Cambridge, 1982.

Bentivoglio, Enzo. "La cappella Chigi." In *Raffaello architetto,* eds. Christoph Frommel, Stefano Ray, and Manfredo Tafuri, 125–42. Milan, 1984.

——. "La cappella Chigi." In *Santa Maria del Popolo,* eds. Enzo Bentivoglio and Simonetta Valtieri, 104–20. Rome, 1976.

——. "Nel cantiere del palazzo del cardinale Raffaele Riario (la Cancelleria): organizzazione, materiali, maestranze, personaggi." *Quaderni dell'istituto di storia dell'architettura* 27 (1982): 27–34.

Berducou, Marie. "Introduction to Archaeological Conservation." In *Historical and Phil-osophical Issues in the Conservation of Cultural Heritage*, eds. Nicholas Stanley Price, M. Kirby Talley Jr., and Alessandra Melucco Vaccaro, 248–59. Los Angeles, 1996.

Bergin, Thomas. *Petrarch*. New York, 1970.

Bergdoll, Barry, and Werner Oechslin, eds. *Fragments: Architecture and the Unfinished, Essays Presented to Robin Middleton*. New York, 2006.

Bertelli, Carlo. "La Madonna del Pantheon." *Bollettino d'Arte* 46 (1961): 24–32.

Biermann, Hartmut. "Raffaello architetto." *Kunstchronik* 41 (May 1988): 247–60.

Bignamini, Ilaria, ed. *Archives and Excavations: Essays on the History of Archaeological Excavations in Rome and Southern Italy from the Renaissance to the Nineteenth Century*. London, 2004.

Bignamini, Ilaria, and Clare Hornsby. *Digging and Dealing in Eighteenth-Century Rome*. 2 vols. New Haven and London, 2010.

Biondo, Flavio. *De Roma triumphante libri decem*. Basel, 1531.

———. *Rome restaurée, Roma instaurata*. Ed. Anne Raffarin-Dupuis. Paris, 2005.

Boëthius, Axel, and J. B. Ward-Perkins. *Etruscan and Roman Architecture*. Harmond-sworth, 1970.

Borsari, Luigi. "Della distruzione di alcuni monumenti romani nel secolo XIV." *Bollettino della commissione archeologica comunale di Roma* 15 (1897): 291–300.

Brand, Stewart. *How Buildings Learn: What Happens after They're Built*. New York, 1994.

Brandi, Cesare. "Theory of Restoration, I." In *Historical and Philosophical Issues in the Conservation of Cultural Heritage*, eds. Nicholas Stanley Price, M. Kirby Talley Jr., and Alessandra Melucco Vaccaro, 230–35. Los Angeles, 1996.

———. *Teoria del restauro*. Turin, 2000.

Brandt, Kathleen Weil-Garris. "Cosmological Patterns in the Chigi Chapel." In *Raffaello a Roma, il convegno del 1983*, 127–57. Rome, 1986.

———. "Michelangelo's Pietà for the Cappella del Re di Francia." In *Il se rendit en Italie: études offertes à André Chastel*, 77–119. Rome, 1987.

Bredekamp, Horst. *Sankt Peter in Rom und das Prinzip der produktiven Zerstörung. Bau und Abbau von Bramante bis Bernini*. Berlin, 2000.

Brentano, Robert. *Rome before Avignon*. Berkeley, 1991.

Brezzi, Paolo. *Roma e l'impero medioevale, 774–1252*. Bologna, 1947.

Brocato, Paolo. "Dalle capanne del Cermalus alla Roma quadrata." In *Roma: Romolo, Remo, e la fondazione della città*, eds. Andrea Carandini and Rosana Cappelli, 284–87. Rome, 2000.

Broise, Henri, and Jean Claude Maire-Vigueur. "Strutture familiari, spazio domestico, e architettura civile a Roma alla fine del medioevo." In *Storia dell'arte italiana: momenti di architettura*, vol. 12, 99–160. Turin, 1983.

Brothers, Cammy. *Michelangelo, Drawing, and the Invention of Architecture*. New Haven and London, 2008.

Bruschi, Arnaldo. *Bramante architetto*. Bari, 1969; 5th ed., Rome, 1998.

———. "Bramante e la funzionalità: il palazzo dei Tribunali, 'turres et loca fortissima pro commoditate et utilitate publica.'" *Palladio* 7 (1994): 145–56.

———, ed. *San Pietro che non c'è, da Bramante a Sangallo il Giovane*. Milan, 1996.

Buddensieg, Tilmann. "Gregory the Great, the Destroyer of Pagan Idols: The History of a Medieval Legend Concerning the Decline of Ancient Art and Literature." *Journal of the Warburg and Courtauld Institutes* 28 (1965): 44–65.

———. "Raffaels Grab." In *Munuscula Discipulorum. Kunsthistorische Studien Hans Kauffmann zum 70 Geburtstag 1966*, 45–70. Berlin, 1968.

———. "Criticism and Praise of the Pantheon in the Middle Ages and the Renaissance." In *Classical Influences on European Culture, AD 500–1500*, ed. R. R. Bolgar, 259–68. Cambridge, 1971.

Burns, Howard. "Raffaello e 'quell'antiqua architectura.'" In *Raffaello architetto*, eds. Christoph Frommel, Stefano Ray, and Manfredo Tafuri, 381–404. Milan, 1984.

———. "Baldassare Peruzzi and Sixteenth-Century Architectural Theory." In *Les traités d'architecture de la Renaissance*, ed. Jean Guillaume, 207–26. Paris, 1988a.

———. "Pirro Ligorio's Reconstruction of Ancient Rome: The Anteiquae Urbis Imago of 1561." In *Pirro Ligorio, Artist and Antiquarian*, ed. Robert W. Gaston, 19–92. Florence, 1988b.

———. "Building against Time: Renaissance Strategies to Secure Large Churches against Changes to Their Design." In *L'église dans l'architecture de la Renaissance*, ed. Jean Guillaume, 107–32. Paris, 1995.

———. "Leon Battista Alberti." In *Storia dell'arte italiana: il quattrocento*, ed. Francesco Paolo Fiore, 114–65. Milan, 1998.

———. "Leon Battista Alberti a Roma: il recupero della cultura architettonica antica." In *La Roma di Leon Battista Alberti: umanisti, architetti, e artisti alla scoperta dell'antico nella città del quattrocento*, eds. Francesco Paolo Fiore and Arnold Nesselrath, 32–43. Milan, 2005.

Burroughs, Charles. *From Signs to Design: Environmental Process and Reform in Early Renaissance Rome*. London, 1990.

Buzzetti, Carlo. "Portus Tiberinus." In *Lexicon Topographicum Urbis Romae*, ed. Eva Margareta Steinby, 5.155–56. Rome, 1999.

Cameron, Averil. *Procopius and the Sixth Century*. London, 1985.

———. "Justin I and Justinian." In *Late Antiquity: Empire and Successor, AD 425–600, Cambridge Ancient History*, vol. 14, eds. Averil Cameron et al., 77–78. Cambridge, 2000.

Camille, Michael. *The Gargoyles of Notre Dame*. Chicago, 2009.

Campbell, Ian. "Rescue Archaeology in the Renaissance." In *Archives and Excavations*, ed. Ilaria Bignamini, 13–22. London, 2004.

Carandini, Andrea. "Variazioni sul tema di Romolo: riflessioni dopo la nascità di Roma (1998–1999)." In *Roma: Romolo, Remo, e la fondazione della città*, eds. Andrea Carandini and Rosana Cappelli, 95–150. Rome, 2000.

Caravale, Mario. "Per una premessa storiografica." In *Alle origini della nuova Roma: Martino V (1417–1431)*, eds. Maria Chiabò et al., 1–15. Rome, 1992.

Caravale, Mario, and Alberto Caracciolo. *Lo stato pontificio da Martino V a Pio IX*. In Storia d'Italia, vol. 14. Turin, 1978.

Carbonetti Vendittelli, Cristina. "Documentazione inedita riguardante i magistri edificiorum urbis nei secoli XIII e XIV e la sua documentazione." *Collection de l'Ecole française de Rome* 170 (1993): 1–42.

Cardilli, Luisa. "Ponte Sisto restaurato, considerazioni in margine." In *Sisto IV: le arti a Roma nel primo rinascimento*, ed. Fabio Benzi, 434–43. Rome, 2000.

Casciato, Maristella. "Lo sviluppo urbano e il disegno della città." In *Roma capitale*, ed. Vittorio Vidotto, 125–72. Rome-Bari, 2002.

Cascioli, Giuseppe. "I monumenti di Roma e la fabbrica di San Pietro." *Dissertazione della pontificia accademia romana di archeologia* 15 (1921): 363–83.

———. *Bibliografia di Tivoli: studi e fonti per la storia della regione tiburtina*. Tivoli, 1923.

Castagnoli, Ferdinando. "Raffaello e le antichità di Roma." In *Raffaello: L'opera, le fonti, la fortuna*, ed. Luisa Becherucci, 2.571–86. Novara, 1968.

Cavallaro, Anna. "Una colonna a modo di campanile facta per Adriano imperatore, vicende e interpretazioni della colonna Traiana tra medioevo e Quattrocento." In *Studi in onore di Giulio Carlo Argan*, eds. S. Macchioni and B. La Greca, 1.71–90. Rome, 1984.

Cecchi, Roberto. *I beni culturali: testimonianze materiale di civiltà*. Milan, 2006.

Ceen, Allan. *The Quartiere de' Banchi: Urban Planning in Rome in the First Half of the Cinquecento*. PhD thesis, University of Pennsylvania, 1977.

Cerasoli, Francesco. "Usi e regolamenti per gli scavi di antichità in Roma, nei secoli XV e XVI." *Studi e documenti di storia e diritto* 18 (1897): 133–49.

———. "Nuovi documenti sulle vicende del Colosseo dal secolo XIII al XVIII." *Bollettino della commissione archeologica comunale di Roma* (1902): 300–15.

———. "I restauri del Pantheon dal secolo XV al XVIII." *Bollettino della commissione archeologica comunale di Roma* (1909): 280–89.

Cessi, Roberto. "La congiura di Stefano Porcari." In *Saggi romani: storia e letteratura, raccolta di studi e testi*, 65–112. Rome, 1956.

Chambers, D. S. "Studium urbis and gabella studii: The University of Rome in the Fifteenth Century." In *Cultural Aspects of the Italian Renaissance: Essays in Honor of Paul Oskar Kristeller*, ed. Cecil Clough, 68–110. New York, 1976.

———. "Lorenzo Pucci." In *Contemporaries of Erasmus*, ed. Peter Bietenholz, 3.123–24. Toronto, 1987.

Chastel, André. *The Sack of Rome 1527*. Trans. Beth Archer. Princeton, 1977.

Cherubini, Paola, Anna Modigliani, Daniela Sinisi, and Orietta Verdi. "Un libro di multe per la pulizia delle strade sotto Paolo II (21 luglio–12 ottobre 1467)." *Archivio della società romana di storia patria* 107 (1984): 45–60.

Chiabò, Maria, et al., eds. *Alle origini della nuova Roma, Martino V (1417–1431)*. Rome, 1992.

Choay, Françoise. *The Invention of the Historic Monument*. Trans. Lauren O'Connell. Cambridge, 2001; first published as *L'allégorie du patrimoine*, Paris, 1992.

———. *Le patrimoine en questions: anthologie pour un combat*. Paris, 2009.

Christian, Kathleen. "The De' Rossi Collection of Ancient Sculptures, Leo X, and Raphael." *Journal of the Warburg and Courtauld Institutes* 65 (2002): 132–200.

———. *Empire Without End: Antiquities Collections in Renaissance Rome, ca. 1350–1527*. New Haven and London, 2010.

Ciaconio, Alfonso. *Vitae et res gestae Pontificum Romanorum et S.R.E. Cardinalium*. 2 vols. Rome, 1677.

Cilento, Nicola. "Sulla tradizione della Salvatio Romae: la magica tutela della città medievale." In *Roma anno 1300*, ed. Angiola Maria Romanini, 695–703. Rome, 1983.

Claridge, Amanda. *Rome: Oxford Archaeological Guide*. Oxford, 1998; 2nd ed., Oxford, 2010.

Coarelli, Filippo. "Il Pantheon, l'apoteosi di Augusto e l'apoteosi di Romolo." *Analecta Romana Instituti Danici, supplementum* 10 (1983): 41–46.

———. *Il Foro Boario: dalle origini alla fine della Repubblica.* Rome, 1988.

———. "Pons Aemilius." In *Lexicon Topographicum Urbis Romae,* ed. Eva Margareta Steinby, 4.106–7. Rome, 1999a.

———. "Pons Sublicius." In *Lexicon Topographicum Urbis Romae,* ed. Eva Margareta Steinby, 4.112–13. Rome, 1999b.

———. *Roma: guide archeologiche Laterza.* Rome-Bari, 2001.

Coates-Stephens, Robert. "The Walls and Aqueducts of Rome in the Early Middle Ages, AD 500–1000." *Journal of Roman Studies* 88 (1998): 166–78.

Colagrossi, P. *L'anfiteatro Flavio nei suoi venti secoli di storia.* Florence and Rome, 1913.

Coleman, Kathleen. "Entertaining Rome." In *Ancient Rome: The Archaeology of the Eternal City,* eds. John Coulston and Hazel Dodge, 210–58. Oxford, 2000.

Conforti, Claudia. "Il cantiere di Michelangelo al Ponte Santa Maria a Roma (1548–1549)." In *I ponti delle capitali d'Europa: dal Corno d'Oro alla Senna,* eds. Donatella Calabi and Claudia Conforti, 75–87. Milan, 2002.

Connerton, Paul. *How Societies Remember.* Cambridge, 1989.

Contardi, Bruno. "Restauro del ponte di S Maria." In *Michelangelo architetto,* eds. Giancarlo Argan and Bruno Contardi, 337. Milan, 1990.

Corazza, Angelo, and Leonardo Lombardi. "L'impianto idraulico." In *Rota Colisei,* ed. Rossella Rea, 46–65. Milan, 2002.

Corbo, Anna Maria. *Cantori, artisti e condottieri alla corte dei papi nel secolo XV.* Rome, 1999.

Cortonesi, Alfio. "Fornaci e calcare a Roma e nel Lazio nel basso medioevo." In *Scritti in onore di Filippo Caraffa,* 277–307. Anagni, 1986.

Croci, Giorgio. *Studi e ricerche sul Colosseo.* Rome, 1990.

Crook, J. A. "Augustus: Power, Authority, Achievement." In *The Augustan Empire, 43 B.C.–A.D. 69,* eds. Alan Bowman et al., 113–46. Cambridge, 1996.

Cruciani, Fabrizio. *Teatro nel rinascimento: Roma 1450–1550.* Rome, 1983.

Cugnoni, Giovanni. "Varietà: diritti del capitolo di S. Maria della Rotonda nell'età di mezzo." *Archivio della reverenda societa romana di storia patria* 8 (1885): 577–89.

Cuno, James. *Who Owns Antiquity? Museums and the Battle over Our Ancient Heritage.* Princeton, 2008.

———. *Whose Culture? The Promise of Museums and the Debate over Antiquities.* Princeton, 2009.

Curran, Brian, and Anthony Grafton. "A Fifteenth-Century Site Report on the Vatican Obelisk." *Journal of the Warburg and Courtauld Institutes* 58 (1995): 234–48.

Curran, Brian. *The Egyptian Renaissance: The Afterlife of Ancient Egypt in Early Modern Italy.* Chicago, 2007.

Curran, Brian, Anthony Grafton, Pamela Long, and Benjamin Weiss. *Obelisk: A History.* Cambridge, 2009.

Dacos, Nicole. *Roma quanta fuit: tre pittori fiamminghi nella Domus Aurea.* Trans. Maria Baiocchi. Rome, 2001.

Dante, Francesco. "Agostino Chigi." In *Dizionario biografico degli italiani,* ed. Alberto Ghisalberti, 24.735–43. Rome, 1980.

D'Arco, Carlo. *Delle arti e degli artefici di Mantova.* 2 vols. Mantua, 1857.

Davies, Paul, David Hemsoll, and Mark Wilson Jones. "The Pantheon: Triumph of Rome or Triumph of Compromise?" *Art History* 10 (1987): 133–53.

De Bartholomaeis, Vincenzo. *Laude drammatiche e rappresentazione sacre.* 2 vols. Florence, 1943.

De Blaauw, Sible. "Campane supra urbem." *Rivista di storia della chiesa in Italia* 47, 2 (1993): 367–414.

De Boüard, Alain. "Gli antichi marmi di Roma nel medio evo." *Archivio della società romana di storia patria* 34 (1911): 239–45.

De Caro, Francesco. "Francesco Armellini Medici." In *Dizionario biografico degli italiani,* ed. Alberto Ghisalberti, 4.234–37. Rome, 1962.

De Fine Licht, Kjeld. *The Rotunda in Rome: A Study of Hadrian's Pantheon.* Copenhagen, 1968.

Degrassi, Donatella. "Insula Tiberina." In *Lexicon Topographicum Urbis Romae,* ed. Eva Margareta Steinby, 3.99–101. Rome, 1996.

De Holanda, Francisco. *De la pintura antiqua.* Ed. Elías Tormo. Madrid, 1921.

Delaine, Janet. "Building the Eternal City: The Construction Industry of Imperial Rome." In *Ancient Rome: The Archaeology of the Eternal City,* eds. Jon Coulston and Hazel Dodge, 119–41. Oxford, 2000.

Delbrück, Richard. *Hellenistiche Bauten in Latium.* 2 vols. Strassburg, 1907–12.

Dello Mastro, Pietro. "Diario e memorie di diverse cose accadute in Roma dal 1422 al 1484." *Buonarroti* 2, 10 (1875).

Delumeau, Jean. *Vie économique et sociale de Rome dans la seconde moitié du XVIe siècle.* 2 vols. Paris, 1957–59.

Denker Nesselrath, Christiane. "Il Colosseo." In *La Roma di Leon Battista Alberti: umanisti, architetti, e artisti alla scoperta dell' antico nella città del quattrocento,* eds. Francesco Paolo Fiore and Arnold Nesselrath, 202–9. Milan, 2005.

De Maio, Romeo. *Michelangelo e la controriforma.* Rome-Bari, 1981.

De Maria, Sandro. *Gli archi onorari di Roma e dell'Italia romana.* Rome, 1988.

De Spirito, Giuseppe. "Pons Lapideus." In *Lexicon Topographicum Urbis Romae,* ed. Eva Margareta Steinby, 4.110. Rome, 1999.

Deswarte Rosa, Sylvie. "Le cardinal Giovanni Ricci de Montepulciano." In *La villa Médicis,* eds. André Chastel and Philippe Morel, 2.110–69. Rome, 1991.

Di Apricena, Marianna Brancia. "La committenza edilizia di Paolo III Farnese sul Campidoglio." *Römisches Jahrbuch der Bibliotheca Hertziana* 32 (1997–98): 411–78.

Di Macco, Michela. *Il Colosseo: funzione simbolica, storica, urbana.* Rome, 1971.

Dio Cassius. *Roman History.* Cambridge and London, 1961.

Dionysius of Halicarnassus. *Roman Antiquities.* Cambridge and London, 1937.

Di Teodoro, Francesco Paolo. *Raffaello, Baldassar Castiglione, e la lettera a Leone X.* Bologna, 2003.

D'Onofrio, Cesare. *Renovatio Romae.* Rome, 1973.

———. *Il Tevere. L'isola tiberina, le inondazioni, i molini, i porti, le rive, i muraglioni, i ponti di Roma.* Rome, 1980.

———. *Visitiamo Roma nel Quattrocento.* Rome, 1989.

———. *Gli obelischi di Roma: storia e urbanistica di una città dall'età antica al XX secolo.* Rome, 1992.

Dorez, Léon. *La cour du Pape Paul III.* Paris, 1932.

Duany, Andres, Elizabeth Plater-Zyberk, and Jeff Speck. *Suburban Nation: The Rise of Sprawl and the Decline of the American Dream.* New York, 2000.

Duchesne, L., ed. *Le Liber Pontificalis.* 3 vols. Paris, 1886.

Edwards, Catharine. *Writing Rome: Textual Approaches to the City.* Cambridge, 1996.

———, ed. *Roman Presences: Receptions of Rome in European Culture, 1789–1945.* Cambridge, 1999.

Egger, Hermann, ed. *Römische Veduten: Handzeichnungen aus dem XV bis XVIII Jahrhundert zur Topographie der Stadt Rom.* 2 vols. Vienna, 1931.

Egger, Hermann, Christian Hülsen, and Adolf Michaelis, eds. *Codex Escurialensis: ein Skizzenbuch aus der Werkstatt Domenico Ghirlandaios.* 2 vols. Vienna, 1906.

Eggert, Paul. *Securing the Past: Conservation in Art, Architecture, and Literature.* Cambridge, 2009.

Emiliani, Andrea. *Leggi, bandi, e provvedimenti per la tutela dei beni artistici e culturali negli antichi stati italiani, 1571–1860.* Bologna, 1996.

Eroli, Giovanni. *Raccolta epigrafica storica bibliografica del Pantheon di Agrippa.* Narni, 1895.

Esch, Arnold. "La fine del libero comune di Roma nel giudizio dei mercanti fiorentini: lettere romane degli anni 1395–1398 nell'Archivio Datini." *Bollettino dell'istituto storico italiano per il medioevo* 86 (1976): 235–77.

———. "Le importazioni nella Roma del primo rinascimento: il loro volume secondo i registri doganali romani degli anni 1452–1462." In *Aspetti della vita economica e culturale a Roma nel Quattrocento,* ed. Paolo Brezzi, 7–80. Rome, 1981.

———. "Roman Customs Registers, 1470–1480: Items of Interest to Historians of Art and Material Culture." *Journal of the Warburg and Courtauld Institutes* 58 (1995): 72–87.

———. *Economia, cultura materiale ed arte nella Roma del rinascimento: studi sui registri doganali romani, 1445–1485.* Rome, 2007.

Esposito, Anna. "Le confraternite del Gonfalone, secoli XIV–XV." *Ricerche per la storia religiosa di Roma* 5 (1984): 91–136.

Fagiolo, Marcello, and Maria Luisa Madonna. "Il possesso di Leone X." In *La festa a Roma dal Rinascimento al 1870,* ed. Marcello Fagiolo, 42–49. Rome, 1997.

Fancelli, Paolo. "Demolizioni e 'restauri' di antichità nel Cinquecento romano." In *Roma e l'antico nell'arte e nella cultura del Cinquecento,* ed. Marcello Fagiolo, 357–406. Rome, 1985.

Fantoni, Marcello, ed. *Carlo V e l'Italia.* Bologna, 2000.

Favro, Diane. "Pater urbis: Augustus as City Father of Rome." *Journal of the Society of Architectural Historians* 51 (March 1992): 61–84.

———. *The Urban Image of Augustan Rome.* Cambridge, 1996.

Fea, Carlo. "Dissertazione sulle rovine di Roma." In *Storia delle arti del disegno presso gli antichi.* Rome, 1784.

———. *Relazione di un viaggio ad Ostia e alla villa di Plinio detta Laurentino.* Rome, 1802.

Fedele, Pietro. "Il più antico documento dei magistri aedificiorum urbis." *Miscellanea per le nozze Crocioni Ruscelloni* (1908): 147–55.

———. "Sul commercio delle antichità in Roma nel xii secolo." *Archivio della società romana di storia patria* 32 (1909): 465–70.

Fentress, James, and Chris Wickham. *Social Memory.* Oxford, 1992.

Fernández Gómez, Margarita, ed. *Codex escurialensis 28–II–12: libro de dibujos o antigüedades.* 2 vols. Madrid, 2000.

Forero-Mendoza, Sabine. *Le temps des ruines: le goût des ruines et les formes de la conscience historique à la Renaissance.* Paris, 2002.

Franceschini, Michele. "La magistratura capitolina e la tutela delle antichità di Roma nel XVI secolo." *Archivio della società romana di storia patria* 109 (1986): 141–50.

———. "Il municipio romano e Sisto V: apparato di rappresentanza o struttura di governo locale." In *Il Campidoglio e Sisto V,* eds. Luigi Spezzaferro and Maria Elisa Tittoni, 33–36. Rome, 1991.

———. "I conservatori della Camera Urbis: storia di un'instituzione." In *Il palazzo dei Conservatori e il palazzo nuovo in Campidoglio: momenti di storia urbana di Roma,* ed. Maria Elisa Tittoni, 19–27. Siena, 1997.

Francia, Ennio. *1506–1606, storia della costruzione del nuovo San Pietro.* Rome, 1977.

Franzoni, Claudio. "Urbe Roma in pristinam formam renascente: le antichità di Roma durante il rinascimento." In *Roma del rinascimento,* 291–336. Rome-Bari, 2001.

Frank, Tenney. *Roman Buildings of the Republic.* Rome, 1924.

Freud, Sigmund. *Civilization and Its Discontents.* Trans. James Strachey. New York and London, 2005.

Friedländer, Ludwig. *Roman Life and Manners under the Early Empire.* 2 vols. London, 1909.

Frommel, Christoph. *Der Römische Palastbau der Hochrenaissance.* 3 vols. Tübingen, 1973.

———. "Francesco del Borgo: Architekt Pius II und Pauls II, Teil 1." *Römisches Jahrbuch für Kunstgeschichte* 20 (1983): 107–54.

———. "Francesco del Borgo: Architekt Pius II und Pauls II, Teil 2." *Römisches Jahrbuch für Kunstgeschichte* 20 (1984): 71–164.

———. "St. Peter's: The Early History." In *The Renaissance from Brunelleschi to Michelangelo,* 399–424. Milan, 1994.

———. "Roma." In *Storia dell' architettura italiana: il quattrocento,* ed. Francesco Paolo Fiore, 374–433. Milan, 1998.

———. "La città come opera d'arte: Bramante e Raffaello (1500–20)." In *Storia dell'architettura italiana: il primo cinquecento,* ed. Arnaldo Bruschi, 76–131. Milan, 2002.

Frommel, Christoph, Manfredo Tafuri, and Stefano Ray, eds. *Raffaello architetto.* Milan, 1984.

Frommel, Christoph, and Massimo Pentiricci, eds. *L'antica basilica di San Lorenzo in Damaso: indagini archeologiche nel Palazzo della Cancelleria (1988–1993).* Rome, 2009.

Frutaz, Amato Pietro, ed. *Le piante di Roma.* 3 vols. Rome, 1962.

Fulvio, Andrea. *Antiquitates urbis.* Rome, 1527.

———. *L'antichità di Roma.* Ed. Girolamo Ferrucci. Rome, 1588.

Fumi, Luigi. *Il duomo di Orvieto e i suoi restauri.* Rome, 1891.

Funiciello, Renato, Leonardo Lombardi, and Fabrizio Marra. "La geologia della Valle dell'Anfiteatro." In *Rota Colisei: la valle del Colosseo attraverso i secoli,* ed. Rossella Rea, 161–67. Milan, 2002.

Fusco, Laurie, and Gino Corti. *Lorenzo de' Medici: Collector and Antiquarian.* Cambridge, 2006.

Gabba, Emilio. *Dionysius and the History of Archaic Rome.* Berkeley, 1991.

Gagliardi, Pasquale, Bruno Latour, and Pedro Memelsdorff, eds. *Coping with the Past: Creative Perspectives on Conservation and Restoration.* Florence, 2010.

Galliazzo, Vittorio. *I ponti romani*. 2 vols. Treviso, 1994.

Gamucci, Bernardo. *Dell'antichità di Roma*. Venice, 1565.

Gargano, Maurizio. "Niccolò V, la mostra dell'acqua di Trevi." *Archivio della società romana di storia patria* III (1988): 225–66.

Gasparoni, Francesco. "Il diluvio di Roma del 7 ottobre 1530." *Arti e Lettere* 2 (1865): 81–131.

Gaston, Robert W. "Merely Antiquarian: Pirro Ligorio and the Critical Tradition of Antiquarian Scholarship." In *The Italian Renaissance in the Twentieth Century*, eds. Allen Grieco et al., 355–74. Florence, 2003.

Gazzola, Piero. *Ponti romani*. 2 vols. Florence, 1963.

Geary, Patrick. *Furta sacra: Thefts of Relics in the Central Middle Ages*. Princeton, 1990.

Gennaro, Clara. "La Pax Romana del 1511." *Archivio della società romana di storia patria* 90 (1967): 2–60.

Gensini, Sergio, ed. *Roma capitale: 1447–1527*. Pisa, 1994.

Ghiberti, Lorenzo. *I commentari*. Ed. Ottavio Morisani. Naples, 1947.

Gilbert, Creighton. "Ghiberti on the Destruction of Art." *I Tatti Studies: Essays in the Renaissance* 6 (1995): 135–44.

Gill, Meredith. "The Fourteenth and Fifteenth Centuries." In *Rome: Artistic Centers of the Italian Renaissance*, ed. Marcia Hall, 27–106. Cambridge, 2005.

Giovio, Paolo. *Lettere volgari di Mons. Paolo Giovio da Como*. Venice, 1560.

Gloton, J. J. "Transformations et réemploi des monuments du passée dans la Rome du XVIe siècle: les monuments antiques." *Mélanges d'archéologie et d'histoire* 74, 2 (1962): 705–58.

Gnoli, Umberto. *Topografia e toponomastica di Roma medioevale e moderna*. Rome, 1939.

Godfrey, Paul, and David Hemsoll. "The Pantheon: Temple or Rotunda?" In *Pagan Gods and Shrines of the Roman Empire*, eds. Martin Henig and Anthony King, 195–209. Oxford, 1986.

Goldman, Norma. "Reconstructing the Roman Colosseum Awning." *Archaeology* 35, 2 (1982): 57–65.

Golvin, Jean-Claude. *L'amphithéâtre romain: essai sur la théorisation de sa forme et de ses fonctions*. 2 vols. Paris, 1988.

Golzio, Vincenzo. *Raffaello nei documenti*. Vatican City, 1936.

Graefe, Rainer. *Vela erunt: die Zeltdächer der römischen Theater und ähnlicher Anlagen*. 2 vols. Mainz, 1979.

Grafton, Anthony. "From Politian to Pasquali." *Journal of Roman Studies* 67 (1977): 171–76.
———. *Leon Battista Alberti, Master Builder of the Italian Renaissance*. London, 2000.

Gramaccini, Norberto. "La prima riedificazione del Campidoglio e la rivoluzione senatoriale del 1144." In *Roma, centro ideale della cultura dell'antico nei secoli XI e XVI*, ed. Silvia Danesi Squarzina, 21–33. Milan, 1989.

Grandazzi, Alexandre. *The Foundation of Rome: Myth and History*. Ithaca and London, 1997.

Greene, Thomas. *The Light in Troy: Imitation and Discovery in Renaissance Poetry*. New Haven, 1982.

Greenfield, Jeanette. *The Return of Cultural Treasures*. Cambridge, 1996.

Greenhalgh, Michael. *The Survival of Roman Antiquities in the Middle Ages*. London, 1989.

———. *Marble Past, Monumental Present: Building with Antiquities in the Medieval Mediterranean.* Leiden and Boston, 2009.

Gregorovius, Ferdinand. *History of the City of Rome in the Middle Ages.* 8 vols. London, 1900.

Grimm, Hermann. *The Destruction of Rome: A Letter from Hermann Grimm.* Trans. Sarah Holland Adams. Boston, 1886; also published as *La distruzione di Roma: una lettera di Ermanno Grimm.* Trans. C. V. Giusti. Florence, 1886.

Gros, Pierre. *L'architecture romaine.* 2 vols. Paris, 1996.

Guasco, Luigi. *L'archivio storico del comune di Roma.* Rome, 1919.

———. *L'archivio storico capitolino.* Rome, 1946.

Guidoni, Enrico. "Roma e l'urbanistica del Trecento." In *Storia dell'arte italiana: dal medioevo al Quattrocento*, 5.309–84. Turin, 1983.

Halbwachs, Maurice. *On Collective Memory.* Chicago, 1992.

Hall, Marcia. "The High Renaissance, 1503–1534." In *Rome: Artistic Centers of the Italian Renaissance*, ed. Marcia Hall, 107–83. Cambridge, 2005.

Halphen, Louis. *Études sur l'administration de Rome au moyen age (751–1252).* Paris, 1907.

Hansen, Mogens Herman. *The Triumph of Time: Reflections of a Historian on Time in History.* Copenhagen, 2002.

Hell, Julia, and Andreas Schönle, eds. *Ruins of Modernity.* Durham, 2010.

Hornblower, Simon, and Antony Spawforth, eds. *The Oxford Classical Dictionary.* Oxford, 2003.

Hülsen, Christian. *Il libro di Giuliano da Sangallo, codice vaticano Barberiniano latino 4424.* 2 vols. Leipzig, 1910; repr. Vatican City, 1984.

———. *Le chiese di Roma nel medioevo.* Florence, 1927.

Hülsen, Christian, and Hermann Egger, eds. *Die Römischen Skizzenbücher von Marten van Heemskerck in Königlichen Kupferstichkabinett zu Berlin.* 2 vols. Berlin, 1916; repr. Soest, 1975.

Infessura, Stefano. *Diario della città di Roma.* Rome, 1890.

Iversen, Erik. *Obelisks in Exile.* 2 vols. Copenhagen, 1968.

Jacks, Philip. *The Antiquarian and the Myth of Antiquity: The Origins of Rome in Renaissance Thought.* Cambridge, 1993.

Jestaz, M. Bertrand. "L'exportation des marbres de Rome de 1535 à 1571." *Mélanges d'archeologie et d'histoire* 75 (1963): 415–66.

Jokilehto, Jukka. *A History of Architectural Conservation.* Oxford, 1999.

Jordan, Henri. *Topographie der stadt Rom im alterthum.* 2 vols. in 4. Berlin, 1871–1907.

Karmon, David. "Renaissance Strategies to Protect the Colosseum: Selective Preservation and Reuse." *Future Anterior* 2, 2 (2005a): 1–10.

———. "Restoring the Ancient Water Supply in Renaissance Rome: The Popes, the Civic Administration, and the Acqua Vergine." *Aquae Urbis Romae* (July 2005b). http://www.iath.virginia.edu/waters/karmon.html

———. "Michelangelo's 'Minimalism' in the Design of Santa Maria degli Angeli." *Annali di architettura* 20 (2008a): 141–53.

———. "Printing and Protecting Ancient Remains in the Speculum Romanae Magnificentiae." In *The Virtual Tourist in Renaissance Rome: Printing and Collecting the Speculum Romanae Magnificentiae*, ed. Rebecca Zorach, 36–51. Chicago, 2008b.

———. "Preservation as Transcendent Vision: Antonio Duca and Santa Maria degli Angeli." In *Faith and Fantasy in the Renaissance: Text, Images, and Religious Practices*, eds. Olga Pugliese and Matt Kavaler, 316–30. Toronto, 2009.

———. "The Colosseum." In *The Classical Tradition*, eds. Anthony Grafton, Glenn Most, and Salvatore Settis, 216–17. Cambridge, 2010a.

———. "Preserving Antiquity in a Protestant City: The Maison Carrée in Sixteenth-Century Nîmes." In *Art, Piety, and Destruction in European Religion, 1500-1700*, ed. Virginia Raguin, 105–40. Aldershot, 2010b.

———. "Archaeology and the Anxiety of Loss: Effacing Preservation from the History of Renaissance Rome." *American Journal of Archaeology* 115, 2 (April 2011): 159–174.

Kimmelman, Michael, and Gaia Pianigiani. "As Rome Modernizes, its Past Quietly Crumbles." *New York Times* (7 July 2010), C1.

Kinney, Dale. "Spolia from the Baths of Caracalla in Santa Maria in Trastevere." *Art Bulletin* 68 (1986): 379–97.

Kleinhenz, Christopher. "Petrarch." In *Encyclopedia of the Renaissance*, ed. Paul Grendler, 4.451-58. New York, 1999.

Kockel, Valentin. "Forum Augustum." In *Lexicon Topographicum Urbis Romae*, ed. Eva Margareta Steinby, 2.289–95. Rome, 1995.

Krautheimer, Richard. "Sancta Maria Rotunda." In *Studies in Early Christian, Medieval and Renaissance Art*, 107–14. New York, 1969.

———. *Rome, Profile of a City 312–1308*. Princeton, 1980.

———. *Rome of Alexander VII, 1655–1677*. Princeton, 1985.

Kuttner, Stephan. "The Revival of Jurisprudence." In *Renaissance and Renewal in the Twelfth Century*, eds. Robert Benson and Giles Constable, 299–323. Cambridge, 1982.

Lalle, Anita. "Il foro di Nerva e il tempio di Minerva: trasformazioni e utilizzo in epoca medievale." In *La Roma di Leon Battista Alberti: umanisti, architetti, e artisti alla scoperta dell'antico nella città del quattrocento*, eds. Francesco Paolo Fiore and Arnold Nesselrath, 230–35. Milan, 2005.

Lancaster, Lynne. "Reconstructing the Restorations of the Colosseum after the Fire of 217." *Journal of Roman Archaeology* 11 (1998): 146–74.

———. *Concrete Vaulted Construction in Imperial Rome: Innovations in Context*. Cambridge, 2005.

Lanciani, Pietro. *Del ponte Senatorio, ora Rotto*. Rome, 1826.

Lanciani, Rodolfo. "Scavi di Roma." *Notizie degli scavi di antichità* (1882): 218–25.

———. "Sulla conservazione dei monumenti di Roma." *Atti della reale accademia dei Lincei, Rendiconti pubblicati per conto dei segretari* 2 (1886): 355–68.

———. *Ancient Rome in the Light of Recent Discoveries*. London, 1888.

———. *The Destruction of Ancient Rome*. London, 1899.

———. "La via del Corso drizzata e abbellita nel 1538 da Paolo III." *Bollettino della commissione archeologica comunale di Roma* 30 (1902): 229–55.

———. *Storia degli scavi di Roma intorno le collezioni romane di antichità*. 7 vols. Rome, 1902–1912; reprint, Rome, 1989–2002.

———. *The Golden Days of the Renaissance in Rome*. London, 1906.

La Regina, Adriano. *Sangue e arena*. Milan, 2001.

Le Gall, Joël. *Le Tibre: fleuve de Rome dans l'antiquité*. Paris, 1953.

Leisching, Peter. "Roma restauranda: versuch einer Geschichte des päpstlichen
    Denkmalschutzrechtes." In *Römische Kurie: Kirchliche Finanzen, Vatikanisches
    Archiv, Studien zu Ehren von Hermann Hoberg*, ed. Erwin Gatz, 425–43. Rome, 1979.

Loercke, William. "Georges Chédanne and the Pantheon: A Beaux-Arts Contribution to
    the History of Roman Architecture." *Modulus: University of Virginia School of
    Architecture Review* (1982): 41–55.

———. "A Rereading of the Interior Elevation of Hadrian's Rotunda." *Journal of the
    Society of Architectural Historians* 49 (1990): 22–43.

Lowenthal, David. *The Past Is a Foreign Country.* Cambridge, 1985.

———. *The Heritage Crusade and the Spoils of History.* Cambridge, 1998.

Lugli, Giuseppe. *Roma antica: il centro monumentale.* Rome, 1946.

———, ed. *Fontes ad topographiam veteris urbis Romae pertinentes.* 4 vols. Rome, 1953.

Macaulay, Rose. *Pleasure of Ruins.* London, 1953.

Macdonald, W. L. *The Pantheon: Design, Meaning and Progeny.* London, 1976.

Madonna, Maria Luisa. "L'ingresso di Carlo V a Roma." In *La città effimera e l'universo
    artificiale del giardino: la Firenze dei Medici e l'Italia del cinquecento*, ed. Marcello
    Fagiolo, 63–68. Rome, 1980.

———. "L'ingresso di Carlo V a Roma." In *La festa a Roma dal Rinascimento al 1870*,
    ed. Marcello Fagiolo, 50–67. Rome, 1997.

Magnusson, Cecilia. "The Antique Sources of the Chigi Chapel." *Konsthistorisk tidskrift*
    61, 4 (1987): 135–39.

Maire-Vigueur, Jean Claude. "Cola di Rienzo." In *Dizionario biografico degli italiani*, ed.
    Alberto Ghisalberti, 21.662–75. Rome, 1982.

———. "Il comune romano." In *Roma medievale, storia di Roma dall'antichità a oggi*,
    117–58. Rome, 2001.

Makarius, Michel. *Ruins.* Paris, 2004.

Manacorda, Daniele. *Crypta Balbi: archeologia e storia di un paesaggio urbano.* Milan, 2003.

Marangoni, Giovanni. *Delle memorie sacre e profane dell'anfiteatro Flavio di Roma,
    volgarmente detto Il Colosseo.* Rome, 1746.

Marchetti-Longhi, Giuseppe. "Le contrade medioevali della zona in Circo Flaminio."
    Archivio della reverenda società romana di storia patria 42 (1919): 401–536.

Marder, Tod. "Specchi's High Altar for the Pantheon and the Statues by Cametti and
    Moderati." *Burlington Magazine* 122 (1980): 30–40.

Mari, Zaccaria. "Via Tiburtina." In *Lexicon Topographicum Urbis Romae Suburbium*, ed.
    Adriano La Regina, 5.161–73. Rome, 2008.

Marini, Gaetano. *Degli archiatri pontifici.* 2 vols. Rome, 1784.

Mark, Robert, and Paul Hutchinson. "On the Structure of the Roman Pantheon." *Art
    Bulletin* 68, 1 (1986): 24–34.

Marliano, Bartolomeo. *Urbis Romae Topographia.* Rome, 1544.

Martines, Giangiacomo. "Argomenti di geometria antica a proposito della cupola del
    Pantheon." *Quaderni dell'istituto di storia dell'architettura* 13 (1991): 3–18.

———. "The Relationship between Architecture and Mathematics in the Pantheon."
    Nexus Network Journal 2, 3 (July 2000). http://www.nexusjournal.com/Martines.html

Mazzocco, Angelo. "Petrarca, Poggio, and Biondo: Humanism's Foremost Interpreters
    of Roman Ruins." In *Francis Petrarch, Six Centuries Later: A Symposium*, ed. Aldo
    Scaglione, 353–63. Chapel Hill and Chicago, 1975.

McCuaig, William. "Biondo, Flavio." In *Encyclopedia of the Renaissance*, ed. Paul
    Grendler, 1.231–32. New York, 1999.

McEwen, Indra. *Vitruvius: Writing the Body of Architecture*. Cambridge, 2003.

Meserve, Margaret, and Marcello Simonetta, eds. *The Commentaries of Pius II*.
    Cambridge, 2003.

Miglio, Massimo. "'Viva la libertà et populo de Roma.' Oratoria e politica a Roma:
    Stefano Porcari." *Archivio della società romana di storia patria* 97 (1974): 5–37.

———. "Il leone e la lupa: dal simbolo al pasticcio alla francese." *Studi Romani* 30
    (1982): 177–86.

———. "L'immagine dell'onore antico: individualità e tradizione della Roma munici-
    pale." *Studi romani* 31 (1983): 252–64.

———. "Roma dopo Avignone. La rinascita politica dell'antico." In *Memoria dell'antico
    nell'arte italiana*, ed. Salvatore Settis, 75–111. Turin, 1984.

———. "Il ritorno a Roma. Varianti di una costante nella tradizione dell'antico: le
    scelte pontificie." In *Roma, centro ideale della cultura dell'antico nei secoli XV e XVI*,
    ed. Silvia Danesi Squarzina, 216–20. Rome, 1989.

———. "Il senato in Roma medievale." In *Il senato nella storia, il senato nel medioevo, e
    nella prima età moderna*, ed. Emilio Gabba, 2.117–72. Rome, 1998.

Millon, Henry. "Michelangelo to Marchionni, 1546–1784." In *St. Peter's in the Vatican*,
    ed. William Tronzo, 93–110. Cambridge, 2005.

Mitchell, Bonner. *Italian Civic Pageantry in the High Renaissance*. Florence, 1979.

Moccheggiani-Carpano, Claudio, and Roberto Luciani. "I restauri dell'anfiteatro
    Flavio." *Rivista dell'istituto nazionale d'archeologia e storia dell'arte* 3, 4 (1981): 9–69.

Modigliani, Anna. "La famiglia Porcari: tra memorie repubbliche e curialismo." In
    Un pontificato ed una città, Sisto IV (1471–1484), eds. Massimo Miglio et al., 317–53.
    Rome, 1986.

———. *I Porcari: storia di una famiglia romana tra medioevo e rinascimento*. Rome, 1994.

———. *Mercati, botteghe, e spazi di commercio a Roma tra medioevo ed età moderna*.
    Rome, 1998.

Montani, Francesco Fabi. *Feste e spettacoli di Roma dal secolo X a tutto il XVI particolar-
    mente nel carnevale e nel maggio*. Rome, 1861.

Moore, David. *The Roman Pantheon: The Triumph of Concrete*. Guam, 1995.

Morolli, Gabriele. *Le belle forme degli edifici antichi: Raffaello e il progetto del primo
    trattato rinascimentale sulle antichità di Roma*. Florence, 1984.

Morrogh, Andrew. "The Palace of the Roman People: Michelangelo at the Palazzo dei
    Conservatori." *Römisches Jahrbuch der Bibliotheca Hertziana* 29 (1994):129–86.

Moscati, Laura. *Alle origini del comune romano*. Naples, 1980.

Mostafavi, Mohsen, and David Leatherbarrow. *On Weathering: The Life of Buildings in
    Time*. Cambridge, 1993.

Muños Viñas, Salvador. *Contemporary Theory of Conservation*. Oxford, 2005.

Muñoz, Antonio. "La decorazione medioevale del Pantheon." *Nuovo bullettino di
    archeologia cristiana* 18 (1912): 25–35.

Müntz, Eugène. "Les monuments antiques de Rome au XVe siècle: Nicolas V, Pie II,
    Paul II, Sixte IV, et Alexandre VI." *Révue archéologique* 2, 32 (1876): 158–75.

———. *Les arts à la cour des pâpes pendant le XVe et le XVIe siècle, Martin V–Pie II
    (1417–1464)*. Vol. 4. Paris, 1878.

———. *Les arts à la cour des pâpes pendant le XVe et le XVIe siècle, Paul II (1464–1471)*. Vol. 9. Paris, 1879.

———. "Raphael, archéologue et historien d'art." *Gazette des beaux-arts* (1880): 453–64.

———. *Les arts à la cour des papes pendant le XVe et le XVIe siècle, Sixte IV–Leon X (1471–1521)*. Vol. 28. Paris, 1882.

———. "Les monuments antiques de Rome à l'époque e la Renaissance: nouvelles recherches." *Révue archéologique* 3, 2 (1884): 296–313.

———. *Les antiquités de la ville de Rome aux XIVe, XVe et XVIe siècles: topographie, monuments, collections d'après des documents nouveaux*. Paris, 1886.

———. "Les monuments antiques de Rome à l'époque de la Renaissance." *Révue archéologique* 3, 9 (1887): 54–175.

Musto, Ronald. *Apocalypse in Rome: Cola di Rienzo and the Politics of a New Age*. Berkeley, 2003.

Nagel, Alexander, and Christopher Wood. *Anachronic Renaissance*. New York, 2010.

Nash, Ernest. *Pictorial Dictionary of Ancient Rome*. 2 vols. London, 1961; 2nd ed., London, 1968.

Natale, Arcangelo. "La felice società dei balestrieri e dei pavesati a Roma e il governo dei bandaresi dal 1358 al 1408." *Archivio della società romana di storia patria* 62 (1939): 1–176.

Nelson, Robert. "Tourists, Terrorists, and Metaphysical Theater at Hagia Sophia." In *Monuments and Memory: Made and Unmade*, eds. Robert Nelson and Margaret Olin, 59–82. Chicago, 2003.

Nesselrath, Arnold. "Raphael's Archaeological Method." In *Raffaello a Roma*, 357–71. Rome, 1983.

———. "Raffaello e lo studio dell'antico nel Rinascimento." In *Raffaello architetto*, eds. Christoph Frommel, Stefano Ray, and Manfredo Tafuri, 407. Milan, 1984.

———. "Il Pantheon." In *La Roma di Leo Battista Alberti: umanisti, architetti, e artisti alla scoperta dell'antico nella città del quattrocento*, eds. Francesco Paolo Fiore and Arnold Nesselrath, 190–201. Milan, 2005.

Newbigin, Nerida. "The Word Made Flesh: The Rappresentazioni of Mysteries and Miracles in Fifteenth-Century Florence." In *Christianity and the Renaissance: Image and Religious Imagination in the Quattrocento*, eds. Timothy Verdon and John Henderson, 361–75. Syracuse, 1990.

———. "The Decorum of the Passion: The Plays of the Confraternity of the Gonfalone in the Roman Colosseum, 1490–1539." In *Confraternities and the Visual Arts in Renaissance Italy*, 173–202. New York, 2000.

Nora, Pierre. *Realms of Memory: Rethinking the French Past*. Trans. Arthur Goldhammer. 3 vols. New York, 1996–1998.

Norman, Diana. "Those Who Pay, Those Who Pray, and Those Who Paint: Two Funerary Chapels." In *Siena, Florence, and Padua: Art, Society, and Religion, 1280–1400*, 169–93. Cambridge, 1995.

Nussdorfer, Laurie. "The Vacant See: Ritual and Protest in Early Modern Rome." *Sixteenth Century Journal* 18, 2 (Summer 1987): 173–189.

———. *Civic Politics in the Rome of Urban VIII*. Princeton, 1992.

———. "The Politics of Space in Early Modern Rome." *Memoirs of the American Academy in Rome* 42 (1997): 161–86.

———. "Il popolo romano e i papi: la vita politica della capitale religiosa." In *Storia-d'Italia, Annali 16: Roma la città del Papa*, eds. Luigi Fiorani and Adriano Prosperi, 241–62. Turin, 2000.

Oldradi, Angelo degli. *Avviso della pace tra la Sant. di N.S. Papa Paolo IV e la maestà del Re Filippo, e del diluvio che è stato in Roma con altri successi e particolarità*. Rome, 1557.

O'Malley, John. "Fulfillment of the Christian Golden Age under Pope Julius II: Text of a Discourse of Giles of Viterbo 1507." *Traditio* 25 (1969): 265–338.

———. "The Theology behind Michelangelo's Ceiling." In *The Sistine Chapel: The Art, the History, and the Restoration*, ed. Carlo Pietrangeli, 92–148. New York, 1986.

Orano, Domenico. "Il diario di Marcello Alberini." *Archivio della società romana di storia patria* 19 (1896): 43–74.

Orlandi, Silvia. "Il Colosseo nel v secolo." *Journal of Roman Archaeology, Supplementary Series* 33 (1999): 249–63.

Otero-Pailos, Jorge. "Mnemonic Value and Historic Preservation." In *Spatial Recall: Memory in Architecture and Landscape*, ed. Marc Treib, 241–59. New York and London, 2009.

Pagliara, Pier Nicola. "Materiali, techniche e strutture in architetture del primo Cinquecento." In *Storia dell'architettura italiana: il primo cinquecento*, ed. Arnaldo Bruschi, 522–45. Milan, 2002.

Pagliara, Pier Nicola, and Suzanne Butters. "Il palazzo Tribunali e Via Giulia a Roma." *Zodiac* 14 (1997): 14–29.

Palermo, Luciano. "Capitali pubblici e investimenti privati nell'amministrazione finanziaria della città di Roma all'epoca di Martino V." In *Alle origini della nuova Roma, Martino V (1417–1431)*, eds. Maria Chiabò et al., 501–35. Rome, 1992.

Palombi, Domenico. *Rodolfo Lanciani, l'archeologia a Roma tra Ottocento e Novecento*. Rome, 2006.

Partner, Peter. *The Papal State under Martin V: The Administration and Government of the Temporal Power in the Early Fifteenth Century*. London, 1958.

———. *The Lands of St. Peter: The Papal State in the Middle Ages and the Early Renaissance*. Berkeley, 1972.

———. *Renaissance Rome, 1500–1559: A Portrait of a Society*. Berkeley, 1976.

Pasquali, Susanna. *Il Pantheon: architettura e antiquaria nel settecento a Roma*. Modena, 1996.

———. "From the Pantheon of Artists to the Pantheon of Illustrious Men: Raphael's Tomb and Its Legacy." In *Pantheons: Transformations of a Monumental Idea*, eds. Richard Wrigley and Matthew Craske, 37–67. Ashgate, 2004.

Pastor, Ludwig Freiherr von. *The History of the Popes from the Close of the Middle Ages*. Trans. Frederick Antrobus. 16 vols. St. Louis, 1898.

———. *Storia dei papi dalla fine del medio evo*, ed. Angelo Mercati. 17 vols. Rome, 1925.

Patterson, John R. "Via Aurelia." In *Lexicon Topographicum Urbis Romae*, ed. Eva Margareta Steinby, 4.133–34. Rome, 1999.

Pavan, Paola. "Gli statuti della società dei Raccomandati del Salvatore." *Archivio della reverenda società romana di storia patria* 101 (1978): 35–96.

———. "La confraternità del Salvatore nella società romana del tre e quattrocento." *Ricerche per la storia religiosa di Roma* 5 (1984): 81–90.

———. "Inclitae urbis Romae iura, iurisdictiones et honores: un caso di damnatio memoriae?" In *Alle origini della nuova Roma: Martino V 1417–1431*, eds. Maria Chiabò et al., 301–10. Rome, 1992.

Pellecchia, Linda. "The Contested City: Urban Form in Early Sixteenth-Century Rome." In *The Cambridge Companion to Raphael*, ed. Marcia Hall, 59–94. Cambridge, 2005.

Perini, Giovanna. "Raffaello e l'antico: alcune precisazioni." *Bollettino d'arte* 89–90 (January–April 1995): 111–14.

Petrarch. "Epistola secunda ad Paulum Annibalensem." In *Poesie minori del Petrarca*, ed. Domenico Rossetti, 2.330–37. Milan, 1831.

———. *Familiarum rerum libri*. Trans. Aldo Bernardo. 3 vols. New York, 1975–85.

Pharr, Clyde, ed. *The Theodosian Code and Novels and the Sirmondian Constitutions*. Princeton, 1952.

Phillips, E. J. "The Roman Law on the Demolition of Buildings." *Latomus* 32 (1973), 86–95.

Pinelli, Antonio. "Feste e trionfi: continuità e metamorfosi di un tema." In *Memoria dell'antico nell'arte italiana*, ed. Salvatore Settis, 2.280–350. Turin, 1984.

Platner, Samuel Ball, and Thomas Ashby. *A Topographical Dictionary of Ancient Rome*. London, 1929.

Podestà, Bartolomeo. "Documenti inediti relativi a Michelangelo." *Il Buonarroti* 10 (1875): 128–37.

———. "Carlo V a Roma nell'anno 1536." *Archivio della società romana di storia patria* 1 (1878): 303–44.

Poole, Reginald, ed. *Ioannis Saresberiensis Historiae pontificalis quae supersunt*. Oxford, 1927.

Povoledo, Elisabetta. "Rome's New Vigilance for Its Buried Treasure." *New York Times* (25 December 2006), E1.

Presicce, Claudio Parisi. "I grandi bronzi di Sisto IV dal Laterano in Campidoglio." In *Sisto IV: le arti a Roma nel primo rinascimento*, ed. Fabio Benzi, 189–200. Rome, 2000.

Price, Simon. "The Place of Religion." In *The Augustan Empire, 43 B.C.–A.D. 69*, eds. Alan Bowman et al., 812–47. Cambridge, 1996.

———, and Peter Thonemann. *The Birth of Classical Europe: A History from Troy to Augustine*. London, 2010.

Procopius. *History of the Wars*. London, 1914.

Prodi, Paolo. *The Papal Prince: One Body and Two Souls, the Papal Monarchy in Early Modern Europe*. Trans. Susan Haskins. Cambridge, 1987.

Purcell, Nicholas. "The City of Rome." In *The Legacy of Rome: A New Appraisal*, ed. Richard Jenkyns, 421–53. Oxford, 1992.

Ramieri, Anna Maria. *I ponti di Roma*. Rome, 2003.

Rawson, Elizabeth. *Intellectual Life in the Late Roman Republic*. London, 1985.

Ray, Stefano. *Raffaello architetto: linguaggio artistico e ideologia nel rinascimento romano*. Rome-Bari, 1974.

Re, Camillo. *Statuti della città di Roma*. Rome, 1880.

Re, Emilio. "I maestri di strada." *Archivio della società romana di storia patria* 43 (1920): 5–102.

Rea, Rossella. "Amphitheatrum." In *Lexicon Topographicum Urbis Romae*, ed. Eva Margareta Steinby, 1.30–35. Rome, 1993.

————. "The Colosseum through the Centuries." In *The Colosseum*, ed. Ada Gabucci, trans. Mary Becker, 161–229. Los Angeles, 2001.

————. "Graffiti e targhe proprietarie." In *Rota Colisei: la valle del Colosseo attraverso i secoli*, ed. Rossella Rea, 231–39. Milan, 2002.

————, ed. *Rota Colisei, la valle del Colosseo attraverso i secoli*. Milan, 2002.

Rea, Rossella, and Giovanni Giacomo Pani. "GERONTI V S: la spoliazione teodericiana." In *Rota Colisei: la valle del Colosseo attraverso i secoli*, ed. Rossella Rea, 153–59. Milan, 2002.

Reynolds, Donald, ed. *Remove Not the Ancient Landmark: Public Monuments and Moral Values*. Amsterdam, 1996.

Reumont, Alfred von. *Geschichte der Stadt Rom*. 3 vols. Berlin, 1870.

Richardson, Lawrence, Jr. *A New Topographical Dictionary of Ancient Rome*. Baltimore and London, 1992.

Ridley, Ronald. *The Eagle and the Spade: Archaeology in Rome during the Napoleonic Era*. Cambridge, 1992a.

————. "To Protect the Monuments: The Papal Antiquarian (1534–1870)." *Xenia antiqua* 1 (1992b): 117–54.

Riegl, Alois. "The Modern Cult of Monuments: its Character and its Origin." Trans. Kurt Forster and Diane Ghirardo. *Oppositions* 25 (Fall 1982): 21–51.

Ritter, Dorothea. *Rom 1846–70: James Anderson und die Maler-Fotografen, Sammlung Siegert*. Heidelberg, 2005.

Rodocanachi, Emanuele. *Les institutions communales de Rome sous la papauté*. Paris, 1901.

————. "Les anciens monuments de Rome du XVe aux XVIIe siècle. Attitude du Saint Siège et du Conseil communal à leur égard." *Revue archéologique*, 4, 21 (1913): 171–83.

————. *Les monuments de Rome après la chute de l'empire*. Paris, 1914.

Roth, Michael, Claire Lyons, and Charles Merewether. *Irresistible Decay: Ruins Reclaimed*. Los Angeles, 1997.

Rowland, Ingrid. "Render unto Caesar the Things Which Are Caesar's: Humanism and the Arts in the Patronage of Agostino Chigi." *Renaissance Quarterly* 39, 4 (Winter 1986): 673–730.

————. *The Culture of the High Renaissance: Ancients and Moderns in Sixteenth-Century Rome*. Cambridge, 1998.

————. "Cultural Introduction to Renaissance Rome." In *Rome: Artistic Centers of the Italian Renaissance*, ed. Marcia Hall, 1–14. Cambridge, 2005.

Ruggieri, Luigi. *L'archiconfraternità del Gonfalone*. Rome, 1866.

Ruskin, John. *The Seven Lamps of Architecture*. Introduction by Andrew Saint. London, 1849; rev. ed., London, 1998.

Salimei, Alfonso. *Senatori e statuti di Roma nel medioevo: i senatori, cronologia e bibliografia dal 1144 al 1447*. Rome, 1935.

Santoni, Barbara Tellini, et al., eds. *Archeologia in posa: dal Colosseo a Cecilia Metella nell'antica documentazione fotografica*. Milan, 1998.

Sanuto, Marino. *I diarii di Marino Sanuto (1496–1533)*. Vol. 34. Venice, 1892.

Satzinger, Georg. "Spolien in der römischen Architektur des Quattrocento." In *Antike Spolien in der Architektur des Mittelalters und der Renaissance*, ed. Joachim Poeschke, 277–308. Munich, 1996.

Scarafoni, Camillo Scaccia. "L'antico statuto dei magistri stratarum, e altri documenti relativi a quella magistratura." *Archivio della società romana di storia patria* 50 (1927): 237–308.

Schiaparelli, L. "Alcuni documenti dei magistri aedificiorum urbis." *Archivio della società romana di storia patria* 25 (1902): 5–59.

Schildgen, Brenda Deen. *Heritage or Heresy: Preservation and Destruction of Religious Art and Architecture in Europe.* New York, 2008.

Schnapp, Alain. *The Discovery of the Past: The Origins of Archaeology.* New York, 1997.

Seabrook, John. "Roman Renovation." *The New Yorker* (2 May 2005): 56–63.

Sear, Frank. *Roman Architecture.* London, 1982.

Schudt, Ludwig. *Le guide di Roma: Materialen zu einer Geschichte der Römischen Topographie.* Vienna, 1930.

Semes, Steven. *The Future of the Past.* New York, 2009.

Settis, Salvatore. "Continuità, distanza, conoscenza: tre usi dell'antico." In *Memoria dell'antico nell'arte italiana,* ed. Salvatore Settis, 375–488. Turin, 1985.

———. *Italia S.p.A.: L'assalto al patrimonio culturale.* Turin, 2002.

———. *Il futuro del "classico."* Turin, 2004.

Shearman, John. "The Chigi Chapel at Santa Maria del Popolo." *Journal of the Warburg and Courtauld Institutes* 24 (1961): 129–60.

———. "Il 'tiburio' di Bramante." In *Studi bramanteschi: atti del congresso internazionale,* 567–73. Rome, 1974.

———. "Raphael, Rome and the *Codex Escurialensis.*" *Master Drawings* 15, 2 (1977): 107–46.

———. *Raphael in Early Modern Sources.* 2 vols. New Haven and London, 2003.

Simoncini, Giorgio. *Roma: le trasformazioni urbane nel Quattrocento.* 2 vols. Florence, 2004.

Smick, Rebekah. "Touch in the Hypnerotomachia Poliphili: The Sensual Ethics of Architecture." In *Sensible Flesh: On Touch in Early Modern Culture,* ed. Elizabeth Harvey, 205–23. Philadelphia, 2003.

Smith, Christine. *Architecture in the Culture of Early Humanism: Ethics, Aesthetics and Eloquence, 1400–1470.* Oxford, 1992.

———, and Joseph O'Connor. *Building the Kingdom: Giannozzo Manetti on the Material and Spiritual Edifice.* Tempe and Turnhout, 2006.

Smith, Leonardo, ed. *Epistolario di Pier Paolo Vergerio.* In *Fonti per la storia d'Italia,* vol. 74. Rome, 1934.

Spezzaferro, Luigi. "La politica urbanistica dei papi e le origini di via Giulia." In *Via Giulia: una utopia urbanistica del Cinquecento,* eds. Luigi Salerno, Luigi Spezzaferro, and Manfredo Tafuri, 15–64. Rome, 1973.

Spezzaferro, Luigi, and Richard Tuttle. "Place Farnèse: urbanisme et politique." In *Le Palais Farnèse: École française de Rome,* eds. André Chastel and François-Charles Uginet, 1.85–121. Rome, 1981.

Stinger, Charles L. *The Renaissance in Rome.* Bloomington, 1998.

Strong, D. E. "The Administration of Public Buildings in Rome during the Late Republic and Early Empire." *Bulletin of the Institute of Classical Studies of the University of London* 15 (1968): 97–109.

Suetonius. *Lives of the Caesars.* London and New York, 1924.

Tafuri, Manfredo. "Via Giulia: storia di una struttura urbana." In *Via Giulia: una utopia urbanistica del Cinquecento,* eds. Luigi Salerno, Luigi Spezzaferro, and Manfredo Tafuri, 65–152. Rome, 1973.

———. "Roma instaurata: strategie urbane e politiche nella Roma del primo Cinquecento." In *Raffaello architetto,* eds. Christoph Frommel, Stefano Ray, and Manfredo Tafuri, 59–106. Milan, 1984.

————. *Ricerca del Rinascimento: principi, città, architetti.* Turin, 1992.

Taylor, Rabun. "Tiber River Bridges and the Development of the Ancient City of Rome." *Aquae Urbis Romae* (2002): 1–36.

————. *Roman Builders: A Study in Architectural Process.* Cambridge, 2003.

Theiner, Augustin. *Codex diplomaticus dominii temporalis S. Sedis: recueil de documents pour servir à l'histoire du gouvernement temporel des états du Saint-Siège.* 3 vols. Rome, 1862.

Theseider, Eugenio Dupré. *Roma dal comune di popolo alla signoria pontificia, 1252–1378.* Bologna, 1952.

Thoenes, Christof. "Sankt Peter als Ruine: zu einigen Veduten Heemskercks." *Zeitschrift für Kunstgeschichte* 49 (1986): 481–501.

————. *Sostegno e adornamento: saggi sull'architettura del rinascimento, disegni, ordini, magnificenza.* Milan, 1998.

————. "Renaissance St. Peter's." In *St. Peter's in the Vatican,* ed. William Tronzo, 64–71. Cambridge, 2005.

Thomas, Edmund, and Christian Witschel. "Constructing Reconstruction: Claim and Reality of Roman Rebuilding Inscriptions from the Latin West." *Papers of the British School at Rome* 60 (1992): 135–77.

Thomson, John. *Popes and Princes, 1417–1517: Politics and Polity in the Late Medieval Church.* London, 1980.

Tiberia, Vitaliano. *La compagnia di S. Giuseppe di Terrasanta nel XVI secolo.* Lecce, 1999.

Tittoni, Maria Elisa. "Il Campidoglio tra potere e potere." In *Il palazzo dei Conservatori e il palazzo nuovo in Campidoglio: momenti di storia urbana di Roma,* ed. Maria Elisa Tittoni, 13–18. Siena, 1997.

Trigger, Bruce. *A History of Archaeological Thought.* Cambridge, 2006.

Tronzo, William. "Il tegurium di Bramante." In *L'architettura della basilica di San Pietro, storia e costruzione,* ed. Gianfranco Spagnesi, 161–66. Rome, 1997.

Tung, Anthony. *Preserving the World's Great Cities: The Destruction and Renewal of the Historic Metropolis.* New York, 2001.

Ughelli, Ferdinando. *Italia Sacra.* Venice, 1717.

Ugonio, Pompeo. *Historia delle stationi di Roma.* Rome, 1588.

Valentini, Roberto, and Giuseppe Zucchetti, eds. *Codice topografico della città di Roma.* 4 vols. Rome, 1940–53.

Vaquero-Piñiero, Manuel. "La gabella dei calcarari: note sulla produzione di calce e laterizi a Roma nel quattrocento." In *Maestranze e cantieri edili a Roma e nel Lazio: lavoro, tecniche, materiali nei secoli XIII–XV,* eds. Angela Lanconelli and Ivana Ait, 137–54. Rome, 2002.

Vasari, Giorgio. *Le vite dei più eccellenti pittori, scultori e architettori.* Ed. Gaetano Milanesi. 10 vols. Florence, 1906.

————. *La vita di Michelangelo nelle redazioni del 1550 e del 1568.* Ed. Paola Barocchi. 5 vols. Florence, 1962.

Vattasso, Marco. *Per la storia del dramma sacro in Italia: le rappresentazioni sacre al Colosseo nei secoli XV e XVI.* Rome, 1903.

Vattuone, Lucina. "Esaltazione e distruzione di Roma antica nella città di Sisto IV." In *Sisto IV: le arti a Roma nel primo rinascimento,* ed. Fabio Benzi, 174–88. Rome, 2000.

Vendittelli, Cristina Carbonetti. "Documentazione inedita riguardante i magistri edificiorum urbis nei secoli xiii e xiv e la sua documentazione." *Rome aux XIII e XIV siècles, collection de l'Ecole française de Rome* 170 (1993): 169–88.

Veranzio, Fausto. *Machinae novae Fausti Verantii siceni* Venice, ca. 1599.

Verdi, Orietta. "Da ufficiali capitolini a commissari apostolici: i maestri delle strade e degli edifici di Roma tra XIII e XVI secolo." In *Il Campidoglio e Sisto V*, eds. Luigi Spezzaferro and Maria Elisa Tittoni, 54–63. Rome, 1991.

———. *Maestri di edifici e di strade a Roma nel secolo XV, fonti e problemi.* Rome, 1997.

Virgili, Paola. "Strutture altomedioevali sulla fronte del Pantheon." *Atti della Pontificia Accademia Romana di Archeologia* 70 (2000): 197–207.

Visceglia, Maria Antonietta. "Cerimoniali romani: il ritorno e la trasfigurazione dei trionfi antichi." In *Storia d'Italia, Annali 16: Roma la città del Papa*, eds. Luigi Fiorani and Adriano Prosperi, 113–70. Turin, 2000.

———. "Il viaggio cerimoniale di Carlo V dopo Tunisi." In *Carlos V y la quiebra del humanismo politico en Europa (1530–1558)*, ed. José Martínez Millán, 2.133–72. Madrid, 2001.

———. *La città rituale: Roma e le sue cerimonie in età moderna.* Rome, 2002.

von Harff, Arnold. *Pilgerfahrt des Ritters von Harff von Cöln.* Ed. Alfred Reumont. Venice, 1876.

Wallace, William. *Michelangelo: The Artist, the Man, and His Times.* Cambridge, 2010.

Ward-Perkins, Bryan. *From Classical Antiquity to the Middle Ages: Urban Public Building in Northern and Central Italy.* Oxford, 1984.

Ward-Perkins, J. B. "Materials, Quarries, and Transportation." In *Marble in Antiquity: Collected Papers of J.B. Ward-Perkins*, eds. Hazel Dodge and Bryan Ward-Perkins, 13–30. London, 1992.

Wataghin, Gisella Cantino. "Archeologia e archeologie: il rapporto con l'antico fra mito, arte, e ricerca." In *Memoria dell'antico nell'arte italiana*, ed. Salvatore Settis, 1.171–217. Turin, 1984–86.

Watkin, David. *The Roman Forum.* Cambridge, 2009.

Weiss, Roberto. "Biondo Flavio archeologo." *Studi romagnoli* 14 (1963): 335–41.

———. *The Renaissance Discovery of Classical Antiquity.* Oxford, 1969; 2nd ed., Oxford, 1988.

Welch, Katherine. *The Roman Amphitheater: From Its Origins to the Colosseum.* Cambridge, 2007.

Westfall, Carroll William. *In This Most Perfect Paradise: Alberti, Nicholas V and the Invention of Conscious Urban Planning in Rome, 1447–1455.* University Park and London, 1974.

Wilkins, Ernest. *Life of Petrarch.* Chicago, 1961.

Wilson-Jones, Mark. *Principles of Roman Architecture.* New Haven and London, 2001.

Wisch, Barbara. "The Passion of Christ in the Art, Theater, and Penitential Rituals of the Roman Confraternity of the Gonfalone." In *Crossing the Boundaries: Christian Piety and the Arts in Medieval and Renaissance Confraternities*, ed. Konrad Eisenbichler, 237–62. Kalamazoo, 1991.

———. "The Colosseum as a Site for Sacred Theater: A Pre-History of Carlo Fontana's Project." In *An Architectural Progress in the Renaissance and the Baroque: Soujourns in and out of Italy*, eds. Henry Millon and Susan Munshower, 94–111. University Park, 1992.

———. "New Themes for New Rituals: The Crucifixion Altarpiece by Roviale Spagnuolo for the Oratory of the Gonfalone in Rome." In *Confraternities and the Visual Arts in Renaissance Italy*, eds. Barbara Wisch and Diane Cole Ahl, 203–24. Cambridge, 2000.

Wittkower, Rudolf. "Nanni di Baccio Bigio and Michelangelo." In *Festschrift Ulrich Middeldorf*, eds. A. Kosegarten and P. Tigler, 248–62. Berlin, 1968.

———, ed. *Le antiche rovine di Roma nei disegni di Dupérac*. Milan, 1990.

Wolf, Lorenz. *Kirche und Denkmalschutz: die päpstliche Gesetzgebung zum Schutz der Kulturgüter bis zum Untergang des Kirchenstaates im Jahr 1870*. Münster, 2003.

Woodward, Christopher. *In Ruins*. New York, 2001.

Wright, John, ed. *The Life of Cola di Rienzo*. Toronto, 1975.

Wurm, Heinrich, ed. *Baldassare Peruzzi Architekturzeichnungen*. Tübingen, 1984.

Yablon, Nick. *Untimely Ruins: An Archaeology of American Urban Modernity, 1819–1919*. Chicago, 2009.

Zanker, Paul. *The Power of Images in the Age of Augustus*. Ann Arbor, 1988.

Ziolkowski, Adam. "Pantheon." In *Lexicon Topographicum Urbis Romae*, ed. Eva Margareta Steinby, 4.54–61. Rome, 1999.

Zöllner, Frank, Christof Thoenes, and Thomas Popper. *Michelangelo: Complete Works*. Cologne, 2007.

Zorach, Rebecca, ed. *The Virtual Tourist in Renaissance Rome: Printing and Collecting the Speculum Romanae Magnificentiae*. Chicago, 2008.

Zucker, Paul. *Fascination of Decay*. Ridgewood NJ, 1968.

Index

Page numbers written in italics denote illustrations.